ROMANTIC GENIUS

D1559672

BETWEEN MEN ~ BETWEEN WOMEN

Lesbian and Gay Studies   *Lillian Faderman and Larry Gross, Editors*

ROMANTIC GENIUS

THE PREHISTORY OF A HOMOSEXUAL ROLE

Andrew Elfenbein

COLUMBIA UNIVERSITY PRESS   NEW YORK

COLUMBIA UNIVERSITY PRESS
Publishers Since 1893
New York   Chichester, West Sussex
Copyright © 1999 by Columbia University Press

Library of Congress Cataloging-in-Publication Data
Elfenbein, Andrew.   Romantic genius : the prehistory of a homosexual role /
   Andrew Elfenbein.
       p. cm. — (Between men—between women)
     ISBN 0–231–10752–8 (cloth : alk. paper). — ISBN 0-231-10753-6
   (pbk. : alk. paper)
      1. English literature—18th century—History and criticism. 2. Homosexuality
   and literature—Great Britain—History—18th century. 3. Homosexuality and
   literature—Great Britain—History—19th century. 4. English literature—19th
   century—History and criticism. 5. Authors, English—18th century—Sexual
   behavior. 6. Authors, English—19th century—Sexual behavior. 7. Romanticism
   —Great Britain. 8. Lesbians in literature. 9. Gay men in literature. 10. Sex in
   literature. I. Title. II. Series.
PR 448.H65E44   1999
820.9'353—DC21   98–54181

∞

Casebound editions of Columbia University Press books are printed on permanent
and durable acid-free paper.
Printed in the United States of America
c 10 9 8 7 6 5 4 3 2 1
p 10 9 8 7 6 5 4 3 2 1

Chapter Three is adapted from material in "Stricken Deer: Secrecy, Homophobia,
and the Rise of the Suburban Man," which appeared in *Genders* 27 (1998), published by *Genders Journal*, copyright © 1998 by *Genders Journal*. Reprinted by permission.

Chapter Five is adapted from material in "Lesbianism and Romantic Genius: The
Poetry of Anne Bannerman," which appeared in *English Literary History* 63 (1996):
929–57, published by Johns Hopkins University Press, copyright © 1996 by Johns
Hopkins University Press. Reprinted by permission.

Illustrations: Figure 1 is reproduced by permission of *The Lewis-Walpole Library,
Yale University*; Figure 2 by *The University of Minnesota Libraries*; Figures 3 and 4
by permission of *The Huntington Library, San Marino, California.*

TO MY SON

CONTENTS

ACKNOWLEDGMENTS

Although geniuses were supposed to be able to create masterpieces all by themselves, writing this book has shown me how wrong such a notion is. I am grateful to the University of Minnesota for providing me with a McKnight Land-Grant Fellowship, a Bush Sabbatical Supplement, and a Single Quarter Leave, and with inexhaustible research assistants: Dan Birkholz, Heejin Kim, Lauren Marsh, Mark Mazullo, and William Young. Among my colleagues at Minnesota, I am lucky to have been helped by Daniel Brewer, Maria Damon, Shirley Nelson Garner, Michael Hancher, Toni McNaron, Ellen Messer-Davidow, and Beth Zemsky. Further afield, I want to thank those who have read or heard portions of the manuscript and given me valuable advice: Leslie Brisman, Kevis Goodman, George Haggerty, Peter J. Manning, Eve Kosofsky Sedgwick, Patricia Meyer Spacks, and Asha Varadharajan. I am especially grateful to Terry Castle, Claudia L. Johnson, and an anonymous press reader for their smart, indispensable comments on my manuscript.

I love libraries, and this book has given me the pleasure of using many. For all the help they have given me, I want to thank the staffs of the Wilson Library at the University of Minnesota; Yale University's Sterling Memorial Library, Beinecke Rare Book and Manuscript Library, and Lewis-Walpole Library; the Newberry Library; the Huntington Library; the Folger Shakespeare Library; the Cambridge University Library; Oxford University's Bodleian Library; the British Library; and the National Library of Scotland. For permission to quote from manuscript material, I especially want to thank the directors of the Lewis-Walpole Library, the Bodleian, and the National Library of Scotland. The editors of *ELH* and *Genders* have kindly allowed me to print versions of material that first appeared in their pages.

Lillian Faderman first directed my attention to Columbia University Press, and I am grateful to her for her encouragement. My editor, Ann

Miller, has been a pleasure to work with, and Roy E. Thomas has been the manuscript editor of my dreams. My parents, Myra and Lowell Elfenbein, and my siblings, Rachel and Eddy, helped me to define my book by never ceasing to ask me what I was writing about.

It is one thing to have a brilliant intellectual companion; it is quite another to have someone to help you survive the millions of tiny things that make getting through the day possible. I have been lucky to have both in the same person, my partner John Watkins, whose intelligence, love, energy, and humor have supported me when nothing else could. The final preparation of this book has been brightened by the arrival of our son, Joseph Dmitri, and I dedicate it to him.

ROMANTIC GENIUS

The advertisement on the World Wide Web shines from my computer screen: "The Invisible Characteristics of Homosexuality and Genius— Detected at Birth!" For $3.99 a minute, I can call a 900 number to learn if "my child or loved one possesses these documented traits that may manifest themselves in the form of Homosexuality and/or Genius." When I call, the man on the taped message explains that, to know for sure, I need a complete natal chart and a qualified astrologer. Even after deciding that I can find other ways to spend four dollars a minute, the advertisement's confidence remains with me: "Potential Homosexual behavior as well as Genius can be known at the birth of a child and any time thereafter during the life of the individual."[1]

For those inclined to experiment, I can promise that sleeping with a member of one's own sex will not produce genius. Nevertheless, an exceptional amount of the artistic hopes, endeavors, and energy of men and women since the eighteenth century has thrived on an obvious fiction, the intimate connection between homosexuality and genius. This book is about the early history of that fiction in eighteenth- and nineteenth-century Britain. It is not a celebration of the genius of homosexual men and women but a discussion of how genius and homosexuality came to be linked in the first place.[2]

The World Wide Web ad demonstrates the extensive reach of the link between homosexuality and genius in popular culture. In the twentieth century, probably its most influential statement has been Sigmund Freud's *Leonardo da Vinci and a Memory of His Childhood*, in which Freud argues that the "atrophy" of Leonardo's sexual life, "which was restricted to what is called ideal [sublimated] homosexuality," led to his "overpowerful instinct for research."[3] For Freud, frustrated male homosexuality found its outlet in artistic and intellectual excellence. His message to his readers was double-

edged: geniuses could be homosexuals, but only if their personal lives atro-
phied. Genius was a curse disguised as a blessing.

Gay activists in the twentieth century have seized the positive side of
Freud's message and ignored the rest, even when they were not consciously
responding to it. For example, to justify what he called "intermediate types,"
the early homosexual rights advocate Edward Carpenter argued that the
"third sex," by which he meant those who combined masculine and feminine traits, took on divinatory roles in "primitive" cultures. He concluded
that "the blending of the masculine and feminine temperaments would in
some of these cases produce persons whose perceptions would be so subtle
and complex and rapid as to come under the head of genius."[4] By the 1920s,
the link between homosexuality and genius was familiar enough that a New
York man imprisoned for homosexuality could tell his prison doctor, "Most
of the world's genius can be traced directly to the homosexual."[5] Even today,
the genius of homosexuals remains inspiring, especially for men and
women wanting to value what may have seemed to them unacceptable. The
Web page for Parents and Friends of Lesbians and Gays, for example, praises the "thousands . . . of genius[es], whose being gay was inherent to their
achievements."[6]

Yet the negative side of Freud's association remains. For those who are
neither geniuses nor homosexuals, the association between the categories
can quickly become a source of resentment. Lanny Poffo, a professional
wrestler from a distinguished wrestling family, adopted "The Genius" as his
wrestling persona and had the label printed on his wrestling shorts. Dressed
in a mortar board and graduation robe, he would preface his bouts by reading poetry about how smart he was, noting in particular how many lan-
guages he had mastered. But in the ring, he proved himself to be less than a
real man because, instead of punching, he would scratch his opponents and,
when he temporarily disabled them, would flutter about in triumph. In the
end, however, he was always reduced to a senseless heap by the more manly
victor.[7] His performances became ritual gay-bashings. Poffo's message was
plain: male geniuses have college educations and are effeminate; ordinary
men who watch professional wrestling do not have college educations and
are straight. In his performances, genius became a wedge for displacing class
conflict onto homophobia.

The negative associations between genius and homosexuality are not
just part of popular culture. As far back as Cesare Lombroso's work, studies
arguing for a connection between insanity and genius have usually included homosexuality as a relevant sign of insanity. Lombroso, in writing about
"insane" geniuses, noted that "all of these great men . . . showed anomalies

of the reproductive functions," which was a nineteenth-century periphrasis for homosexuality. William Hirsch's *Genius and Degeneration* argued against Lombroso by distinguishing true geniuses, who were sane, from pseudo-geniuses, who were Lombroso's madmen. Hirsch thought that most modern writers were pseudo-geniuses, whom he also called degenerates. Homosexuality was a distinguishing mark of their work: "Other abnormal impulses, especially of a sexual origin, appear in the work of degenerates."[8] Even when Hirsch argued against Lombroso, he still reinforced the connection between artistic distinction and homosexuality.

It would be easy to dismiss Lombroso and Hirsch as believers in now-exploded anthropological concepts. Yet versions of their findings are everywhere in much recent writing about genius and creativity. Janine Chasseguet-Smirgel's *Creativity and Perversion*, for example, reads like a Freudian updating of Lombroso. Examining the "need to create which gains a hold on so many a pervert," she decides that it results from a fixation on the anal-sadistic stage: "Let me say that the pervert will attempt to give himself and others the illusion that anal sexuality (which is accessible to the little boy) is equal and even superior to genital sexuality (accessible to the father), by erasing from the sexual scene all those elements that might act as obstacles to his conviction."[9] For Chasseguet-Smirgel, preferring anal to genital sexuality is an obvious illusion, although one that fosters creativity. In her terms, male homosexuals who prefer anal sexuality are trapped in immaturity.

Another psychiatrist, Arnold M. Ludwig in *The Price of Greatness*, constructs a quasi-scientific apparatus, complete with charts and graphs, for evaluating the genius of one thousand men and women, ranked according to a "Creative Achievement Scale." He discovers that "there are marked differences in sexual orientation among the various professions. Poets, fiction writers, companions, and social figures are more likely than others to be homosexual (10 to 14%)." Ludwig does not attach evaluative language to his statistics, but other psychiatrists are less reticent. Albert Rothenberg in *Creativity and Madness* discusses "the homosexual disorder" and creativity. Although he admits that many great artists have been homosexuals, he worries about endorsing a connection between this supposed disorder and the work of genius: "To the degree that a person's homosexuality arises from psychopathological processes, lack of choice, and intense rigidifying conflicts, there is impairment in that person's creative processes." Rothenberg's evidence for the bad effects of homosexuality is his work with "a noted homosexual poet." Writing a poem about riding a horse, the poet found himself facing a mental block as long as he imagined the horse to be male.

Once he changed the horse's gender, he completed the poem. Rothenberg notes, "Although he surely could have written about frank homosexual attachment in this poem, as he had done in others, he intended to describe a more universal experience of intimacy, accord, and loss. That more universal feeling and aesthetic intent were finally achieved by the change of sex from stallion to mare." According to Rothenberg's analysis of his case study, heterosexuality is "universal" and stimulates creativity, while homosexuality causes "serious blocks" in artists.[10] Although he concedes that many homosexuals have been outstanding creators, his analysis implies that they would have been even better if they could have gotten past their disorder to the more universal language of heterosexuality.

Lori Reisenbichler of the Center for the Study of Work Teams has found in Rothenberg's discussion of homosexuality important evidence about the future of capitalism. In "Creative Tension: A Crucial Component of Creativity in the Workplace," she argues that workers resist creativity because they think that "creativity is a special gift of the homosexual." Yet she reports that a "controlled empirical study in 1977," cited in Rothenberg's book, "demonstrated that homosexual individuals did not score higher on creativity tests than did heterosexuals, but in fact scored significantly lower."[11] She reassures heterosexuals who might want to be creative that their creativity does not mean that they are really homosexuals. In her work, the link between genius and homosexuality becomes an excuse for examining "the homosexual" as a measurable quantity of behaviors, and then proving mental inferiority on the basis of it. More generally, her report rescues creative heterosexuals from the presumably horrific fate of believing that they might have anything in common with homosexuals.

As these examples reveal, the link between homosexuality and genius has a dark side. It encourages the continued pathologizing of homosexuality as disease, madness, or disorder. The implied message of the pathology is that, while homosexuals may be rewarded with genius, they are also punished for it with lives of suffering, poverty, neglect, and psychic trauma. Most important of all, their suffering means that they do not pass on their genius to another generation, so that their genius entails gay self-extinction. As Ernst Kretschmer noted in *The Psychology of Men of Genius*, "One of the strangest biological facts is the rapid way in which the stock of genius disappears, as if by a simple law of nature. Many geniuses have been unmarried or childless; some have been weak in the sexual impulse, or perverted."[12] A homophobic society has turned Kretschmer's observation into a source of aesthetic pleasure. No drama is more enjoyable for this audience than the untimely death of a promising young gay man or, more rarely, a lesbian, whose genius guarantees an early demise. AIDS has provided a hideous new tool to support the continuing myth of gay genius's biological obsolescence.[13]

Another dark side to the link between homosexuality and genius is its misogyny. It is no coincidence that my discussion has been mostly about men. As Christine Battersby has argued, artistic genius has from its inception been defined as male. Traditional concepts of genius hide lesbian history and achievement by suggesting that only men are significant enough for their deviance to be worth noticing. In the rare cases when female geniuses are acknowledged, they run the risk of being labeled as too masculine. Kretschmer, for example, notes that a masculine side "betrays the abnormal, contrary, sexual component in psychopathic women. And this mixture of masculine and feminine feelings is found equally in most of the great women of history."[14] Such characterizations send the double message of female genius: although masculine women are abnormal, only they can achieve anything valuable because merely feminine women are worthless. This misogynistic tradition did not prevent writers like Mary Wollstonecraft from appropriating the link between homosexuality and genius for lesbian representation. But the cult of genius has been a serious obstacle in the path of women artists trying to gain stature and recognition.

Although many critics have demystified the ideology of genius, they have not loosened its hold on the popular imagination.[15] In the roughly two hundred and fifty years since the concept of genius attained its present form, it has embedded itself in the practices and rhetoric of a variety of disciplines in ways that its first theorists would never have suspected. Even though the basic concept has changed little, its uses have multiplied unexpectedly.

Genius, for the most part, remains a term of unqualified praise. I use it throughout the book in the fairly simple senses given by Webster's: "Great mental capacity and inventive ability; esp., great and original creative ability in some art, science, etc." and a person with such capacity and ability.[16] For the most part, I confine myself to genius within the creative arts rather than in the sciences. Even though men and women in both fields have been recognized as geniuses, genius has carried a greater weight in the arts because science provides other measures of accomplishment, such as accuracy of discovery. In the arts, genius alone is supposedly enough to guarantee merit.

Genius has become a favorite noun in bourgeois aesthetics because it reinforces a myth of individualism. As a quasi-mystical gift that simply occurs, with no help from society, genius points to pure greatness, divine inspiration in a secularized world. Yet since daring, originality, and creativity threaten any status quo, genius is also dangerously unpredictable. As Reisenbichler's report shows, the capitalist workplace is both eager for creativity and terrified of it. A genius might invent a gadget that could make millions, but he/she might also be crazy enough to refuse to collaborate with an oppressive economic order. Creativity earns loud applause, but its potential threats to the system need to be crushed. The popular association between genius and homosexuality provides one form of containment by giving genius's deviance a name. The full threat of genius is too strong to be brought into language, so linking it to homosexuality is a second best, a supposedly familiar form of deviance brought in to stand in for a more mysterious one. Homosexuality is less a cause or prerequisite for genius than an imperfect metaphor for it.

As such, genius may seem like a strange category for a scholar interested in the history of homosexuality to investigate. If the link between homosexuality and genius is an obvious fiction, why not just avoid it and concentrate on real people? I choose to focus instead on aesthetic issues and objects like poems because they have had so great an influence on the history of homosexual representation and the perception of homosexual character. Through the work of several distinguished historians, more material is now available about British same-sex eroticism in the late eighteenth and early nineteenth centuries than ever before.[17] Trials records, obscure poems, little-known medical texts, manuscript letters and diaries, and other archival sources have been ransacked for evidence about the lives of men and women who had sex with members of their own gender. Although my book relies heavily on such research, I believe that by concentrating on these marginal sources, historians have avoided mainstream writing that ultimately had a greater effect on perceptions of homosexuality. Without ever mentioning sex between men or women, eighteenth-century treatises on genius set in motion an image that would play a large role in defining the homosexual's supposed character. For example, when asked by a customs officer what he had to declare, Wilde did not mention his homosexuality but purportedly answered, "I have nothing to declare except my genius."[18]

As a result, this book argues for the unexpected importance of aesthetics to lesbian and gay history. Michel Foucault left aesthetics out of the first volume of his *History of Sexuality*, although it plays an important role in his later works about the classical world. For him, the truth of sexuality in the modern world moved from the priest to the doctor. Only these professionals were licensed to hear confessions in which sexual secrets could be told: "Beginning in the sixteenth century, this rite [of confession] gradually detached itself from the sacrament of penance, and . . . emigrated toward pedagogy, relationships between adults and children, family relations, medicine, and psychiatry."[19] In this book, I want to place a literary stage between Foucault's religious and medical/domestic ones. Geniuses intervened between the priest and the doctor as the privileged interpreters of the human soul and its sexual secrets. They never showed themselves to be more daring, original, and creative than when they broke sexual taboos. Homosexuality guaranteed the truth of geniuses' confessions, since without it they would have had nothing to confess.

Whether or not geniuses actually slept with members of their own sex, they took on the mantle of mixed fear and admiration that has historically characterized homosexuals since the eighteenth century. It might be more accurate to speak of the homosexualized genius than of the homosexual one. Like homosexuals, geniuses became a privileged repository for all the behaviors exiled from respectable society. They inspired a mixture of envy and relief because they were able to experience all that ordinary people could not. For everyone to live the life of a genius would be too exhausting, but knowing that someone was living it reassuringly kept alive a range of possibilities for human behavior, even if most people never exercised them.

I also concentrate on aesthetics partly because of an odd development within my discipline, English literary studies. Through a lucky mix of favorable institutional conditions and gifted scholars, the study of English literature has been at the forefront of queer studies. Yet with this luck has come some embarrassment at the status of literature itself. Scholars have used fictional works, especially novels, to corroborate or complicate the image of homosexuality found in nonliterary works. While few critics treat literary texts simply as mirrors of social mores, they often view literary works as both indexes to and shapers of larger sociological trends. The result is that English professors have not explained what might look like their obvious point of departure, the overwhelming number of gay and lesbian authors. They have used literature to analyze everything about homosexuality except why it has such a large place in literary history.

As I will argue, something about literature's construction has proved exceptionally inviting to homosexuality, and that "something" is genius. It would be inadequate to claim that homosexuals have become writers simply because so many homosexuals had already been writers. The cult surrounding genius has created an analogy between the situation of the alienated, marginalized artist who rebels against social norms by shattering conventional gender categories and that of the homosexual man or women in a homophobic world. Homosexuality is not intrinsically creative, but the situations in which many homosexuals have found themselves have offered all the disadvantages required by successful genius.

Having discussed genius and homosexuality, I want to turn to the word *prehistory* in my subtitle. It points to a larger problem in queer history, which concerns how to talk about homosexuals in a century when the word did not exist. *Genius* is far less controversial because plenty of eighteenth-century writers wrote about it, and the continuity between their discussions and twentieth-century ones is striking. While continuities also exist between eighteenth- and twentieth-century writing about homosexuality, especially in terms of homophobic perceptions, fundamental assumptions about sexuality are available in the twentieth century that were not in the eighteenth. Eighteenth-century writers did not speak of "sexuality," defined as a quasi-medical term for an ingrained aspect of the human psyche. Instead, their discussions are dominated by the terms of gender. They could be quite explicit about same-sex eroticism, but their language was often that of gender inversion: a man who had sex with a man was feminine, and a woman who had sex with a woman was masculine.[20] Frequently, gender-typing aligned active/passive sexual roles with masculine/feminine gender traits. A woman who penetrated another woman with fingers or dildos was masculine, since she took the active role; a man who was penetrated by another man was feminine, since he was supposedly passive.

Yet writers were not consistent. They did not always make such fine distinctions between active and passive, and might label two male partners effeminate, or two women masculine. In addition, other traditions complicated any neat patterns that twentieth-century historians might want to impose. As I discuss in the first chapter, effeminacy had a long, complicated history that gave it a possible but never certain link to homosexual behavior. Pedophilic conventions of sex between active men and passive boys positioned the boy as feminine but left the man's gender identity ambiguous. Likewise, one popular strand of misogyny treated women as inherently unstable, sexually voracious, and excessive. Lesbianism in this tradition was less an assertion of female masculinity than a natural extension of women's inherently unnatural traits. Using gender to describe sexual behavior did not guarantee clarity of definition.

A further complication in the eighteenth-century sex / gender system was the vexed relation between visible signs and assumed practices. Although writers often described men who had sex with other men as being feminine, no one could assume that feminine traits in a man necessarily signaled that he had sex with other men. A woman who dressed like a man might be giving clues that she had sex with other women, but the conclusion was not certain. Eighteenth-century representations, especially satirical or derogatory ones, were expert at playing with such ambiguities. They left readers wondering about the exact sexual practices of those described in ways that may have been more damaging than outright libel.

I take a fiery denunciation from 1757 as an example of how complicated eighteenth-century works about same-sex activity could be, even at their most explicit. I quote the discussion of what it calls "effeminacy" in full:

> If we do but take the Trouble of looking into human Life a little, we may observe some Characters of a peculiar Cast, who are so obnoxious in their Natures, that, upon being once acquainted with their Vices, the manly Bosom shudders, even at the Thoughts of such unnatural Appetites, much more the contemptible Means of putting them in Practice; which are, indeed, so monstrous and indecent, that I should look upon it as defiling my Paper, to give a literal Description of it; but the Judgment of the Reader will as easily conceive what is meant, when I tell him it is too shocking and unnatural to describe. I am sorry to say, that in *England* there are as many of the abominable Sect, as any where in the World. Besides several Clubs and Assemblies of these Wretches that are publickly known, there are many private Ones, where Effeminacy revels in all its Impurity of filthy Vice and detestable Practices: Nor is there a public Place, but something of this Nature shews itself with the most shocking Aspect. We may often observe the sudden Transition of a smooth-faced young Fellow, who but just before was Servant to the same noble Personage who has now made him his Companion; and what reason, can one think, would induce a Man of Quality to so much Condescension as to prefer the Company of a Rascal, who the other Day used to ride behind his Coach in the Character of a Footman?
>
> Nor does Effeminacy, wherever it governs the Monster, who possesses a plentiful Fortune, stop at the most absurd and inconsistent Actions. The *He-Minion* of a certain Nobleman, before now, has been seen sometimes in the Character of a modern Belle, at others in that of a rural Maiden, and very often in a loose Morning-Dress, in Imitation of a Lady of Pleasure; but what appears the most horrible and detestable to human Nature is the *Sham Lying-in*, where the Lady-looking Gentleman is brought to Bed with all the Formality of a real Labour; the *Spouse* of the fair-faced *Incubus* affects as great Care and Concern at the feigned Pangs of his Beloved, as if it was the real Wife of his Bosom; the *He-Midwife* is no less assiduous in his Part, the *Male Nurse* is likewise making great Preparations, while the *Gentleman Gossips* are all in full Employ, and lending their Assistance to the screaming *Minion*.

Can anything in the World equal the ridiculous Absurdity of such a Scene? What End can it produce, or what Satisfaction can be reaped from an Affair of this kind? But it is impossible for any one, but of the same Stamp, to entertain the least Idea of any Pleasure that can derive itself from such mean and filthy Practices: Nay, so opposite is the noble and manly Nature to that of the effeminate Kind, that some Men would never believe that there were such Creatures upon Earth, and perhaps would have still persisted in their Incredulity, had not Time and incontestable Instances demonstrated to the contrary.

But we shall not pretend to confine the Vice to any particular Rank, for within these few Years it has shewn its frightful Aspect among all Sorts of People. Grave Citizens and Tradesmen have been found guilty of it, and others of that Denomination are still known to be so; and it is not only confined to the Laity, but the solemn Order of the Gown has been, at Times, dishonoured. But it is to be hoped, that those Few, whose Natures were too vile to appear under that Sanction, cannot reflect their Scandal upon the Whole; yet the lower Sort of People are always glad of one Example, and by that Means would find an Opportunity, if they could, to condemn the rest.

But among Dissenters there are several Instances of this Vice, even in their pious Pastors, not forgetting the reverend Gentleman, who some Time ago made an Attempt of this Nature, in his own *Meeting*, with a pious Lamb of his own Flock; and the grave and worthy Person, who was expelled, by his Congregation, near *Lincoln's-Inn-Fields*; but yet even these known Proofs are not sufficient to cast a Scandal on the rest of that Fraternity, for undoubtedly there are a great many good People among them.

The inferior Sort of People, who are given to this filthy Vice, have been found in the Fact in open Streets, Lanes, Alleys, and empty Houses, Houses of Office, or any other Places most convenient for their wicked Purposes; but such is the Nature of this shocking Crime, that it requires the Mantle of Night, as it is too monstrous to appear in the Face of Day.[21]

Several conventions of homophobic representation tumble together in this diatribe. The first is that of religious invective, present less in the description itself than in the title of the pamphlet, *The Ten Plagues of England, Of Worse Consequence Than Those of Egypt*, written by a "Well-Wisher." The title of this particular plague, "Effeminacy," flatly contradicts the claims of some critics that effeminacy "only very rarely" meant homosexuality in this period.[22] The Well-Wisher has interpreted St. Paul's assertion in 1

Corinthians that effeminates will not enter the kingdom of heaven as a religious justification for condemning men who have sex with men.

The Well-Wisher does not care in the least about internal consistency or subscribing to one model of same-sex eroticism. He shuttles between blaming the effeminates' "Vices," as if he saw them in moral or ethical terms, and describing them as if they had determined personalities in their "Natures" or "Stamp." Foucault's distinction between a religious understanding of sodomy in terms of practices and the medical understanding of homosexuals as personality types blurs here. For the Well-Wisher, the sodomite is not a "temporary aberration," as Foucault claims.[23] Although he does not use medical language, he sees these men as a distinct and dangerously widespread minority.

Initially, he treats this minority as aristocratic. The familiar language of antiaristocratic polemic appears when he attacks the confusions in ranks consequent upon the "sudden Transition of a smooth-faced young Fellow" from "Servant" to "Companion." But his class-based polemic crumbles when he notes that effeminacy belongs to "all Sorts of People," not just to aristocrats. Class analysis gives way to a more miscellaneous categorization that includes "Grave Citizens and Tradesmen," "Dissenters," and the "inferior Sort of People" and thereby mixes morality, occupation, religion, and rank.

Other inconsistencies fill the Well-Wisher's account. He thinks that the effeminates' practices are so horrifying that they cannot even be described, since to do so would defile his paper. Yet he also admits that everyone must already know about them since they are so publicly visible. Similarly, he attacks the lower ranks for being too hostile to effeminacy and for being not hostile enough. They are too hostile because they are eager to take one wrongdoing priest and thereby "find an Opportunity, if they could, to condemn the rest." They are not hostile enough because "the inferior Sort of People" are so vulgar that they indulge the "Vice" of effeminacy in "open Streets, Lanes, Alleys, and empty Houses." They do not even have the shame to hide their actions.

The Well-Wisher is least consistent in his tone. His vocabulary begins with words and phrases of outrage: "manly Bosom shudders," "so monstrous and indecent," "too shocking and unnatural," "detestable Practices." Yet, as he continues, he includes other phrases that point to comedy or ridicule: "absurd and inconsistent," "ridiculous Absurdity." His religious outrage dwindles to petty sniping at the "*Sham Lying-in*": "What End can it produce, or what Satisfaction can be reaped from an Affair of this kind?"[24] As if realizing that his question is trivial, since the scene that he describes is obviously meant to be comic, he suddenly changes direction by announcing that only one "of the same Stamp" could enjoy "such mean and filthy Practices." Reading his description, it is as if, for a brief second, he allows himself to be seduced by the comedy of the scene. His recoil is defensive, as if he realizes that even describing the "*Sham Lying-in*" potentially implicates him in the effeminates' practices. For someone who finds them so detestable, he thrives on writing about them.

The more he implicates himself in their activities, the more naked his outrage becomes. By the end of the passage, he has called the effeminates every bad thing possible, whether doing so is consistent or not. Covering all positions from which he might attack them matters more to him than the logical coherence of his positions. Academic analysis sometimes points to contradictions and gaps in a work as if these necessarily undercut or subverted its message. Yet, as this document reveals, hostility overcomes a wealth of faulty arguments. The Well-Wisher makes the point, intentionally or not, that logic and reason are not necessary or even appropriate when confronting as supposedly outrageous a group as the effeminates. For gay and lesbian historiography, merely teasing out the various discursive strands in a given record may not account fully for a work's effect. Eighteenth-century homophobia thrives even in the face of blatant contradictions.

The Well-Wisher's account also reveals that no single model of sex/gender roles can encompass all the complexities of surviving eighteenth-century evidence. The search to uncover and define such models has become something of an obsession in lesbian and gay historiography. To avoid essentializing lesbian and gay experience, historians have constructed narratives in which, at some specified historical moment, an older model of a homosexual role gives way to a newer, supposedly more modern version. The prototype of this narrative is Michel Foucault's famous location in the nineteenth century of the transposition of homosexuality from "the practice of sodomy onto a kind of interior androgyny, a hermaphrodism of the soul."[25] In eighteenth-century studies, Randolph Trumbach has found a similar "great transition" around 1700 from the bisexual libertine, who could have sex with boys or women without losing his masculinity, to the "molly," who took on stereotypical feminine roles and, as an adult man, was the passive partner in homosexual sex.[26] Similarly, he locates at the end of the eighteenth century the emergence of the "modern" lesbian role, the "tommy," which he argues parallels the earlier "molly" role for men.[27]

In *Epistemology of the Closet*, Eve Sedgwick has criticized such narratives by arguing that the "historical search for a Great Paradigm Shift" can "obscure the present conditions of sexual identity." For her, claiming that homosexuality used to look one way and has now attained its "modern" form falsely assumes the obviousness of sexuality in the present. Her alternative is to move away from "a unidirectional narrative of supersession" to a history of "relations enabled by the unrationalized coexistence of different models during the times they do exist."[28] Yet her criticisms could be pushed further. Even the idea of a "model" presumes more coherence than eighteenth-century materials often present. Craig Patterson, in discussing texts about the mollies, describes them as "shifting" and "unreliable" in ways that "render difficult any confident pronouncements about the existence of new identities."[29] I agree, because, as the Well-Wisher's account reveals, assumptions about gender and identity were in such flux during the century that any supposed paradigms of homosexual roles need to be treated with caution.

Sex / gender representations can never be fully analyzed merely by fitting them into one model or another, or even by treating them as sites for the coexistence of different models. Eighteenth-century writers appropriated existing conventions for specific purposes, criticized or altered them, or invented new ones. Even the most commonplace images varied in function, tone, and style from work to work. One of my goals in this book is to counter the possible overemphasis in recent lesbian and gay historiography on paradigm shifts with attention to the peculiarities and idiosyncrasies of specific textual representations.

Consequently, I avoid constructing a diachronic argument about this period and instead describe a general situation in the first chapter about genius and homosexuality in the eighteenth century and follow it with six chapters about the effects of this situation on eighteenth- and early nineteenth-century writing. As the meaning of "genius" in the eighteenth century increasingly came to describe an extraordinarily gifted creator, the new definition had surprising effects. Men and women who wanted a literary career but who lacked a university education, London connections, or inherited wealth seized the role of untutored genius to justify their entitlement to authorship. In striving to present their works as the works of geniuses, they needed to find ways to demonstrate the daring and wildness that, according to eighteenth-century treatises, geniuses supposedly possessed. Eighteenth-century treatises often associated this daring and wildness with androgyny and with unsuitability for traditional domestic arrangements. Although they stopped short of connecting androgyny with homosexuality, men and women aspiring to the role of genius did not. I argue that a frequent strategy for such authors was to challenge contemporary codes of sexual propriety in their works and, in some cases, in their lives. They used transgressive sexual representations, especially those of same-sex eroticism, to mark their perceived superiority to authors who merely reproduced codes of sexual propriety.

The next six chapters then show how this potential intersection between genius and sexual transgression shaped the careers of men and women producing literature. Authors range from the semicanonical (Beckford and Cowper) to the unknown (Damer and Bannerman) to the familiar (Blake and Coleridge). They cover a range of sexual behaviors, from Beckford's pedophilia to Cowper's celibacy, from Damer's probable lesbianism to Bannerman's unknown sexuality, from Blake's marriage to Coleridge's messy love life. I have avoided one much-investigated genre in studies of gender and sexuality, the Gothic novel, in order to concentrate on work that has been given less attention. In particular, since genius supposedly found its highest written expression in poetry, many, though not all, of my authors are poets. They are also different enough that, at the risk of turning this book into six mini-theses, the relevance of genius to each varies. What they share is that their careers, in different ways, help to answer the little-examined question of how genius became so closely linked to homosexuality.

After the first chapter, I turn to two authors who could not have been more different, William Beckford and William Cowper. William Beckford's *Vathek* was one of the first works that put into practice the qualities that eighteenth-century theorists associated with genius. Yet it did more, because genius in *Vathek* belonged not to producers but to consumers. The work responded to eighteenth-century luxury debates by examining the moral effects of consumerism run wild. It both idealized and criticized a paradise of consumption whose highest form was pedophilia.

The reclusive, deeply religious William Cowper had neither Beckford's wealth nor his flamboyance. Unlike Beckford, he never claimed genius for himself and preferred to represent himself as a humble amateur. Yet he became more influential than Beckford because his masterpiece *The Task*, one of the most widely read poems of the period, modeled for the nineteenth century the figure of what I call the suburban man. This man prided himself on the domestication of genius, the ability to create a unique personal self with which to judge a world from which he was set apart because of his unique sensitivities. As represented by Cowper, this uniqueness was the product of mysterious traumas, which *The Task* pointed to but never explained. After his death, as knowledge of his madness grew, he was increasingly assimilated to the cult of genius, which he had repudiated in life. The more that he seemed like a genius, the more that rumors about his possible sexual deviance arose to explain the traumas hinted at in *The Task*.

My chapter places these rumors in the context of the role of genius and corrects long-standing errors about Cowper's supposed hermaphroditism.

The next two chapters examine women writers, the novelist and sculptor Anne Damer and the poet Anne Bannerman. Like Cowper, Damer never claimed genius for herself, but others were happy to see her as one because of her accomplishments in sculpture, which were unprecedented for a British woman. The scandalous death of her husband started a persistent series of rumors about her sapphism. Damer's artistic activities heightened the credibility of these rumors for her contemporaries. Any woman with artistic ambition was liable to be suspected of infractions against proper gender roles, and a woman who sculpted was especially open to suspicion. The more Damer could be seen as an artistic genius, the more likely she was to be perceived as a sapphist. I analyze the rumors and Damer's responses to them in terms of a crisis in the symbolic value of the aristocratic woman. Two competing narratives about Damer arose. Those who accused her of lesbianism read her unconventional dress and life through a narrative of improper sexual behavior, which was sometimes linked to her artistic activities. In response, Damer represented herself as a virtuous woman of the upper class who was at the patriotic center of her society. Yet the activities through which Damer asserted her innocence—her sculpture, her acting, and her novel *Belmour*—provided more fuel for her detractors because they seemed to flout bourgeois norms of propriety.

Bannerman lacked the privilege and education that Anne Damer had. Acknowledging the cult of genius allows Bannerman's poetry to be analyzed as lesbian writing even in the absence of information about her personal life. As a poor young woman in Edinburgh, she had virtually no other way of making her mark as a poet than to take on the role of genius. In so doing, she followed the path of other women writers, most notably Mary Wollstonecraft, who used lesbian representation as a mark of distinction. Bannerman, like other women who adopted genius, infused the role with far more seriousness and intensity than most male writers did. Her work avoids the demystifying irony of Beckford and instead appropriates the sublimity associated with genius for a woman writer.

The final two chapters turn to two Romantic writers, Blake and Coleridge. By the time of their writing, the role of genius had become virtually mandatory for those wanting to make a literary mark. Blake, like Bannerman, had little other than his claims of genius to distinguish him from other engravers of the period. Using the framework of the long-standing investment in Blake by gay male writers, I challenge the heterosexism that has prevailed in Blake criticism for much of this century. His epic

Milton is his most extended attack on the way that writers like William Hayley had diminished genius's potential. In the character of Ololon, usually misread as Milton's Emanation, Blake restored the radical power of genius by imagining a character who transcended gender roles, psychological motivation, and logical coherence. Only through Ololon's multiple agencies can Blake conceive of apocalyptic fulfillment in *Milton*.

Coleridge took genius in a new direction after he received an annuity that freed him somewhat from the demands of the literary marketplace. He was one of the first writers who was paid to be a genius and who faced the heavy burden of producing work that justified his role. The result was a series of highly experimental and daring poems, most notably *Christabel*. I trace the evolution of *Christabel* out of bawdy, eighteenth-century lesbian representation and argue that the poem takes one of the eighteenth century's most overdetermined images, sex between women, and reduces it to an enigma. Doing so provided a precedent for the production of high art out of obscene materials by severing them from their conventional political and religious associations. In Coleridge's hands, lesbianism for the first time became the occasion for art that defied contemporary canons of acceptability.

Thinking about genius offers the chance to conceive of literary history not from the point of view of mainstream taste but from the perspective of writers who did not quite fit in, even though some of them, like Cowper, became quite influential. The prominence of various modes of homosexual representation in their works, lives, and receptions meant that they positioned themselves far from the established taste of the day. For the writers in this book, genius was not a category that implied serene confidence in their creative powers. Instead, it was a highly defensive, troubled posture that was either assumed with great pains or anxiously thrust on them. These anxieties became part of the long history by which homosexuals and homosexuality came to take a leading role in defining the history of literature and of authorship.

CHAPTER ONE

The Danger Zone: Effeminates, Geniuses, and Homosexuals

By the second half of the eighteenth century, the male genius and the sodomite had become, if not doubles, close relations. On the surface, they seemed to be complete opposites. The male genius was the eighteenth century's most admired cultural other, while the sodomite was its most despised. The male genius produced artistic masterpieces, and the sodomite did not. The male genius was fiercely independent, while sodomites supposedly clustered in suspicious, cultlike assemblies.

Nevertheless, they were more alike than they seemed. While both male genius and sodomy had always been seen as categories that could apply potentially to all men as well as to just a few, popular representations increasingly put geniuses and sodomites together in a different, marginal segment of society. This marginality arose from their association with lawless excess: the sublime originality of the male genius, often figured as enthusiastic possession, and the sodomite's lack of self-control. These identities were so strong that they overrode class or rank. Any man could be a genius, and any man could become a sodomite. Conservative critics attacked both partly because their open ranks seemed to veer toward democracy.

Most important, both the male genius and the sodomite occupied a shadowy space in terms of sex / gender definition. Male geniuses had feminine traits. This femininity had a dense web of associations, but it generally floated uneasily between older, negative associations with excess and lack of self-discipline and newer, more ambivalent ones with sensibility, imagination, and passion. Sodomites were also feminine because their sexual desire for other men was supposed to indicate a hermaphroditism of the soul. Heightening the similarity between the two was the stereotype that male geniuses, like sodomites, were bad husbands and preferred friendships with men.

Even more, artistic geniuses often demonstrated their daring wildness by portraying, or at least hinting at, unconventional sexual possibilities, including same-sex desire, in their works. A male artist had little purpose if he imagined commonplace things. He existed to let the reading public experience vicariously what it would never know in real life, and no arena was more open to experiment than sexual desire. While neither the genius nor the sodomite was equivalent to the twentieth-century homosexual, neither fit comfortably into the role of respectable, married man that conduct books, novels, medical discourses, and religious texts advocated vigorously in the eighteenth century.[1]

I have emphasized the maleness of genius because most eighteenth-century treatises assumed that it was male.[2] Yet writers' frequent insistence that it arose from nature rather than from education had a consequence they may not have intended. Men *and* women who did not belong to the conservative establishment appropriated the role of genius to stake a claim to attention. Artists most invested in appearing as geniuses were not the men dominating London's literary scene. Instead, they were the outsiders for reasons of gender, education, nationality, or even health. Genius gave them an opening into what seemed the hitherto closed system of literary production. With it they could make up for not having what traditional authors were supposed to have, such as a classical education.

Since such outsiders were the most eager to appear as geniuses, their work is the best place to see how the sex / gender unconventionality of genius encouraged eighteenth-century writers to rebel against heterosexual norms. Although this rebellion first appeared as a quality in geniuses' work, it later became an expected aspect of their lives, since their works supposedly reflected their experience. In some cases, such as William Beckford or Mary Wollstonecraft, authors both wrote about same-sex desire and experienced it personally. Yet same-sex passions did not become part of their writing simply because they wanted to confess themselves. Instead, the role of genius, to which both Beckford and Wollstonecraft aspired, encouraged them to toss out conventional sexual roles as one means of establishing their perceived superiority to merely respectable authors.

It might seem that a critic interested in the relation between literary history and homosexual representation ought to concentrate on explicit treatments of sodomy and sapphism and not on the vaguer sexual representations of would-be geniuses. While I will not ignore explicit same-sex representations, they were not what later authors found interesting in eighteenth-century writing. For the most part, overt treatments of sodomy and sapphism continued long-established homophobic patterns. In many cases, they are more accessible and better known today than they were in the eighteenth century. But the forays of genius into underexplored forms of human desire were far more compelling to contemporary and later audiences. I concentrate on them because they have the most to tell us about why literature has played such a large role in the history of understanding homosexuality.

CROSSING THE SEX/GENDER SYSTEM

The relation between the genius and the sodomite in the eighteenth century arose in the larger context of gender-crossing. Although recent critics have separated sexuality and gender, the distinction did not exist in the eighteenth century.[3] Male sodomy and sapphism were seen not as departures from proper sexuality but as transgressions against natural gendered roles. Henry Fielding in *Amelia,* for example, described a sodomite in prison as "a Man who was committed for certain odious unmanlike Practices, not fit to be named." When denouncing sapphism in *The Female Husband,* he claimed that "if modesty be the peculiar characteristick of the fair sex, it is in them most shocking and odious to prostitute and debase it."[4] In both cases, he treated same-sex practices as a betrayal of a gender role, not as part of a distinct sexual identity.

Yet noting that eighteenth-century writers linked same-sex love to gender infractions does not explain their attitudes completely. Gender definitions were in such flux throughout the century that the significance of transgressing gendered behavior also varied.[5] In the late seventeenth century, it had been possible for rakes like Rochester to write about having sex with boys without losing their manliness, and this possibility did not entirely disappear in the eighteenth century.[6] Likewise, a writer of erotica like John Cleland could represent women having sex with other women without suggesting that they had lost their femininity.[7] Changing understandings of same-sex desire arose in relation to changing treatments of gender.

Eighteenth-century writers had a huge variety of sources to provide them with images for proper and improper gendered behavior. Yet it is most useful to think of gender in the period less as a topic in itself than as an element in larger networks of political, religious, legal, and medical discourses. For my purposes, two of the most important such networks were those of civic and civil humanism, as defined by J. G. A. Pocock and developed by Catherine Gallagher. Civic humanism or republicanism, the older of the two models, had its roots in classical political rhetoric. Its ideal was the good man, understood as a "citizen, virtuous in his devotion to the public good and his

engagement in relations of equality and ruling-and-being ruled, but virtuous also in his independence of any relation which might render him corrupt."[8] The keys to the good man's virtue were moderation, self-discipline,
and restraint, through which his behavior became a model for the state's.
The civic humanist understanding of manly virtue appeared throughout
eighteenth-century writers, often, though not exclusively, in conservative
ones.[9] When Pope, for example, described his father as an ideal man, he used
the clichés of classical moderation: "By Nature honest, by Experience
wise, / Healthy by Temp'rance and by Exercise."[10]

In the civic humanist model, if virtue was moderation, vice was excess. It
threatened to disrupt the citizen's ability to contribute to the public good by
destabilizing his sense of his proper behavior toward the state. Depending on
the writer, gendered descriptions of vice floated between unmanliness and
femininity. This confusion arose from the Aristotelian assumption that the
female body was not distinct from the male, but merely an imperfect version
of it. Unmanly behavior, therefore, was not just unmanly but also potentially
feminine. If men acted excessively, they were effeminate. If women acted
with noble self-restraint, they might be praised as manly, as when Pope, for
example, praised Martha Blount as "a softer Man."[11] Ordinary femininity
was less admirable. In Number 191 of *The Rambler*, Johnson took on the
voice of "Bellaria," a young lady confined to bed by a cold. When her aunt
brings her *The Rambler* to teach her "to moderate [her] desires and to look
upon the world with indifference," she responds, "But . . . I do not wish nor
intend to moderate my desires."[12] Johnson, like Pope, generalized that every
woman was at heart a rake.[13]

Effeminacy had a long history in civic humanism as an image of corrupt-
ed manliness. An effeminate man gave himself over to intemperance, typi-
cally at the cost of neglecting public good for private indulgence. His
intemperance might involve sodomy, because taking the passive position in
sex with another man was supposedly an example of immoderation. Yet it
might just as well involve "subservience to a wife or mistress, lecherousness,
or the compulsive pursuit of sexual experience to the neglect of more 'manly'
activities, excessive attention to fashion and coiffure in an attempt to attract
women more effectively, or conversely, such personal vanity and self-absorp-
tion as to preclude any but the feeblest interest in sexuality at all."[14]

Writers usually associated such effeminacy not only with personal corruption but also with civic decay.[15] A characteristic usage appears in Sir
Robert Thorold's translation of Plutarch's "Agis": "When Gold and Silver
(the great Debauchers of Mankind) had once gain'd Admittance into the
Lacedemonian Commonwealth, 'twas quickly follow'd by Avarice, baseness

of Spirit, and all manner of Frauds in the possession, by Riot, Luxury, and Effeminacy in the use."[16] Effeminacy here has nothing to do with same-sex passion, but is a general term for irresponsible spending. As such a term, effeminacy appears often in eighteenth-century writing. Charles Wesley, for example, complained of the "Softness and Effeminacy" found "even among those who have kept themselves pure from" what he calls "grosser Abomi-nations."[17] By distinguishing "effeminacy" from "grosser Abominations," he did not equate it with sodomy.

Nevertheless, certain developments in the eighteenth century helped to push effeminacy closer to sodomy. First, Protestant attention to scripture underscored the importance of Paul's list in 1 Corinthians 6:9 of the damned. Paul specified that "neither fornicators, not idolaters, nor adulter-ers, nor effeminate, nor abusers of themselves with mankind" would enter heaven. He did not say exactly who the "effeminate" and the "abusers" were, but eighteenth-century commentators in Bibles designed for family reading did. They defined the "abusers" as sodomites, and, without quite making the "effeminate" equivalent, they implied that the two groups were similar. Matthew Henry glossed them as the "*Effeminate*, and *Sodomites*"; E. Har-wood, as "the libidinous" and "the sodomite"; and John Guyse, as "Males of lascivious Tempers and Practices" and "those that are guilty of the most unnatural, detestable Sin, for which the Men of *Sodom* were destroyed by Fire from Heaven."[18] The move from juxtaposition to identification was small. While "effeminate" and "sodomite" never became perfect synonyms, Paul's text guaranteed that suspicions of sodomy might cluster around any given use of "effeminacy."

In addition, sodomy was often described in terms of hermaphroditism. For example, in Ben Jonson's *Volpone*, Lady Politic Would-Be accuses her husband of associating with "Your Sporus, your hermaphrodite."[19] Her apposition suggests that she understands a boy-lover (Sporus) as being not quite masculine: he hermaphroditically blurs two genders. Whereas Lady Would-Be associates only the boy, the passive partner, with hermaphro-ditism, in the eighteenth century it became just as likely for both partners in sodomy to be understood as unmanly "he-strumpets."[20] For example, Pope accused Addison and Steele of sodomy by labeling them "a couple of Her-maphrodites."[21] Cleland's Fanny Hill, after a voyeuristic scene in which she describes two men having sex, dismisses them as "unsexed male misses."[22] All these quotations treat the sodomite as a feminized man.

In some cases, effeminacy could refer quite specifically to sodomy, as in *The Ten Plagues of England*, quoted in my introduction. Similarly, the author of *Faustina; Or, the Roman Songstress*, attributed to Henry Carey,

gave his work the subtitle, "A Satyr on the Luxury and Effeminacy of the
Age." In it, he made clear that "luxury and effeminacy" included sodomy:

> They look like Females, dress'd in Boys' Attire,
> Or Waxwork Babies, activated by Wire:
> And if a Brace of powder'd Coxcombs meet,
> They kiss and slabber in the open Street;
> Curse on this damn'd *Italian*, Pathic mode,
> To *Sodom* and to Hell the ready Road.[23]

In such a work, effeminacy's meaning is more specific than mere intemperance. It has become "this damn'd *Italian*, Pathic mode." Texts like *Faustina* complicate Alan Sinfield's argument that "up to the time of the Wilde trials . . . it is unsafe to interpret effeminacy as defining of, or as a signal of, same-sex passion."[24] It would be more accurate to claim that meanings of "effeminacy" hovered between uses that had nothing to do with sodomy, those that had everything to do with it, and those somewhere in between.

Effeminacy became even more complex during the eighteenth century because the newer political rhetoric of civil humanism increasingly competed with the older one of civic humanism. As Gallagher notes, this new model "accepted that the worthy man would have private interests and commercial dealings as well as a private life in which he cultivated himself merely for the sake of personal cultivation; the earlier civic model eschewed commerce and justified property and leisure primarily on the grounds that they freed one for service to the state, not for the development of a multifaceted self."[25] The crux of the difference between the models might be encapsulated by that between virtue and politeness.[26] As Britain became ever more clearly a commercial society, a new code arose to define properly polite behavior for economic men and women.

The consequences for models of female behavior were dramatic. As Gallagher notes, the civil humanist model created "a newly positive assessment of women and new anxieties about them."[27] Whereas the civic humanist model assumed there was one right mode of behavior—manly discipline and self-control—to which men and women might aspire, the civil humanist model posited a sharp distinction between male and female forms of virtue. It treated "men and women as two species of humanity, endowed by God with distinct traits expressed in their characters and destinies. Men, strong of body and mind, are intended for feats of courage and intellect, for converse with God, and for the making of history. Women, delicate and graceful, are intended for the ministrations of comfort and delight, for deference to men, and for the making of a home."[28] This model located differences between men and women not merely in externals, such as clothing, but in deep, internal traits belonging to masculine and feminine essences. As Addison noted, "Men and Women ought to busie themselves in their proper Spheres, and on such Matters only as are suitable to their respective Sex."[29] Conservative as this model appears today, it often appeared in the eighteenth century in progressive or Whig writers. It let them conceive of a positive role for femininity to replace its wholly negative associations in the civic humanist model.[30]

The reason for the mixed feelings noted by Gallagher was that, once masculine and feminine natures could have desirable qualities, it became unclear how much each might borrow from the other without becoming ridiculous. Edward Lovibond took an extreme position when he dreamed of becoming female and sharing a virtuous friendship with a woman. After imagining his "soft Aspasia" as a man, he fantasized about changing his gender:

> But ah! my sweeter downy hours,
>   Had I been chang'd, not you;
> What tranquil joys, if kinder powers
>   Had made me woman too!
>
> Made each the other's softer care,
>   One table then had fed,
> One chamber lodg'd the faithful pair,
>   Ah, do not blush!—one bed.[31]

Lovibond acknowledges the attractiveness of taking on the "sweeter" character of a woman, although his concern that his auditor might "blush" at his fantasy reveals his own lingering discomfort with such gender-crossing. Yet the possibilities represented by his poem were relatively new in the eighteenth century. In the civic humanist model, it was not possible to be masculine and feminine at once because no one could be both moderate and excessive. Gender fantasies like Lovibond's became possible only with the civil humanist model.

Eighteenth-century authors never tired of searching for an image of a man who could take on feminine politeness and refinement without sacrificing manly courage and valor.[32] The most telling sign of their new interest in androgyny was the man of feeling, whose qualities made him not an effeminate object of satire but a figure for sympathy and admiration.[33] For example, in Sterne's *A Sentimental Journey*, one of the most popular representations of the man of feeling, the hero Yorick describes his reaction to the death of Father Lorenzo: "I burst into a flood of tears—but I am as weak as a woman; and I beg the world not to smile, but pity me."[34] Yorick as a feminized man, rather than being ridiculously comic, is here a model of sensitivity. Far from deserving the reader's contempt, he deserves "pity," although Sterne's phrasing suggests that less enlightened readers might still "smile" at this womanish hero.

Critics have debated just how feminine the man of feeling was. Michael McKeon argues that the man of feeling "strategically reclaimed a now recognizably *feminine* model of virtue as a distinctively male possession, reincorporating the newly normative *gender* traits within what a patriarchal culture persisted in seeing as the normative *sex*." Claudia L. Johnson takes this argument further to claim that the man of feeling masculinized gender traits that had been perceived as feminine. For her, "affective practices" of eighteenth-century sentimentality mattered "*not* because they are understood as feminine, but precisely and only insofar as they have been recoded as masculine."[35]

While I agree with these critics that the man of feeling did not threaten patriarchal power, I differ slightly in the degree to which I think the man of feeling became a widely accepted model of proper masculine behavior. He was always something of a novelty, and a rather suspect one because his undisciplined emotions brought him suspiciously close to the older model of effeminacy. Even sympathetic representations, such as Sterne's *Sentimental Journey* or Henry Mackenzie's *Man of Feeling*, register loud anxieties about his weaknesses. A character in Robert Bage's *Hermsprong* sums up the ambivalence surrounding the man of feeling: "The manly manners of our more immediate ancestors, we have exchanged for the manners of women. We have gained in gentleness and humanity; we have lost in firmness of nerve, and strength of constitution."[36] While many eighteenth-century writers agreed that refinement was a valuable marker of progress, it carried with it the specter of unmanliness and a nostalgia for an earlier age of "real" men.

The man of feeling's challenges to masculinity in some cases extended to his sexual behavior. He was utterly unsuited for the conventional roles of husband, father, or lover. At times, as with Sterne's Uncle Toby, he appeared as an aged child who ventured into sexual relations at his peril. For younger men of feeling, their closest bonds were not with women but with other men, as in Yorick's relation to his servant LaFleur.[37] Even louder hints of homoeroticism appear in Henry Brooke's *The Fool of Quality*. At its conclusion, the hero's devoted male attendant suddenly reveals that he is really a woman, and the hero marries her. While the man of feeling could never be simply equated with homoeroticism, neither could he be entirely divorced from it. As George Haggerty has argued, male-male desire was "the open secret of sensibility."[38]

For women, competing models of gender produced different results. Since in the civic humanist model, femininity was lack of moderation, a rampant sexual appetite was naturally feminine. In the case of Johnson's Bellaria, this appetite extended merely to coquettishness. But Juvenal's notorious and much-translated Sixth Satire showed that a woman's craving for sexual variety might lead her to have sex with women as well as with men.[39] Sapphism in this model was not a transgression against feminine excess but an extension of it. Although Saint Paul harshly condemned sex between women, the sense that, in having sex with other women, women were only fulfilling their natural sexual voraciousness helps to explain the light view of sapphism in eighteenth-century texts like *Venus in the Cloister* and John Cleland's *Fanny Hill.*

As long as sapphism did not involve any element of masculinity, it was not threatening. As soon as women began to cross-dress or to use phallus substitutes like dildos, however, male authors were ready to condemn them harshly. Women having sex together were far less worrisome than women seeming to act like men.[40] For example, while Cleland's *Fanny Hill* presented sex between women as a comic introduction to the more "substantial" pleasures of heterosexuality, Cleland was far harsher about sapphism in his translation of a work about the cross-dressing Catherine Vizzani. She, unlike Fanny Hill, engaged in masculinizing practices, like using a dildo, that Cleland termed "nauseous" because they involved the appropriation of phallic power. Likewise, when William King slandered the Duchess of Newburgh, he wrote a poem in which he cast her as a lesbian. Yet, as he represented her, her crime was less having sex with women than wanting to rival men, and the poem eventually rewarded her with a phallus.[41] Sapphism was a threat not to reproduction or to the family but to gender hierarchies.

The rise in the civil humanist model of gender made it unlikely by the end of the century for a woman to be praised for having masculine characteristics. As James Fordyce noted, "A masculine woman must be naturally an unamiable creature. . . . Any young woman of better rank, that throws off all the lovely softness of her nature, and emulates the daring intrepid temper of a man—how terrible!"[42] Numerous works repeated that men should be manly, and women, womanly. Theatrical cross-dressing was increasingly frowned upon as a violation of femininity.[43] Even as radical a thinker as William Blake included as one of his Proverbs of Hell a call for distinct gender roles: "Let man wear the fell of the lion, woman the fleece of the sheep."[44]

Just as the civil humanist model of gender guaranteed that a sodomite was a man with feminine desires, so a woman who had sex with other women had to have masculine ones.[45] To a degree, it seems that lesbians from this period also understood themselves in cross-gendered terms. Three of the most public examples of women known for loving other women, Anne Damer, Lady Eleanor Butler, and Anne Lister, all adopted masculine dress and manners. The women who occupied the proto-*femme* roles in lesbian relations were far less visible, and the degree to which they even conceived of themselves as transgressing conventional sexual roles remains an unanswered question for historians.

At the same time, it would be too simple to claim that women with masculine traits were entirely stigmatized. Admittedly, overtly masculine women in late eighteenth-century novels usually appear as figures of ridicule, descendants of the conventional virago. Yet prominent female novelists of the late eighteenth century did not create female heroines who simply embodied the new, determinate ideal of feminine behavior found in the conduct books.[46] Late eighteenth-century heroines are often not submissive, passive, and obedient. Instead, as Patricia Meyer Spacks has argued, they have "energy of mind," a mixture of high intelligence and strong feeling that challenges the stereotype of the angel in the house.[47] Ann Radcliffe's Ellena in *The Italian*, for example, when imprisoned in a tower, gains from the surrounding landscape a sublime strength that convinces her of her ultimate rightness: "She would experience, that [man's] utmost force was unable to enchain her soul, or compel her to fear him, while he was destitute of virtue." To John Aikin, the heroines of the 1790s seemed so masculinized that, in his "Literary Prophecies for 1797," he predicted that "a novel, by a lady, will make some noise; in which the heroine begins by committing a rape, and ends with killing her man in a duel."[48]

Admittedly, even as such novels made mental energy a heroine's most attractive quality, they forced her to lose it in order to become a suitable wife. Nevertheless, the energetic minds of these heroines, without making them masculine, distinguished them firmly from the bland icons of the conduct books. Just as the man of feeling bonded with men rather than with women, late eighteenth-century female heroines, as Claudia Johnson has argued, had friendships with other women that were stronger and more certain than those with men: Ellena's relation to Olivia in Radcliffe's *The Italian*; Mary's love for Ann in Mary Wollstonecraft's *Mary: A Fiction*;

the friendship between Mrs. Arlbery and Camilla in Frances Burney's *Camilla*; and the sisterhood of Marianne and Elinor in Jane Austen's *Sense and Sensibility*.[49]

A highly tentative acceptance of the feminized hero and the energetic heroine in no way increased tolerance for male or female homoerotic activity. The potentially blurry line between the femininity of the man of feeling and that of the sodomite made it all the more necessary to distinguish firmly between the two. Arrests for sodomy rose dramatically at the end of the eighteenth century and beginning of the nineteenth.[50] While sapphism was not legally recognized as a crime, the work of Randolph Trumbach and Lisa Moore has revealed a growing public recognition and stigmatization of women believed to have sex with other women.[51] The collision of the civic and civil humanist ideologies helped to create the odd double bind of homosexuality, in which the admired behavior of the man of feeling and the energetic heroine was only a hair's breadth away from the most despised behavior of the sodomite and sapphist.

THE GENDER OF GENIUS

Genius in the eighteenth century seems initially to have nothing to do with gender-crossing. No eighteenth-century writer overtly connected the two. The earliest link that I have found is Samuel Taylor Coleridge's dictum that "a great mind must be androgynous," first published in 1835 but derived from a notebook entry of 1820.[52] Nevertheless, Coleridge's statement had a long prehistory in the eighteenth century. With the new meanings that genius acquired came new images for the gender of art and artists.

I will avoid repeating the many critics who have traced the history of genius through its origins in Roman cults and its development in British criticism by Dryden, Addison, Young, and others.[53] By the eighteenth century, genius had roughly five meanings: "(1) genius as an attendant spirit, (2) genius as inclination, bent, or bias, (3) genius as mental endowment, (4) genius as the person endowed with superior faculties, and (5) genius as superior ability to succeed in some particular art."[54] Although the second meaning is probably the most common in eighteenth-century writing, this book is primarily concerned with the fourth and fifth meanings. In particular, I am interested in the development whereby genius came to stand for a small group of people. By the end of the eighteenth century, the genius as an almost magically gifted individual had largely supplanted genius as the peculiar characteristics of any person, place, or thing.

Previous critics have written the history of genius by looking at the many treatises about it, such as William Sharpe's *Dissertation on Genius*, William Duff's *Essay on Original Genius*, and Alexander Gerard's *Essay on Genius*. While these treatises are important and I rely on them heavily, looking only at them assumes that genius was always a precisely defined philosophical category. Actually, it was a loose term of praise in poems, reviews, biographies, broadsides, collections, portraits, novels, and educational tracts. Like "effeminacy," its power came partly from its vagueness. Rarely a carefully defined concept, genius was a general and usually positive term whose meaning was taken to be self-evident.

Writers often linked genius to two equally vague categories: originality and sublimity. Although the association with sublimity is more important for my argument, it depended on a prior association with originality. Writers never tired of repeating that true genius was original: "It is invention, and that alone which deserves the name *genius*"; "*Originals* can arise from Genius only"; the "degree of Genius" that has "superior excellence, deserves the name of ORIGINAL"; "In general, the first rank is assigned to those who have invented, when there was no example or model of which they could avail themselves"; "the characteristic of genius is *invention, a creation of something not before existing*"; genius "is the introduction of a new element into the intellectual universe."[55]

The difficulty with praising originality was the impossibility of defining how one recognized it. From a strictly logical point of view, the demand for originality was meaningless. As Joel Weinsheimer notes about Young's *Conjectures*, "If the original is inimitable, this consequence necessarily follows: that all imitations are original; and thus the entire edifice built upon the dichotomy of the two must inevitably dissolve."[56] Yet originality did not become a rallying-cry because of its logical rigor. Instead, it answered an important need in the eighteenth-century literary system about the author's status.

Martha Woodmansee and Catherine Gallagher have shown the importance of genius and originality for the emergence of concepts of copyright and intellectual property. According to Paul Hiffernan, writing in 1770, the genius virtually poured himself whole into his art: "Enthusiasm irradiates his glowing fancy, and operates an immediate transition of the poet into each character he draws."[57] Such an association proved useful for authors wanting to claim that their work belonged to them alone. The origin of a work of genius came from the personality of the genius, who infused himself or herself into the text.

If genius helped to link authorship to private property, it also helped booksellers to turn books into commodities. Books no longer appeared as collections of general information but as repositories of individual genius, an intangible quality that lay behind the words. To buy genius was far more exalted than merely buying words. By the latter part of the century, "genius" was prominent in titles such as *The Beauties of Goldsmith; Or, the Moral and Sentimental Treasury of Genius* (1782) or *The Beauties of Swift; Or, the Favourite Offspring of Wit and Genius* (1782). Such titles promised not miscellaneous poems or essays but direct contact with an ideal world of artistic excellence. Although the *Cabinet of Genius* (1787) was only a collection of illustrated poems, the title proclaimed a whole that genius would make greater than the sum of its parts. Similarly, Thomas Tomkins's 1806 anthology *Rays of Genius Collected to Enlighten the Rising Generation* taught that children should read great authors not, as in older anthologies, to improve their grammar or to practice elocution, but to be inspired "with a love of their genius."[58]

Original genius also helped eighteenth-century writers to weaken the perceived stranglehold of the classics. As Annette Wheeler Cafarelli argues, the debate on genius shifted "the moribund ancient-and-modern polemic to the question of what kinds of literary powers can prevail over time."[59] While original geniuses could appear at any time and place, the association between genius, originality, and nature encouraged writers to find the purest forms of genius in supposedly less civilized ages. William Jackson spoke for many when he noted that "the early stage of society . . . is most favourable to Genius, and the advanced state of mankind to Taste."[60] While Homer was always cited as the exemplar of primitive genius, genius rehabilitated the literature of other "primitive" times as well, such as the Middle Ages. As Richard Hurd asked rhetorically, "May there not be something in the Gothic Romance peculiarly suited to the views of a genius, and to the ends of poetry?" In his Dedication to his *Reliques of Ancient English Poetry*, Percy likewise wrote that "the infancy of genius" was "nurtured and advanced" by the bards he describes.[61] The association between genius and the primitive even fostered an appreciation for Eastern literature. For example, in arguing that "ORIGINAL GENIUS always discovers itself in Allegories, Visions, or the invention of ideal Characters," William Duff maintained that the best examples could be "drawn from the Eastern and the *Egyptian* mythology."[62]

Genius had to be sublime as well. Theoretically, a genius could be original but not sublime, and a sublime writer could be neither a genius nor an original. Yet most eighteenth-century writers were not interested in such logic-chopping. Since Young had suggested that works of original genius were like the sublime in being characterized by their limitless power, super-human strength, and superiority to convention, it was only a small step to suggest that the content of works of genius should also be sublime. For eighteenth-century writers, it was a commonplace that the originality of genius was manifest in the sublimity of its creations, which refused all boundaries and became laws unto themselves.[63] For example, genius was described in sublime terms as "the supreme arbiter and lord of Nature's whole domain; her superior, her king, her god."[64] A poetic genius, according to Duff, manifested this superiority through sublime qualities, "an IRREGULAR GREATNESS, WILDNESS and ENTHUSIASM of Imagination."[65] No systematic criticism was adequate to genius, so a writer like Shakespeare was "not to be tried by any code or critic laws."[66] Poets never tired of highly conventional paeans to the superiority of genius over convention.[67]

The association between genius and the sublime is particularly useful in explaining how male genius came to be perceived as having feminine qualities. Both genius and the sublime were associated with excess. As William Combe noted in 1784, genius "soars above, and it grovels below, without resting for a moment in the middle path of Discretion"; according to Burke, the sublime "in all things abhors mediocrity."[68] Both, as a result, went directly against the Aristotelian praise of the mean. Under the civic humanist model of gender, the excessiveness of genius and the sublime placed them much closer to femininity than to masculinity.

In linking the sublime to femininity, I part company with many critics who link it to masculinity.[69] Femininity in its older garb as all that is excessive, outrageous, and unbounded haunts the most famous eighteenth-century discussion of the sublime, Burke's *Enquiry*.[70] In particular, Burke treats several supernatural female beings as causes of the sublime, including harpies, Virgil's Fame, and Homer's Discord. He quotes Lucretius as feeling delight ("*voluptas*") and shuddering ("*horror*") when he sees the sublime and feminized spectacle of Nature laid open and unveiled ("*Natura tua vi / Tam manifesta patet ex omni parte retecta*"). Burke similarly mentions "the terrible picture which Lucretius has drawn of religion, in order to display the magnanimity of his philosophical hero in opposing her."[71] He makes religion a "her" rather than an "it," thereby feminizing religion's sublimely "terrible" qualities. Throughout Burke's text, the associations of femininity in the civic humanist model, which had traditionally appeared as ludicrous or comic, are revalorized as sources of strong aesthetic sensation.

Traces of the Burkean association between an older mode of femininity and the sublime appeared throughout eighteenth-century descriptions of genius, as when William Duff argued that a poetic genius is "like the *Delphi-an* Priestess" in being "animated with a kind of DIVINE FURY."[72] More generally, genius resembled the sublime in that, despite its purported masculinity, its excessiveness associated it with feminine figures. Young, for example, explicitly masculinized genius when he sneered at Pope for having taken the "*masculine* melody" of Homer's genius and covered it with the "*effeminate* decoration" of rhyme.[73] Yet a countertext of similes in the *Conjectures* reveals that, for Young, genius is less masculine than it seems: "The pen of an *Original* Writer, like *Armida's* wand, out of a barren waste calls a blooming spring" (872–73); "An Adult Genius comes out of Nature's hand, as *Pallas* out of *Jove's* head, at full growth, and mature" (876); "An inventive Genius may safely stay at home; that, like the Widow's cruse, is divinely replenished from within" (878); "During his happy confusion, it may be said to [the genius], as to *Eve* at the Lake, *What there thou seest, fair creature! is thyself*" (879). In no case is the explicit purpose of Young's similes to feminize genius. Yet these local examples have a cumulative effect of suggesting that the genius, if not feminine, is not quite masculine either.[74]

Images of gender-crossing surface frequently in discussions of genius. Isaac D'Israeli suggests that when the work of a genius "is received with favor," he is like a mother proud of her daughter; the genius "resembles Latona . . . who contemplated with secret joy, her daughter Diana . . . whose appearance was taller, and more lovely than her companions." Gerard's distinction between a genius for the sciences and a genius for the arts arises from a masculine / feminine polarity. While the scientific genius "can receive no assistance from the passions" because "truth is the object" of his investigations, the artistic genius is a feminized bundle of sensitivities who needs "an imagination easily affected by the passions."[75] More generally, poetic representations of genius often followed the old tradition of presenting inspiration as female. While Samuel Johnson sternly told an author of a poem on the genius of Britain, "Here is an errour, Sir; you have made Genius feminine," many others made the same "errour."[76] Genius appeared to be a necessary feminine component of the male creative mind.[77]

Christine Battersby has argued that in the eighteenth century "the stock descriptions of women and of genius were so close as to suggest that if only women could be released from domestic duties, they would prove an important reservoir of future genius."[78] Like women, geniuses were associated with fertility, pregnancy, imagination, passion, and nature.[79] Yet this similarity, in Battersby's account, resulted only in the male appropriation of these qualities, not the flowering of female genius. She argues that male genius purchased its femininity at the cost of real female geniuses, and describes the many conduct-book writers, doctors, and philosophers who denied the possibility of female genius.

I want to complicate Battersby's account in two ways. First, as I will show in chapters 4 and 5, interest in female genius was greater than she claims. Concentrating on statements about its impossibility, she bypasses the male and female writers who praised female genius. Second, and more important, by using a model of gender appropriation, she ignores issues of sexual identity. In many cases, male writers appropriated feminine characteristics and remained firmly ensconced within patriarchal, heterosexual patterns. Yet for male and female writers, this appropriation was more troubled than Battersby allows, largely because genius created a possible breakdown in the assumption of natural heterosexual desire. While a man with feminine characteristics might desire a woman, as men of feeling did, there was always the lurking suspicion that the sublime excessiveness of genius might lead to less conventional sexual possibilities. Like the effeminates described in *Faustina*, the genius knew no moderation. The peculiar gender status of genius meant that heterosexual desire could not be taken as a given. Isaac D'Israeli's *Essay on the Manners and Genius of the Literary Character*, a major document in the eighteenth-century definition of the artistic genius's character, demonstrates this suspicion.

Like many eighteenth-century authors, D'Israeli treated geniuses as otherworldly creatures, unsuited to the mundane activities of ordinary men.[80] One sign of this otherworldliness was that geniuses did not marry, or at least not happily. For D'Israeli's genius, domestic life was a disaster: "If we contemplate the domestic life of a man of genius, we rarely observe him placed in a situation congenial to his pursuits." Geniuses suffered at home from not being "surrounded by persons of analogous ideas, who are alone capable of drawing forth their virtues and affections." Consequently, they were "undutiful sons," "disagreeable companions," and "indifferent husbands." D'Israeli gave particular weight to the last possibility by noting that he "would never draw conclusions from particular circumstances, such as, that Addison describes his lady under the character of Oceana, and Steele delineates his wife under that of Miss Prue; the one was a stormy ocean, and the other a stagnated stream."[81] Even though D'Israeli claimed that he would not draw a general conclusion from these instances, merely describing them showed that marriage hindered genius. Addison and Steele were a particularly charged example of the problem of genius and marriage since, as I noted earlier, no less than Pope had branded them "a couple of Hermaphrodites."

If, according to D'Israeli, domesticity and marriage hurt the man of genius, he found relief in his male friends:

> Two atoms must meet, out of the vast mass of nature, of so equal a form that when they once adhere, they shall appear as one, and resist the utmost force of separation. . . . Each must live for the other, decide with one judgment, and feel with one taste. . . . The greatest inconvenience attending such a friendship, is to survive the friend; nor are there wanting instances in which this has not been suffered, and the violence of grief has operated like a voluntary death.[82]

Three pages of examples from the lives of literary geniuses backed D'Israeli up. Although he drew on a long tradition of praising male friendship, the increased prominence of husband and father as naturalized male roles by the late eighteenth century made such friendships as described by D'Israeli potentially anomalous. If ordinary men lived contentedly with their wives and children, geniuses, according to D'Israeli, were happier with their own sex.

Although D'Israeli's book provides the clearest evidence that geniuses were expected to depart from respectable social codes, images of the genius's indifference to women appear throughout much late eighteenth-century literature. The period's two most widely disseminated images of genius were the biographical one of Thomas Chatterton and the fictional one of James Beattie's Edwin in *The Minstrel; Or, The Progress of Genius*. Chatterton inspired passionate debate because he, more than any previous writer, seemed to have suffered the alienation and neglect that were the supposed fate of genius.[83] His suicide inspired floods of elegiac tributes to him as a genius, such as "Neglected Genius; Or, Tributary Stanzas to the Memory of the Unfortunate Chatterton." When Chatterton's critics attacked his supposedly loose behavior with women, one of his champions countered by arguing that, for at least part of his life, he had not cared for women at all. He "was for a considerable time remarkably indifferent to females. He declared to his sister, that he had always seen the whole sex with perfect indifference, except those whom nature had rendered dear."[84] Beattie's much-reprinted poem (inspired by Percy's *Reliques*) similarly described Edwin's indifference to women. In his solitary rambles, Edwin is educated by the beauty of nature around him and by the folktales he hears from an "ancient dame." Yet heterosexual love never becomes part of his education. While other "village-youth" dance in heterosexual pairs, "Edwin, of melody aye held in thrall, / From the rude gambol far remote reclined."[85] Beattie pointedly removed erotic longing from the genius's education. Without being sodomitical, neither Chatterton nor Edwin was a conventional heterosexual lover, husband, or father.

The ascetic image of a poet's Hippolytus-like indifference to women haunted even William Wordsworth's early career, from his "Lines Left Upon a Seat in a Yew Tree" to his portrait of the Wanderer in *The Excursion*.[86] As Marilyn Butler notes, "narcissism and asexuality" became "the commonplaces of the day in critics hostile to Wordsworth" because they registered Wordsworth's use of commonplaces about the genius's ascetic disposition.[87] They might also have noted that in Wordsworth's poetry, as in D'Israeli's treatise, close homosocial bonds flourished in the absence of heterosexual love. Of the Wanderer, for example, the narrator of *The Excursion* notes, "He loved me; from a swarm of rosy boys / Singled out me," and the narrator claims that it was his "best delight / To be his chosen comrade."[88]

The treatises on genius and images like those of Chatterton and Edwin produced two models for genius, both of which avoided conventional male roles. The treatises suggested that the greatest geniuses were so excessive and unbounded that they possessed feminine qualities, especially ones associated with the Burkean sublime. The biographical images of the character of the male genius, on the other hand, underscored his unconventional sexual sides: his unsuitability for domestic arrangements, his intense friendships with other men, and his problematic relations with women. In no cases have I found that any eighteenth-century writer explicitly associated the feminized or antidomestic genius with the sodomite. Yet the step from one to the other was small. A man who had feminine traits, never married, and preferred the company of men possessed all the visible signs of a man who had sex with other men. Even if the visible signs were not an accurate index of his sexual practices, they were enough to be suggestive.

Eventually, the character of genius would offer the best available metaphor for the supposed character of the homosexual. Although the eighteenth-century theorists who wrote about genius never intended to limn the homosexual character, the image that they created would replace the religious image of the sodomite and would provide an image of the homosexual for late nineteenth-century sexology. In the late eighteenth and early nineteenth centuries, the link between genius and homosexuality was never as sharp as it later became. Instead, late eighteenth-century images like the man of feeling, the antidomestic genius, and the feminized creator provided alternatives to the conventional images of the heterosexual husband, father, and lover. As such, they always teetered on the brink of associations with effeminate sodomy, although these associations rarely, if ever, became explicit. This ambiguous position made such roles invaluable for emerging writers who wanted to represent themselves as geniuses.

POLITICS OF GENIUS

By the middle of the century, writers began to use the category of genius to describe themselves as well as others. Established male writers, as if recognizing the potential egotism of such a claim, often made it with considerable self-mockery. George Colman, for example, began in 1761 a series of articles in the *St. James's Chronicle* written by a character who announced, "I am Myself an acknowledged GENIUS." He gave a comic portrait of himself as "an adept in every art; [who] acquires learning without study; improves his good sense without meditation; writes without reading; and [is] full well acquainted with one thing as another." James Boswell, likewise, signed his pamphlet on Samuel Foote's play *The Minor* as "a Genius" and noted about his style, "We *Geniuses*, you know, are frequently absent,—a little given to reverie, or so;—but you must excuse it, you must excuse it."[89]

Other writers took their claim to genius more seriously. Elizabeth Gilding presented herself in her volume *Breathings of Genius* as an isolated genius: "Unhappy in crowds, I have always preferred the society of a few, and the charms of solitude. . . . A despiser of an empty head . . . I devoted those hours to reading and composition, which too many of my sex spend in studying the modes of fashion." For Gilding, the solitary, alienated genius was a powerful role model long before the start of what has usually been considered the Romantic period. Her self-description initially appears to be self-deprecating: "My genius led me to Poetry. I scribbled. It pleased myself. After which a hope arose, that 'The Breathings of my Genius' might not be unacceptable to the public."[90] Her phrase "my Genius" seems to use "genius" in its older sense, meaning her particular character or nature. Yet in the title of her volume, *Breathings of Genius*, in which the possessive pronoun drops out, "genius" seems to have its newer sense of the special talent belonging to a gifted soul. The poems announce themselves not merely as the breathings of her genius, but as those of genius itself.

Whereas literary men like Colman and Boswell claimed genius lightheartedly, a woman like Gilding, with no connection to the contemporary literary scene, was much more serious. Conservative writers lampooned the cult of genius because it seemed to empower writers like Gilding who came from groups that traditionally had been kept out of literary production. Although I have concentrated on the sex / gender anxieties surrounding the

role of genius, its democratizing aspects troubled eighteenth-century writers far more. As Colman noted in his column, although a genius was "a
character purely modern," it had suddenly "become almost universal."[91]
Literary excellence, formerly the preserve of the well-educated elite, was
threatened by the emergence of hordes of would-be geniuses.

Concern over this universality arose partly from a fear that natural
genius might challenge hierarchies of rank. James Currie introduced the
poetry of Robert Burns by noting that "this original genius . . . was in reality what he has been represented to be, a Scottish peasant."[92] Gregory's *Life
of Thomas Chatterton* noted that "the ancestry of men of genius is seldom
of much importance to the public or their biographers" because genius "is
almost a perfect democracy, in which the rise or promotion of individuals
is generally the consequence of their respective merits."[93] If Burns's example held and Gregory was right, then anyone could be a genius, regardless
of rank, blood, or education.[94]

Conservative authors in the late eighteenth century used several strategies to combat this supposed democratic onslaught. One was satire. Thomas
Busby in his *The Age of Genius!* complained of genius, "All *think* they have
it—nay, who has it *not*? / In *courts* it shines, in *senates*, and the *schools*, / And
clears the world of *dunces* and of *fools!*" In language that anticipates the
Blackwood's attacks on Keats, he grumbled that even "th'Apothecary makes
Castalian doses! / And Madam turns Musician and *composes!*"[95] For Busby,
genius was a Trojan horse, an attractive concept that contained within it the
potential to overthrow traditional artistic and social hierarchies.

Didactic literature sternly warned young people not to presume that they
were geniuses.[96] The speaker of "On the Preference of Virtue to Genius"
happily sacrificed "the Muses' love" in order to offer "the pleasing praise" to
Virtue's shrine.[97] A broadside addressed to "Young People of great genius in
any art or science, (MUSICK in particular) who swallow praise too greedily"
informed them that "the wonder" that they excited "belongs to the age, and
not to the abilities." Music appeared as a particular danger in encouraging
some to "demand, or rather extort, precedency by self-sufficiency and intol-
erance."[98] Frances Burney in *Camilla* showed the seeds of Lionel Tyrold's
corrupt character when he, as a youth, "conceived the highest ideas of his
own premature genius," and Maria Edgeworth in *Belinda* similarly blamed
genius for Clarence Hervey's flaws: "He had been early flattered with the
idea that he was a man of genius; and he imagined that, as such, he was entitled to be imprudent, wild, and eccentric." Hannah More told young ladies
aspiring to virtue that they must "renounce the desire of any celebrity" with
"noble indignation," although she added an escape clause maintaining that

"no censure is levelled at the exertions of real genius, which is as valuable as it is rare."[99]

Perhaps the most telling attempt to block the spread of genius was the insistence that genius could not be purely natural because it needed education. Without arguing against genius per se, conservative writers argued against the often-repeated claim that it was inborn, which Hugh Downman in 1806 had take so far as to link to brain formation.[100] They maintained that natural abilities could not develop unless properly taught. According to J. Cawthorn, "Whate'er of genius we inherit, / Exalted sense, and lively spirit, / Must all be disciplin'd by rules, / And take their colour from the schools." Abraham Purshouse in his *Essay on Genius* insisted that "Self-promis'd bards, that for perfection strive, / Must knowledge from each copious fount derive."[101] For such writers, education or its lack differentiated the genius from the dullard.

Just as the antisodomy tracts of the eighteenth century played as great a role in fostering homosexuality as in suppressing it, so the attacks on genius helped in turn to disseminate its cult. Even the insistence on education had a double edge because radical writers used it to argue for a more democratic educational system. According to them, only if education was universal could Britain guarantee that seeds of genius, wherever they sprang up, had proper nourishment. The larger stakes in this debate involved the nature of the educational curriculum and the challenge to tradition posed by experimental educational systems that "emphasize[d] reason and judgment over rote learning."[102] The haunting lines in Gray's churchyard elegy describing unrealized genius, the "mute inglorious Milton," were a battle cry to authors like William Godwin and John Weddell Parsons who advocated educational reform. Parsons, for example, noted angrily, "But how can that be called a state of political refinement, which suffers the greater part of natural genius, only born for works of high contemplation, to be wasted away in common with that order of capacities, which rise no higher than to carry into execution works of manual labor?"[103] For Parsons, if genius needed education, then the state ought to provide it.[104]

All the authors that I will be discussing in this book partook of genius's "outsider" status insofar as they were not professional writers, or at least did not look upon the works that I will be considering as moneymakers. Neither were they part of the gentlemanly, amateur elite that dominated much late eighteenth-century authorship.[105] Instead, they belonged to the growing group of literary outsiders whose justification for publishing was that their work demonstrated genius. When they wrote poetry, they wrote works that were ambitiously experimental, unlike the tidy, well-turned verses that

amateurs sent to periodicals. When they wrote prose, they wrote in a dar-
ingly unusual and even wild style, unlike the well-proportioned sentences of
the Addisonian essay. They occupied the innovative margin of the eighteenth-century literary system. In all cases, the experimental quality of their
work linked it to the aesthetic qualities associated with genius rather than to
pleasant conventions of gentleman authors or the supposed audience-pleas-
ing vulgarity of professional writers.

Given the conservative attack on genius, the stakes were high for these
writers to demonstrate that they were not mere pretenders like Busby's
apothecaries. They needed to guarantee that their works would have an
unmistakable effect on their audience, so that no one could take them as
anything other than works of genius. Their experimentalism is the product
of this pressure to show that they were special. In the following chapters, I
will argue that they used sex / gender representations as a key site of experimentation. Since a writer like D'Israeli had made an unconventional
sex / gender role part of the literary genius's character, writers striving for
this character had to demonstrate to their audience that they too did not fit
the usual mold. Their goal was not to make their audiences think that they
were sodomites or sapphists, but to indicate through their treatments of
desire that they had access to a far greater range of emotional experience
than that of their audiences. Only thus could they be recognized as geniuses.

While I suspect that many of the writers I discuss were conscious of the
pressures created by the cult of genius, the peculiarities of their representations of desire were not ends in themselves but part of a larger strategy
whereby they might infuse their works with the qualities of genius. But
given the way that so many writers had described the character of genius,
the likelihood of using unusual sexual representations as a marker of genius
was high. Since a genius's work was supposed to reflect his or her life, these
writers ran the risk of drawing onto themselves suspicions of being
sodomites or sapphists. But part of the work of genius was to challenge the
audience to accept such risks as part of the experience of art. A faint trace
of possible scandal only heightened the symbolic value of a work of art and
the supposed genius of its creator.

CHAPTER TWO

William Beckford and the Genius of Consumption

Many eighteenth-century writers insisted that taste and judgment had to chasten the wildness of genius. Some, including William Beckford, forgot about taste and judgment and concentrated instead on the wildness. Since, as I suggested in the first chapter, this wildness included breaking down conventional gender roles, the aesthetics of genius spurred some writers to daring and transgressive representations of love. Beckford's *Vathek* tossed taste, judgment, and heterosexuality to the winds in favor of rampant consumerism, boy love, and necrophilia. It is no coincidence that Beckford, a man who paid for his unconventional sexuality with a lifetime of social ostracism, wrote a work that took the aesthetics of genius to the limit.

"Genius" seemed the right word for *Vathek* from the start. One of its first reviewers wrote in 1786 that it was a "work of real genius." He liked the tale's moral, but was most excited by its qualities of genius: "A machinery, not only new but wild and sublime, seizes on the mind, and pervades the whole composition."[1] For him, *Vathek* drew on the exciting new trends in eighteenth-century aesthetics: sublimity, boundlessness, powerful imagination. When it was reprinted in 1815, reviewers used the same language: "The wildness of imagination displayed in it, and that property of genius which elicits from readers a corresponding train of thought . . . claim for the author of *Vathek* . . . our praise"; "In fertility of imagination, and richness and liveliness of description, we have but seldom met with any production that would be raised in our estimation, by being put in competition with the history of *Vathek*."[2] Later in the nineteenth century, John Edmund Reade echoed established opinion: "It will maintain its position among the most original efforts of human genius; the mind that conceived it could conceive anything."[3]

Beckford himself enshrined the perception of his tale as a work "composed in a passionate fit of genius" by making up the story that he dashed it off in three days.[4] His myth drew on a common motif in the eighteenth-century cult of genius: all creation was autobiographical. A genius's works were the effluence of his personality, not carefully crafted artifacts. They were not composed so much as poured onto the page because they were mere extensions of their creator. Beckford further encouraged readers to think that he was his hero by telling his first biographer, Cyrus Redding, that he had used people and places from his life in *Vathek*.[5] To special friends, he read *Vathek*'s unpublished episodes, as if knowing them meant knowing his most hidden secrets.[6]

Many, though not all, twentieth-century readings of *Vathek* have followed Beckford's lead by reading it as autobiography. At their most basic, such readings match characters to people in Beckford's life, so that Gulchenrouz, a beautiful boy, is read as his idealization of William Courtenay, the young aristocrat he loved; the scandal that wrecked his life occurred when the two were caught having sex together.[7] While some critics have avoided Beckford's life in the interpretation of *Vathek* and discussed its sources or ironies instead, gay studies have once again put Beckford's life in the foreground. George Haggerty, for example, reads *Vathek* as "a testimony to the horror with which [Beckford] contemplated his own internal paradox of innocent love and damning desire," while Adam Potkay interprets the tale's exaltation of pederasty in terms of "Beckford's anarchic denial of the need to grow up."[8]

In this chapter, I want to question the assumption that Beckford's writing comes from his "personality," of which his sexuality is one aspect, if his personality is supposed to be a coherent, autonomous object outside of history and society. Instead, I want to reinterpret Beckford through the social and aesthetic forces that conditioned his reasons for writing in the first place. My argument is neither that Beckford adopted the role of genius because he was a pedophile, nor that he became a pedophile once he adopted the role of genius. Instead, I will examine the conditions that made the roles of genius and pedophile so closely intertwined for him that neither can be said to have caused the other.

THE PURSUIT OF LUXURY

Vathek links three hotly debated eighteenth-century categories: effeminacy, genius, and luxury. While I have described effeminacy and genius in the first chapter, Beckford was a serious participant in the luxury debate as well. He entered it partly through the luck of being absurdly rich. As he knew, he was a highly visible example of proper or improper spending, and he chose to become the champion collector of his day. For the twentieth-century reader, Beckford looks like an early example of the stereotypical gay man who loves antiques, china, lacquer, manuscripts, paintings, bookbindings, and much else. Before Beckford, collecting on a grand scale did not necessarily involve associations with homosexuality, but he foreshadowed shopping for beautiful things as a distinctively gay option.

Throughout the luxury debate in which Beckford was involved, writers used economic, moral, religious, and political analyses to understand England's unprecedented wealth. While, as Lorna Weatherill notes, "Advertising and fashion in the eighteenth century played a part in fostering the image of a society falling over itself to consume clothes, furniture, houses, possessions and leisure," opinions about the effects of this image varied widely.[9] Conservative authors, drawing on the civic humanist tradition, feared that consumerism would corrupt society by making citizens focus their energy on private interests, not public ones. As one writer noted, "Where every one is snatching all he can from the public, and, where there is a general neglect of national interest; they grow luxurious, proud, false, and effeminate."[10]

More generally, satirists assumed that consumerism would ruin social hierarchy because it would let anyone with money become a fake aristocrat. They liked to mock members of the lower classes who eagerly aped their betters. For example, R. B. Sheridan's Fag in *The Rivals* knowingly tells a fellow servant Thomas, "None of the London whips of any degree of *ton* wear wigs now." In *The Task*, Cowper shows the collapse of rural virtue through a "rural Lass" whose head is "adorn'd with lappets pinn'd aloft" and whose "tott'ring form" is "ill propp'd upon French heels," as if she were "of a rank / Too proud for dairy-work or sale of eggs." Samuel Johnson discovered the decay of hierarchy even in advertisements, because in them "the noblest objects may be so associated as to be made ridiculous."[11]

On the "pro" side of the luxury fight were such writers as Bernard Mandeville, David Hume, and Adam Smith.[12] In *The Wealth of Nations*, Smith agreed with Hume that "the natural progress of things toward improvement" arose from the "effort of every man to better his condition" by accumulating property. This effort led to "public and national, as well as private opulence."[13] Smith distinguished bad opulence from good by contrasting two paths that a rich man might take:

A man of fortune . . . may either spend his revenue in a profuse and sumptuous table . . . or . . . he may lay out the greater part of it in adorning his house or his country villa, in useful or ornamental buildings, in useful or ornamental furniture, in collecting books, statues, pictures; or in things more frivolous, jewels, baubles, ingenious trinkets of different kinds; or, what is most trifling of all, in amassing a great wardrobe of fine clothes. (310)

As an economist, Smith prefers durable goods because they support more "productive hands" (308). As a moralist, however, the Mandevillian argument is not easy for him because, as he recognizes, such collecting did not produce a good person: "Especially when directed towards frivolous objects, the little ornaments of dress and furniture, jewels, trinkets, gewgaws, [it] frequently indicates, not only a trifling, but a base and selfish disposition" (312). The luxury needed for the spread of wealth did not encourage individual virtue.[14] Smith could justify it only because it maintained "productive hands" and therefore was conducive "to the growth of public opulence" (312).

Like the theorists of genius that I discussed in the first chapter, Smith thought that productive labor created a healthy state. Yet he conflicted sharply with the theorists over what counted as productive. The core of the fight was whether progress arose from mental or manual production. Whereas the theorists of genius argued that social order depended on "the distribution of mental faculties and the accumulation of works of genius," Smith countered that it depended on the desire "to truck, barter, and exchange."[15] *The Wealth of Nations* had little respect for all activities that did not contribute directly to increasing a nation's opulence. In Smith's view, artists were marginal because they could not compete with trade and industry as contributors to national wealth. Even the man of fortune's idle luxury was better than artistic genius because it at least maintained productive labor and increased durable goods.

Beckford's *Vathek* imagines a world in which the base and selfish dispositions despised by Smith have become the law of the land. Everyone, from the Caliph Vathek to the lowliest of his subjects, longs to collect beautiful items: slippers, knives, sabres, beautiful slaves, jars of apricots from the Isle of Kirmith. Even children, left to themselves, spend their time "culling flowers, or picking up shining little pebbles that attracted their notice."[16] We never see anyone making such objects, so the desire for them cannot be justified, as in Smith, by claiming that they create jobs. Rarely do they have a use value: their attraction is their beauty, and their fate is to become part of a collection. In a Smithian economy obsessed with usefulness, collecting is perversely unproductive and self-enclosed. Beckford's *Vathek*, however, responds to Smith by putting collecting in a new and positive light. Rather than being a source of jobs, it becomes a sign of genius.

All the qualities of genius, including wildness, potent imagination, and soaring ambition, belong in *Vathek* not to creators but to consumers. The results of such laissez-faire consumerism, as Beckford reveals, are catastrophic to society. Yet *Vathek*'s commitment to society's health is weak. For Beckford, if society suffers from the ambitious consumption of its leaders, that may be too bad for society.

By linking the aspirations of genius to collections of pretty things, Beckford created an early version of what Colin Campbell terms Romantic consumerism, a "distinctive form of autonomous, self-illusory hedonism" that stems from "daydreaming, longing and the rejection of reality, together with the pursuit of originality in life and art."[17] Consumerism in *Vathek* involves more than the desire to buy. It demands a commitment to qualities fundamental to bourgeois aesthetics: "the rare, the distinguished, the chosen, the unique, the exclusive, the different, the irreplaceable, the original."[18] Like the romantic genius, the Beckfordian consumer longs for secular transcendence, the possibility of rising to a higher, more exalted plane by accumulating things. The collection is the logical outlet for this desire because only unique and irreplaceable objects are worth collecting. Possessing them should be a sure sign of having escaped the grubby cycle of everyday production and consumption.

BECOMING A GAY COLLECTOR

The Beckfords were not aristocrats, nor even gentry, although Beckford asked Benjamin West to invent pictures of his grandparents as if they had been.[19] Like many eighteenth-century nouveaux riches, the Beckfords' money came from slave labor in Jamaica. Beckford's father, Lord Mayor of London and MP for the city, would have given eighteenth-century satirists a good example of how the spread of wealth threatened social hierarchies. He used his wealth to ape the manners of the aristocracy; to build a spectacular home, pretentiously called Fonthill *Splendens*; and to marry into "one of the first families in the land, which could claim descent from the blood royal of Scotland."[20] Traditionally, aristocratic displays of wealth were signs of political power and the magnanimity appropriate to a ruling class. Beckford's father, however, diluted this tradition. In his hands, luxurious objects lost their associations with political magnificence and appeared instead as secondhand images of vulgar display.

Although Beckford was educated to be an extraordinary man who would follow his father's political footsteps, he rebelled against a political career almost immediately. Even before the Courtenay scandal, William Combe's

R[oya]l Register had rebuked him: "A man who lives in a state of active and zealous opposition to the friends of his father's fortune, is guilty of ingratitude both to the living and the dead."[21] Yet Beckford strove for ingratitude. Since his father died when he was ten, he had only his father's reputation to rebel against, and consequently worked all the harder to show how different he was from his father. While sons of traditional aristocratic families had no need to work for distinction since their blood gave it to them intrinsically, he got from his father nothing more than vast wealth. He had to earn distinction, or he would appear as merely an ordinary man lucky enough to have a rich father.

He dedicated his entire life to showing that he was a true original. Since his father had been a gruff man of business and politics, Beckford became the exact opposite, a hyper-refined being who never succumbed to ordinary expectations. As he wrote in his journal for 1779, "Every thing like originality either in taste or conversation is always thrown by the English world into a tub of whimsies—a most contemptible situation in their eyes, of course an eligible one in mine."[22] His fortune helped him to advertise his "originality" since it allowed him to have "the *prestige* of vastness about all his conceptions," as his first biographer wrote.[23] Beckford could use money to try to transcend money.

For Beckford, traditional male roles were a bore. In 1777 he sneered at three gentlemanly possibilities. The first, "*un homme comme il faut*" was "mighty civil, well-bred, quiet, prettily Dressed and smart"; Beckford regretted "how often" he was "doomed to be" such an "Animal." The second, the man of "good sound Sense," would "despise poetry and venerable Antiquity, murder Taste, abhor imagination, detest all the charms of Eloquence unless capable of mathematical Demonstration"; Beckford felt that he was "sometimes doomed" to be this man. The third and worst man would "smell of the stable, swear, talk bawdy, eat roast beef, drink, speak bad French, go to Lyons, and come back again with manly disorders"; this type Beckford was "determined not to be."[24] Least comfortable with the last and most masculine role, he had little desire even to be the more civilized *homme comme il faut.*

Beckford instead worked to be ultra-unmanly. Like fictional men of feeling, he worshipped childhood and boasted that he had "resolved to be a Child for ever!"[25] He displays his trembling sensitivity as often as possible in his early letters, as George E. Haggerty has shown.[26] He denounced "dull impertinent Society" and preferred his "phantastic visions": "I am determined to enjoy my dreams my phantasies and all my singularity, however irksome and discordant to the Worldlings around. In spite of them I will be happy, will employ myself in trifles, according to their estimation."[27] Such visions gave him all the qualities of genius, as he noted reading Ariosto: "Surely those must have every feeling of Genius blunted who are not seized with a kind of enthusiasm upon reading such an assemblage of beautiful Fictions."[28]

Yet while fictional men of feeling rhapsodized in the woods or cried over calamities that they encountered, Beckford took a different road. He adapted his sensibility and feeling to defiantly feminized behavior. In particular, he became a virtuoso collector. He imagined a friend reproaching him by saying, "For God's Sake, William, leave the contemplation of plates and dishes, what will people think if these are the objects that chiefly attract your attention."[29] What people would have thought was that he was behaving like a woman. Although such scholars as Laura Brown and Beth Kowaleski-Wallace have emphasized the importance of women as the eighteenth century's dominant image of the new consumer, Beckford's career draws attention to the importance of male consumption as well.[30] As Dennis Altman has argued, the prototypical modern consumer may not be the woman but the gay man, who has more disposable income and is less restricted by traditional roles.[31] Female puffs, powders, and patches signaled consumption still enslaved to use value, the need to attract men. Beckford's Limoges, lacquer, and libretti freed collecting for true pointlessness.

Beckford played the effeminate consumer most self-consciously in the role of opera lover. As Elizabeth Carter noted, when he "so extravagantly and ridiculously addicted himself to music, all prospect of his becoming great or respectable was over."[32] Carter's link between music and decadence appears throughout Beckford's letters. He writes from Venice to acknowledge that he has been enjoying the lures of pedophilia, his "soft but criminal delight." For him, its cause was his favorite castrato, Pachierotti: "Such Musick—O Heav'n, it breathes the very soul of voluptuous effeminacy." He mentions its "enervating" effects, "fatal style," and "dangerous melody," and suggests that, "were it not for the O[pera]," his "spirits" might be "re-established" enough for him to become a sturdy heterosexual.[33]

For Beckford, such effeminate behavior was more than mere posturing. It was a longing for a kind of salvation in which he could create a timeless, dead world, of a type that Pope had savagely attacked in his treatment of collectors in Book IV of The Dunciad. At twenty Beckford dreamed of a life in which "every month we shall invent some new Ornament for our Apartments and add some exotic rarity to its treasures."[34] He later realized this dream at Fonthill Abbey by accumulating extraordinary collections of china, books, Japanese lacquer, art, and manuscripts.[35] His tastes guaranteed that he had no time for ordinary activities: "I fear I shall never be . . . good for anything in this world, but composing airs, building towers, forming gardens, collecting old Japan, and writing a journey to China or the moon." Creating a world apart, a "lofty Tower" in which he could breathe "an air uncontaminated with the breath of wretches, the objects of our contempt and detestation," was a more attractive goal.[36] Although Beckford married and had two daughters, he truly reproduced himself not through biology but through art.

In *On Longing*, Susan Stewart writes about collecting as if she had Beckford in mind. She treats collections as a "paradise of consumption" because objects in collections represent "the aestheticization of use value." This aestheticization springs from the collector's personality, not the history of the objects collected, because they are divorced from everything except the collector's particular aesthetic taste: "Not simply a consumer of the objects that fill the decor, the self generates a fantasy in which it becomes the producer of those objects, a producer by arrangement and manipulation."[37] Beckford's collections projected an image of self-sufficiency in which objects had meaning only as signs of his personal wealth and taste.

Boys were a particularly seductive taste for Beckford: "It's cruel to hear talk of fair boys and dark Jade vases and not to buy them."[38] Boy love and luxury had a long association in literature. Charles Churchill's antisodomitical satire *The Times*, for example, imagines the pedophile Apicius decking a "smooth, smug stripling" with "a solitaire," "nicest ornaments," and "gay, gaudy trappings," as if seducing the boy meant turning him into a glittering trinket.[39] For Beckford, lovely youths were the ultimate rare objects to be collected. In 1782 he wrote an opera that allowed him to go to Covent Garden to gather "seven or eight stray choristers" who opened "their coral lips very plausibly" in his piece. He also noted tartly that many " 'potent, grave and reverend Seignors' " were "on the 'qui vive' to witness this charming expansion of buds and blossoms."[40] According to him, "respectable" men were as eager as he was to inspect his collection of boys, though they may have been too hypocritical to admit their desire.

Both Beckford's pedophilia and his collections rebelled against the Smithian demand for productivity. Just as Beckford's collections plucked objects from their original, useful context and froze them into tasteful arrangements, so his pedophilia denied the temporal thrust of reproductive sexuality. Especially in his later life, boys were most attractive when they could be assimilated as closely as possible to a consumerist ideal of perfect, dead objects. Since the less subjectivity the boys had, the better, Beckford even seems to have largely given up physical sex for fantasy. As for an interest in homosexual activities among older men, Beckford cared about them insofar as they could form a collection. Specifically, for most of his adult life, he kept scrapbooks with newspaper clippings about virtually every homosexual scandal or execution in Britain.[41]

For Beckford, the pedophile as collector bordered on the necrophile. What Freud generalized as the repetition compulsion and the death drive in *Beyond the Pleasure Principle* appear in Beckford as modes of consumerism. The Beckfordian collector controlled the death drive by surrounding the self with objects that were forever static, including boys. Necrophilia filled Beckford's professions of love for Courtenay: "O Ciel, que me puis-je mourrir dans ses embrassements et plonger mon ame avec le sien dans le bonheur ou les peines qui ne doivent jamais finir [O Heaven, might I die in his embraces and steep my soul with his in happiness or pains that should never end]"; "If anything could reconcile me to death twould be the promise of mingling our last breaths together and sharing the same grave."[42] In themselves, these quotations could be seen as expressions of heterosexual *Liebestod* adapted to homosexual pedophilia. Yet in the context of Beckford's collections, they point to a necrophilic drive for repetitive stasis.

Beckford's "Idyllium of Hylas," a hitherto unpublished manuscript reproduced in this chapter's appendix, demonstrates Beckford's connection between pedophilia and necrophilia. He wrote it in Switzerland in 1778; according to Boyd Alexander, it "appears to be a psychological document of some importance."[43] On first reading, what is most striking about "Hylas" is its style. It is prose aspiring to the condition of china, a block of writing polished to a high sheen. Although a tissue of literary clichés, it uses them to create a self-sufficient space of fantasy. Like the scenes on Keats's Grecian Urn, it is desire frozen for permanent consumption.

Yet "Hylas" is no mere stylistic exercise. It contrasts two representations of desire. The first is the "long friendship" between "godlike" Hercules and Telamon. This bond between adult men is an intellectual relation, in which the friends "discourse" in solitude, separated from other heroes. The other, more exciting desire appears when the nymphs grab Hylas: "A hundred twinkling arms sprung forth, and, grasping his tender limbs, snatched him to their embraces." Despite their embraces, the nymphs do not have sex with Hylas. Instead, they go sex one better by giving him an immortality that is a perpetual death. In Hylas's death-in-life, he becomes the nymphs' prized collection of one, the perfect item that will never need duplication because he will never pretend to meet their desires. As a result, he remains for the nymphs, as "Hylas" remained for Beckford, a fixed reminder of desire possessed but not quenched. The idyll presents the beautiful, dead boy as the ultimate limited edition.

Collecting, necrophilia, pedophilia: all were ways for Beckford to show that he was different from and better than ordinary people. His personality echoed characteristics that eighteenth-century writers associated with genius. In his *Essay on Original Genius*, for example, William Duff had argued that an original genius possessed "IRREGULAR GREATNESS, WILDNESS, and ENTHUSIASM of Imagination." Irregular greatness was a "native grandeur of sentiment which disclaims all restraint"; wildness showed itself in "grotesque figures, in surprising sentiments, in picturesque and inchanting description"; and enthusiasm involved "intenseness and vigour."[44] Duff here might be giving a sketch of how Beckford wanted himself perceived.

The single difference between Beckford as I have thus described him and the man described by Duff was productivity. For Duff, the qualities that he described "distinguish" the "productions" of original genius.[45] Beckford, in contrast, was a consuming genius rather than a creating one. For him, irregularity, wildness, and enthusiasm went into collecting already existing objects rather than producing new ones. Even though, as Stewart suggests, collecting depends on a kind of production, it transforms what already exists rather than doing what genius was supposed to do, inventing ex nihilo.

Much of Beckford's writing advertises his brilliance as a collector, not his original genius as a producer. His first work, *Memoirs of Extraordinary Painters*, showed an exceptional knowledge of art history for a boy of sixteen. As he told Redding, he was able to write it because he grew up "amidst a fine collection of works of art."[46] Kevin L. Cope has analyzed Beckford's early, unpublished work, "The Dome of the setting sun," as a collection of classical passages about the sunset, which he sees as exemplary of Beckford's "explorations of the collecting mode."[47] His *Dreams, Thoughts, and Waking Incidents*, which he revised much later in life as *Italy, Spain, and Portugal*, was not an original work but a revision of his travel diaries. It showed his ability to collect and record interesting and extraordinary impressions. Even "Hylas" is less an original work than a collection of Hellenistic clichés. Likewise, his later satires, *Azemia* and *Modern Novel Writing*, showed how many novels he had read through the skill with which he parodied them.

Only *Vathek* and its episodes were a partial exception. Like Beckford's other works, *Vathek* showed how much knowledge he had collected. As many of its first readers noted, its notes were packed with more information about the Orient than virtually any other eighteenth-century Oriental tale, and Beckford could show off this knowledge because he had a large collection of Oriental manuscripts. At the same time, *Vathek* was more than a catalogue of facts. It was the product of the genius of consumption, in which all the traits of genius belonged to consumers, not producers. Duff's *Essay* had argued that genius wrote in "ALLEGORIES, VISIONS, or in the creation of ideal figures" and singled out "the Eastern manner of writing" as especially appropriate to genius.[48] While most eighteenth-century Eastern tales were sober didactic fables or thinly veiled erotica that hardly conformed to Duff's description, Beckford in *Vathek* came closer to what Duff might have deemed the true genius of Eastern writing.[49]

But Beckford had a queasy, hesitant relation to his own writing, which resulted from a critical flaw in the role he had created for himself. A true genius, according to eighteenth-century theorists, was autonomous. Edward Young noted that imitators had to "travel far for food" while a genius could "safely stay at home," since his power, "like the Widow's cruse," was "divinely replenished from within."[50] The genius needed no approval from any except himself. In a much-repeated myth, the death of genius in poverty and neglect proved that artistic greatness did not depend on pleasing an audience. On the contrary, ideal geniuses wrote only for themselves and for a dimly imagined posterity.

Beckford, in contrast, had no autonomy. While the genius's imagination was supposedly able to produce something out of nothing, no consumer can consume what does not exist. A genius of consumption depends on others to provide objects. Beckford's money came from Jamaican slave labor; his goods needed dealers and traders to procure them; and his proud indifference to the opinions of others meant little unless others recognized it. As George Eliot notes in *Daniel Deronda*, the "state of not-caring, just as much as desire, required its related object—namely, a world of admiring or envying spectators."[51] Half the fun of having sex with boys was shocking others with having done so. Throughout his life, Beckford was caught in the paradox that wanting to be beyond the opinions of others enslaved him to them.

The paradox of wanting and not wanting attention led Beckford to act as if he wanted to publish and not publish at the same time. He wrote several works anonymously or under pseudonyms and wanted to pull both *Dreams, Thoughts, and Waking Incidents* and *Vathek* when they were about to be published. It was as if his ideal would be for everyone to know that he had written something, but for no one to know what it was. That way, he could have the reputation of being a writer but would not have to let anyone see or comment on what he had done. Experience gave him some hard lessons. In the case of *Dreams, Thoughts, and Waking Incidents*, after his friends read the manuscript, they urged him to pull it, and he did: "It was feared by Lettice and other friends that the extravagantly enthusiastic tone of the book might lend colour to the ugly rumours which were being circulated about Beckford."[52] Similarly, Beckford asked Samuel Henley not to publish his translation of *Vathek* in 1786, although he justified his hesitation by claiming that he wanted it to appear with its accompanying "Episodes," which he had not completed. In the event, Henley published his translation anyway and forced Beckford to bring out editions of his original French text.[53]

Yet he never published the three "Episodes" of *Vathek*, and claimed that he had destroyed one because "he thought it would be deemed too wild."[54] The "Episodes," which he read to his close friends, were perhaps the closest he came to his ideal of publishing and not publishing. To need an audience was to admit defeat because it was a reminder of the painful truth that genius could not disseminate itself. Beckford's solution in *Vathek* was to write in so ironic, demystified a mode that the author remained elusive despite the perceived genius of the story. Nowhere does Beckford lower himself to anything so vulgar as a statement of belief. One of *Vathek*'s charms is its ability to wriggle out of easy critical generalizations. Faced with his paradoxical enslavement to an audience he wished to transcend, Beckford found strategies to reveal himself without quite revealing himself.

CONSUMPTION AND ITS DISCONTENTS

Vathek's characters, like Beckford, believe that it is possible to become more than human not by creating things but by collecting them. As Alan Liu notes, "Luxurious particulars (useless in themselves) appear as if they were useful parts in some higher but as yet unsensed whole" to which the characters aspire.[55] Yet *Vathek* also wittily skewers any illusions of consumerist transcendence. Its paradise of consumption looks more like hell than heaven. Beckford's writing opens a fantasy space in which he can both display and keep a critical distance on the enchantments of consumption, to which he seemed to have succumbed in life. To convey the double sense of consumerism, at once grand and absurd, Beckford presents a gendered opposition. Like the satirists before him, he associates the purest, most sublime drive toward consumption with female characters, especially Nouronihar and Carathis, and with heterosexuality.[56] The male characters, especially Vathek and the Giaour, undercut this sublimity by showing how thoroughly consumption fails as a mode of transcendence.

The story of the novella's heroine Nouronihar is about the pure seductiveness of things. In a critical scene, she sees an elaborate spectacle at which voices tell her to leave her childhood love Gulchenrouz for the great Caliph Vathek. If she gives herself to Vathek, "then all the riches this place contains, as well as the carbuncle of Giamschid, shall be hers" (71). Although the voices also promise her "glory" and she occasionally wishes for power, she longs for the carbuncle during most of the novella. Power and ambition mean little for her next to things themselves. After Vathek's long and ardent declaration of love, she is disappointed that he has not "discovered more ardour for the carbuncle of Giamschid" (85). He later describes her as a woman "enamoured of carbuncles; especially that, of Giamschid; which hath also been promised to be conferred upon her" (94). Like the nymphs in "Hylas," she longs for the perfect collection of one item. Although she has a few passing moments of regret for losing Gulchenrouz and abandoning her father, she is, until the end, ready to lose her soul for the carbuncle. While Beckford does not take her pursuit wholly seriously, his tone is complex enough to hint that he might share with her such single-minded devotion to things. Risking everything for the sake of one durable item is for Beckford at once a noble destiny and a ridiculous goal.

For Vathek's mother Carathis, in contrast, objects in themselves mean nothing next to her search for power. Like traditional overreachers, her ambition makes her an ascetic in terms of bodily consumption. She needs "no common aliment" (91) to nourish her, and is "chastity in the abstract, and an implacable enemy to love intrigues and sloth" (92). In itself, her ambition is conventional. Beckford may have made her "a Greek" (8) to recall the hubris of Greek tragedy, although her name also mangles Christian "caritas." What saves her from being a commonplace overreacher is the blithe sangfroid with which she pursues her goals, as when she indulges hobbies like meeting "select parties" of the ladies of the city, poisoning them with scorpions, and "now and then amus[ing] herself in curing their wounds" (38–39). She has the cool unflappability of evil devoid of conscience.

While Nouronihar longs for a beautiful carbuncle, Carathis is vulgar enough to be a utilitarian. She needs the items that she collects, such as "oil of the most venomous serpents; rhinoceros' horns; and woods of a subtile and penetrating odour, procured from the interior of the Indies, together with a thousand other horrible rarities" (31), for her magic spells, through which she hopes to achieve world dominion. Only such items let her summon the powers of darkness to aid her quest for power. She is also the tale's most eager necrophile in her taste for "dead bodies, and every thing like mummy" (42), although these, too, matter to her only because they are ingredients for magic.

In the end, once she reaches the dwelling place of the evil spirits, Carathis demonstrates how little she needs her horrible collections by burning them. Nor does she need Vathek, although she spends much of the tale urging him forward. Having reached the halls of Eblis, she promptly abandons him. Her final punishment is a fit reward for her lust for intangible power. Like all the consumers in the halls of Eblis, she suffers the *contrapasso* of having her own heart consumed in flames. Yet she has the added punishment of glancing "off in rapid whirl" and continuing "to revolve without intermission" (119). While an obvious punishment for her restless ambition, her whirling invisibility is also appropriate for one who has longed for abstract power beyond merely visible things.

Both Carathis and Nouronihar know that the success of female consumption ultimately depends entirely on men. They are powerless without the cooperation of Vathek because he alone can lead them to the best items. Indeed, despite her plans, Carathis only reaches the halls of Eblis because Vathek, in an afterthought, remembers "it is but right she should have her share" of his perdition (115). Vathek himself has a far more complicated relation to consumption. Liu explains it in terms of Vathek's ambiguous desires. He argues that "the significance of Vathek's consuming orality is that to eat one's way through life is to be existentially *incorporative*, to seek to transcend the self by converting all external reality into the self."[57] In this way, Vathek might be thought of as combining aspects of Nouronihar and Carathis. Like Nouronihar, he is fascinated with material objects and consumption. Like Carathis, he has transcendent ambitions and longs for the infinite. Yet, as Liu also notes, Vathek's restless search is plagued by a haunting "awareness of possible inauthenticity" in a way that Carathis's activity is not.[58] He cites the scene in which Vathek, having built his tremendous tower, looks up to find that the stars are still "as high above him as they appeared when he stood on the surface of the earth" (4). No matter how high Vathek aspires, he will never reach the stars' infinity.

Liu implies that Vathek's chief impediment to solipsistic, consumerist bliss is self-doubt. Beckford, however, reveals a simpler but more serious problem. In succumbing to the allure of things, Vathek binds himself to those who can get them for him. Whereas the creative genius of eighteenth-century treatises depended on no one but himself to produce masterpieces, a genius of consumption needed others to create, distribute, and market luxury items. Where Liu sees Vathek's difficulties as internal ones, the tale puts as much emphasis on the difficulties created for Vathek by other people. The lack of autonomy that a genius of consumption would rather ignore constantly confronts him. He makes various gestures at avoiding it by alienating his subjects, as when he meets three holy men from Mecca while perched in "an apartment by no means adapted to the reception of embassies" (39). Yet his efforts are ultimately futile. When, irritated with the Giaour for making him "dance attendance, too long already," he asks, "Besides, who shall prescribe laws to me?" (53). The answer is, virtually anyone. In succumbing to the allure of things, Vathek succumbs to those who can get them for him.

Beckford represents this economic enslavement as a homoerotic one. Vathek's passion for the Giaour hinders all Vathek's aspirations toward sublime limitlessness because only the Giaour can get the best things for him. At the same time, Beckford goes the cult of genius one better by making their relationship an especially bizarre version of the casual homoeroticism endemic to market relations themselves, in which men must attract other men to buy them. The tale illustrates Luce Irigaray's contention that since "the trade that organizes patriarchal societies takes place exclusively among men . . . , homosexuality is the law that regulates the socio-cultural order."[59] The homoeroticism of Vathek's relations with the Giaour lets Beckford manifest his genius through his utter indifference to respectable modes of desire. Yet this indifference also lets him show, in an exaggerated and grotesque form, the relationships between men that are everywhere present in his society. In Beckford's hands, the genius that was supposed to transcend society becomes most ingenious when it exposes a pervasive homoeroticism that society would rather not acknowledge.

Initially, Vathek loves the Giaour's "extraordinary . . . merchandize," including slippers, knives, and sabres of "dazzling radiance" that "fixed, more than all the rest, the Caliph's attention" (5–6). When the Giaour and his goods vanish, Vathek mourns not for lost opportunities but for lost objects: "Where are thy sabres? thy golden key? thy talismans?" (29). Later, when his mind has wandered from his purpose, he is recalled to his quest by "the remembrance of the Giaour, the palace of Istakar, the sabres, and the talismans" (94). Although the talismans are supposed to "control the world" (22), Vathek, like Nouronihar, cares about them less because they bring power than because they are valuable objects. Moreover, as Eblis explains, the talismans are only keys to more objects. Their power can "compell the dives to open the subterranean expanses of the mountain of Kaf" where Vathek's curiosity can find "sufficient objects to gratify it" (111).

Yet Vathek is also his mother's son and feels the lure of immaterial things as well. Through Beckford's fine irony, the more he desires abstract power, the more he is enslaved to the Giaour's hideous body. When he is tortured by thirst, the Giaour gives him a "draught" to cure him, then continues, "To satiate the thirst of thy soul, as well as of thy body, know, that I am an Indian; but, from a region of India, which is wholly unknown" (14). Having learned that the Giaour can quench the thirst of the soul, Vathek "leaped upon the neck of the frightful Indian, and kissed his horrid mouth and hollow cheeks, as though they had been the coral lips and the lilies and roses of his most beautiful wives" (15). As the Giaour well knows, he has hardly satiated Vathek's soul. By revealing his origins in "unknown" India, he makes himself even more tempting to Vathek because he claims to have access to unknown lands. His origins make him a sign for the infinity that Vathek wants to swallow, as Liu notes. Yet the more infinite Vathek's desire, the more he is riveted to the dreadful concreteness of the Giaour's body.

The homoerotic current of their love continues in hints of anal eroticism. While the Giaour identifies himself as an "Indian," Beckford gives him a forehead and body "blacker than ebony" and an "enormous" paunch (6). When Vathek and his followers, exasperated with the Giaour's silence, kick him violently, the Giaour collects "himself into a ball" (18). In a suggestively obscene image, all the people of the city, with an "eagerness beyond conception" (18), are impelled to kick the huge black ball until it disappears down "an immense gulph" (20). Although Vathek cannot descend into the gulf, after he promises the Giaour to abjure Mohammed, the earth opens and he sees "at the extremity of a vast black chasm, a portal of ebony, before which stood the Indian, holding in his hand a golden key" (23). Such imagery suggests a proto-Freudian connection between anal eroticism (Vathek's desire to penetrate the Giaour's chasm) and relations of consumer exchange (Vathek longs to control the place from which the Giaour's beautiful things come).

The historical reference of the Giaour's color gives an extra edge to his seductions. Despite his Indian origins, his blackness associates him, like Carathis's negresses, with the slaves whose labor supported Beckford's plantations.[60] Although the Giaour's "beautiful commodities" appear magically, with no reference to production, his blackness indirectly recalls the slavery that was the source of Beckford's money. The Giaour nightmarishly literalizes and eroticizes Beckford's own subservience to the slaves over whom he seemed to have power, and, more generally, reminds his audience how much of English luxury came from slave labor. The more grotesque and distasteful Beckford can make the relations between the Giaour and Vathek, the more accurate they appear as parodic inversions of England's everyday slave economy.

The most important interchange between the Giaour and Vathek is also the most complicated because Beckford pulls a Fielding-like stunt. An event occurs which at first seems to have one kind of significance; much later in the novel, we are given more information about it that dramatically alters its meaning. The initial meaning, the revised meaning, and the process of complicating the first with the second all become part of the interpretive process. Specifically, the Giaour sets up an exchange with Vathek. He promises Vathek access to his secret treasures if Vathek will provide him with "the blood of fifty children" (23). Vathek sends fifty boys to their deaths, one at a time, while the Giaour "incessantly repeat[s]; 'more! more!' " (27). Yet, after having dispatched them, Vathek discovers that he has been duped and still cannot enter the cave with the Giaour's treasures.

Initially, this episode appears to be one about erotic competition between men. The Giaour is ultimately less interested in eating the fifty boys than he is in ensnaring Vathek. Having captivated the caliph with his merchandise and his hideous body, he lures him on by making promises that he does not keep. The circulation of goods depends on the intersection of male desires, in which men seduce through the strategic display and withholding of information.

Yet, near the end of the novel, Beckford puts the episode in a different light. The Giaour, it turns out, really has not eaten the boys after all, because a "good old genius" with a "fondness for the company of children" had "made it his sole occupation to protect them" (97). He rescues each child just as the Giaour is about to eat him. As a result, the Giaour did not open his cave to Vathek because he did not get the children he wanted. Yet, in the end, the entire exchange is shown to be a farce. The Giaour's bizarre appetites are nothing more than a masquerade he puts on as part of his job, and whether or not they are fulfilled is ultimately irrelevant. He is the servant of Eblis, lord of *Vathek*'s underworld, and all his actions promote Eblis's goal of collecting human souls. The tale's most chilling moment occurs when the Giaour finally reveals that Vathek means nothing to him. As soon as he knows that Vathek's heart will "be kindled like those of the other votaries of Eblis," he dismisses him callously with the words, "As for me, I have fulfilled my mission: I now leave thee to thyself" (114). What had looked like teasing erotic competition is unmasked as a routine, even bureaucratic, procedure.

Only once in the tale does Vathek find a plausible alternative to the Giaour as an object of erotic interest when he falls in love with Nouronihar, "the object that enthralled his soul" (63). For a brief time, the two have a small idyll in which Vathek's curiosity about the Giaour disappears before "all the attractions of Nouronihar" (87). Although Vathek claims that she has enthralled him, he knows that he really holds the power in the relationship: "Your lovely little person, in my estimation, is far more precious than all the treasures of the pre-adamite sultans; and I wish to possess it at pleasure" (84). But what at first seems like a distraction from the Giaour becomes another step to Vathek's damnation. Although Carathis breaks up the love tryst by reminding Vathek of his duty to pursue the Giaour and his merchandise, Nouronihar is as eager as Carathis for Vathek to follow the Giaour and reach the beautiful objects in the halls of Eblis. Vathek's love for Nouronihar, which initially distracted him from the Giaour, ultimately spurs him on to commit the greatest atrocities in pursuit of the Giaour's goods.

Vathek remains touchingly loyal to Nouronihar, but his love does him no good because heterosexual loyalty counts for little in *Vathek*. Immediately before the final descent to Eblis, a good Genius warns Vathek to return Nouronihar to her father and to abandon his quest. Through this episode, Beckford gives Vathek the miscreant's traditional final warning to prove that he damns himself of his own free will. In accordance with tradition, Vathek scorns the Genius's warning: "I have traversed a sea of blood, to acquire a power, which will make thy equals tremble" (105). Somewhat less traditionally, he adds gallantly, "Deem not . . . that I will relinquish [Nouronihar], who is dearer to me than either my life, or thy mercy" (105). Yet his loyalty to her means nothing in the long run. One of the tale's few moments of pathos occurs when Vathek and Nouronihar realize that their love will not survive in what Jorge Luis Borges called "the first truly atrocious Hell in literature."[61] They end up hating each other when their hearts are at last consumed by flames.

The tale's final vision is the halls of Eblis, who is the tale's master collector and its true genius of consumption. Although his halls are packed with sumptuous luxuries, their real prize is Eblis's collection of "adorers": "Some stalked slowly on; absorbed in profound reverie: some shrieking with agony, ran furiously about like tigers, wounded with poisoned arrows; whilst others, grinding their teeth in rage, foamed along more frantic than the wildest maniac" (110). All differences vanish in this prized display, which literalizes the collapse of hierarchies feared by the eighteenth-century opponents of luxury. Those who try to consume more than they should are themselves consumed when their hearts are set on fire; those who try to collect more than they should are themselves collected.

Only the beautiful boy Gulchenrouz escapes Eblis's hell. Although Beck-ford is careful to indicate that Vathek himself never desires Gulchenrouz, who is "the most delicate and lovely creature in the world" (65), the text treats him as a pedophilic fantasy. As Hester Piozzi noted, "Mr. Beckford's *favourite Propensity* is all along visible I think; particularly in the luscious Descriptions given of Gulchenrouz."[62] Carathis wants to employ this lus-ciousness by feeding Gulchenrouz to the Giaour, for whom "there is noth-ing so delicious . . . as the heart of a delicate boy palpitating in the first tumults of love" (95). Yet the good Genius rescues Gulchenrouz just as he had earlier rescued the fifty boys. Although Gulchenrouz initially loves Nouronihar, his cousin and double, after the good Genius takes him to his paradise he quickly forgets her and "the inconstancy of women" (97). Instead, in the "mansions of eternal peace" (97), he receives "the boon of perpetual childhood" (98).

Most critics have agreed with Piozzi that Gulchenrouz reflects Beckford's own preferences. Yet Beckford's representation is not quite so simple. The text subjects Gulchenrouz to a stream of criticism. The voices in Nouroni-har's cavern condemn him as "a giddy child, immersed in softness, and who, at best, can make but a pitiful husband" (71). Vathek complains that Gulchenrouz is "inefficient and nerveless" (74), "has been brought up too much on milk and sugar" (85), and is "a girl dressed up like a boy!" (85). Beckford also makes Gulchenrouz look ridiculous, as in the episode in which he is "persuaded he should actually be damned for having taken too many little freedoms, in his life-time, with his cousin" (87). In the end, the fate of Gulchenrouz mirrors exactly that of the bad characters: he becomes an item in the collection of a powerful master-collector. I agree with Liu when he notes that "we wonder . . . whether childish ignorance is really bliss or itself a species of damnation."[63]

The problem with Gulchenrouz is that he has subjectivity at all. As a pure object, he succeeds admirably in being "the most delicate and lovely creature in the world." When he stops being an object who can be collected or con-sumed and becomes a character judged in terms of his subjectivity, his desires, and his capacity to act, he becomes ridiculous. In the end, he, like Hylas, becomes the perfect pedophilic icon at the cost of losing his subjec-tivity. In the necrophilic paradise of the good Genius, he is happily relieved of the need to be anything more than a beautiful object who passes "whole ages in undisturbed tranquillity" (120).

The real genius of *Vathek* may be not the genius of consumerism but the genius of demystification.[64] What is boundless, original, and sublime in the

tale is the degree to which it reveals the utter worthlessness of the characters' desires, even as it encourages the readers' sympathy with their ambitions. In *Vathek* all desires are empty, yet their emptiness paradoxically
becomes their greatest lure. The novella wanders from episode to episode,
in which every aspiration is undercut with a gesture, and every gesture subverted with a droll detail. Nothing reveals the desirability of the narcissistic
world of consumer exchange more than Beckford's pains to undercut its
every seduction. In one of the first works written to conform to the cult of
genius, Beckford simultaneously provides one of genius's most effective
undercuttings. For later authors, criticizing the cult of genius demanded a
stern moral tone and an indictment of potential narcissism and self-indul-
gence. Beckford, in contrast, offers no sermonlike didacticism. Instead, he
demonstrates with chilling clarity the potential complicity of genius with
an emerging consumer economy and the ability of that economy to subvert
all that genius was supposed to represent.

Given the sublime extent of Beckford's efforts at demystification, it
might seem as if his own life might have escaped some of the traps that he
mocks in his characters. It did not. With unnerving accuracy, he lived out
to the smallest detail the comic deflations of *Vathek*. Through the excesses
of Fonthill, he earned the reputation that he wanted as a man who lived on
a different scale from that of ordinary people. The author of a two-penny
pamphlet about Beckford noted in 1823 that "the minds most nearly allied
to genius, are the most apt to plunge into extremes, and no man at present
can make higher pretensions to a mind of this cast, than the founder of
Fonthill Abbey."[65] Yet Fonthill was also an image of futility. Its huge tower
was built shabbily, mostly so that Beckford could watch it collapse. Yet when
it did collapse, he was not there to see it, so that having prepared for waste
on a grand scale, he could not enjoy it.

In an anonymous article for the *Weekly Entertainer*, published in 1824,
the author imagines "An Unpublished Episode of Vathek," which turns out
to be a thinly veiled account of the sale of Fonthill, forced upon Beckford
by the collapse of the Jamaican sugar trade. "Bekfudi," the "most ambitious
rival" of Vathek, loses his fortune, is forced to sell his palace, and watches as
the people of Samarah come "with money in their vests to purchase some
relic of the magnificent Bekfudi." All are happy except Bekfudi, who
"writhed under the mortifications of his pride, and the outrages upon his
taste" as his palace is "metamorphosed into one large bazaar."[66] The splen-
did collections that Beckford had wanted to place him outside of time and
apart from the world reentered the world as a magnificent auction where
all could gape. Finances forced Beckford into the situation that many

aristocrats of the period adopted voluntarily: making their spectacular collections available to the public, as if the art belonged to the nation even though it was in private hands.[67]

After the collapse of Fonthill and the reduction of his fortune, Beckford still did not give up collecting. When Cyrus Redding visited him at Bath, he noted that Beckford's "fancy seemed to be that in every room in the house there should be articles of the same description, so that if he wanted to look at fine old china, Etruscan vases, Limoges ware, Rafaelle china, books, missals, or prints, in whatever room he might be, there were always specimens of each."[68] It is harder to know for certain how long in his later years he continued to collect boys, although he never stopped collecting newspaper clippings of homosexual scandals.

Yet at the end of his life, a peculiar turn occurred in his life whereby it became clear that he would achieve lasting fame not as a collector but as an author, even though he had devoted far more of his life to collecting than to writing. Although publishers had ignored him for decades, in the 1830s Richard Bentley "foresaw the chance of a 'boom' in Beckford's works."[69] In 1834 he published a revised version of *Dreams, Thoughts, and Waking Incidents* as *Italy, Spain, and Portugal*; the third edition of *Biographical Memoirs of Extraordinary Painters*; and an edition of *Vathek* as part of Bentley's Standard Novels. The next year, he brought out *Recollections of an Excursion to the Monasteries of Alcobaça and Batalha*.

This new prominence ensured Beckford's presence as an icon for a new generation of writers interested in the connection between genius and homoeroticism. Byron had already acknowledged his indebtedness to Beckford in *Childe Harold's Pilgrimage*. Now Beckford saw his work influence Benjamin Disraeli and helped Catherine Gore with her definitive representation of the effeminate dandy, *Cecil; Or, the Adventures of a Coxcomb*. He found that he would achieve immortality not through his vast collections but through the writings that he had earlier been so hesitant to publish. Although they reduced him to the level of an object for consumption, they also guaranteed his continued presence as an influence on English literature, especially among readers with a taste for the outré.

Not surprisingly, even Oscar Wilde's *Picture of Dorian Gray* admits the seduction of Beckfordian collecting. When Dorian needs his picture hidden, he asks an art dealer and his assistant to move it to the top floor of his house. The dealer obliges, but also hopes that he can interest Dorian in a "beauty of a frame" that he has just acquired, adding, "Came from Fonthill, I believe."[70] For a moment, Wilde holds out the Beckfordian past as a temptation to his hero.

Yet Wilde does not allow Dorian to accept the frame. For all Dorian's fascination with external objects, his ultimate temptation for Dorian is not what lies outside of himself, as it is for Vathek, but the blurring of inside and outside represented by his picture. Whereas Vathek's chief tempter and double was the Giaour, Dorian's is himself. It is only fitting that Dorian not accept the external object from Fonthill, because he has already internalized Beckford's connection between love of things, of self, and of other males. But at the end of the novel, in a profoundly Beckfordian twist, Dorian is known by his luxury items. After the servants and police find his hideous dead body, they recognize its identity only from "the rings" on Dorian's hands.[71] Beckford would particularly have liked the collector's excessiveness of "rings," a sign of desires ranging far beyond those signified by a wedding band.

APPENDIX

"Idyllium of Hylas"
(Transcribed from Bod. MS. Beckford d. 21)

The Pleïades, rising with the sun, began to diffuse their genial influence on the pastures, when Jason and his divine companions ascended the Argo. Hercules joined the band: and Hylas attended his footsteps, the breeze waving, as he moved, the soft flow of his golden hair.

No adverse wind obstructed the progress of the vessel: no omen depressed the exultation of the heroes, who soon perceived the Hellespont lessening on their sight.

Thus, impelled by propitious gales, they glided, towards the close of day, by those extensive meads which form the shores of Propontis. Here, numerous herds fed on fresh springing herbage; and clear rivers gleamed in the western sun. The heroes, pleased with the vernal scene, resolve to land; and, casting anchor in a bay, leap cheerfully ashore.

Now, traversing the meads, they chuse some sheltered spot of greensward; and there, amidst cypress and flowering rushes, prepare their beds with the spoils of formidable animals.

Whilst some are reclining peacefully beneath the serene expanse of ether, others prepare the viands, and scatter the ground with canisters of bread.

Hercules and Telamon, whom a long friendship had endeared to each other, retired, as they were wont, from the train of heroes; and spread their repast upon a solitary bank. Hylas did not long remain behind with the multitudes; but hastened towards the godlike friends, and sat gracefully listening to their discourse; until Hercules gave him his vase and bade him fill it with the waters of some neighbouring fountain.

He arose. He cast a look on his sandals; and, crossing the plains with the speed of a young hind, reached a sequestered dale.

It was dark—and no fount appeared. As he listened—a ripling sound caught his ear. Guided by the noise, he descended amongst leafy thickets; and perceived at length a spring almost hidden by its cove. There, the cerulean of the celandine, with the verdure of the adiantum were reflected in the deep clear waters; above which rose mossy rocks that cast a grateful shade. Imagine not these scenes were unpossessed of divinity. 'Twas here the ever wakeful Naïads held their evening revels, to the frequent alarm of benighted travellers.

"Mark, sisters," murmured Eunica from beneath the limpid mirror, "what footsteps press the herbage of our grot?"—"Some youthful Argive," answered Malis, "puts aside the celandine with lovely hands!"—"Ah, could we but seize him!" replied Nychea, Eunica, and all the chorus, with one voice.

As they spoke—the heedless Hylas stooped o'er the brim of the fountain, and immerged the vase he bore into the stream.

That instant, a hundred twinkling arms sprung forth, and, grasping his tender limbs, snatched him to their embraces.

In vain did they braid his hair with fragrant lilies, such as bloom alone in the hallowed recess of their grottos—in vain did they lavish on the youth the gift of immortality—he sighed, he wept, he refused consolation.

They led him trembling to their pumice thrones, whence oozed the rill which fed their fountain. There he remains lost in wonder. At length he begins to remark the polished pavement, where innumerable rills shone like veins of the purest silver. Now, scarce venturing to breathe, he starts at the sight of waters flowing above his head and streaming down the arches of the caves, in whose chambers he descries a thousand fishy forms, with bright scales quivering in the gloom. Now, by the pale light admitted through the watery medium, he perceives the features of the Naïads, flushed with desire. Fain would he fly from their importunities; but, alas, how could a mortal escape!

In the midst of his afflictions, the well-known voice of Hercules descended faintly through the waters. Thrice did the lovely captive reply; and thrice did the unavailing sound rise bubbling from below.

The malicious Naïads sported with his perplexity: and, as he sat dejected on a mossy fragment, danced wantonly around. And now, the moon rising to illuminate that world to which he never could return, gleamed brightly on the spring, and darted her lustre on the humid realms below. Shadows without number, reflected from th'impending vegetation, glanced on the playful group and chequered their lucid forms: but Cynthia, disgusted by their wantoness, soon lost herself in clouds.

Hylas now mourned in darkness—the springs murmured in vain—nor could the lulling song of the Naïads soothe him to repose!

CHAPTER THREE

The Domestication of Genius: Cowper and the Rise of the Suburban Man

Few writers of the second half of the eighteenth century would provide a more dramatic contrast with William Beckford than William Cowper. Unbounded narcissism and endless vistas of luxury fill Beckford's work; Cowper's is tame, small-scale, and carefully restricted. *Vathek* proudly takes on all the clichés of genius, even as it shows the ultimate vanity of its characters' endeavors. Cowper never claims genius for himself and insists on Evangelical Christianity as his inspiration. Beckford was a cult author known only to a few until well into the nineteenth century. Cowper was one of the most widely read poets in Britain, capable of appealing to writers as different as Mary Wollstonecraft and Jane Austen, William Hone and Robert Southey. No writer could have striven less for the spectacular wildness and daring supposedly characteristic of eighteenth-century genius. Whereas the genius was so extraordinary that he was supposedly inimitable and unique, Cowper became a model for respectable domestic behavior.

Yet the cult of genius eventually caught up with Cowper, despite his efforts to avoid it. After his death, his poetry increasingly came to be read in light of the clichés of the genius. The appropriation of Cowper for genius depended partly on the knowledge of his struggle with mental illness, which first gained widespread currency in William Hayley's *Life and Posthumous Writings of William Cowper* (1803–1804). Madness rarely inspired Cowper. For the most part, he wrote his poetry to distract him from madness, and his spells of insanity stopped his work. Yet the mere fact that he had had spells of madness allowed readers to fit him into the model of the unhappy, isolated, tortured genius that eighteenth-century writers like Isaac D'Israeli had popularized. Following the classic pattern of genius, Cowper's life became more interesting for his readers than his work, and the autobiographical moments in his poetry became the most prized. Not surprisingly, given the associations that I discussed in my first chapter, rumors of sexual

anomalies soon accompanied the image of Cowper as mad genius. By the
1830s he was rumored to have been a "hermaphrodite," and such rumors
have survived until today in scholarship about him.

It might seem that Cowper as mad genius is simply a misreading to be
blamed on nineteenth-century readers. Yet, for all Cowper's avoidance of the
cult of genius, it is no coincidence that he could be made to fit its clichés so
easily after his death. I am going to concentrate on the nineteenth century in
this chapter, even though Cowper is an eighteenth-century writer, because I
believe that Cowper's nineteenth-century reception reveals aspects of his
work and of emergent aspects of eighteenth-century masculinity that have
thus far been invisible to scholars whose purview ends at 1800. He demonstrated what I will call the domestication of genius, a translation of the rebellious originality and autonomy of genius into the coziness of the domestic
sphere. This domestication proved fundamental to the developing role of the
suburban man, for which Cowper provided a model to generations of readers.[1] Yet the role of the suburban man was highly vexed because it was never
clear how original and autonomous a man might be in his own house without stepping over the line, as Cowper had, into unacceptable behavior. In
particular, given Cowper's bachelorhood, the suburban man was especially
vulnerable to fears that his perceived specialness might be interpreted as the
wrong kind of specialness, sexual deviance. Life in the suburbs had as a precondition the ability to distinguish sharply between the respectable character
of the suburban man and the deviant character of the homosexual.

Not coincidentally, the nineteenth century witnessed a marked increase
both in suburban populations and in the systematic surveillance and persecution of men who had sex with other men. As Louis Crompton notes,
"During the period 1805–1835, when the annual number of executions for
all crimes dropped from about seventy to thirty, sodomy was the only crime
for which the number of hangings remained more or less constant."[2] By
1885, while sodomy was no longer a capital crime, the Labouchère amendment to the Criminal Law Amendment Act increased the courts' ability to
punish sex between men by making acts of "gross indecency" illegal when
they occurred not only in public, as had been the case previously, but also
in private.[3]

While few critics have described the historical relation between homophobia and the suburbs, several have noted that the rise of industrial capitalism, the precondition for suburbia's growth, affected nineteenth-century
sexual roles. Such critics as Barry D. Adam, Guy Hocquenghem, David Fernbach, and John D'Emilio argue that privileging the nuclear family as the
kinship structure best suited for the reproduction of an industrial workforce

led to a vigorous condemnation of homosexuality: "Homosexuality . . . was cast, by the terms of the capitalist discourse, as a violation and failure, a betrayal of masculine virtues necessary for success. Any male temptation toward sexual polymorphism would be contained by the monogamous family."[4] While condemnations of homosexuality were hardly new to the nineteenth century, turning the nuclear family into a norm, according to these critics, made homosexuality appear more deviant than ever.

While I agree that industrial capitalism profoundly altered sexual roles, the arguments of these critics do not fully explain the existing evidence of British homophobia in the nineteenth century. If the nuclear family was an ideal supposedly endangered by homosexuality, we would expect to find writers condemning sex between men because it had no place in the normative roles of husband and father. Yet medical writers from this period were far more worried about masturbation than homosexuality as a danger to masculinity.[5] Despite the sacred aura with which nineteenth-century writers surrounded the family, they did not express concern that homosexuality might threaten its stability until the Wilde trials near the century's close. For the most part, individual male writers rarely justified their homophobic attitudes through appeals to the family. Nor did they invoke any of the other medical, religious, or legal associations that they might have used to stigmatize homosexuality.

Instead, the rhetoric of their reactions is far more immediate and personal. Nineteenth-century condemnations of sex between men are striking because writers seem so deeply affected by the topic. Their comments combine disgust and anxiety in a vocabulary of queasy nervousness. While the "unspeakability" of homosexuality was originally part of a religious formula ("crimen inter Christianos non nominandum"), by the nineteenth century it was more of a social embarrassment. For example, when Percy Jocelyn, the Bishop of Clogher, fled the country after he was found having sex with a soldier, a writer for the *Times* noted that "mingled feelings of sorrow, humiliation, and disgust" had almost prevented him from writing at all.[6] Contemplating the pedophilia of classical Greece, Percy Shelley thought that "the laws of modern composition scarcely permit a modest writer to investigate the subject with philosophical accuracy."[7] Reacting to Byron's separation from his wife, widely rumored to have been caused by his homosexuality, Macaulay noted in 1816, "You have heard of course of the abominable, unmanly, conduct of the Peer-poet to whom we once paid such admiration"; in 1835, William Macready noted that when dinner conversation turned to the topic of Byron's separation, "some observations were made which occasioned me disagreeable sensations; being evidently perceived, it made me quite embarrassed."[8] W. H. Thompson in 1868 thought that "it seems impossible that Plato can seriously have entertained the paradox that the παιδῶν ἔρως [love of boys] was a necessary step toward moral perfection."[9] David Lester Richardson read Shakespeare's sonnets "accompanied by [a] disagreeable feeling, bordering on disgust," and Henry Hallam noted that "it is impossible not to wish that Shakespeare had never written them."[10] In all cases, these men did not turn to abstract discourses to justify their distaste. Instead, they assumed that readers would recognize personal embarrassment as the only appropriate reaction to love between men.

Eve Kosofsky Sedgwick's theory of homosexual panic best explains the convention of acute discomfort that characterizes such comments. Where other critics have assumed that men fear homosexuality because it differs from respectable norms, Sedgwick's theory suggests that homophobia arises from fears not of difference but of similarity. Male homosocial bonds that followed from splitting off the public from the private sphere in the eighteenth century allowed homophobia to regulate all male behavior: "Because the paths of male entitlement, especially in the nineteenth century, required certain intense male bonds that were not readily distinguishable from the most reprobated bonds, an endemic and ineradicable state of what I am calling male homosexual panic became the normal condition of male heterosexual entitlement." Although men had to form bonds with other men to succeed in public life, the ambiguity of those bonds led to a combination of "acute *manipulability*" arising from fear of potential homosexuality and "a reservoir of potential for *violence*" to enforce a distinction between homosexuality and heterosexuality blurred by the homosocial spectrum.[11] Sedgwick's theory of homosexual panic accounts for the discomfort of nineteenth-century homophobic rhetoric in a way that the other theories do not. It describes why men stigmatized homosexuality not from allegiance to abstract causes but from urgent personal need.

Yet Sedgwick's theory also has a weakness. It does not explain how social structures could have implanted in men the fear of their own potential deviance in the first place. Her argument assumes that the prevalence of homosocial bonds would be enough to lead men to fear and to react against their own potential for homosexuality. Yet, given the normative nature of homosocial bonds, men could be in them without ever noticing what she takes to be obvious, that the lines between these bonds and homoerotic affections were ambiguous. In the nineteenth century, conventional patterns of socialization in schools, the military, and the workplace made the ambiguity of homosocial desire invisible.[12]

For the panic she describes to have occurred, as I believe it did, other social practices must have existed that encouraged middle-class men to understand themselves as at least potentially "different." Only then could they worry that they might appear to resemble other "different" men, and react against that perception. The work of Pierre Bourdieu, a sociologist not usually associated with theories of gender or sexuality, is useful in explaining such practices.[13] Bourdieu is best known to Anglo-American readers for *Distinction*, his sociology of taste in twentieth-century France. In it, he explains how the struggle for "symbolic capital," defined as "the acquisition of a reputation for competence and an image of respectability and honourability," structures social hierarchy. According to Bourdieu, members of the bourgeoisie display symbolic capital by demonstrating their superiority to whatever they perceive to be merely commonplace. A range of intellectual and educational institutions encourages

> the cult and culture of the "person," that set of personal properties, exclusive, unique, and original, which includes "personal ideas," "personal style" and, above all, "personal opinion." It could be shown that the opposition between the rare, the distinguished, the chosen, the unique, the exclusive, the different, the irreplaceable, the original, and the common, the vulgar, the banal, the indifferent, the ordinary, the average, the usual, the trivial . . . is one of the fundamental oppositions . . . in the language of bourgeois ethics and aesthetics.[14]

These oppositions are so fundamental because they spring from the theories of genius that I described in the first chapter. What Bourdieu describes as the "cult and culture of the 'person'" is a transformation of the language of genius so that it applies less to creators of artistic works than to creators of a personal lifestyle. To adapt Bourdieu's analysis, bourgeois society places on every individual who desires distinction the responsibility to arrange his or her life so as to achieve an "exclusive, unique, and original . . . personal opinion." I call this responsibility the "domestication of genius," whereby the eighteenth-century demand for originality in art became the nineteenth-century middle-class demand for originality in living.

The domestication of genius means that genius is no longer the province of a privileged group of artists in a Bohemian romance. Instead, all respectable people have to be geniuses to the extent that they can invent themselves as unique, special, and original. The greatest fear of the domesticated genius is to be commonplace or to mouth secondhand opinions. The greatest success is to know that a special personal style infuses every aspect of one's life and gives one special prestige in the eyes of the world. Since the capitalist workplace privileges a high degree of uniformity, regularity, and efficiency, the domesticated genius flourishes most freely in the private space of the home, in which specialness can be safely indulged without interfering with business. The suburban house, which has traditionally depended on an absolute split between public and private spaces, became the ideal space for nurturing the domesticated genius.

Bourdieu associates the cult of the person with the bourgeoisie in twentieth-century France, but it also existed as a slowly developing ideal of the members of Britain's newly enfranchised middle classes in the nineteenth century. Whereas an older aristocratic hierarchy had distinguished itself from the common people through a mystique of blood, a middle-class man distinguished himself from commonness through the capacity to assert his personal judgment on matters of taste. In the early nineteenth century, the writings of William Hazlitt most vividly foreshadowed the mode of distinction described by Bourdieu. Hazlitt poured scorn on commonplace people as those "who have no opinion of their own and do not pretend to have any." An individual gained an identity through the ability to distinguish himself: "Good nature and common sense are required from all people: but one proud distinction is enough for any one individual to possess or to aspire to!" The goal of life was to be able to claim at least one such "proud distinction."[15]

In the first half of the nineteenth century, valorizing individual difference came to seem a national trait of the English, owing in part to Protestantism's traditional emphasis on private judgment as opposed to received authority. Two case studies in the development of cultural competence, James Buzard's discussion of tourism and my work on Byron's reception, document how members of the middle classes sought to "lay claim to an aristocracy of inner feeling, the projection of an ideology of originality and difference" in their responses to mass cultural phenomena.[16] Nineteenth-century writers often described the desire for distinction in terms of the supposedly English ability to "think for oneself." Edward Lytton Bulwer, for example, claimed in 1833 that "men now think for themselves. That blind submission to teachers, which belongs to the youth of Opinion, is substituted for bold examination in its maturity." By 1859, Samuel Smiles found that "one of the most marked characteristics of the Englishman" was "his strong individuality and distinctive personal energy." In the same year, John Stuart Mill elevated the desire to be distinguished from the commonplace into a moral imperative: "It is not by wearing down into uniformity all that is individual in themselves, but by cultivating it and calling it forth, within the limits imposed by the rights and interests of others, that human beings become a noble and beautiful object of contemplation."[17] Englishmen were proud of the extent to which they had become domesticated geniuses.

Critics examining gender in the nineteenth century have largely ignored how the atomizing need for distinction tempered the construction of normative gender roles. For men in particular, distinction may have conflicted with the pressure on them to conform to the recognized roles of husbands and fathers struggling valiantly to provide for their families. As Mill's qualifying phrase "within the limits imposed by the rights and interests of others" suggests, men had to be different enough to validate their cultural competence, but not different enough to estrange themselves from bourgeois norms of masculine behavior and family structure. The cult of the person had within it a lurking danger that masculine distinctiveness might be carried too far and cross the invisible yet critical line between acceptable difference and unacceptable deviance. In this context, even the most hallowed language for describing individual distinction, such as the Protestant convention whereby each man identified himself as the worst of sinners, might seem dangerous. John Bowdler, editor of *The Family Shakespeare*, worried that Christians who dwelt too explicitly on the "deep depravity of their hearts" and spoke of themselves as "the vilest of sinners" were indulging a practice "liable to considerable perversion" that might "lead to some serious dangers."[18]

Nineteenth-century suburbia embodied the paradoxical but fundamental demand that the middle-class man be distinctive without being too distinctive. According to Olsen, in the nineteenth century, "the ordinary suburb assumed, if it did not impose, at least outward conformity of behavior; but in planning and in the symbolism it tried to see to it that such conformity took place by individuals and families cut off from the obtrusive society or inspection of their fellows." Bulwer thought that Englishmen had become so attached to privacy that they had become recluses. Domesticity had given them the habit "of viewing with indifference all the sphere beyond, which proverbially distinguishes the recluse, or the member of a confined coterie."[19]

This reclusive privacy encouraged men to lead a double life split between the world inside and outside the home. At home, men could domesticate genius by cultivating what Mill calls "all that is individual in themselves" as a compensation for the supposed conformity demanded by the public world of labor.[20] Similar as the houses may have been, each could be modified to suit the taste of its particular owner: "Through judicious selection of materials and styles, and appropriate arrangement of tectonic elements such as windows, porches, and chimneys, a house could represent much of the personality, occupation, or heritage of the inhabitant."[21] Dickens's *Great*

Expectations provides the best-known representation of the fantasy of the domestic genius in the figure of John Wemmick, a man of virtually no personality in public who has a richly eccentric and hidden life at his home, a modest cottage decorated as a castle. When asked if his employers know about his home life, Wemmick says, "No; the office is one thing, and private life is another. When I go into the office, I leave the Castle behind me, and when I come into the Castle, I leave the office behind me."[22] In this essay, I use the phrase "suburban man" to indicate a Wemmick-like model of masculine selfhood that encouraged men to cultivate in their homes a "true," distinctive inner self that was separate from the public identity supposedly forced on them by their occupations.

In the nineteenth century, men in the suburbs were not the only ones leading double lives. Although Ed Cohen has described the double life as the master trope in late nineteenth-century narratives by and about homosexuals, the anonymous *Don Leon* (c. 1830) suggests that it was associated with men who had sex with other men far earlier.[23] When *Don Leon*'s author wanted a rhetoric in which to deplore the harsh treatment of sodomy, he defended sodomites by claiming that at least they kept their practices secret. Their "secret haunts were hid from every soul." Only the legal system insisted on dragging them into the public light, since their "one propensity . . . always hides / Its sport obscene, and into darkness glides, / Which none so brazen'd e'er presumed to own, / Which left unheeded, would remain unknown."[24] *Don Leon* made evident the potential analogies between the nineteenth-century's suburban man, cultivating his distinctiveness in private, and the nineteenth-century sodomite, indulging his passions in darkness. Both led lives divided between a public exterior of conformity and a secret, hidden life that flourished with little regard for the world's opinion.

This analogy suggests that Sedgwick's theory of homosexual panic might lead to a theory of suburban panic. Like Sedgwick, I agree that the homophobia of nineteenth-century middle-class men had a paranoid element based on the fear of potential similarities between "normal" men and "deviant" homosexuals. Yet I would locate the source of this paranoia not in the homosocial spectrum, as Sedgwick does, but in the special, distinctive existence to which suburban ideals encouraged all middle-class men to aspire. Homosexuality would be more likely to provoke embarrassed reactions not if it were something entirely alien to middle-class experience but if the possibility of a secret life hit uncomfortably close to home. Every man's castle might turn out to be some men's closet.

Although I locate this development in nineteenth-century Britain, I hesitate to specify too sharply a date for the emergence of suburban panic and of the kind of homosexual behavior with which it was associated. In his *History of Sexuality*, Michel Foucault suggests that 1870 "can stand" for the "date of birth" of the homosexual defined "less by a type of sexual relations than by a certain quality of sexual sensibility." While he takes his argument about this definition seriously, his casualness about the date gently mocks a naive historical positivism, as does Sedgwick when she questions the usefulness of fighting over a "Great Paradigm Shift" in the history of homosexuality.[25] Although much of this essay will concentrate on events between 1780 and 1880, I would not treat this period as a distinct phase. Just as British suburbia gradually spread throughout the nineteenth century, so its effects on masculine behavior and homophobia should be understood as a slow but pervasive dissemination of norms of masculine respectability associated with a new living environment.

As Cohen argues, "If one of the ways that the stability and dominance of normative masculinity has been shored up over the last century is by (re)producing it in opposition to its antithetical 'other(s),' then the (violent) repudiation of those who are categorically defined as antagonistic to it can be imagined by those interpellated as 'manly men' to fix the vicissitudes of their own subjectivity."[26] In particular, writers loudly insisted that individual distinction was a manly characteristic. "Unmanly" men who had sex with other men were represented, in contrast, as faceless members of a cult. Given the association of homosexuals with cultlike groups, it was particularly important for men wanting to appear manly to underscore their personal discomfort with homosexuals. In the middle-class imagination, if homosexuality was a mark of succumbing to a group mentality, homophobia was a mark of individual character. Consequently, nineteenth-century men made sure that their homophobia looked like the spontaneous expression of personal embarrassment rather than behavior mandated by an array of social, medical, legal, and religious practices and institutions. By repudiating men who had sex with other men, the suburban man could draw a line between being different and being deviant.

WILLIAM COWPER AND THE SUBURBAN MAN

To develop the history of the suburban homophobia and the domestication of genius, I turn to William Cowper and to his most famous poem, *The Task* (1785). Cowper may seem a strange choice for a discussion of nineteenth-century masculinity since he is an eighteenth-century writer whose poetry has traditionally been read in the context of eighteenth-century literary developments. I base my choice on the work of Leonore Davidoff and Catherine Hall in *Family Fortunes*. According to them, Cowper and Hannah More were the most influential writers on members of the nineteenth-century middle class. While More concentrated on female behavior, Cowper, especially as he presented himself in his most famous poem, *The Task*, became the most widely loved role model for middle-class men. By citing a variety of archival sources, Davidoff and Hall create an impressive portrait of the range of Cowper's appeal. He was accessible as an ideological paragon to virtually all who could read or who could have others read to them.[27]

I am struck by the sheer unlikeliness of Cowper as a model suburban man. He had no job, wife, or children; suffered paralyzing bouts of religious mania; lived as a virtual recluse in rural England; and was supposedly a hermaphrodite. Yet legions of readers looked to him and his work to help them understand what a man's happy home should be. My purpose in this chapter is not to offer a literary analysis of *The Task*. Rather, I want to draw on Raymond Williams's characterization of the dynamic interrelations of a cultural system in terms of dominant, residual, and emergent elements to examine aspects of Cowper's work most important for middle-class masculinity.[28] Since the study of Cowper generally has fallen to scholars of the eighteenth century, they have treated his work in terms of its dominant elements, such as its Evangelicalism or sensibility, or its residual elements, such as its indebtedness to Augustan satire.[29] Yet, except for Davidoff and Hall, scholars of the nineteenth century have overlooked the emergent elements of Cowper's work at the cost of ignoring a formative writer for nineteenth-century manhood.

Nineteenth-century reactions to Cowper repeatedly emphasized that he provided the perfect image of domestic life. In 1800, *The Monthly Magazine* noted that *The Task*'s most memorable passages were those "in which the charms of rural life, and the endearments of domestic retirement are described." The poem's reputation was "established by universal consent." For Francis Jeffrey in 1803, Cowper was popular because of "the minute and correct painting of those home-scenes and private feelings with which every one is internally familiar."[30] In 1816 the *Quarterly Review* rose to a small rhapsody: "We share his walks, or his fire-side, and hear him comment on the newspaper or the last new book of travels; converse with him as a kind familiar friend, or hearken to the counsels of an affectionate monitor. We attend him among the beauties and repose of nature, or the mild dignity of private life." An encyclopedia entry of 1838 explained that "by inspiring a feeling of intimacy, a kind of domestic confidence in his readers, he made his works 'household words.' "[31] While it was unlikely that everyone in

England had the income to sustain the happy home described by Cowper, his work was so popular and so widely read that it became a touchstone.

Cowper's home in *The Task* was not in the suburbs but in the rural village of Olney. Yet, as Robert Fishman demonstrates, Cowper's domestic ideal inspired the Evangelical founders of Clapham, the "prototypical suburban community" and model for later British suburbs. They organized a living environment that balanced closeness to the city with what Cowper had represented as the desirable solitude of the country.[32] Cowper also inspired J. C. Loudon, the nineteenth-century writer who had the most influence on the layout and appearance of British villas, gardens, and suburban homes. Loudon loved Cowper's poetry and frequently quoted his work, especially *The Task*. In works like his *Suburban Gardener and Villa Companion*, Loudon adapted a Cowperian vision for Britain's middle classes by explaining how men living near the city could retain the healing refuge of domesticity and nature. So important were Loudon's works that Melanie Simo maintains "there is scarcely a nineteenth-century town or village in the English-speaking world that shows no trace of Loudon's . . . influence." Loudon guaranteed the truth of Thomas Shaw's claim that Cowper was "the painter of domestic life" whose views had been "deeply incorporated" into nineteenth-century "household existence."[33]

In discussing Cowper, Davidoff and Hall overlook an important and unexpected aspect of his writing: he was a bachelor. Work on domesticity has so emphasized the role of middle-class women that it comes as a surprise to note that neither wife nor children appear in *The Task*. Although some analyses of bachelors assume that they threatened gendered norms of domesticity, *The Task*'s representation of a bachelor's life, surprisingly, became *the* model for the English home.[34] *The Task* presents no father reading to or playing with children, no husband counseling his wife, and no family enjoying meals together, and yet it came to define domestic life. The poem does occasionally mention Cowper's female companions. Mary Unwin appears as his friend in Books I and IV, but Cowper never names her, never gives her voice, and barely sketches her. Lady Austen inspires the poem by suggesting that Cowper write about the sofa, but she, too, vanishes from the poem after his opening invocation. He treats his female friends in such a cursory way that he increases rather than decreases the impression of his solitude.

In representing himself as a solitary, Cowper was not being radical: he drew on the long Horatian tradition recounting a single man's pleasure in rural retirement.[35] Nevertheless, it might seem that other eighteenth-century works would have provided more suitable models for nineteenth-century

middle-class men, especially books emphasizing the importance of husbands and fathers to the domestic unit. Yet the overwhelming evidence of
Cowper's popularity suggests that the roles of husband and father were not
the only ones available to men for their home lives. While Davidoff and Hall
suggest that "the real reward for the private man would, of course, be in the
world to come," *The Task* showed instead that men might find internal, spiritual rewards in homes that belonged to this world.[36] Cowper's self-portray-
al was an emergent representation of the suburban home's supposed ability
to nurture a man's sense of privileged distinction from the outside world.

In accordance with the Horatian tradition, Cowper locates his home on a
moral map that associates the city with luxuriousness and effeminacy and the
country with health and truth. London has some virtues, but for the most
part is a sink of iniquity, the seat of "ambition, av'rice, penury incurr'd / By
endless riot; vanity, the lust / Of pleasure and variety" (3.811–13).[37] In the
country, "virtue thrives as in her proper soil" (1.600). Its purest essence
appears in Cowper's home, where "domestic happiness" is the "only bliss / Of
Paradise that has survived the fall!" (3.41–42). It contrasts in every way with
London's corruptions and violence.

Cowper describes how he learned to value the blessings of home in what
became the poem's most famous passage. Rather than being a joyful
account of domestic pleasure, his story is one of personal trauma and partial recovery:

> I was a stricken deer, that left the herd
> Long since; with many an arrow deep infixt
> My panting side was charged when I withdrew
> To seek a tranquil death in distant shades.
> There was I found by one who had himself
> Been hurt by th'archers. In his side he bore,
> And in his hands and feet the cruel scars.
> With gentle force soliciting the darts
> He drew them forth, and heal'd and bade me live.
> Since then, with few associates, in remote
> And silent woods I wander, far from those
> My former partners of the peopled scene,
> With few associates, and not wishing more.
> Here much I ruminate, as much I may,
> With other views of men and manners now
> Than once, and others of a life to come.

(3.108–22)

Cowper draws on the familiar story of Christian conversion, a shortened version of the exodus narrative that dominates English spiritual biography.[38] Yet if he conforms to the conventional role of the Christian man, what is most striking about the passage is how subdued his promised land is. The joy and comfort in Christ and incorporation into the church that the redeemed man should conventionally find in his salvation are eerily absent. Christ is at the center of the episode, yet as the passage describes it, he functions less as the center of Cowper's spiritual life than as a liminal figure carrying Cowper into a new understanding of his isolation. Though Cowper proudly reconceives of himself as a man whose solitude authorizes his "other views of men and manners" and "others of a life to come," an undercurrent of mysterious loneliness persists. His haunting repetition of the phrase "with few associates" (a Miltonic effect put to utterly un-Miltonic uses) emphasizes "few" so as to make the associates figures of absence, not presence.

Part of Cowper's mystery derives from his use of the stricken deer emblem itself, which implies that he could narrate a more detailed history than the one he shares with the reader. In masking the specifics of his situation, he seems to be holding back details that might explain the full truth of the situation. Why did he have to leave "the herd"? What were the "arrows" that wounded him? Why has he not returned to society? Why, if he has been saved, does he still refer to himself as if he suffered from depression? If Cowper is a domestic everyman, then the history of the domestic everyman is markedly secretive. Not everything about the passage is mysterious: the deer is obviously Cowper and the "one" who rescues him is obviously Christ. Yet Cowper does not reveal how or why he was wounded and what the historical reference for the allegorical darts might have been.

The Task intensifies the secrecy of the stricken deer passage by suggesting that Cowper has not fully recovered from his experience. For example, he praises writing poetry for its ability to "steal away the thought / With such address, from themes of sad import" (2.299–300) without explaining what the themes are. In the middle of a description of England's climate, he notes that its gloom "disposes much / All hearts to sadness, and none more than mine" (5.463–64) without explaining why. When faced with "fierce temptation," he claims that "to combat may be glorious, and success / Perhaps may crown us, but to fly is safe" (3.684, 687–88). These lines set up the expectation that he will describe the true Christian's ability to resist temptation, but he startlingly concludes by recommending flight. For unknown reasons, naked fear blanks out more exalted theological considerations. While such scattered references to Cowper's distress appear as diversions from topics at hand, they cumulatively heighten the sense that he is with-holding key aspects of his personality.[39]

Throughout *The Task*, Cowper lets his audience know enough about him-self to suggest that he is harboring secrets. At a general level, Cowper's secre-cy effect anticipates a "deep" selfhood never fully available to language that would become a nineteenth-century commonplace, typifying a major strand in the romantic representation of subjectivity from Wordsworth and Byron to Freud. Michel Foucault's work has provided the most influential account of the construction of this subjectivity. In *The Order of Things*, he traces a shift from eighteenth-century "order" to nineteenth-century "history," which involved the construction of "a depth in which what matters is no longer identities . . . but great hidden forces developed on the basis of their primi-tive and inaccessible nucleus, origin, causality, and history." In *The History of Sexuality*, Foucault argues that the discourse of confession gave such depth to subjectivity itself. Confession created a literature about "the infinite task of extracting from the depths of oneself, in between the words, a truth which the very form of the confession holds out like a shimmering mirage." For Foucault, the chief signifier of the depths of subjectivity was sex: "It is in the confession that truth and sex are joined."[40]

While I agree with Foucault about the rise of a "deep" model of subjec-tivity, I question the assertion that the truth of this subjectivity arose solely through a discourse about sex. At least before Freud, sexual desire was not assumed to provide an incontestably adequate index to the full depths of the inner self. Instead, it was an always inadequate means to gauge a depth that lay beyond language. While sex, as Foucault suggests, may have been a privileged theme of confession, it was never the only one and never the one that necessarily carried with it the full revelation of truth. I would posit a more tentative relation between sexuality and subjectivity: a discourse of sexual desire existed as a possible but never absolutely certain means of knowing mental depths that were potentially immune to any explanation. If psychic knowledge was in the first place sexual knowledge, it was also true that knowledge of sexuality did not necessarily exhaust knowledge of subjectivity.

I note the possible distinction between knowledge and sexuality to avoid the too hasty reduction of Cowper's secrecy effect in *The Task* to sexual secrecy. Instead, it is useful to explore its significance quite apart from its potential sexual associations, although I will turn to these later in the essay. In itself, the association between confession, secrecy, and inner depths was not new to the late eighteenth century. Yet it had new effects in Cowper's work because his poem was so overtly autobiographical. While many eighteenth-century poets wrote about themselves and their feelings, they often did so within the conventional lyric decorum of a generalized "I." Cowper, unlike such writers as Gray or Collins, exchanges the lyric "I" for an autobiographical narrator who describes his daily activities, his opinions of the world, and even, as in the stricken deer passage, his past. Personal self-revelation led Cowper to be loved for what were perceived to be his personal qualities even more than for his verse.[41]

As Cowper presents himself in the stricken deer passage, what he has gained from his mysteriously traumatic conversion experience is a sense of being different. Without ever invoking the cult of genius, he has achieved the domestication of genius that I described earlier, in which his finest accomplishment is the creation of himself as a unique and special individual. Cowper is privileged because he can believe that he is better than the larger community from which he has set himself apart. In the Horatian tradition, the mere fact of being in the country gave the solitary man a sense of privileged superiority. But since Cowper eventually finds that even the country is imperfect because "the town has tinged the country" (4.553), he internalizes the privileged vision of the rural solitary.[42] For him, his distinction arises from the internal changes he underwent after the experience described in the stricken deer passage, not from his location in Olney. His secrecy effect is a continual reminder of the mysterious process whereby a man who was once a member of a herd has developed in solitude "other views of men and manners now / Than once, and others of a life to come." However painful his experience was and still is, it allows him to claim a sense of distinction because he knows that his perspective is different from and superior to that held by merely ordinary men.

Cowper's domestication of genius reveals itself not in how he creates art but in how his sense of his own specialness permeates all his activities, down to the most mundane. For example, when he reads the newspaper, he feels how fully his "other views" separate him from the public world that it represents:

> 'Tis pleasant through the loop-holes of retreat
> To peep at such a world . . .
> Thus sitting and surveying thus at ease
> The globe and its concerns, I seem advanced
> To some secure and more than mortal height,
> That lib'rates and exempts me from them all.
> It turns submitted to my view, turns round
> With all its generations; I behold

The tumult and am still. The sound of war
Has lost its terrors 'ere it reaches me,
Grieves but alarms me not. I mourn the pride
And av'rice that make man a wolf to man,
Hear the faint echo of those brazen throats
By which he speaks the language of his heart,
And sigh, but never tremble at the sound. (4.88–89, 94–106)

The newspaper, by translating the public world into a network of textual
signs, allows him to imagine it as something from which he is cut off but
which provides him with material for reflection. Cowper resembles the
reader that Jon Klancher describes as being fashioned by early nineteenth-
century periodicals: "The individual reader must be defined as a textual
presence in a discourse where he constitutes himself as a 'reader' by becoming aware of his distinction from all social, collective formations that he
learns to 'read' as a social text."[43] Not only is Cowper separate from the
social text of the newspaper; he is also superior to it, "advanc'd / To some
secure and more than mortal height." He revalues his social marginality as
a position that earns him privileged interpretive power. Because he is not
involved in the morass of politics, he can see the true littleness of contemporary leaders in ways that commonplace men who lack his depth of mysterious experience cannot.

Cowper in *The Task* is a specifically masculine model. When he reads the
newspaper, the action belongs to him and not to his female companions.
He is "fast bound in chains of silence, which the fair, / Though eloquent
themselves, yet fear to break" (4.53–54). Reading the paper becomes a peculiarly masculine form of self-discipline and concentration, a chaining in
silence, that women are forbidden to interrupt. The passage is typical of the
ways in which the home allows Cowper to cultivate an internal life that
seems to transcend history itself. Although in his home he may not have
achieved "immortal fame" (6.933), he insists that he obtains "fresh triumphs
o'er himself / And never-with'ring wreaths, compared with which / The
laurels that a Caesar reaps are weeds" (6.937–39). The self-discipline that he
exercises genders the inner life of the home as a masculine mode of con-
quest superior to military victory.[44]

Although when Cowper wrote in the 1780s, modern suburbs had not yet
appeared in England, for his later audiences the suburban home provided
the ideal space in which to develop and refine the domestication of genius,
since it valued privacy above all else: "The most satisfactory suburb was that
which gave [the Englishman] the maximum of privacy and the minimum of

outside distraction."[45] Whereas previously men had sought distinction by proving themselves in the public world, Cowper suggested that a man gained his true distinction only at home. Since few men had the financial resources to take Cowper literally and abandon public life altogether, the suburbs allowed them both to earn the money necessary to maintain a suburban home and to live far enough away from the city that it could be perceived as a refuge. At home, they might follow Cowper's example, which suggested that the home could soothe the secret wounds produced by the public world's demands for conformity. Whether or not men actually thought that their public lives hurt them as Cowper says his life did, *The Task* taught them that the private sphere was a space of compensation.

It may seem misleading for me to suggest that the compensation Cowper found in the home was that of internal distinction or the domestication of genius since many of his readers would have recognized his opinions as commonplaces of Evangelical Christianity. Nevertheless, Cowper avoided seeming to be merely the spokesman for a religious movement, although his Christianity played an important role in his canonization as a model domestic poet. Nowhere in the poem does he ever admit that an Evangelical revival has occurred or that he is part of a larger Evangelical community. Although relations with other Evangelicals mattered greatly to him, they play no part in *The Task*. Instead, he takes his Protestant stance to such an extreme that he presents his opinions as if they belonged to him alone, although he always insists that they have divine sanction. His opinions look like the inspired meditations of a reflective Christian rather than the platform of an aggressive and well-organized educational, religious, social, intellectual, and political movement.[46] By 1834, a non-Evangelical writer like Sir Egerton Brydges could note that "Cowper, from a singleness of thought, sentiment, and expression, which comes home to every one's business and bosom, will always keep possession of the public interest."[47] While Brydges acknowledges Cowper's attractive "singleness," he does not connect it to Protestant nonconformity. Instead, he understands that Cowper became a shared ideal not because of his religion but, paradoxically, because of his particularity.

Yet the desirability of "singleness" like Cowper's was not unambiguous. While I earlier suggested that his secrecy did not necessarily have to be interpreted in sexual terms, I want now to turn to the aspects of the poem that encouraged such an interpretation in the nineteenth century. The domestication of genius brought with it the aura of possible sexual deviance that eighteenth-century writers had attributed to genius. Just as one sign of the genius's rebellion against convention lay in his rebellion against fixed gender categories, so the domestic genius might find his privileged specialness arising from sexual nonconformity. Yet such non-conformity was never a conscious strategy for Cowper, as it was for a writer like Beckford. Instead, if Cowper's secrecy anticipated romantic subjectivity, it also anticipated the homosexual closet in ways that had important effects for the suburban man's relation to homoeroticism. In a complex definition, Sedgwick notes that " 'closetedness' itself is a perfor-mance initiated as such by the speech act of a silence—not a particular silence, but a silence that accrues particularity by fits and starts, in rela-tion to the discourse that surrounds and differentially constitutes it."[48] Cowper's secrets in *The Task* surrounded him with many silences, not solely ones about his sexuality. Yet certain aspects of his self-representa-tion provided clues for later readers about his possible sexual deviance.

As critics have long recognized, Cowper's self-presentation in the strick-en deer passage has much in common with the eighteenth-century man of feeling, such as his "virtually helpless, passive, 'feminine' " characteristics.[49] As I noted in the first chapter, the man of feeling's putative femininity did little to challenge heteronormative sexual roles.[50] Cowper, however, differed from men of feeling like Laurence Sterne's Yorick and Henry Mackenzie's Harley by avoiding displays of heteroerotic attachment. *The Task* begins with his taking up his friend Lady Austen's challenge to write about the sofa, a piece of furniture associated in eighteenth-century literature with illicit or violent sex. Cowper's mock-epic history drains the sofa of its sexu-al associations, an act characteristic of his desire for "a world in principle as chaste / As this is gross and selfish" (6.836–37). He is a bachelor markedly uninterested in the possibilities of women as objects of erotic sympathy.

No eighteenth-century writers that I have discovered found any scandal in Cowper's self-representation as a bachelor, probably because the reflec-tive, solitary man was such a literary commonplace after the success of such works as John Milton's "Il Penseroso," Edward Young's *The Complaint; Or, Night Thoughts on Life, Death, and Immortality*, and Thomas Gray's "Elegy Written in a Country Churchyard." Yet Cowper differed from these writers in one respect: by placing his solitary in a setting so closely associated with women, marriage, and the family, he drew attention to his anomalous celibacy. While this anomalousness did not affect his eighteenth-century reception, perceptions about Cowper changed dramatically in the nine-teenth century. In the next section, I will trace how reactions to him point to a crisis in the formation of the suburban man's identity. Cowper's link between secrecy and distinction could be read as one between secrecy and sexual deviance in ways that made the violent repudiation of homosexual-ity necessary for the suburban man to maintain his masculine authority.

THE STRICKEN DEER AND THE HERMAPHRODITE

In the years following *The Task*'s publication, Cowper's readership spread as he was taken up by the Evangelicals and their periodicals, reprinted in numerous editions, acquired by lending libraries, excerpted in schooltexts, copied in commonplace books, and generally treated as an unexceptionable author for the respectable home. From the start, readers wanted to know the answers to the mysteries with which he surrounded himself. The *Gentleman's Magazine*'s comment in 1785 held true for readers at least until the end of the nineteenth century: "All who read [Cowper] must be curious to know him and his communication, and grieve that such a writer, such a man, ever had an 'arrow' in his side."[51] The solution to the identity of the mysterious "arrow" that received most attention from early biographers was not Cowper's sexuality but his insanity. Almost immediately after his death, accounts of his madness began to appear, which provoked a stormy controversy between Evangelical and anti-Evangelical readers about whether Evangelicalism had created or cured it.[52]

Part of Cowper's success depended on his readers' assimilation of him to the role of poetic genius. Even though he never used the word to describe himself, it quickly became a standard part of descriptions of him, as when John Blain Linn included Cowper in his poem *The Powers of Genius*. The publication of William Hayley's *Life and Posthumous Writings of William Cowper* did the most to place Cowper in the cult of genius. First, hoping to calm the argument among religious groups about Cowper's madness, Hayley printed hundreds of Cowper's letters for the first time. He commented that they "must render all who read them intimately acquainted with the Writer, and the result of such intimacy must be . . . an increase of public affection for his enchanting character."[53] Hayley's project worked better than he might have dreamed. Cowper's letters became extraordinarily popular because, like *The Task* itself, they made readers familiar with the everyday life of an exemplary domestic man. As one reviewer wrote, "What imagination can be so dull, after having read these letters, as not to . . . behold him in the act of writing and in that of reading aloud to the ladies, or in the humbler employments of feeding his birds and his tame hares, winding thread, working in the garden, and even mending kitchen windows?"[54] The letters may even have increased Cowper's readership because they were less heavily infused with Evangelical doctrine than his poems were. If in *The Task*, Cowper located the authority of his personal opinions in his exemplary Christianity, the exemplarity of the letters arose because they were supposed to be the genuine productions of a model man.

Yet Hayley also produced what looks at first like a curious split in Cowper's reception. Even as Cowper was the model domestic man in his letters, he also became, in Hayley's hands, a tortured genius:

> The smothered flames of desire uniting with the vapours of constitutional melancholy, and the fervency of religious zeal, produced altogether that irregularity of corporeal sensation, and of mental health, which gave such extraordinary vicissitudes of splendor and of darkness to his moral career, and made Cowper at times an idol of the purest inspiration, and at times an object of the sincerest pity.[55]

After Hayley's biography, calling Cowper a genius was no longer simply a casual word of praise. It signified instead that Cowper manifested all the melodramatic traits with which the eighteenth century had endowed genius. Poetic responses to Hayley revealed how deeply his portrait of Cowper's madness touched contemporary readers. For example, while addressing the "Ill-fated Minstrel!" Bernard Barton lamented that "the feverish dream / Of mental anarchy, with dreadful gloom, / Obscur'd the light of hope's celestial beam." By 1833, Cowper had become a standard example of mad genius, as the nearly one-hundred-page analysis of him in R. R. Madden's *Infirmities of Genius Illustrated* demonstrates. His supposed personality had become inseparable from his work.[56]

Discomfort at the split between Cowper as a masculine role model and Cowper as insane genius became especially pronounced with the 1816 publication of his *Memoirs*. Although many late twentieth-century critics have found this text to be his most compelling, early nineteenth-century readers disliked the specificity with which Cowper described his madness and his suicide attempts: "We do not like to be carried back to all the particulars of his early offences. . . . When they are pressed once more upon our notice, with all their minuteness, they have a tendency . . . to detract somewhat from our respect"; "The secret sufferings of the gifted but most unhappy subject . . . were detailed with a minuteness, which nothing but the unsocial and indelicate taste of *methodism* could for one instance have endured."[57] Just as Bowdler had warned, if a man told too much about what made his suffering distinctive, he would not be admired. Cowper's memoir strained the ability of his audience to distinguish between the glamorous insanity of genius and the sheer wretchedness that Cowper described.

One might suppose that such a strain would have ended Cowper's popularity. If Cowper the bachelor seems an unlikely model for suburban masculinity, Cowper the mad genius seems impossible. Yet the actual reactions of nineteenth-century readers were more complex. Among Evangelicals, he remained an irreproachable standard of piety. While Southey's 1837 anti-Evangelical edition of Cowper sold 6,000 copies, the Rev. T. S. Grimshawe's 1835 Evangelical edition sold 32,000.[58] For William Blake, the Romantic link between madness and inspiration encouraged him to see Cowper as an inspired visionary.[59] What prevented Cowper from losing his audience entirely was the increasing perception of his femininity. Rather than seeing him as a sharp satirist, as his first readers tended to do, he came to seem a man who for various reasons appeared interestingly feminine. This femininity prevented the potential division between Cowper the domestic model and Cowper the lunatic. Those who admired Cowper the domestic man could praise his feminine meekness, gentleness, and domesticity. At the same time, they could admit that, at certain moments, Cowper's feminine side had unfortunately become too strong and had allowed him to descend into madness. Those who wanted to see Cowper less as a moral model and more as an aesthetic genius could praise his feminine side, which eighteenth-century treatises had insisted was part of the genius's character.

Not all readers were happy with Cowper's supposedly feminine side. Hazlitt complained of the "effeminacy about [Cowper], which shrinks from and repels common and hearty sympathy." Frederick Denison Maurice worried that the "gentleness of [Cowper's] life might lead some to suspect him of effeminacy," but he assured them that "the old Westminster school-boy and cricketer comes out in the midst of his Meditation on Sofas."[60] For both writers, "effeminacy" had lost its older associations with civic humanism and had come to mean a man who has the characteristics of femininity in civil humanist discourse, as discussed in the first chapter. In defending Cowper, Maurice did not suggest that Cowper really possessed adult masculine characteristics. Instead, he projected backwards into the eighteenth century the aggressive masculinity associated with Victorian public schools. Better for Cowper to be a boy than to be effeminate.

Yet the distaste that Hazlitt and Maurice felt for Cowper's effeminacy was far less common among readers than a recuperation of Cowper as a man who, while flawed in many ways, still remained a model. Toward his "feminine" aspects, critics who treated him as a model domestic man maintained an amiable condescension. Jeffrey praised his "feminine gentleness and delicacy of nature, that shrank from all that was boisterous, presumptuous, or rude," and George Saintsbury commented on his "slightly feminine" nature.[61] Even those who did not use "feminine" used feminizing phrases to describe him, such as "delicate in constitution, and timid in his disposition"; they praised his "peculiar naïveté" and "tender, generous and pious sentiments."[62] The long-term effects of this condescension are still evident, as in the *Norton Anthology*'s description of him as a poet whose "sensibility" is "delicate" and whose "gentle talk" can "re-create for us the serenity and simplicity of life in an English village."[63]

This condescension reveals more about uncomfortable perceptions of relations between masculinity and domesticity than it does about Cowper. Labeling Cowper as feminine let nineteenth-century writers imply that they, in contrast, were masculine. Nevertheless, they respected Cowper's femininity insofar as it distinguished him from vulgarity. Nor did they ever treat Cowper exclusively as feminine, but as a man who had masculine and feminine qualities: he united "the playfulness of a child, the affectionateness of a woman, and the strong sense of a man."[64] The only supposedly masculine quality with which readers were eager to associate him was his patriotism: "Cowper is the poet of a well-educated and well-principled Englishman"; "When the shame of England burns in the heart of Cowper, you must believe him; for through that heart rolled the best of England's blood."[65] Likewise, Cowper's love of domesticity and his strong faith earned him "many simple and honest readers who turn to books for sympathy and fellowship" because "Cowper is one of the strongest instances, and proofs, how much more qualities of this kind affect Englishmen than any other."[66] If Cowper's gender identity was unusual, his national representativeness was not, since identifying with this vulnerable and feminized man was a mark of English manhood.

For those interested in Cowper's genius, his femininity might be recuperated as the source of his aesthetic distinction. As Henry Neele noted, in comparing Cowper to Thomson, "His range is neither so wide, nor so lofty, but, as far as it extends, it is peculiarly his own. . . . The pictures of domestic life which he has painted are inimitable." Macaulay thought that Cowper had rejected eighteenth-century clichés to become the "forerunner of the great restoration of our literature" represented by the Romantic movement. For William Michael Rossetti, "in point of literary or poetic style, Cowper was mainly independent."[67] This independence could even be valued as a form of masculinity: "His language has . . . a masculine, idiomatic strength"; Cowper had "a manliness of taste which approached to roughness."[68] In the eyes of these writers, problematic as Cowper's personality may have been, at least he was independent enough to think for himself.

Nevertheless, Cowper's perceived mixture of masculine and feminine qualities had within it the seeds of scandal that haunted the character of genius. There was always the possibility that this mixture would be recognized not as distinctive and even admirable eccentricity but as alarming deviance. The most dramatic evidence for this possibility arose in the 1830s while Robert Southey was writing his Cowper biography. He heard of a letter supposedly by Cowper's mentor John Newton that disclosed "something regarding Cowper much more remarkable than anything that is publicly known concerning him."[69] According to the memoirs of Charles Greville, the letter claimed that Cowper "was an Hermaphrodite; somebody knew his secret, and probably threatened its exposure."[70] Southey pondered the significance of the letter, but did not include the rumor in his biography. It leaked out through "the sensation-mongering editor of a small journal, the *Literary Times*," though it received little public attention.[71] Later in the century, it resurfaced with the publication of Southey's letters and of an expurgated version of Greville's memoirs, which changed Greville's language to say that Cowper had "some defect" in his "physical conformation."[72]

The most intriguing aspect of this incident is trying to understand precisely what these men thought was wrong with Cowper. The 1874 editors of Greville's memoirs assumed that Cowper's hermaphroditism was a physical condition, presumably of the sort that Alice Domerat Dreger has shown received considerable attention from Victorian doctors.[73] Yet Southey decided otherwise. According to Southey, if Cowper possessed an actual physical deformity, "no parent would or could have sent him to a boarding school," as Cowper's parents had done.[74] Instead, Southey treated Cowper's hermaphroditism as evidence not of biological deformity but of mental instability: "He fancied that he was an androgyne"; "It occurs to me that the most probable solution is to suppose it a mere conception of madness, not the real and primary cause of his insanity, but a hypochondriacal and imaginary effect of it."[75] By treating hermaphroditism as a figment of Cowper's mind rather than a fact about his body, Southey suggests that Cowper's gender deviance was a psychological rather than a physical trait. He assimilates Cowper to the role of the mad genius whose imagination overpowers his reason. For Southey, Cowper's delusion that he had a body combining male and female biological traits must have stemmed from a prior confusion about gender identity related to his mental illness.

Greville's remark in his memoir that Cowper was a "hermaphrodite" with a "secret" that might have been exposed suggests that, for him, Cowper's "hermaphroditism" had a different significance. Since the Renaissance, the term *hermaphrodite* had hovering around it an ambiguity similar to that surrounding the adjective *effeminate* in the eighteenth century. If applied to a man, it might mean that he was a man who had sex with other men, but it did not necessarily do so.[76] In the case of the quotation from Greville, the association of "hermaphrodite" with same-sex passion seems probable because of its link to secrecy and exposure. By the 1830s, a series of scandals had accustomed the British public to understand sex between men as the most shameful secret that could possibly be exposed. Crompton discusses the most famous of these in his accounts of William Beckford, the Bishop of Clogher, and Lord Byron.[77] These cases took place against the backdrop of many lesser-known examples of men forced to flee the country because of their "disgraceful conduct," as well as cases in which men who had sex with other men submitted to blackmail to keep their behavior secret.[78] Such events suggest that Greville understood Cowper as a man worried about keeping his sexual desires closeted. For him, Cowper looked more like a closeted homosexual than like a model suburbanite.

The history of the hermaphrodite rumor took a surprising turn in 1837 after Southey had seen the supposedly incriminating letter about Cowper. He was shocked to discover that it referred not to his Cowper but to one of Cowper's relatives with the same name:

> I obtained from Ingles a sight of the sealed letter. How little are men's memories to be trusted upon points of which they have no cause to take particular notice at the time! . . . The facts of the disappearance, the tracing of the lost person to France, and the supposed cause of his thus absconding, relate to the *other* William Cowper, as clearly ascertained by the date. What then becomes of all the collateral traditional evidence respecting *my* Cowper's real or supposed malformation? . . . Did *my* Cowper apply to himself what was reported of his kinsman, and engraft this miserable imagination upon his other delusions?[79]

Presumably the other William Cowper disappeared and fled to France after a homosexual scandal. In any case, this letter makes clear that the hermaphrodite rumor about Cowper the poet arose from a case of mistaken identity. No evidence existed for it whatsoever.

It may look as if the hermaphrodite rumor should be dismissed as telling more about Southey and later readers than about Cowper. Yet doing so would lose the insight that the rumor provides into the nineteenth century's use of the poetic genius to construct masculinity in relation to homosexuality. Southey, once he learned that the rumor was groundless, still wondered about the "collateral traditional evidence" of Cowper's "supposed malformation." Even without the specific evidence of Cowper's hermaphroditism, Southey still suspected that Cowper harbored a secret about gender deviance. He even thought that it was possible that Cowper believed himself to have engaged in same-sex passion, as the earlier Cowper evidently had.

Even more remarkably, twentieth-century scholars have entirely overlooked the evidence of Southey's letter and proceeded as if the hermaphrodite rumor really applied to Cowper the poet. It persists in the most recent and authoritative accounts of Cowper, even though it arose from a mistake. Scholars have produced a wealth of theories and denials in relation to the rumor, including the possibility that Cowper was a latent homosexual.[80]

The rumor's durability is no mere accident. It reveals how little distance might exist in the nineteenth century between the model suburban man and the sexual deviant. In Cowper's case, his supposed feminine qualities overdetermined the possibility of seeing him as having a secret identity as a "hermaphrodite" or "androgyne." Tellingly, Southey and Greville never described him as a "sodomite" or a "bugger," but used words that pointed specifically to feminine traits in a man. For Greville, if Cowper were a "hermaphrodite," he had sex with other men. For Southey, Cowper the "androgyne" might at least have thought, in his insanity, that he had homoerotic desires.

In terms of Cowper's larger significance to the history of masculinity, the hermaphrodite rumor reveals the potential danger in the domestication of genius as a model for male behavior. In the 1780s, Cowper had defined himself as a stricken deer who had earned his unique perspective on the world through painful but mysterious experience. The secrets with which Cowper surrounded himself could by the 1830s be taken as evidence of homosexuality, or at least of gender dysfunction. *The Task* taught nineteenth-century suburban men that any man who wished to aspire to the special viewpoint fostered by the domestic sphere needed to have his share of secrets. Yet this secrecy effect could seem potentially scandalous after "one particular sexuality . . . was distinctively constituted as *secrecy*," as Sedgwick notes of homosexuality.[81] Although the hermaphrodite rumor was not widely known in the nineteenth century, it reveals the anxieties for nineteenth-century men lurking beneath the model for the suburban man represented by Cowper. The question marks potentially surrounding masculine secrecy as the mark of a distinctive inner life meant that the suburban man had to find a way to differentiate his secrecy from the kind that could make him look "hermaphroditic."

The solution to these anxieties in nineteenth-century writing was to recreate the stricken deer narrative as a specifically masculine story of achievement. Like Cowper, nineteenth-century heroes underwent secret inner struggles that earned them a distinctive, individual perspective on the world and separated them from the supposedly less sensitive mass of commonplace men. Yet far from feminizing them, this process gave them masculine character.[82] In *Sartor Resartus* (1833–34), for example, Carlyle notes approvingly about his hero, Diogenes Teufelsdröckh, that "what ragings and despairing soever Teufelsdröckh's soul was the scene of, he has the goodness to conceal under a quite opaque cover of Silence."[83] From these secret ragings emerge Teufelsdröckh's self-assertions as a prophet who feels, like Cowper, that he sees beyond the commonplace, everyday appearances to eternal truth.

While Carlyle writes Teufelsdröckh's story in an extravagant, hyperbolic style that seems hardly appropriate for the Victorian suburbanite, a more likely model was Thomas Hughes's Tom Brown. Brown is the archetypal Victorian man, product of Thomas Arnold's Rugby and then an Oxford education. While he may initially appear to be the polar opposite of the "feminine" Cowper, he ends by emphasizing that he is not "some one who found the world a very good world, and was satisfied with things as they are." Like Cowper's stricken deer, he is "full of all manner of doubts and perplexities, who sees little but wrong in the world about him, and more in himself."[84] Brown's self-doubt is supposed to be a mark of his masculine character because it distinguishes him from the complacency of Philistines who are satisfied with things as they are. As with Cowper, the exact content of Brown's "doubts and perplexities" remains vague, but his secrets are not to be despised because they manifest his distinctively masculine inner struggle.

Once Cowper the stricken deer could be rewritten as a masculine model, the secret of homosexuality had to be connected not to men of individual character but to men who lacked such character. Writers located such homosexuals in cities, far from the isolating world of the suburban home: "These wretches have many ways and means of conveying intelligence, and many signals by which they discover themselves to each other . . . by means of these signals they retire to satisfy a passion too horrible for description, too detestable for language."[85] A Victorian work entitled *The Yokel's Preceptor* warned those new to London to beware of groups of men who "generally congregate around the picture shops, and are to be known by their effeminate air, their fashionable dress."[86] Reactions to Oscar Wilde treated him likewise as the leader of a cult. *Punch* noted that when Wilde's plays were performed, "nightly the stalls were fulfilled by Row upon Row of neatly curled Fringes, surmounting Buttonholes of monstrous size."[87] When testimony at his trials revealed his involvement with same-sex activity, the newspaper commented that "this curse of an outrageous cult" had at last been exposed.[88] Even in British colonial experience, the homoerotic anxieties surrounding the possibility of "going native" can be seen as a version of the paranoia surrounding secrecy. As in the attacks on Wilde or the Tractarians, anxieties about masculinity arose when men faced the possibility of submerging their individual personality within an eroticized, larger body, such as the secretive mass that writers like Kipling represented as India.

This mode of homophobia remains familiar today in the attacks by the religious right on the gay agenda. Homosexuals supposedly threaten the fundamental value of individualism insofar as they are represented as a cult eager to recruit new members rather than as an oppressed minority. The suburban domestication of genius continues, with the proviso that the required uniqueness never be the wrong kind of uniqueness. At the same time, a gay man's story can be acceptable if it follows an archetypal individualist narrative, as in Jonathan Demme's film *Philadelphia* (1994). Its hero is a latter-day Cowperian stricken deer whose secret is not madness but AIDS. The contradiction whereby a violently homophobic culture can praise and reward a film that sympathetically represents a gay man has its roots in Cowper's model of suburban masculinity and the discomfort surrounding its nineteenth-century reception. Cowper's poem installed the structure of the closet at the center of the middle-class suburban psyche in ways that made homophobia more useful than ever as a means of reinforcing the fragile borders of bourgeois masculine subjectivity.

CHAPTER FOUR

Anne Damer's Sapphic Potential

Like William Cowper, Anne Damer was an artist who never claimed genius for herself, but who had the label thrust on her. As the most famous female sculptor in England, she received numerous tributes to her genius. Horace Walpole thought that she was "a female genius" and "the greatest Female artist ever known."[1] In his description of her bas-relief inspired by *Coriolanus*, Edward Jerningham wrote that "this high, heroic task, by Genius plann'd, / Avows th'impression of a female hand."[2] Yet in many ways, the label was a problem. Unlike other artists in this book who strove to be geniuses, Damer was, with few exceptions, a traditional neoclassicist. Little in her work aimed at the overreaching wildness that was the eighteenth-century genius's trademark. Also, unlike other aspiring geniuses, she was no outsider to eighteenth-century society.[3] She never knew the grinding poverty faced by Blake or the ostracism of Beckford and Cowper. Yet the fact that she was a woman and distinguished herself as a sculptor was enough to earn her praise as a genius.

When an admirer like Walpole applied "genius" to Damer, he did so chiefly as a synonym for "fine artist" rather than as a marker of perceived sublimity and originality. Jerningham's praise, however, comes closer to the eighteenth-century convention of the genius's androgyny. He initially associates genius with masculinity and the "high, heroic task" of sculpting Coriolanus. Yet he notes that Damer's "female hand" has executed this masculine plan, as if to marvel at this seemingly discordant gender mix. Even as he praises Damer, he sustains traditional gender roles in which an implicitly masculine "Genius" originates; the secondary, female hand carries out orders. Jerningham's comment overlays the gender-crossing characteristic of genius with a standard hierarchy that gives priority to supposedly masculine capacities.

For those who did not admire Damer, the perceived gender-crossing associated with the female sculptor fueled rumors about her purported sapphism. Initially, these rumors had nothing to do with her art and arose in
relation to the scandal surrounding the suicide of her husband. Yet they persisted long after his death and owed much of their perceived credibility to
her artistic activities. Her career demonstrates the double-standard of genius.
Whereas male geniuses could be admired for not fitting into conventional
domestic roles, a woman labeled a female genius was at risk of being perceived not only as masculine but also as a sapphist. Even though Damer's
work did nothing to plant clues about her sexuality of the kind that Beckford
put in *Vathek*, the mere fact of her outstanding artistic activity, especially as a
sculptor, was enough to heighten the suspiciousness of her character.

Because of the rumors about her sapphism, Damer has figured significantly in recent accounts of female homosexuality in the eighteenth century
by such writers as Randolph Trumbach, Emma Donoghue, and Rictor Norton. Trumbach in his influential essay "London's Sapphists" uses Damer to
argue for "the emergence of the tommy's role" in the 1770s as a lesbian equivalent of the molly for homosexual men.[4] For him, Damer represents a pivotal
moment in lesbian history, a critical transition to what he calls the modern
lesbian role. I agree with Trumbach that Damer is an important figure for lesbian history. Yet I will argue that her career has rather different implications
from those that have been previously derived from it. By looking at a much
wider range of material by and about Damer, I want to question how useful
Trumbach's formulation is as a description of Damer or as a marker of lesbian history. He assumes that lesbian history needs to model itself on gay
male history. Since in other essays he identifies a transition to what he con-
ceives as a proto-modern gay male identity in the early eighteenth century, he
assumes that lesbian history has to play catch-up. Damer is his missing link
who proves the internal coherence of homosexual history across genders.

But the evidence about Damer is not as neat as Trumbach suggests and
frustrates the desire to make her fit a preconceived role, especially one based
on the supposed shape of gay male history. If, instead of looking only at a
few diary entries and libelous poems, we look at the numerous other writings about Damer, her letters, her visual art, her novel *Belmour*, and her
theatrical roles, it is harder to be quite so certain about where she belongs.
Rather than coming to a univocal reading of the evidence, I want to read
Damer's historical significance in terms of its uncertainties. It may be less
useful to debate whether Damer truly was or was not a prototypical modern lesbian than to see in her career a new kind of uncertainty about how to
interpret behavior as a key to sexual practice. My goal is not to remove the

uncertainties about Damer, but to describe a historical moment when these uncertainties surfaced in a new way because Damer, unlike many previous women, responded directly to the accusations leveled at her. In so doing, she presented her own self-construction to counter the libelous representations of her contemporaries.

Interpreting Damer's life demands investigating a vexed area of queer historiography, the valid reading of evidence. Almost anyone working in queer studies has encountered hostile readers for whom the mere presence of words like *homosexual, gay,* or *lesbian* guarantees an argument's flimsiness. Such readers assume a conservative version of a historian's relation to evidence, of the kind enunciated by Arnaldo Momigliano:

> The historian works on evidence. Rhetoric is not his [*sic*] business. The historian has to assume ordinary commonsense criteria for judging his own evidence. He must not allow himself to be persuaded that his criteria of truth are relative, and that what is true for him today will no longer be true for him to-morrow.[5]

Although the best work in gay and lesbian history has come from scholars who have ignored such pronouncements, their work has remained controversial largely because of their use of evidence. While it would be tempting to argue that, after the work of Foucault, Ricoeur, and others, no one working in any historical field, let alone queer history, could agree entirely with Momigliano, his standards nevertheless haunt debates over the gay and lesbian past.[6]

Martha Vicinus has addressed such problems in her article "Lesbian History: All Theory and No Facts or All Facts and No Theory?" In it, she describes two directions for lesbian history. One, which she criticizes, looks for women who had sex with other women as a distinct historical minority. Vicinus sees in this approach an excessive concern with "knowing-for-sure," whereby " 'lesbianism' continues to depend upon the evidence of sexual consummation, whereas heterosexuality is confirmed through a variety of diverse social formations." Her alternative is "a continuum of women's sexual behaviors, in which lesbian or lesbian-like conduct can be both a part of, and apart from, normative heterosexual marriage and childbearing." Keeping such a continuum in mind should allow historians of lesbianism to move away from an overemphasis on "the visible markers of lesbian sexuality."[7]

While I agree with Vicinus's insistence on the centrality of lesbianism to women's history, I want to complicate her argument. She explicitly distinguishes herself from Adrienne Rich's understanding of a lesbian continuum because she wants to retain "an irreducible sense of the dangerous difference implicit in homosexuality."[8] But doing so seems to defeat the purpose of having the continuum in the first place. A continuum cannot describe the historical power of a model of lesbian sexuality that casts it as a sharp break into deviance, perversity, and the unnatural. Any historian looking for a lesbian continuum needs to account for the sexual imaginary that for so long has distinguished sharply between "bad" women who have sex with other women and "good" women who do not.

Emma Donoghue's *Passions Between Women*, the most complete survey of eighteenth-century lesbian representation, copes with these historiographic problems by adopting a broad understanding of what counts as lesbianism. She documents eighteenth-century treatments of female hermaphrodites, female husbands, cross-dressing women, romantic friendships, long-term partnerships between women, female-female seductions, and sexual communities of women.[9] What is most striking about her material is that it sorts itself most neatly into the categories not of real lesbians versus everything else, but of good women versus bad ones. The more overtly a relationship between women depended on sexual consummation, the more likely it was to be condemned as sapphist. As Lillian Faderman has shown, the more platonic such relations appeared, the more likely they were to be praised as a romantic friendship.[10] The Ladies of Llangollen were a well-known example of how sharply sexual behavior split perceptions about morality. For differing viewers, they were either a touchstone of virtuous friendship or a scandalous precedent.[11]

Considerable debate has swirled around how to interpret literary representations of the kind that Donoghue presents as indices to actual historical practice. Virtually no affirmative representations by women of physical sex between women exist in Britain until the diaries of Anne Lister in the early nineteenth century. This lack in no way means that women did not have sex together or think of themselves as women who primarily desired other women. They did not, however, associate themselves with the cultural category of sapphism because doing so would have meant taking on its bad associations. If women tried to reappropriate sapphism and give it a more positive significance, historians have not yet found evidence of it before Lister. Women who are known to have slept with other women in the eighteenth century are for the most part accessible to a historian not in their own words but in the derogatory language of men who wrote about them.

Anne Damer is one of the few eighteenth-century women who, when accused of sapphism, responded. Although Donoghue notes that "an accusation of lesbianism in this period usually came not as a direct labeling but in the form of juxtaposition of several elements which on their own would not seem criminal," Damer was directly and publicly labeled.[12] For her, the objection to being associated with sapphism was above all a moral one. Since she believed herself to be a virtuous woman, it was impossible for her to acknowledge that she resembled the depraved woman portrayed by the scandal-mongers. In the face of their abuse, she insisted on her propriety and used her art to establish it.

Doing so, however, involved changing the grounds of the debate from sexual morality to social status. Accused of improper sexual behavior, she represented herself as a proper member of a ruling elite. The gap between the accusation and the defense meant that she never quite stifled the rumors about her sapphism, although she did not let them ostracize her, stop her artistic career, or cut her off from her friends. In the case of a writer like William Beckford, even though he denied his specific guilt in the Courtenay scandal, his self-representation in his letters and tales did not counter the public perceptions of his pedophilia. Likewise, even though Anne Lister hated negative public representations of herself, she freely confessed in her diary to having sex with women.[13] In Damer's case, the gap between what others wrote about her and her self-presentation, at least in the material that has survived, was far more pronounced. She battled for much of her life to live down the rumors that threatened to blight her happiness.

Neither the rumors about Damer nor her denials of them can be taken at face value. While her strongest emotional ties were with women and there is no reason to believe that she did not sleep with them, the libelous rumors about her relationships with other women were often either demonstrably untrue or quite vague. It would be wrong to read the libels as documentary fact and to ignore their larger context: the late eighteenth-century battle about the aristocratic woman's significance in general. For Damer, the battle had three parts: (1) the initial attack on her in the 1770s, which was part of a larger campaign against the aristocracy, in which the supposed misdeeds of upper-class women signaled the perceived degeneracy of the whole class; (2) her artistic activities beginning in the 1780s, which projected her image as a respectable, patriotic woman who belonged to the best circles of society; and (3) a renewed attack on her in the 1790s, in which the artistic activities that she organized to counter the rumors about herself paradoxically encouraged them to continue. As for her denials, she certainly denied sapphism, in the eighteenth-century sense of morally depraved sex between women. Yet she never acted in the ways that might have crushed the rumors entirely, such as remarrying or possibly giving up her art. Doing so would have made her seem less of a genius and more of an ordinary woman. Much as she hated the abuse, she preferred to suffer the rumors that surrounded a supposed female genius.

SAPPHIC ACCUSATIONS

Damer's lineage was eminently respectable. Her father, Field-Marshal Henry Seymour Conway, was an outstanding soldier and a major Whig politician. He also had literary interests: he wrote a play, employed David Hume as his secretary, encouraged George Crabbe, and was Horace Walpole's longtime friend.[14] Her mother, Lady Ailesbury, was the daughter of a Duke of Argyll and the widow of the third Earl of Ailesbury. Anne, born in 1748, was set to be a model Whig lady with money and high connections, including Walpole's friendship. Her first slight deviation from expected activities occurred as a child, when she developed what became a lifelong interest in sculpture. She studied with Giuseppe Ceracchi and John Bacon and took a course in anatomy with William Cruikshank, the surgeon who attended the dying Samuel Johnson.

A turning-point in her life was her marriage at nineteen to John Damer, the eldest son of Lord Milton. He looked like an eligible match since he stood to inherit £30,000, but the marriage was a catastrophe. Damer was a compulsive gambler and ran up huge debts. Anne spent little time with him, and instead became a luminary of London's bon ton, along with her friends Lady Melbourne and the Duchess of Devonshire.[15] Like other women in her situation, she spent lavishly and traveled extensively. Her social appearances were dazzling. One contemporary recorded that her earrings "cost four thousand pounds" and that she was presented at court "extremely well dressed *a la mode de Paris*."[16] Another noted that the Duchess of Devonshire's sixteen-inch plumes had "so far outdone all other plumes, that Mrs Damer, Lady Harriet Stanhope, &c., looked nothing."[17] Damer's gambling debts, probably made worse by Anne's spending, continued to mount, and, when his father refused to pay them, he shot himself through the head in August 1776. The scandal was the talk of British high society. Lord Milton made sure that Anne kept none of her husband's possessions. She was left with a jointure of £2,500, which was not paid regularly, and she gave up the first year of it to help pay her husband's debts.

After her husband's suicide, Damer never remarried and devoted herself instead to sculpture. Her best-known works are the headstones of the Thames and the Isis on the bridge at Henley, which are still visible. Yet she also sculpted many animal figures and images of her friends, including Horatio Nelson and Charles James Fox, whose marble bust she presented to

Napoleon in 1815. An ardent Whig in politics, she assisted the Duchess of Devonshire in the notorious 1784 elections, during which she, the Duchess, and Mrs. Crewe publicly canvassed for Charles James Fox, much to the outrage of their contemporaries. Upon his death in 1796, Horace Walpole left her Strawberry Hill, along with a yearly income of £2,000. There, she distinguished herself as an actress in private theatricals, as she had a decade earlier at her brother-in-law's estate at Richmond House, and published her novel *Belmour* in 1801. In later life, she was noted for her championship of Queen Caroline, for whom few other women of comparable rank had much respect. Although she seems to have planned to publish some of her papers and those of her father, she ordered them all to be burned at her death. She was buried in 1828, accompanied by the ashes of her dog Fidèle, her sculpting tools, and her working apron.

Damer's life would have been relatively typical of other eighteenth-century Whig celebrities were it not for the libels about her that began to appear shortly after her husband's death. Would-be wits promptly blamed Anne and suggested that something must have been wrong with her sexual behavior. Obscene libels about her provide some of the most interesting eighteenth-century representations of sapphism because their truth value is the most complicated. Bawdy fictions like *Fanny Hill* and *Venus in the Cloister* were fantasies; accounts of cross-dressing women like Fielding's *Female Husband* presented themselves as documentary fact, although with highly biased commentary. Obscene libels fell somewhere in between. In the early eighteenth century, impartiality had little place in obscene libels because they were usually tools of party politics. As Catherine Gallagher has noted about the period, "Party politics and ministerial government, the very forces that were bringing the libel prosecutions against controversial publications, were also feeding on, stimulating, and subsidizing the marketplace in those very publications."[18] During Queen Anne's reign, for example, Whigs used ballads and pamphlets about her sexual relations with Abigail Masham to counter Tory attacks on Sarah Churchill:

> However for sweet Service done,
> And Causes of great Weight,
> Her Royal Mistress made her, Oh!
> A Minister of State.

> Her Secretary she was not,
> Because she could not write;
> But had the Conduct and the Care
> Of some dark Deeds at Night.[19]

The fact that such libels were weapons in a political war hardly invalidates them as evidence of Anne's lesbian activity. Yet lesbian activity alone may not have been enough to cause them. In Anne's case, lesbianism became interesting to her enemies only insofar as it could be imagined to have political consequences: "The ways in which monarchs combined or separated business and pleasure have always had significant political consequences because they decide such things as who controls access to the monarch and how offices get distributed."[20] The libels about her were less judgments on sexual propriety than on the supposed bad influence that her favorites might have on her political judgment.

Although political libels against certain women continued into the second half of the eighteenth century, the poems about Damer took a different direction. While traces of political squabbles remained in them, they were less obviously enmeshed in local political debates. Rather than taking a stand on a specific issue, they made sweeping attacks on the mores of aristocrats, male and female. Their agenda was social rather than political because they reinforced an image of the British aristocracy as a collection of moral degenerates.

The libels about Damer began appearing after her husband's suicide in 1776. William Combe's couplet satire *The First of April; Or, the Triumphs of Folly* (1777) seems to have been the first such libel. It is set at a pageant in honor of Folly, modeled on the spectacular masquerade balls at Carlisle House and the Pantheon in the 1770s.[21] Combe's poem makes no pretense at impartiality. He wrote it for revenge on the Marquis of Hertford, a relative of Damer's, who had supposedly betrayed him.[22] The poem attacks Hertford and as many of Hertford's relatives as Combe could include. Even though Folly addresses the crowd gathered to pay tribute to her as "Ye High, ye Low,—ye Vulgar, and ye Peers!" the people in the poem all belong to the upper classes.[23] Damer appears as one of a series of bad upper-class women, and her most obvious crime is not lesbianism but lack of grief for her dead husband. Although she produces a "loud lament, and bitter moan . . . not for a husband, but a Title gone," she is comforted by "the *Modern Messalina*" (Lady Harrington), who

> told of joys which blooming Widows share;
> Whose easy life no haughty Ruler knows;
> Who, when th'awaken'd passion wanton grows
> May, where her fancy leads, allay the flame,
> Nor fear a husband's threats or ruin'd fame.

The Queen of Folly encourages Damer to dry her eyes and take comfort because she still has friends, including "the *virtuous H[arring]ton*" and "the *wedded H[orneck]*," who will never "forget the proofs of *former love*."[24] She concludes by assuring Damer, "Never shall you more lament the name of Wife; / The Widow's joys will crown your future life."[25]

As the quotations suggest, although Combe nowhere names Damer as a sapphist, he makes such an interpretation likely. The "*Modern Messalina*" gives no pronouns when she described "th'awaken'd passion" that Damer will enjoy and mentions the "joys which blooming Widows share" so as to suggest that they share them with each other. They need fear no "haughty Ruler," meaning most obviously a husband, but hinting also at independence from men in general. More tellingly, the Queen of Folly comforts Damer by naming female friends who remain with her. Mrs. Horneck's "*Former Love*" is the closest that the poem comes to hinting at sapphist activities, although it is careful to keep its references veiled.

A different and more graphic treatment of Damer appeared in James Perry's *Mimosa; Or, The Sensitive Plant* (1779).[26] This poem eschews Combe's satiric panorama for a one-note joke, the wonders of the sensitive plant as a metaphor for the penis: "To rich and poor; to high, and low, / Doth this sweet plant in common grow; / To prince, as well as peasant" (16). Although Perry claims that everyone is interested in the plant, when it comes to naming names, he, like Combe, concentrates on the upper ranks. He singles out three people who inexplicably challenge the plant's dominance:

> Can Botanists find out the cause,
> That contrary to nature's laws,
>   Some people can abuse it?
> ST—T claps it in his valet's b—m;
> H–LL fingers it, and some
>   Like DAM—R never use it.

> (*Mimosa*, 16)

Here Damer appears not in a Juvenalian fantasy but in a more exclusive group of sexual outsiders: sodomite, masturbator, and lesbian. While in Combe, Damer did not differ much from other women in Folly's court, in Perry she is the only woman of the three abusers of the sensitive plant. In noting that she does not use the plant, Perry underlines that he does not simply mean that she is celibate: "This lady's late elopement with the Countess du B—e will explain this."

This charge, which appears in a footnote, is based on a garbled version of events in Damer's life. In the summer of 1778, she met the Viscount du Barry, the nephew of the famous Countess du Barry, and his wife at Spa. At the time, the Viscount was dying. In search of healing waters, he and his wife went to Bath in October, and Damer accompanied them. After the Viscount's death in November, she went to Paris with the Viscountess. Although little evidence survives about the relationship between Damer and the Viscountess except that they traveled together before and after the Viscount's death, Perry treats the trip with the Viscountess as a "late elopement."[27]

In terms of truth claims, Perry's work is more risky than Combe's, who is obviously out for revenge on Hertford. Perry has less personally at stake, and his footnotes show that he has evidence to back up his characterizations. For example, in his note to "H—LL," he drops the dashes, identifies him as "General Hall," and locates his actions in Covent Garden. Likewise, by specifying Damer's partner as the "Countess Du B—e," he implies that he has a specific scenario in mind about her and is not just accusing randomly. Nevertheless, like the ballad about Queen Anne, Perry's specific language about lesbianism is vague. To claim that Damer does not "use" a phallus is far less tangible than accusing a man of clapping it in his "valet's b—m" or of "fingering" it. Perry dodges the question of exactly what he is accusing Damer of doing by noting that her elopement "will explain this," as if what "this" referred to were obvious.

The third and most damaging libelous poem about Damer was *A Sapphick Epistle, from Jack Cavendish to the Honourable and Most Beautiful Mrs. D***** (1778?).[28] Unlike the others, this poem gave her greater prominence by putting her name in the title, though only as a capital D followed by asterisks. At first glance, it seems that the naming of Jack Cavendish returned the poem to the early eighteenth-century tradition of politically motivated libels. John Cavendish was a major Whig politician, like Damer's father, and uncle to the husband of Damer's famous friend, Georgiana, Duchess of Devonshire.[29] Since he was unmarried when the poem was written, the author imagines him addressing Damer as a potential spouse. Yet, despite the poem's references to well-known Whig figures, few specifically political battles enter it. As with *Mimosa*, it entertains male bourgeois readers with juicy gossip about the lives of the upper classes.

The poem's running joke is that Cavendish, although male, is writing a "sapphick" epistle because he recognizes both how unattractive men must usually be to women, and how unattractive women who run after men become. In his eyes, sapphism, far from seeming unnatural as it does in *Mimosa*, seems the obvious right choice for a woman. He praises Sappho in the poem's first part for turning to women after Phaon has proved "most untrue."[30] Since man is a "rough, unwiedly [sic] bear," Cavendish recommends that women pursue his "plan" by turning "upon the monster man" (10). Doing so would free them from the coarseness of phallic sex. Yet Cavendish regrets that too many women nevertheless long for it, and praises Damer because she is willing to "resign a husband's life / To raise a Sapphick name" (14). After listing several women base enough to prefer heterosexuality to sapphism, he turns at last to Damer and offers himself as a suitor:

> May I not hope—dear, lovely, Fair
> Of you to have some little share?
>   For if report is right,
> The maids of warm Italia's Land,
> Have felt the pressure of your hand,
>   The pressure of delight.
>
> (22)

This passage is as close as Cavendish gets to specifics about Damer's behavior, and he is even less direct than Perry in *Mimosa*. The nearest he comes to mentioning lesbianism is the obscene innuendo about the "pressure of your hand." Unlike Perry, he even emphasizes that he is relaying gossip that may or may not be true when he adds, "if report is right."

Cavendish hopes that, by proving that he is different from ordinary men, he will lure Damer into loving him. Yet, by the end, he discards the veil of politeness for crude assertion: "But if obdurate you will prove / Deaf to the language of my love, / Take *that* you cannot give" (25). After spending most of the poem acknowledging the attractions of lesbian love, he reestablishes phallic dominance by asserting his ability to make Damer "take" the penis that she cannot "give" to other women. Since, according to Cavendish, Damer resists sex with men, it must be forced on her. Although the poem has earlier attacked lascivious women like "Lady G[rosveno]r," in the end, Damer is supposedly the most unnatural woman described, not because she runs after men but because she does not (18).

Poems like *The First of April*, *Mimosa*, and the *Sapphick Epistle*, rather than being written by the flunkies of major political figures, came from hacks eager for quick money. While it is hard to know exactly who read them, they seem to have appealed to the London manufacturing and professional classes. The *Monthly Review* gives some clue to the readership when it noted of the *Sapphick Epistle*, "Were a court of criticism to be held by the rakes and debauchees of this wicked town, a *Sapphic Epistle* would afford them matter for a capital investigation: nor should we, queer old Square-toes! presume to approach the verge of their jurisdiction."[31] Although this critic shies away from this "jurisdiction," he suggests that the poem is less for real rakes or debauchees than for readers who may believe themselves to be "old Square-toes" but who fantasize about being rakes and debauchees.

Whoever read such poems, writers like Combe and Perry evidently did not worry about reprisals. The fact that a journal as respectable as the *Monthly* even noticed the *Sapphick Epistle* suggests that men were comfortable reading and acknowledging it.[32] To read such works is to conclude that eighteenth-century writers had declared open season on aristocratic women, and a woman like Damer could do little about it. These women came to stand for all the stereotypical flaws of the aristocracy, such as luxury and sexual profligacy. Novelists had adapted this misogynistic tradition by taking what had been traits of all women and giving them only to aristocratic ones as foils to the good, middle-class heroine. From Richardson's Lady Davers and Fielding's Lady Booby to Austen's Lady Catherine de Burgh, the amount of venom that eighteenth-century writers could summon in attacking women of the upper classes is striking.

Yet the aristocratic status that made Damer an easy target for slurs also created channels for her defense. Other aristocratic women did not appreciate seeing abuse hurled at one of their own, especially because, in their view, Damer had acted properly after her husband's death. Although these aristocratic women did not publish their defenses, they did circulate them in their letters. Within their own ranks, they could establish a proper view of Damer, whatever others thought about her. As Lady Sarah Lennox wrote about her, "She did everything in regard to [her husband's] servants that show'd respect & regard for his memory, for she paid all she could." For Lady Sarah, such behavior led her to conclude, "As for the *abuse* she has met with, I must put such nonsense out of the question, and in everything else her conduct is very proper." For her, no "*abuse*" could be true about a woman whose conduct was so "*strictly right*."[33] Lady Louisa Conolly disliked Damer and found her "cold in her nature." Yet, having learned that Damer planned to "give up £1,500 a year of her jointure" to pay her husband's debts, she added, "I never heard of anything more noble and if it was necessary am glad she should do it, as it must stop every ill-natured idea about her."[34] Her assumption seems to have been that if Damer were a sapphist, she would have hated her husband and not wanted to clear his name by paying his debts. Since, however, Damer had nobly honored her husband's memory, she would therefore succeed in stifling the rumors of her sapphism.

Yet Damer did not leave her defense solely to such women. Despite the image problems that aristocratic women as a group suffered in the late eighteenth century, the cultural field for women in general had opened up as never before. As Jacqueline Howard notes, "Women contributed to a 'feminization' of values, language, and literature that empowered them over succeeding decades and favoured their development as authors. With the concomitant shift in the notions of 'genius' and 'author,' they actively promulgated and legitimized their lore, tastes, judgments, and feelings as the fit subject-matter of literature."[35] By the 1770s and 1780s, women occupied a significant place in the publishing industry.[36] Howard adds that the cult of genius helped to establish this place by allowing women writers who lacked a traditional literary background to claim significance for themselves. Although, as I have noted, Damer as a sculptor did not attempt to align her work with the characteristics that genius was supposed to possess, the mere fact that she was a female sculptor automatically brought her into the circle of those who might be considered as geniuses. As an aristocrat, artist, and perceived genius, Damer had the means and talents to create a public image of herself through which she could respond to the representations of her spread by obscene libels.

A VIRTUOUS ARTIST

In 1791 William Combe talked with Damer's friend Edward Jerningham about apologizing to her and revising his works to omit derogatory references to her. Damer wrote about Combe's plan to her best friend, Mary Berry:

> Mr. Combe can *not* redress the wrong he has done me. It is only a melancholy speculation to trace, in this instance, one, possibly *the* original author, as far as newspapers, of calumny and a long train of persecuting abuse. At the time he first began his writing, a word, a bow, from me, or the least accidental attention or acquaintance, might have made him lavish as much unmerited praise as he has barbarous abuse. Now, were he to write, to swear, to disavow his injuries in the most formal manner, ten to one it would be said that I had bought this man, and all his testimonies laughed at.[37]

Nevertheless, she decided to accept his offer. Berry, however, strongly urged her not to: "I do *earnestly* entreat you to let no persuasion, no good humour, no carelessness prevail with you ever to allow him to approach you . . . his praise would be as indiscriminate, & hardly less disagreable [*sic*] than his abuse."[38] On reflection, Damer changed her mind and sided with Berry, adding, "My aversion and contempt for such productions [as Combe's poem], even when I guessed not half their mischief, made me never seek them, and I had no one who *could* and *would* show me the necessity of, in some measure, attending to them."[39]

Such letters show that she was even more aware of her abuse than she was comfortable admitting. When she learned that a newspaper, *The World* (London), had printed more innuendos about her, she wrote, "Think of their putting into another of the newspapers that I was modelling Lady Cadogan's arm!"[40] Her surprise was justified insofar as there is not a shred of evidence that she sculpted Lady Cadogan or even knew her. Having become the target for such fantasies, she relied on Jerningham to silence them, since he was a friend of the *World*'s publisher and could influence him.[41] Yet, as Damer knew, Jerningham's influence would never be enough: "Malice does not wither nor die away of itself when unsupported by truth, as I had imagined, but the baneful seed, once sown, grows and flourishes and overruns all."[42] Although she could intervene in specific instances, she was helpless to stop the overall scandal.

Maybe the darkest moment came when rumors threatened to wreck even her friendship with Mary Berry. In the summer of 1794, Berry wrote to Damer in panic after what seems to have been the accusation that she and Damer were lovers:

> Do not think f[ro]m what I have wrote that we are to be separated, God almighty forbid—but a change of manner, a less frequency of meeting, a something must be done. . . . You see, my friend, for *my friend* you are, & ever must be, & no power on Earth, but *yourself*, ever can, or shall make you otherwise—You see the necessity of all & *double all* the caution I enjoyned, [*sic*] & of which, would to heaven! you had not recieved [*sic*] so severe a conviction—[43]

Damer's response does not survive, but, given her closeness to Berry during the 1790s, the loss of her friendship would have been a personal disaster. Eventually, Berry decided that she had overreacted, because "upon blameless, & prudent conduct & virtuous friendship it is impossible malice can *long* act with such balefull [*sic*] effect."[44] Yet the fact that the newspapers could threaten a relationship as close as Damer's with Berry indicates the stress of living with the constant danger of degrading public notice.[45]

Just as truth has little to do with the poems about Damer, so it has little to do with why she objected to their abuse. Whether or not the rumors about her sexual activities with other women were true, they represented her as a morally corrupt woman whom it was dangerous for other women to know. For a woman of Damer's rank, such public notice was profoundly distasteful, and her strategy for coping with it was complex. When contemplating her response to Combe, she wrote to Berry, "For the world, we can never now be upon more than civil terms, but while I have another and a dearer interest than my own to consider, I will, with scrupulous care, attend even to that world, and to the best of my judgement do all it requires."[46] Having suffered from the likes of Combe, she writes as if, if it were entirely up to her, she would be happy to forget the world. Yet, because she and Berry are friends, she cannot forget it, because ignoring the world might put herself beyond the pale of respectable acquaintance for Berry. Since Berry's social and financial positions were precarious, she had to be scrupulous about her acquaintance. Berry's maintenance depended on friends' charity, especially Horace Walpole's, and she could not afford to be seen as a disreputable woman. Although Damer's "scrupulous care" was not enough to stop rumors about herself and Berry, Damer emphasizes that, insofar as she could counteract them, she would.

To do so, she used her artistic abilities to give to the public an alternative image to the one presented by the scandalous poems. The most prominent element of her self-image was her status as a sculptor, and as such she became a tourist attraction for the upper classes, much as the American lesbian sculptor Harriet Hosmer would become in the nineteenth century.[47] With some asperity, she recounts in her letters to Berry the kinds of comments that she heard when she was at work: "*Dumby*'s whole conversation was, 'Lord! what a charming scaffold! What a delightful scaffold! So clever; was there ever anything so clever, so well contrived?' and Lady A— [Damer's mother], 'Look at her figure, what a good figure; well, I do admire her figure, and how well she does look.' "[48] Damer complained of being "teazed and tired to death with the number of persons coming to see" her.[49] Yet letting herself be seen at work meant that, whatever abuse might be hurled at her by the papers, she was no social outcast like William Beckford. On the contrary, she showed that she had more visitors than she knew what to do with. Since they belonged to the best families, they confirmed that Damer belonged to a privileged class even though she had an unladylike occupation.

The subjects of her sculpture similarly asserted her place at the center of her society. Like the male members of the aristocracy eager to present themselves as guardians of national culture, Damer used her art to immortalize important Britons, most of whom were her friends and acquaintances: Charles James Fox (1802), Sir Joseph Banks (1806), Sir Humphry Davy (1813), Princess Caroline (1814), and others. Some sculptures were busts for private collections, like the one of Mary Berry (1793) for Horace Walpole, but others were for highly visible sites, such as the Royal Academy's annual exhibitions. She presented her bust of Nelson (1803) to the Corporation of London, which placed it in the Common Council Room of Guildhall. Upon her uncle Lord Frederick Campbell's commission, she executed a statue of George III (1794) for the center of the Register Office in Edinburgh. Her most famous works, the keystones of the Thames and Isis (1785) on the bridge at Henley, occasioned several poems in her honor.[50] The statue of herself as the muse of sculpture, sculpted by her teacher Ceracchi, went to the British Museum.[51] With such sculptures, she offered to the nation a massive legacy of British heroes preserved in marble.

A second artistic path through which Damer demonstrated that she belonged to the best members of society was acting. At her brother-in-law's estate, Richmond House, and later at Strawberry Hill, she distinguished herself in the private theatricals that were a late eighteenth-century fad. These theatricals were highly exclusive because tickets were available by invitation only, and only to the best members of society. The Royal Family attended the performances at Richmond, and debate in Parliament was even suspended when the first play opened. Such exclusivity promoted aristocratic class consciousness and let the audience escape the noisy, crowded public theaters. Since most of the plays were fashionable comedies, they provided the titillating spectacle of aristocrats playing aristocrats, instead of supposedly upstart actors mimicking what they took to be fashionable manners. For the aristocratic actors themselves, the theatricals let them show off. Contemporaries commented on the splendor of the sets, costumes, and jewels.[52] Those close to Damer even wrote some of the scripts: her father's *False Appearances*, adapted from a French play, was performed at Richmond House in 1788, and Mary Berry's *Fashionable Friends*, at Strawberry Hill in 1801.

If Damer had wanted to present herself as a woman interested in challenging gender boundaries, eighteenth-century plays might have given her many chances.[53] Yet while it is not certain how much influence she had in the choice of plays or roles, she avoided risky parts. The women that she played were not always good or admirable, but they were all definitely interested in men. For example, in Arthur Murphy's *The Way to Keep Him*, the play that opened the Richmond House theater, she played the heroine, Mrs. Lovemore. This character discovers that she has been at fault for her husband's philandering because she has merely been virtuous, when she needed to be entertaining as well. In such a role, Damer did nothing to support rumors about her supposed sapphism: she appeared as a good, heterosexual woman whose chief goal in life was to please her husband.[54]

In Damer's more interesting roles, she played bad women. In George Colman the Younger's *The Jealous Wife*, for example, she was Lady Freelove, a woman of questionable reputation. Her final speech, after her bad intentions are unmasked, must have been telling for Damer's audience: "But the reputations of women of quality are not so easily impeached—My rank places me above the scandal of little people, and I shall meet such petty insolence with the greatest ease and tranquillity."[55] In Colman's play, Lady Freelove's speech is merely the bravado of a woman who has been found out, but in Damer's mouth, it may well have turned into her self-defense against her libelers.

Perhaps her strangest role was in Mary Berry's *Fashionable Friends*, which attacks "the exaggerated expression of false feelings . . . accompanied by a dereliction of all real duties," and especially "false feelings" between women.[56] Lady Selina (played by Damer) pretends to be the close friend of Mrs. Lovell (played by Berry) only because she wants Mr. Lovell for herself. Several scenes between Lady Selina and Mrs. Lovell parody romantic friendships between women. After they enter "Arm in Arm," Mrs. Lovell gushes, "The charm of seeing you thus unexpectedly—," and Lady Selina interrupts, "Can only be guessed by those who, formed to pass their lives together, have *suffered* separation for a long month!" (17). Speaking of men, Lady Selina claims that "they have none of them any idea of the delicacy, the disinterestedness of female friendship; and to friendship I have resolved to dedicate my future life" (20). Yet the play quickly unmasks Lady Selina's sentiments as hypocrisy. When she and Mrs. Lovell are alone together, Mrs. Lovell comments, "How charming, if the world, and all its tedious forms, allowed one to pass more evenings like this, in the calm enjoyments of friendship," to which Lady Selina responds, "You know how peculiarly suited they are to my pensive turn of mind.—(*Yawns.*)—Thus agreeably situated, I could positively forget all time—I have no idea how long we have already been together—(*Yawns.*)—Pray, my dear, what o'clock is it?" (71). In the end, Lady Selina is found out and leaves for Italy, while Mr. and Mrs. Lovell reaffirm their love.

Given Berry's fears about her friendship with Damer, the play looks like her attempt to distance herself from sapphic rumors by criticizing romantic friendships harshly. It supports Lisa Moore's argument for the "conflict between approbatory accounts of" female friendship in the period and "the virulent eighteenth-century discourse about the present dangers of female homosexuality in such relationships."[57] Yet in the play, the danger of romantic friendship is not that it leads to lesbianism but that it masks heteroerotic intrigue. In playing Lady Selina, Damer presented herself as a woman who seemed dedicated to female friendship, but was really scheming to get a man. For the play's viewers, it offered the titillating possibility of seeing Damer and Berry play at being romantic friends, only to reveal them in the end as true heterosexuals who valued relations with men above those with women.[58]

These theatricals gave Damer some power over her public visibility. Even when she played bad women, she still controlled who perceived her and how. Since the libelous poems had made her a public spectacle, acting in plays gave her the opportunity to present a competing image of a woman who, far from being at the margins, belonged to the cream of high society. If she truly were as scandalous as the poems said, she would not be received in such company. Presumably, any woman who was a nonprofessional actress yet who was respectable enough to perform for the Royal Family could not possibly be a sapphist.

Damer's third method for countering rumors about her was her novel *Belmour*, published anonymously in 1801 and republished in 1827.[59] It presents the adventures of the young Lord Belmour and his protracted pursuit of Emily Melville, who appears and disappears strangely during the first part of the novel, piquing Belmour's interest and frustrating his desire to know her. Eventually, the two live happily ever after, but only after numerous examples of the novel's two obsessive motifs, unhappy marriages caused by fashionable expectations or happy matches cut short by death. *Belmour* can be classed with other psychological novels of the 1790s, such as those of Elizabeth Inchbald, which avoid the spectacular incidents of Radcliffe and concentrate instead on tracing characters' interior states. The reviewer for the *Monthly Review* accurately noted, "Considerable talents are here displayed in the support and delineation of characters; accompanied by many just reflections, and a knowledge of the world."[60]

As a potential response to rumors of sapphism, *Belmour* extends the strategy of Damer's sculpture. It denies the marginality that such rumors imposed on her by showing her ability to participate in major literary trends of the day, such as the psychological novel. If anything, *Belmour* is remarkable for avoiding incidents that might have made it controversial in the charged political atmosphere of the 1790s. As critics like Marilyn Butler,

Claudia Johnson, and Gary Kelly have shown, novels of the 1790s were political war zones that championed and criticized competing political philoso-
phies.[61] Although Damer was an ardent Whig and an admirer of Fox and
Napoleon, she avoided overt politicization in *Belmour* except for a few pro-
Fox remarks. The novel's pile-up of bad marriages never leads to a polemic
against marriage as an institution of the sort found in Wollstonecraft's
Maria; Or, The Wrongs of Woman. For the most part, *Belmour* contains neutral versions of motifs and characters put to more polemical uses in other
novels of the 1790s.

Damer was confident enough of *Belmour*'s respectability to make it a
regular gift to female acquaintances. The Lewis-Walpole Library has two
autographed copies, one to "Louisa Johnson 1818 from the Author" and the
other "à son Excellence Madame La comtesse de Stahremburg." The copy in
the University of Minnesota's Wilson Library has a similar dedication:
"From The Authoress To Miss Davenport and may She in her Marriage, as
She equals her in Virtue and every distinguished quality of the mind, experience all the Well deserved happyness of *Emily*." Damer's comment suggests that she treated her heroine's marriage as a model to which young
women might aspire. Miss Davenport may well have known that there was
a slight sting in the compliment because Anne Damer herself had never
known Emily's "Well deserved happyness," yet the comment hardly presents Damer or *Belmour* as rebels against respectability.

RESPONDING TO THE FEMALE GENIUS

To a degree, Damer's writing and art created an enduring image of her as
an "ingenious" woman who rose above a bad marriage to achieve creative
success. Poems like Robert Merry's *Diversity* (1788), Erasmus Darwin's *The
Botanic Garden* (1799), and Jerningham's *The Shakespeare Gallery* (1806)
paid tribute to her talents as a sculptor and disseminated a somewhat con-
descending representation of her as an aristocratic artist "in talent rich, in
feeling warm."[62] Throughout the nineteenth century, many accounts
repeated this image, including the notice of her in the *Annual Biography
and Obituary* for 1829 and such Victorian celebrations of femininity as
Samuel Mossman's *Gems of Womanhood* and A. T. Thomson's *Queens of
Society*.[63] Percy Noble's 1908 biography, *Anne Seymour Damer: A Woman of
Art and Fashion*, provided the most complete version of the myth of
Damer's respectability.

When some nineteenth-century writers attacked Damer, they did so because she was a female sculptor, not because she was a lesbian. Allan Cunningham's discussion of her in his *Lives of the Most Eminent British Painters and Sculptors* says nothing about her sexuality but has little admiration for a woman trespassing on the supposedly masculine reserve of sculpture.[64] Although he notes that "her sex and situation render it difficult to estimate her real merits as an artist," he does so anyway. After asserting, on slender evidence, that she used assistants to do her serious work, he adds, "Those works which we *know* to have been actually carved in marble by her own hand, are all rude in execution. There is no ease of hand—none of that practised nicety of stroke—that undulating rise and fall of flesh, which every one feels to be necessary, and which no one can hope to reach without great knowledge and practice."[65] Cunningham here envisions the skilled sculptor as a feminized figure who works with "ease" and "practised nicety" to create an "undulating rise and fall," but a real woman evidently cannot attain this feminized skill. For him, Damer was a woman deluded by a belief in her own cleverness into tackling subjects far beyond her powers. Although Leslie Stephen's notice of her in the *Dictionary of National Biography* is less damning than Cunningham's, it repeats his charge: "It was whispered that she received assistance from 'ghosts.' "[66]

Despite the comments of Cunningham and Stephen, Damer achieved at least a partial triumph over her libelers because, after her death, she was remembered as an artist rather than as a scandalous woman. Not until the twentieth century and the appearance of such works as Katharine C. Balderston's edition of *Thraliana* did rumors about Damer's sexual behavior become easily accessible to scholars. Yet Damer was luckier with her reputation after her death than during her lifetime. Despite all her efforts, the rumors that first appeared about her in the late 1770s resurfaced in the 1790s.

They did so for several reasons, but one of them was the suspicion about gender that any woman asserting herself in the artistic sphere was likely to attract. Whereas before, Damer had been guilty of being an aristocrat, she was now guilty of being an artist. In the 1790s fears about the possible effects of the French Revolution caused a widespread crackdown on gender nonconformity in British society, and they targeted female artists in particular. Richard Polwhele notoriously attacked Mary Wollstonecraft and others as "unsex'd females" because they had dared to assert the equal rights of men and women to rationality.[67] Damer as a sculptor was especially open to such attacks because, given the impossibility of sculpting while wearing eighteenth-century female outfits, she wore certain stereotypically masculine clothes. As Joseph Farington noted, "She wears a Mans hat, and Shoes, and a Jacket also like a mans—thus she walks ab[ou]t, the fields with a hooking stick."[68] Yet eighteenth-century writers hardly needed the inspiration of Damer's clothes. The metaphoric possibilities in the figure of the female sculptor gave them rich satiric material.

If Damer looks like the first modern lesbian to historians like Trumbach, that may be less because she really was so than because she combined two of the most notorious eighteenth-century female roles: aristocrat and artist. As such, she was uniquely poised to join two categories of improper female behavior that had not always gone together: the woman who slept with other women (as a licentious aristocrat) and the masculinized woman (as an artist). The attacks on Damer brought together the sexual license traditionally associated with the aristocratic woman and the gender infractions increasingly associated with female artists. The result was to associate a particular kind of gender "unnaturalness" with a particular mode of sexual "perversion." As such, Damer resembles uncannily the fictional figure who has done so much to define twentieth-century lesbian identity, Radclyffe Hall's Stephen Gordon, the heroine of *The Well of Loneliness*. Gordon, like Damer, is an artist and an aristocrat. Yet Gordon can acknowledge herself as a lesbian in a way that Damer never could, because Damer was trapped in a situation in which she was doomed to abuse.

This abuse reemerged in a print of 1789 entitled "The Damerian Apollo" (figure 1).[69] While nothing in the print implies that Damer sleeps with other women, it represents her as a phallic woman who triumphantly penetrates male bodies. In the print, Damer is shown not in her work clothes but as a woman of fashion whose chisel takes aim at Apollo's buttocks. Her mallet arm is raised high, and she looks confidently at the strategically placed chisel. Although Damer's female assistant, also dressed fashionably, supports Apollo so as to cover his phallus, his spear is distinctly erect. He nevertheless looks quite unhappy about Damer's actions and points to the group of statues on the left. Entitled "Studies from Nature," they show a male and female nude gazing at each other longingly. Their "natural" love contrasts with the implicitly "unnatural" actions of the print's center. While nothing about Damer's body itself looks masculine, her pose projects a masculine, phallic power that the drawer of the print assumes his audience will find unnerving and ridiculous. This print was available from William Holland, one of the three major caricature publishers who dominated the trade in late eighteenth-century London. Damer's image would have been visible to the broad range of viewers who came to laugh at the images in Holland's exhibition room in Oxford Street.[70]

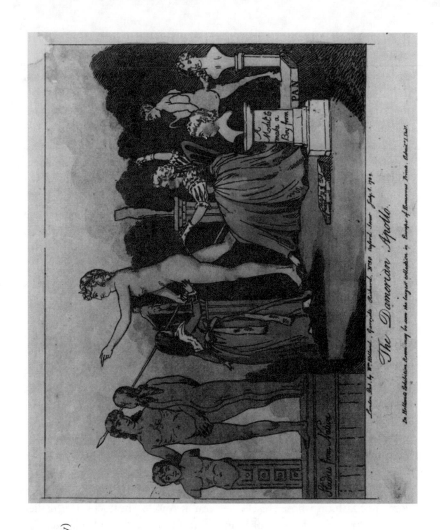

FIGURE 1.
"The Damerian Apollo." (Courtesy of the Print
Collection, Lewis–Walpole Library, Yale University)

Perhaps as a defensive move, women writers were especially active in disseminating the print's image of Damer as a woman associated with gender transgressions. Mary Robinson's *Modern Manners* (1793) presented a poetic version of such gender accusations. It included Damer in a list of the follies to which fashion condemned society: "When BANKS delights in BUTTERFLIES and FLEAS, / And DAMER forms the PARIAN HERCULES!"[71] Robinson's grouping implies that fashion creates gender confusions. Sir Joseph Banks, the famous botanist, reduces himself to a figure like those in Book IV of the *Dunciad* who delights in trivia, while the female Damer takes on masculine ambition by sculpting Hercules. Rather than being a sign of genius for Robinson, such gender-crossings are one more absurdity of "modern manners." Although Damer never actually sculpted a Hercules, Robinson is not targeting a particular artwork by Damer. Instead, she questions the propriety of a woman interested in sculpture of any sort, especially that involving the male body.

Hannah Cowley in *The Town Before You* (1795) based the character of Lady Horatia Horton on Damer. Horton is a female sculptor who consorts with women of dubious femininity and who "seeks for models only in the graces of her own sex, the daughters of Britain and the matrons of Greece."[72] Although Cowley carefully emphasizes that Horton does indeed love a man, whom she accepts as her spouse at the end of the play, she includes many veiled references in her portrayal to Damer's supposed transgressions against normative femininity. At the play's beginning, the ingenue Georgina has fallen under Horton's spell and describes the kind of women that she meets at Horton's house, who seem especially affected by female opera singers:

> When I was last at Lady Horatia Horton's, a countess from the Opera came in, thus [*striding across, and sitting down abruptly.*]—Bless me, Lady Horatia, how cou'd you be at home to-night? I gallopp'd sixty miles to-day, have kill'd one coach-horse, and spoiled another, merely to hear the Banti—O! the Banti! (12)

Cowley underscores that the countess's admiration for the Banti has a sexual element: "O! Her upper tones!—and, O! her under tones!" (13). It is as if Cowley displaces some of Damer's problematic femininity onto Horton's friends, rather than showing it directly through Horton herself. The countess's gruff manner and her transports establish her as a masculinized woman who has developed an erotic obsession with the Banti.

Eventually, in the latter part of Damer's life, the image of her as a woman of questionable femininity mellowed into an image of her as an amiable eccentric. Just as Cowper dwindled from a mad poet into a sweetly feminine man, so Damer dwindled from the threatening woman aiming a chisel into a "character." Evidence for this development appears in Susan Ferrier's *Marriage*. When Ferrier showed an early version of some of the material to her friend Charlotte Clavering, a distant relation of Damer's, Clavering identified one of the characters as a version of Damer: "First of all, I must tell you that I approve in the most signal manner of 'Lady McLaughlan.' . . . Do I know the person who is the original? The dress was vastly like Mrs. Damer. . . . Her kissing Lady Juliana and holding her at arm's length is capital. Now you must not think of altering her."[73] In the novel, Lady Maclaughlan appears in what Ferrier calls "masculine habiliments," dressed much as Farington had described Damer's clothes.[74] Although she has a flowered skirt and petticoats, she also sports "a pair of worsted stockings and black leather shoes, something resembling buckets" along with "a black beaver hat" and "a gold-headed walking-stick" (42–43). Upon meeting the pretty but spoiled heroine Lady Juliana, Lady Maclaughlan examines her closely: " 'So—you're very pretty—yes, you are very pretty!' kissing the forehead, cheeks and chin of the youthful beauty, between every pause" (43). For most of the novel, Lady Maclaughlan, who also has a "voice like thunder" (50) and a "marble aspect" (105), is treated affectionately as an eccentric rather than as an evil or threatening woman. Only in this one passage between her and Lady Juliana does Ferrier hint at the connection between Damer's masculine appearance and her supposed sapphic preferences. Anyone reading the novel who did not know that Lady Maclaughlan was based on Damer would not have guessed solely from Ferrier's representation that Damer had been suspected of sapphism. For others, they may have been amused at seeing how the scandalous woman of 1778 had dwindled into the eccentric curmudgeon of 1818. Nevertheless, Ferrier's portrait contains the vestigial traces of earlier scandal in ways that reveal that Damer never completely stifled the rumors about her. As she herself knew, they had a life of their own.

Eighteenth-century materials thus present two stories about Damer, one by her "abusers" and one by herself, neither of which is entirely reliable. The libelous descriptions of her, which arose from a complicated mix of events in Damer's life, the gender-bending mystique of genius, late eighteenth-century misogyny, and antiaristocratic stereotypes, are vague and sometimes simply untrue, as in the rumor about her and Lady Cadogan. At the same time, so much evidence about Damer's strong emotional relationships to other women survives that their association of her with same-sex desire cannot be dismissed entirely. Although Damer denied specific instances of abuse, she never, in the documents that survive, directly denied the accusations that she was more emotionally invested in women than in men. Given the moral ugliness attached to sapphism, it is not surprising that she wanted to distance herself from the term, but nothing in her life rejected same-sex desire per se. She defended herself by emphasizing her respectable social affiliations, but not by proving her heterosexuality.

The challenge of Damer's biography is deciding how to narrate it, given the split in the way that she represented herself and the way that others represented her. The most convenient hypothetical narrative is the one most familiar to lesbian and gay studies: a narrative of repressed creativity. I want first to explore what such a narrative might look like if constructed around Damer and then discuss how it might be complicated. A narrative of repressed creativity would depend on assumptions inherited from the eighteenth-century cult of genius: the artist's work reflects her life, and the most important aspect of her life was sexual. In it, Damer appears as a genius in spite of herself, a proto-romantic split subjectivity. Whereas her social situation demanded her conformity, her "true" genius, which she was not able to articulate explicitly in her work or letters, and perhaps not even to herself, supposedly rebelled against the constricting behavior demanded of respectable women.

Finding evidence for the narrative of Damer as reluctant genius would demand reading her work as biography, especially a biography of desire. Her most important documents would be her most autobiographical ones, her letters to Berry. Although Berry is best known as the woman whom Horace Walpole loved at the end of his life, neither Berry nor Damer felt for Walpole what they felt for each other. Berry's letters to Damer survive only because Damer compiled four notebooks full of extracts of them, and statements of mutual love fill their correspondence. A typical one from Damer to Berry addresses Berry as "my only hope and comfort on earth."[75] Berry's letters to Damer are even more passionate: "What would I have given to have wept for half an hour without constraint in your bosom!"; "Judge then what that dread must be of any thing *but death*, seperating [*sic*] us"; "Your friendship I never will either conceal, or disown—from it I still look for the comfort and support of my future life."[76] For both, no emotional relationship in their lives was more important than their love for one another.

In the hypothetical narrative of lesbian genius, Damer's friendship with Berry would appear as the key to the truth of her inner self, the real lesbian that she could supposedly not express more openly. Her art might also be taken to provide similar clues, since it, like her friendship with Berry, would be treated as if distorted by social censorship. The uncomfortable relationship between Emily and Mrs. Stainville in *Belmour* might be seen as an example of such a coded distortion of authentic feeling. It begins when Emily develops a crush on the older woman: "Mrs. Stainville's conversation was lively, intelligent, and agreeable, and her manner even fascinating, when she wished to please, which being now the case, Emily was enchanted with her."[77] As for Mrs. Stainville, "she was delighted with Emily, and that something, which she thought *romantic*, in thus unexpectedly meeting with a creature so superior, lodged hitherto in obscurity, added much to the interest, with which she was inspired for her."[78] The relationship later deteriorates when Mrs. Stainville becomes jealous of Emily. Like Berry's *Fashionable Friends*, Damer's novel shows that heterosexual love destroys female intimacy. Yet even this episode in *Belmour* could be made to fit a narrative of genius if Damer is imagined as using her novel as a smoke screen whereby she could present a negative version of what could be taken to be her real emotional life.

A similar decoding of Damer's art might look to her terra-cotta bas-relief of Cleopatra's death from *Antony and Cleopatra*, designed for John Boydell's Shakespeare Gallery (figure 2). The lesbian visibility of this scene becomes especially clear next to Henry Tresham's representation of the same scene in the gallery.[79] In Tresham's engraving, Charmian is the image's focus. She stands above Cleopatra and turns to silence the invading soldiers. In Damer's bas-relief, no soldiers appear. Instead, an imposing Cleopatra dominates the middle, drawn larger-than-life as an image of royalty, and Charmian clasps her tightly. Cleopatra's arm falls against Charmian's inner thigh, and Charmian holds it with her hand. Whereas Tresham's image is about Charmian's request that the dead be respected, Damer's is about physical intimacy between women. In the hypothetical, proto-romantic reading of Damer that I am exploring, this sculpture could be interpreted as Damer's appropriation of a high cultural event, the Boydell Shakespeare Gallery, to envision an image of a marginal sexuality. The deaths of Charmian and Cleopatra provide just enough censorship to make the image respectable.[80] The moment's extremity could be seen to justify a physical intimacy that, at least for a heterosexist viewer, might be less appropriate under more ordinary circumstances.

FIGURE 2.
Antony and Cleopatra, Act 5, Scene 2. Engraving
after Anne Damer.
(Courtesy of Special Collections and Rare
Books Department, University of Minnesota
Libraries)

The approach to Damer's life that I have been exploring helps to explain much about her life and illuminates particular moments in her art. Yet coding, although the dominant biographical model in gay and lesbian studies for relating art to life, has serious drawbacks. Once the subject's sexuality becomes the omnipresent but unspeakable truth lurking beneath his or her work, the critic becomes a latter-day Poirot / Marple, hunting for clues to say what the artist could not. Doing so assumes a coherent sexuality as a psychic category, encourages using conclusions as evidence, and leads to a reductive, repetitive way of reading. The interpreter of Damer's work is forced to hunt for coded signs and is always left wondering how aggressively such coding can be pursued in works that, on the surface, seem to have nothing to do with sexuality at all.

I want to complicate a narrative of coding by considering what other narratives about Damer might be possible. Any narrative about her that considers all the surviving evidence must acknowledge the centrality of female-female relations to her life. Yet the narrative of tortured lesbian genius tends to cast Damer entirely as a victim of repression. It leaves her with little agency and with the ability to express herself only in brief flashes in her art. It also entirely ignores her own narrative about herself as a virtuous, respectable woman whose art was largely dedicated to celebrating British national heroes. Most of all, it bypasses the degree to which Damer's life was not just about love and genius. It was also about money and the privileges available to a woman who had more money than most in eighteenth-century England.

However miserable the rumors about her sapphism made Damer, she never stopped them partly because she did not have to do so. In particular, she did not need to make herself acceptable to a man in order to support herself. In 1792 a man who seems to have been named William Fawkener proposed to her. Although Damer was not enthusiastic, Berry urged her to accept. After noting that Damer was not likely to get a second offer, Berry added, "It would destroy in a moment all the vile mistakes of the world in your regard, for depend upon it, in a month's time, such an idea would never more be thought of, and you would become as respectable in their eyes as you have always been in your own."[81] Damer thought otherwise: "With regard to the world, were I inclined to buy its uncertain favour, I much doubt if any step of this sort would now have the effect you imagine, as I do maintain it, undone as I am, it is by malice, not by the sober or confirmed opinion of any living creature" (96). Whether or not Damer was right about marriage, her unwillingness to "buy" the world's "uncertain favor" was enough to persuade her not to marry Fawkener.

When Damer explained why she refused him, she did so in terms of personal objections: "Could you . . . see his character, dissimilar as it is to mine, ill calculated to afford me real comfort or real happiness" (95). But her ability to object depended on a prior fact. She, unlike many women in Georgian England, could turn down suitors because she had enough money that she did not need them. Her independence arose as much from her status as a widowed member of the aristocracy as it did from her personal sexual desires. As novels of the period demonstrate, many women had to take what they could get for a husband or face a miserable existence living off charity. Paradoxically, Damer, as an aristocrat, could invoke bourgeois standards of love and compatibility to justify turning down a suitor in a way that most actual bourgeois women could not. Her wealth and connections also brought her further wealth, as when Walpole left her Strawberry Hill in his will. Given the question marks surrounding Walpole's own sexuality, his gift to her points to a possible bond between two people who may both have been marginalized by their sexual practices. In leaving her his estate, he may tacitly have acknowledged her unorthodox sexuality by allowing her to continue to support herself without the need of a husband. Aristocrats could help each other preserve their ability to transgress sexual codes in a way that most people could not.

Only Damer's wealth allowed her to sustain long-term friendships with women like Mary Berry because she did not have to worry about a husband's approval. When Damer justified refusing Fawkener, she wrote to Berry, "I am enjoyed to think that I shall pass this evening alone, for I want quiet, and I do protest that, however distant, it is the next step to passing it with you. This is one of the comforts the disposal of which you would have me deprive myself" (98). Damer blames Berry for encouraging her to marry Fawkener because if she did so, Damer could no longer write to her at her leisure.

Likewise, the artistic activities so important to Damer's self-representation depended on her wealth. Unlike most authors striving to be geniuses, who needed only pen and paper, Damer became skilled in an activity available only to a privileged few because of its prohibitive expense and the need for time and training. She could use her sculpture to demonstrate her place in England's elite only because she was already a member of that elite. Similarly, her acting also depended on her prior acceptance by the upper-crust of the British aristocracy. The interest in watching her play aristocratic roles was that she was a real aristocrat.

Yet the wealth that brought her so many privileges also had a drawback. Insofar as it allowed her to distinguish herself from ordinary women, it fueled rumors about her sapphism. Paradoxically, all the activities through which Damer asserted her position as a respectable member of the upper classes could be read by bourgeois readers as signs that she was not respectable at all. For unfriendly viewers, Damer's sculpture looked not like the activity of a wealthy amateur but that of a woman who aspired to masculine power. Her mallet, chisel, and partly masculine attire seemed to prove that she really was an unfeminine woman and therefore one potentially involved in sapphism.

Damer's acting was even more controversial. Like sculpture, acting demonstrated her place in an elite, but it also brought her into contact with the most suspicious women in eighteenth-century society, actors. Her work with the famous comic actor Elizabeth Farren provided grist for the gossip mill. The most public comments came in Charles Pigott's *The Whig Club* (1794), which attacked major Whig figures. It has a section on Lord Derby, in which it abuses Farren, his mistress. All London society knew that Lord Derby was waiting for his wife to die so that he could marry Farren, who notoriously had refused to sleep with him until then:

> His Lordship impatiently waits the moment of her decease, that he may at last reap the harvest he has long promised himself from a marriage with a well-known fashionable actress. . . . But though the vanity of the Comedian must be interested in the event, her amorous passions are far from being awakened by the idea. Superior to the influence of MEN, she is supposed to feel more exquisite delight from the touch of the cheek of Mrs. D—r, than from the fancy of any *novelties* which the wedding night can promise with such a partner as his Lordship.[82]

In a section on Sir William Mordaunt Milner, Pigott continues the rumors about Damer and Farren in the course of attacking Milner for being an alcoholic:

> He has for some years receded from the rites of the latter [Venus] to attach himself to those of Bacchus; and when warmed with a bottle, he does not hesitate to declare, "That Lady M—r, though a charming woman, is cold." No wonder that any woman should be to an habitual sot, whose only praise is, that he can walk off with five bottles. Yet there is another reason assigned for Lady M—r's indifference to the caresses of Sir William; and by those who are intimate at N—n she is supposed to be a formidable rival to Mrs. D—r for the affections of Miss F—n. (60–61)[83]

Although the men that Pigott attacked could easily shrug off such comments, they were far more devastating to the women involved.

The motives of *The Whig Club* were obviously political. Pigott wrote explicitly in his introduction about this "club" that "it is in the public and private characters of its chiefs, that its designs are to be traced; from their conduct or condition, we may form some conjecture of what they aim at" (4). Yet when he attacked men like Derby and Milner for the sexual behavior of women with whom they associated, he moved out of the political arena into sex scandal. He located himself somewhere between the political tract and the gossip column. For readers who followed the doings of the aristocracy, the rumors about Damer and Farren might have had more credibility than earlier poems about Damer because her friendship with Farren was no secret. Farren supervised the amateur theatricals at Richmond, and Damer had made a bust of her as Thalia that was part of the set.[84] Given the widespread associations of sapphism with aristocratic women and female actors, who distinguished themselves from respectable bourgeois women because of their public visibility, rumors about Damer almost inevitably revived as soon as she came into contact with Farren.[85] They were made even more credible because Damer's activities as a sculptor and, for her admirers, her artistic genius, had already associated her with activities not typical of ordinary women.

Whether or not Pigott's insinuations were true, they spread enough in London society so that Hester Piozzi recorded them twice in her diary. Her entry for June 17, 1790 noted,

> Mrs *Damor* [*sic*] a lady much suspected for liking her own Sex in a criminal Way, had Miss Farren the fine comic Actress often about her last year; and Mrs Siddons's Husband made the following Verses on them.

> > Her little Stock of private Fame
> > Will fall a Wreck to public Clamour,
> > If Farren leagues with one whose Name
> > Comes near—Aye very near—to *Damn her.*[86]

Five years later, Piozzi still thought that the rumor was current: " 'Tis a Joke in London now to say such a one visits Mrs Damer. Lord Derby certainly insisted on Miss Farren's keeping her at Distance & there was a droll but bitter Epigram while they used to see one another often—." She then repeats a different version of the epigram in which the last two lines read, "If Far-

ren herds with her whose Name / Approaches very near to *Damn her*."[87]
Piozzi's comments reveal that rumors about Damer's supposed behavior
had entered into the oral culture of the English upper classes. Since female
actors were supposed to be sexually licentious, and especially since Elizabeth Farren was notorious for not sleeping with Lord Derby until she could
marry him, the gossip already existing about Damer and Farren plus their
work as actors made them easy targets.

Belmour did not have much positive or negative effect on the rumors
about Damer, even though I have suggested that it contained a lesbian subtext. It did, however, reveal that Damer belonged to a class of women for
whom the bourgeois rules of marriage did not apply. Much as the writer for
the *Monthly Review* liked the novel, he admitted that he could not find the
"author's moral sentiments *quite* correct." Specifically, he did not approve
of the characters' attitudes toward marriage: "We must except . . . the libertine behaviour of Lord Belmour, in violating the rights of honour and hos-
pitality by his criminal intimacy with Lady Roseberg. . . . Nor can be com-
mended in a virtuous wife, as Emily Courtenay is described to be, her
expressions of tenderness towards her former admirer, and still giving him
hopes of their future union."[88] For the reviewer, marriage was a sacred and
inviolable bond between husband and wife, and female adultery was an
unthinkable horror. Damer's attitude in *Belmour* was far more casual, in
keeping with the morality of an aristocratic class for whom marriage and
love did not obviously go hand in hand. For example, her hero, Belmour,
has an affair with a married woman, Lady Roseberg. Although Lady Roseberg is revealed to be a bad woman, Damer suggests that nothing is wrong
with the adulterous affair per se. Belmour's father, for example, "did not at
all disapprove of a connection of that sort, which he thought might contribute to form his son, and keep him out of worse company."[89] The heroine, Emily, marries Mr. Courtenay even though she secretly loves Belmour.
When Belmour visits them, she encourages him in a way that, as the reviewer notes, a perfectly respectable heroine would not. Damer leaves throughout *Belmour* signs that she came from a class with enough money that she
did not have to follow bourgeois norms of marital respectability.

I emphasize Damer's rank and economic privilege because these tend to
drop out of the hypothetical narrative about thwarted lesbian genius that I
described earlier. Letting them disappear bypasses the degree to which
Damer was not merely a victim of her society. She was also a woman who
had the means at her disposal to counter its homophobic standards, develop her artistic skills, and spend time with the women she loved. Without
money and rank, she would have been potentially far more of a victim and

would probably not have distinguished herself in a way that her contemporaries would have noticed.

The bigger point that the evidence about Damer reveals is the centrality of economics in lesbian history. If evidence about lesbianism is difficult to find, this absence suggests not that lesbianism is a recent invention but that few women have historically had the economic independence to be able to counter the sexual practices enforced by a patriarchal society. If some lesbians like Mary Hamilton cross-dressed, they did so not merely because they were "masculine" women but because doing so allowed them to earn a living and have the economic wherewithal to sustain a relationship with another woman. In terms of the homophobic imaginary, resentment of lesbians has arisen partly from the hatred of women who have not been "properly" subdued by a patriarchal economy. In a world in which women were supposed to be wives and mothers, women who for various reasons had the economic wherewithal to avoid these roles came to be explained as woman who were openly hostile to them. The fact that many women who slept with other women in the eighteenth century may well have been wives and mothers is a fact that seems intuitively obvious but is exceptionally difficult to document. Only women who avoided these roles became visible as sapphists.

The conflicts over the evidence about Damer might be taken to represent a transition between the death of the aristocratic woman and the birth of the lesbian as the bourgeois woman's dark other. The key to the transition was an unconventional relation to middle-class economics that permitted an unconventional relation to middle-class sexual mores. As possibilities of female economic independence increased, the possibilities of a sustained lesbian identity increased as well. Damer points to the origins of the stereotype of the aristocratic lesbian, the woman who could afford her independence. I emphasize that I generalize only about women of the educated classes and ignore the different formations that lesbianism took among women of the working classes. But the presence of women like Damer pointed up the merely contingent relations between patriarchy and capitalism that bourgeois writers liked to believe were inevitable. Middle-class writers treated activities that for Damer were part of her class prerogative as actions of a sexually depraved sapphist. She had the money and the talent to produce counterrepresentations of herself in the late eighteenth-century cultural marketplace, which had expanded enough to provide certain opportunities for women. Yet the activities that she used to defend herself paradoxically increased her vulnerability to attack.

To return to the issues raised by Vicinus about lesbian historiography, the material about Damer suggests an alternative to her model of the lesbian continuum. Such a continuum assumes that the most important aspect of lesbian history is women's relations to other women. Commonsensical as such a focus must seem, Damer's career suggests that it is equally important to examine the ways that women who had sex with women did not have to be part of a continuum. They possessed certain traits, especially economic independence, that rendered them different. I would suggest the value of historicizing the category of deviant women as a category containing women who, because of economic reasons, did not have to conform to the roles of wife and mother. So much has been written on the role of the proper bourgeois woman in the eighteenth century that it may be useful to look for a history of lesbianism in the history of women who did not need to play this part.

CHAPTER FIVE

Lesbianism and Romantic Genius: The Poetry of Anne Bannerman

The poet on whom I concentrate in this chapter, Anne Bannerman, contrasts strikingly with Anne Damer. Damer was an artist with strong emotional ties to other women, yet she avoided the cult of genius. Her work is impersonal and, with few exceptions, rebuffs attempts at a proto-romantic reading of repressed lesbianism. Anne Bannerman's work, in contrast, invests in all the clichés of genius, such as sublimity, obscurity, medievalism, and enthusiasm. Part of her investment is a pointed avoidance of conventional heteroeroticism. Like Beckford and Blake, she uses sexual representations in her poetry to distinguish herself from merely conventional writers. Yet whereas we know a moderate amount about Damer's personal life, we know little about Bannerman's. The ideology of genius seems to demand a biographical reading of her work, in which her poetry's sexual deviance might be reflected in her life. The archival record offers enough details to allow us to piece together her brief career, but it tells us nothing about her personal life. It is tempting to imagine an artist who had Damer's life and wrote Bannerman's poetry, because such an artist would allow us to read the life through the work. Instead, this chapter will examine how the cult of genius provides a framework for interpreting Bannerman's poetry as lesbian writing despite the absence of information about her personal life.

Bannerman wrote at the end of a brief period in the second half of the eighteenth century when certain women successfully appropriated the cult of genius. As Christine Battersby has argued, definitions of genius drew heavily enough on conventionally feminine characteristics that some women "managed to benefit from the Romantic notion of genius, despite the fact that male supremacists have wielded this concept like a metal bar to try and beat back the female hordes invading the male space of European Culture."[1] I discuss Elizabeth Gilding in the first chapter as the first woman that I have found who used "genius" in the title of her volume of poetry.

Many women followed her lead and were far more overt in claiming it. Mary Robinson's "Ode to Genius," for example, boasted about the importance of genius as a weapon for those who lacked conventional educations:

> *I'VE SEEN THEE*, spurning *SOLEMN FOOLS*,
>   Mock the vaunted lore of schools;
>   And laugh to scorn the *PEDANT'S* art,
> That hides, in *LEARNING'S GARB, THE DULL*
>   *DECEITFUL HEART!*[2]

A woman with such genius might feel superior to male writers who had merely learned the "vaunted lore of schools." Anna Seward likewise wrote a pair of sonnets on genius that underscored its attraction. Although her first sonnet questions the value of genius since it could lead to false hopes, the second sweeps such doubts aside: "Yet who would change / The powers, thro' Nature and thro' Art that range, / To walk the bounded, dull, tho' safer plain / Of moderate intellect."[3] Echoing Milton ("For who would lose, / Though full of pain, this intellectual being, / Those thoughts that wander though Eternity"), Seward implies that she is no writer of "moderate intellect" but a woman of genius with powers that span the full range of experience.[4]

Most tellingly, Ann Yearsley, a poet from the laboring classes, praised the inspiration of natural genius in "To Mr. —, an unlettered Poet, on *GENIUS UNIMPROVED*": "Deep in the soul live ever tuneful springs, / Waiting the touch of Ecstasy, which strikes / Most pow'rful on defenceless, untaught Minds."[5] Yearsley maintains that minds without the clutter of education will be more open to the visitations of genius. Education appears in her poem as a wall that dulls the mind to its sources of inspiration. Only those without it can be most sensitive to its "touch of Ecstasy."

Many male writers also recognized and encouraged female genius, although their tributes rarely escaped condescension. William Belsham countered the charge that genius belonged only to men: "It does not appear that the claim of man to superiority in this view rests upon any very just foundation."[6] William Hayley's "Ode to the Countess de Genlis" praised her role as a female genius: "For O! beneath whatever skies / Records of female genius may arise, / Those records must enfold thy fair and fav'rite name."[7] Alexander Thomson composed a poem celebrating "Sappho and the Triumph of Female Genius," in which he lauded Mary Wollstonecraft because she had impelled "her sex to dare / And with bold voice assert their equal right, / In ev'ry mental task with man to share."[8] The abstract idea of female genius and concrete examples of its accomplishments were widespread in late eighteenth-century British culture.

Yet female genius was hardly uncontroversial. Many commentators enjoyed making fun of the sudden efflorescence of women writers who made large claims for themselves. Hester Piozzi commented acidly about women and the cult of genius that "ladies have therefore as good a chance as People regularly bred to science in Times when fire-eyed fancy is said to be the only requisite of a popular poet."[9] In an anonymous preface to Miss Cutherbertson's *Anna*, the author imagines how the play's audience might be inspired by the idea of female genius:

> A Smirking Matron, strikes upon my View
> "—I wish, She cries, my Polly had been here
> She's such a Genius—such a witty dear
> —Twould suit her vastly, this here play To night
> And if it do, 'twou'd goad Poll on to Write."

Yet a neighbor explains to this "matron" that female writers are not as glamorous as she might think. She describes her visit to a female author, an antidomestic nightmare with "uncurl'd hair" and nails bitten "in Spite, when no kind Muse supply'd / The wonted Thought."[10] For this author, female genius was incompatible with women's supposedly proper femininity. Hannah More had a similar message for women who aspired to fame. A virtuous woman, in her view, should "renounce the desire of any celebrity" with "noble indignation." Yet More adds an interesting escape clause: "No censure is levelled at the exertions of real genius, which is as valuable as it is rare."[11] She admits the possibility of female genius, although she wants to ensure that it is not too easily available.

The central objection to female genius was that it was an oxymoron: genius supposedly belonged to men, and women who tried to assume it were trying to masculinize themselves. The most notorious statement of such an objection was Richard Polwhele's attack on Wollstonecraft in *The Unsex'd Females*. For all its misogyny, Polwhele's poem is less of an indictment of female writers than is often assumed, and it concludes with a detailed paean to many British women writers. Polwhele even admits that Wollstonecraft has "a mind by Genius fraught, by Science stor'd." Yet he blames her, along with such writers as Mary Robinson and Charlotte Smith, for abandoning a properly female role for a masculine one: "A female band despising NATURE's law, / As 'proud defiance' flashes from their arms, / And vengeance smothers all their softer charms."[12]

Although Polwhele objects specifically to these women's Jacobin politics, he also implies that writing itself has the power to challenge gender roles. At a biographical level, this challenge arose partly because few women writers of the period had conventional marriages. Often, women had literary careers because they needed to support themselves in the absence of a husband. Charlotte Smith, Jane Austen, Mary Robinson, Joanna Baillie, Anna Seward, Mary Hays, Felicia Hemans, Mary Shelley, L.E.L., and many others either were not married or lived most of their lives without husbands. I am not claiming that their writing arose solely from not having a husband, nor that their unmarried state necessarily testified to a hostility toward marriage. Yet it did mean that they almost automatically occupied an anomalous gender position in a society that expected women to marry.

Mary Poovey's work has stressed the degree to which some women writers felt the pressure to be proper ladies and to mask the potential oddity of their position.[13] Yet others acknowledged and exploited their presumed oddity through overt experiments with gender-crossing. Charlotte Smith translated Petrarch's sonnets to Laura and wrote sonnets in the voice of Goethe's Werter. Seward and Robinson also wrote works in the voice of Petrarch that, in Robinson's case, included intense expressions of passion: "Fix'd to earth, with trembling zeal I gaz'd. / Each passion madden'd, and each sense amaz'd! / Involuntary sight too soon confess'd / The struggling tumults lab'ring in my breast."[14] Through the persona of Petrarch, Robinson wrote fervently emotional verse about love for another woman. Given the gender-crossing that eighteenth-century writers had frequently associated with male genius, it is telling that Robinson was one of the writers most invested in the cult of genius. Adopting Petrarch's voice was one way to demonstrate that she had the female equivalent of the male genius's supposed ability to transcend conventional gender boundaries.

The writer who used genius most boldly to challenge the sex / gender system was Mary Wollstonecraft. Her novella *Mary: A Fiction* presented itself as a story of female genius in its epigraph from Rousseau: "L'exercice des plus sublimes vertus élève et nourrit le génie" [The exercise of the most sublime virtues elevates and nourishes genius]."[15] In a letter written in 1787, she likewise maintained, "It is a tale, to illustrate an opinion of mine, that a genius will educate itself."[16] Although Wollstonecraft avoided simply making Mary a masculine woman, she, far more than other women writers, used genius to justify the leap from gender-crossing to homoeroticism. Mary falls in love with Ann, whose illness provokes her to cry, "I cannot live without her!—I have no other friend; if I lose her, what a desart [*sic*] will the world be to me."[17] Although after Ann's death, Mary proceeds to fall in love with a man named Henry, I agree with Claudia Johnson that "Henry is

Ann resexed, beloved not insofar as he is different from Ann, but rather insofar as he is like her."[18] In *Mary*, Wollstonecraft created a vivid association between the female genius and lesbian desire.

Most other writers of the day were far less comfortable with this association. In her memoirs, Mary Robinson, despite her claims to genius, carefully insisted on the importance of her domestic life and her love for her daughter. In writing Wollstonecraft's life, William Godwin worked hard to feminize the woman he called a "female Werter." He admitted that her friendship with Fanny Blood, on whom Wollstonecraft based her depiction of Ann, was "so fervent, as for years to have constituted the ruling passion of her mind." Yet for Godwin, Wollstonecraft's later passions for Henry Fuseli, Gilbert Imlay, and finally himself demonstrated her increasing feminization.[19] After Wollstonecraft, de Staël's *Corinne* largely eradicated the traces of masculinity and lesbianism that clustered around the late eighteenth-century image of the female genius. For all Corinne's talent, independence, and unconventionality, she poses no serious threat to patriarchal sex / gender hierarchies. She provided an image of the truly feminine female genius that nineteenth-century writers like Felicia Hemans and L.E.L. found more acceptable than that of the troubling lesbian genius who hovered in writing like Wollstonecraft's.

Anne Bannerman occupied the brief space when the lesbian possibilities made available to female genius by Wollstonecraft were still a reality and de Staël's *Corinne* had not yet swept them away. Unlike the women poets who followed her, Bannerman had little interest in cultivating a respectable image as a conservative poetess. Instead, she, like Wollstonecraft, used the category of genius to justify pushing the boundaries of sex / gender representation. Godwin's image of Wollstonecraft as a female Werter usefully introduces Bannerman because she, like Charlotte Smith, wrote a series of sonnets based on Goethe's novella in which she spoke as Werter. In them, she left no doubt about the nature of the desire involved:

> Ah! not on me she turn'd her wand'ring eyes!
> On me who saw but her, but her alone;
> Yet still I thought! Alas! my soul relies
> On airy phantoms, when its peace is gone.
> Yes! I would go! could this devoted breast
> Give back her image?—but in vain I rave:
> For ever present, on my brain impress'd,
> Her eye's dark lustre lights me to the grave![20]

In her notes, Bannerman reproduces the quotation from Goethe's novel on which she based her sonnet: "I watched Charlotte's eyes, they wandered from one to the other, but did not light on me; upon me, who stood there motionless, and who saw nothing but her" (218). Including this passage highlights the contrast between the sonnet's passionate vehemence and what looks in comparison like the novella's emotional blandness. Where the accusation of being a masculine woman horrified writers like Hannah More, Bannerman invites that perception by writing overtly as a male character, Werter. Even more, she foregrounds the lesbian possibility that had always hovered around the woman writer by expressing passionate desire for another woman. In the next section, I will explain how and why Bannerman used lesbianism in her Werter sonnets and other poems to convince her audience that she possessed the impassioned imagination that Wollstonecraft had associated with genius.

THE TRIALS OF GENIUS: BANNERMAN'S BIOGRAPHY

If Bannerman addressed her sonnets to an actual Laura or Charlotte, that woman has vanished without a trace. Available facts about Bannerman herself are slight. She was born around 1780 and, according to William Beattie, her "spirit" was "greatly superior to her birth or fortune; but she received an excellent education, and was highly accomplished."[21] The critical turn in her career occurred when she met a leading figure of Scottish Romanticism, Robert Anderson (1750–1830), presumably in the late 1790s.[22] Anderson had edited a *Works of the British Poets* (1792–1807) that was pioneering in two ways. It was the first extensive collection of British poetry cheap enough, at £8, for a person of moderate income to afford. Wordsworth, Coleridge, and Southey used it.[23] Second, unlike earlier collections, particularly Johnson's, it included such pre-Miltonic authors as Chaucer and Spenser.[24]

Anderson's edition was so successful that he was invited to edit the *Edinburgh Magazine*. He used it to publish promising young Scottish authors, usually those from poor, working-class backgrounds. Many benefited from his encouragement, most famously Thomas Campbell, who dedicated his *Pleasures of Hope* (1799) to Anderson, but also lesser-known writers such as Thomas Brown, William Erskine, James Grahame, David Irving, John Leyden, and Jessie Stewart.[25] He also had an extensive correspondence with leading antiquarians and men of letters, including William Wordsworth, James Hogg, and Walter Scott. Bannerman's connection with Anderson probably arose when two sonnets and her translation from Rousseau appeared in *Edinburgh Magazine* for 1798 under the pseudonym "Augusta."[26]

Probably with Anderson's encouragement, she published her *Poems* in the spring of 1800 with the Edinburgh firm of Mundell. Although she had initially tried to publish with the prestigious London firm of Cadell and Davies, she had to settle for Mundell, who published the work of most writers in Anderson's circle, including Thomas Campbell and Alexander Thomson, quoted earlier.[27] Bannerman's volume never went into a second edition, but periodical reviewers and Anderson's friends praised it highly.[28] The *Edinburgh Magazine* and the *Morning Chronicle* reprinted pieces from it.[29] Anderson's connections opened doors for Bannerman to publish several poems in Richard Davenport's *Poetical Register* and to contribute translations to the works of Joseph Cooper Walker, an Irish antiquarian who wrote on Irish and Italian literary history.[30]

Through the efforts of another of Anderson's friends, the antiquarian and editor Thomas Park, Bannerman published her next book, *Tales of Superstition and Chivalry* (1802), with a London publisher, Vernor and Hood, who had just scored a great hit with Robert Bloomfield's *Farmer's Boy*.[31] Unlike her first volume, it was published anonymously. Although the volume's weird, fragmented tales appear today as her most interesting work, they did not sell well and fared badly with critics.[32] On top of this disappointment, her mother died in 1803; her brother, in 1804.[33] Since her mother had supported Bannerman on an annuity which stopped at her death, she was left penniless.

For the next four years, Anderson and his friends struggled to support Bannerman. They considered putting together a volume of her poems by subscription; begging the powerful Henry Dundas, Lord Melville, to give her an annuity; asking various aristocrats to be her patrons; and finding a situation for her with the Princess of Wales.[34] Although Joseph Cooper Walker interested Lady Charlotte Rawdon (sister of the Earl of Moira) on Bannerman's behalf, Lady Rawdon never succeeded in getting Bannerman an annuity.[35] While the precise reasons for her rejection are not known, Bannerman's Whig politics could not have endeared her to the staunchly Tory Dundas.[36]

In 1807, Bannerman published by subscription with Mundell a handsome quarto volume dedicated to Lady Rawdon. It had about three hundred subscribers and consisted of most of her previously published poems, in some cases substantially revised.[37] It also marked the end of her literary career because, in the same year, Anderson's connections procured for her a position as governess for the daughter of Lady Frances Beresford.[38] After this time, the scarce materials on Bannerman grow even scarcer. She seems to have returned to Edinburgh at least by 1810 and lived in the home of a Mr. Hope, perhaps also as a governess.[39] In 1815, when the editor of the *Poetical Register* asked for a contribution from her, Anderson intimated "that it would be useless to solicit *her* for *original* poetry."[40] In 1816, she rescued the papers of John Leyden, the poet, linguist, and close friend of Walter Scott, from oblivion and gave them to Leyden's biographer, James Morton, although neither Morton nor anyone else who wrote on Leyden ever thanked her publicly.[41]

Presumably she continued to live in Edinburgh as one of Anderson's acquaintances. In her final years, she became a companion of Anne Grant, herself a distinguished writer, who described Bannerman as "a feeble invalid at Portobello; but with all this external decay, her shattered frame is illuminated by a mind bright with genius and rich in stores of intelligence."[42] Bannerman died in September 1829. In the same year, a poem by her but not in her 1807 volume appeared in *The Casket: A Miscellany*.[43] Since *The Casket* was supposed to contain unpublished poems from manuscript, the poem's appearance suggests that Bannerman may have continued to write after 1807. If she did, her papers have vanished. The National Library of Scotland owns seven large volumes packed with manuscript letters to Anderson, yet they contain not one by Bannerman, nor do the six volumes of David Irving's correspondence at Glasgow's Mitchell Library, even though Irving was Anderson's son-in-law and Bannerman's friend.[44]

In looking at Bannerman's life in light of her poetry's sexual representations, it is impossible to determine what kinds of relations she may have had with other women. Certain facts are striking, more in terms of what she did not do than of what she did. She never married and is never mentioned in any record that I have seen as being romantically involved with a man. Most strikingly, when her means of support disappeared at her mother's death, neither Anderson nor any of his circle hinted at the obvious answer to her financial woes: marriage. Her unsuitability for the marriage market may have arisen partly from physical disability. Sydney Smith refers to her cruelly as a "crooked poetess" characterized by "ugliness and deformity."[45] These traits may have intensified her felt alienation from "respectable" female sexual roles. It is certainly possible that Bannerman's use of thinly veiled lesbian eroticism in her poems arose from her sense of her sexuality. Yet I want neither to assume on the basis of her poetry that she definitely had erotic relations with other women nor to dismiss her poetry's lesbian representation because the "truth" of her sexuality cannot be proved. Instead, based on the evidence that exists, I want to concentrate on factors that helped to determine why Bannerman wrote as she did.

Bannerman repeatedly struck readers and acquaintances as bearing "strong marks of genius," as Joseph Cooper Walker and Anne Grant noted.[46] While she never used the word "genius" to characterize herself, she used its near-synonym "enthusiast" when she presented herself in one poem as "the lone Enthusiast, wrapt in trace sublime" who hopes to "soar, unfetter'd by the bounds of time" ("Verses on an Illumination," 61). The imagery in responses to Bannerman's work was a feminine version of the gender-crossings that eighteenth-century writers usually associated with masculine genius. Readers often resorted to masculinizing adjectives like "bold" and "sublime." A reviewer of Bannerman's 1800 volume wrote, "We are accustomed to characterise the sublimer and more energetic strains of poesy as the productions of a *masculine spirit* . . . but we may be permitted to observe that Anne Bannerman's Odes may be quoted as an irrefragable proof that the ardour . . . which gives birth to lofty thought and bold expression may glow within a female breast."[47] William Preston praised her in cross-gendered terms as a poet "who female sweetness joins to manly worth."[48] For critics, *The Genii* was "a very bold attempt"; her poems united "vigour, harmony, and taste"; her poetry was "Miltonic" and reached "the true *sublime*"; her imagination was "lively and bold."[49]

Reactions to the perceived masculinity of Bannerman's writings were not always positive. After reading the *Tales*, Preston complained that she had deserted feminine beauty for masculine sublimity: "Why with thy Pen delight to Wound? / Why call the gliding Spectres round, / In all the Pomp of Death array'd?— / Our Pangs should from thy Glances flow, / Our Terrors lighten on thy Brow."[50] Another member of the Anderson circle, Thomas Brown, wrote to her as if she threatened manhood itself: "Ah! then, aspirer! let thy strain / Man's humbler powers no longer tell him! / The equal wreath let Woman gain; / But let her, let her—not excel him!"[51] For these men, Bannerman's writing departed unnervingly from the poetry that ladies were supposed to write.

Although Bannerman might have aspired to genius in writing, her life could not sustain the independence that such genius implied. In her lack of autonomy, she provides a stark contrast with Anne Damer. Thomas Park, on learning of Bannerman's initial resistance to becoming a governess, complained, in a tellingly cross-gendered image, of her "loftiness of feeling, which I frankly confess is too Chattertonian to enhance my respect or admiration."[52] Anderson too was irritated by Bannerman's mind, which was "so lofty and unaccommodating" that it was difficult "to do her any reasonable service."[53] Social circumstances eventually forced Bannerman's "lofty and unaccommodating" mind to submit to male patronage and patronizing.

For example, since her *Tales* were printed in London, she had little supervision over their engravings. The fourth engraving represented a female nude and, tame as it looks today, it caused a scandal in Edinburgh. As Park wrote in 1802, "The wits of Edinburgh are complotting to give the fair authoress disgust, or to make the work misprised." Park vowed in return that he was "ready to commence knight-errant" for her and had the illustration pulled from the volumes that the press had not already distributed.[54] Such feminization of Bannerman intensified after her mother's death. Walker was typical when he wrote, "There cannot, perhaps, be a more affecting spectacle, than a young and lovely woman, indued with fine talents, and exquisite sensibility, lamenting a parent, and at the same time, struggling with adversity."[55] When Bannerman at last accepted the position of governess, Anderson noted sententiously, "She is now to earn her livelihood like other females in her circumstances." "In the judgment of all her friends," he stated chillingly, her decision reflected "more credit on her than all her poetry can do."[56] Bannerman's "genius" went for nothing next to the supposedly greater good of becoming like other women.

Even if we recognize the sincere efforts that Anderson and his circle made to provide for Bannerman so that she could keep writing poetry, their words reveal discomfort with her work and eventual relief that she would write no more. They turned their attention instead to the more conventionally feminine work of Jessie Stewart, who wrote sentimental sonnets under the pseudonym "Adeline."[57] Contrasting Bannerman's career with those of other female writers reveals how few options were open to her after her mother's death. Unlike Anne Damer, she had no inherited wealth to support her work. Living far from London, she had little opportunity of getting work as a journalist or as a dramatist, unlike Mary Wollstonecraft, Elizabeth Inchbald, or Hannah Cowley. No records suggest that she ever tried to write novels, as Charlotte Smith did when she needed to make more money than she had from poetry. While this absence of novel-writing may have arisen from Bannerman's personal inclination, it was overdetermined by the lack of opportunities for publishing. Novelists were strikingly absent from Anderson's circle and, with a few exceptions, from writers living in Scotland during the height of Bannerman's career. Nor did the two publishers with whom she was most closely associated (Mundell, and Cadell and Davies) publish many novels.

In this light, the intensity with which Bannerman's poetry developed the role of the female genius seems less like vanity or adolescent histrionics and more like the only way, given her isolation, that she could claim significance for her writing. Only if her writing could convince the reader that she was a

genius entirely unlike other women writers could it succeed. As such, she
might be thought of as a female version of William Blake, and her work
shares several characteristics in common with his: it draws eclectically on a
wide range of sources and shows a particular interest in mythological alternatives to the traditional Greek and Roman models; deranges conventional
narrative chronology to differentiate itself from the mode of the contemporary novel; and strives for the loftiest expression of the sublime.

Perhaps most hauntingly of all, a sense of loneliness pervades the work of
Blake and Bannerman, a feeling that they are writing in a vacuum for an
audience that will probably not be receptive. As would-be geniuses, they
build their own failure into their poetry. For all that Bannerman includes
passionate expressions to other women and avoids any representation of
conventional heterosexuality, she remains the "lone Enthusiast." Enough of
the traditional ascetic aspects of genius remain in her poetic self that she
does not imagine long-term same-sex friendships that a writer like Isaac
D'Israeli thought were essential to masculine genius. To a degree, this loneliness is a self-glorifying cliché of the cult of genius because it proves that the
genius is superior to any worldly attachments. Yet, insofar as the character of
the genius entwined with that of the homosexual, Bannerman's poetry also
suggests the origins of the image of gay and lesbian life as perpetually unful-
filled and lonely. Whereas for so many women writers of the late eighteenth
and early nineteenth centuries, social relationships formed the major subject
of their poetry, Bannerman remains even more solitary than the major male
romantic poets.

SEXUALITY AND THE POETRY OF FEMALE GENIUS

Bannerman never wrote a love poem to a man or even one that represented
erotic relations between a man and a woman in an admiring or approving
way. Her avoidance of heteronormativity varied from poem to poem:
addressing a woman as the object of erotic attraction; speaking as a natural
or supernatural force whose desires cannot be categorized as masculine or
feminine; and imagining supernatural female characters who for various
reasons avoid heterosexual relations. Insofar as the role of female genius
encouraged Bannerman to counter prevailing heterosexual norms for female
writers and characters, her writing manifests the kinds of cross-gendering
that the eighteenth century associated with female sexual impropriety.

The dominant sonneteer of the 1790s was Charlotte Smith, whose *Elegiac
Sonnets* appeared in 1784, and Bannerman knew Smith's work well.[58] As I

have noted, Smith provided Bannerman's precedent for translating sonnets
from Petrarch and writing sonnets in the voice of Goethe's Werter.[59] Since
Smith's sonnets, unlike Bannerman's, never provoked the anxieties about
cross-gendering that were so marked a feature of Bannerman's reception, it
is worth comparing Smith's with Bannerman's to see how they differ:

> Tho' my fond soul to heaven were flown,
>   Or tho' on earth 'tis doom'd to pine,
> Prisoner or free—obscure or known,
>   My heart, O Laura, still is thine.
> Whate'er my destiny may be,
> That faithful heart still burns for thee![60]
>
> (Smith)

> O Laura! Laura! in the dust with thee,
>   Would I could find a refuge from despair!
>   Is this thy boasted triumph, Love! to tear
> A heart, thy coward malice dare not free,
>   And bid it live, when every hope is fled,
>   To weep, among the ashes of the dead?[61]
>
> (Bannerman)

The contrast between the bland sensibility of Smith's translations and the
fiercer passion of Bannerman's brings home the difference between what
Wollstonecraft calls "sickly delicacy" and the "impassioned imagination" of
genius.[62] Smith's mild tetrameters flow smoothly, with few enjambments and
little violence of expression. The climactic statement is merely that the speaker's "faithful heart still burns" for Laura. Bannerman's poem, with its strong
internal caesurae ("Laura! Laura!"), dramatic enjambment ("to tear / A
heart"), and active verbs or verbal forms ("find a refuge," "tear / A heart,"
"dare not free") produces a far more violent effect. Reviewers praised such
language as "the breathings of ardent genius" flying "with the intrepid pinion
of an eaglet."[63] Smith, in contrast, provoked no one to call her an eaglet.

   It is tempting to explain the differences between the sonnets in essential-
ized terms by arguing that the "heterosexual" Smith's is merely conventional while the "lesbian" Bannerman's is somehow more sincere. But the language of both is equally traditional. Nothing prevents us from believing
that Bannerman's sonnet *could* be the product of a woman forced to use
sleights such as translations to express her love for another woman. Yet,

given the lack of biographical evidence about Bannerman, I want to emphasize instead how the evidence that does exist can help to explain her writing. Smith, an upper-class lady who married a wealthy man, was an outstandingly talented originator of the vogue for polite, vaguely melancholic
women's poetry during the Romantic period. Yet she never carried her
melancholy so far as to imply that she was entirely cast out from society.
Her sonnets return repeatedly to the image of her dead daughter Anna to
emphasize the importance of a maternal role to her inspiration. Even
though her husband had reduced the family to penury, she wrote as a proper lady who identified herself on the title page with the name of the estate
where she had grown up.

Bannerman, in contrast, did not and could not pretend to belong to
Smith's station. She rejected the proper lady's authorial stance for the more
radical one of cross-gendered female genius. The speaker's intensified passion in the sonnets for the female addressee appears as a marker of Bannerman's difference from, and implied superiority to, Smith. Bannerman, the
female genius from Scotland, shows Smith, the polite lady from England,
how passionate writing to another woman ought to look. The result of this
literary rivalry is a series of sonnets by a woman that declare violent love
for another woman. While they are labeled as being inspired by Petrarch
and Werter, nothing in the poems' language indicates that the speaker is
male. What the reader sees is a series of poems by Miss Bannerman to Laura
and to Charlotte.

The sonnets are Bannerman's most immediately striking work in terms
of locating female-female desire, but they are not the only example of
how the cult of genius leads her to flout heteronormativity. Her 1800 volume also includes "The Nun," a long dramatic lyric based on Madame de
Genlis's drama *Cécile; Ou, Le Sacrifice de l'Amitié*. In this drama, Cécile is
about to become a nun so that her sister will receive an inheritance adequate to let her marry the man she loves. At the last minute, the sister rescues Cécile from the convent because an uncle conveniently dies and
leaves Cécile a fortune also. Bannerman, however, changes this happy ending so that no rescue occurs and Cécile becomes a nun. As the poem
opens, her initial enthusiasm for her sacrifice has worn off, and she is horrified at her choice.

Despite the overt debt of "The Nun" to de Genlis, the more obvious subtext for the poem, as one reviewer recognized, is Pope's "Eloisa to
Abelard."[64] Both poems are dramatic lyrics in heroic couplets by women
immured in convents who rail against the injustice of their fates.[65] Yet in
Pope, the situation depends on heterosexual relations: Eloisa speaks inces-

santly of her love for Abelard. Bannerman's heroine never mentions her
longing for a man. The pathos of her story depends on the convent's threat
to her genius: "Enwrapt in superstition's iron chains, / How the blood rushes thro' my shivering veins! / The sick'ning spirit wears the powers away, /
Which Genius kindled with his brightest ray" (88). The heroine at such
moments appears as Bannerman's figure of her own biographical situation,
a female genius trapped in a hostile environment. Her solitude literalizes
the uniqueness that Hannah More attributed to "real genius." The nun is
utterly alone, just as a female genius had to be in order to demonstrate her
difference from ordinary women writers.

   Yet for the nun, imprisonment has stimulated her genius because it
encourages her cross-gendered identifications with male figures. She maintains that "like some sad wreck, by tempests blown, / Forlorn and desolate,
I stand alone" (90) only after a strange visionary passage in which she
describes two men who represent her ideal of freedom. The first is an
African savage whose "giant soul, / Indignant, mocks the shadow of con-
troul" (87); the second, an Icelandic fisherman who knows that, despite his
"hard and laborious" lot, "still, still, his heart can tell him—he is free!" (88).
These male figures represent the freedom that she contrasts with the imprisoning power of Catholicism. The contemptible "pallid Sisters" pour "tears,
in torrent, from their eye-lids," and their lachrymose femininity contrasts
sharply with her masculine self-identification.[66]

   She acknowledges only one social tie, which is to the sister for whom she
has sacrificed herself:

> O! Sister of my soul! I seek you here;
> In vain I seek you, thro' the caverns drear;
> Falsely I triumph'd, when I bade adieu
> To social life, to happiness,—to you.
>
>   (77–78)

She later asks, "Art thou not dearer to this aching breast, / Than joy, and
freedom, happiness, and rest?"[67] This bond with another woman is the closest the speaker comes to acknowledging eroticism. Admittedly, sisterly affection is present in Bannerman's source, de Genlis's drama; Cécile says, "Le
premier & le seul objet auquel j'aye pu m'attacher, c'est ma soeur" [My sister
was the first and only person to whom I was able to become attached] and
leaves at the end proclaiming, "Je vais suivre ma soeur, & pour ne jamais me
séparer d'elle" [I will follow my sister, never to quit her].[68] Yet, even though
the erotic undertones of such professions are transparent, de Genlis's comic

style and Cécile's desire to use her sister to escape from the nuns nevertheless prevent her love from being taken too seriously.

In Bannerman's version, however, the professions of sisterly attachment
acquire more weight because the speaker has accomplished her self-sacrifice for her sister. The only erotic attachment acknowledged by this self-
professed female genius, with her cross-gendered imaginary identifications,
is to another woman. In the case of both Bannerman's sonnets and this
monologue, it is possible to dismiss female-female desire as something else:
a translation of a male voice in the sonnets, a sisterly attachment in the
monologue. Yet doing so ignores how Bannerman chooses situations that
require passionate addresses from one woman to another. In all cases, such
addresses arise from her stance as the female genius who marks her uniqueness by avoiding the conventions of heteronormativity.

Even when Bannerman's poems do not express same-sex desire, they still
pointedly unsettle the conventional position of woman as object of heterosexual love. In romantic poetry, such a position is notoriously linked to the
equation between femininity and nature. As Margaret Homans has argued,
such an equation invites the silencing of the female voice by absorbing it
into the environment.[69] Although many Romantic women writers nevertheless described and appreciated nature in their work, in Bannerman's
most striking poetry she unsexes nature by envisioning it as a force unavail-
able to heterosexual desire.

For example, the speaker of Bannerman's "Spirit of the Air" is an all-
powerful deity who glories in transcending the elements: "Encompass'd
by the raging storm, / I smile at Danger's threat'ning form; / I mock
Destruction on his tow'ring seat, / And leave the roaring winds, contend-
ing at my feet" (9). Through such personifications, Bannerman represents
the vast and transcendent power stereotypically associated with the
Burkean sublime. Yet even as she does so, she revises it by suggesting a
more humane side to this impersonal force. Transcendent as the Spirit is,
it still recognizes the misery of women, especially those of different races.
The Spirit notices the anguish of an African woman who throws herself
overboard when she realizes that she cannot spare her son from slave
traders. While suffering African mothers were stock characters in abolitionist poetry, Bannerman revises Burke's association between sublime
emotions and horror of blackness.[70] For Bannerman's sublime being,
an African is not a spectacle of horror but of misery demanding sympathetic action.

While the Spirit cannot revive the black woman, it takes its revenge on
white traders by transforming her into a spectral image of vengeance:

Now, for your happy homes prepare;
But, curb your joy—I meet you there.
Then, as your friends, your infant race,
Rush wildly to your fond embrace,
Before your eyes a ghastly form shall stand,
And o'er her infant weep, and wave her beck'ning hand.

(5)

The Spirit vows to destroy the domestic bliss of the traders, their "happy homes," by presenting them with the African mother's ghost. Bannerman's Spirit produces this image of the ghastly sublime to demonstrate that the traders' domesticity is built upon destroying mother-child bonds. In so doing, the Spirit combines sublime masculine transcendence and power with beautiful feminine sympathies for the suffering of other women. Like Wollstonecraft's genius, it confounds gender categories.

A similarly transcendent woman appears in Bannerman's dramatic lyric "The Mermaid." Its epigraph from *The Rambler* tells the story of two lovers, Anningait and Ajut: "Anningait was seized . . . by the Genius of the Rocks, and . . . Ajut was transformed into a *mermaid,* and still continues to seek her lover, in the deserts of the sea" (20). One might expect that a poem based on this story would be a heterosexual romance about the mermaid's endless quest for her lost love. Yet heterosexual romance plays no part in Bannerman's poem. Her mermaid has lost all interest in her male lover: "Yes! I am chang'd.—My heart, my soul, / Retain no more their former glow" (21). Instead, she has become a sublime spirit who aids the "avenging ministers of wrath" (23) in order "to lure the sailor to his doom" (22).

The mermaid's murderous address to the spirits of death leads to some of Bannerman's best poetry:

To aid your toils, to scatter death,
    Swift, as the sheeted lightning's force,
When the keen north-wind's freezing breath
    Spreads desolation in its course,
My soul within this icy sea,
Fulfils her fearful destiny.
Thro' Time's long ages I shall wait
To lead the victims to their fate;
With callous heart, to hidden rocks decoy,
And lure, in seraph-strains, unpitying, to destroy.

(24)

Although Bannerman's elevated diction often can seem strained, it is appropriate to the mermaid's character. The mermaid achieves a negative exaltation in her treachery that makes much other poetry of the period by women seem bland in comparison. Bannerman's skillful manipulation of the meter also helps to vary the pace of her high-flown diction. She begins the stanza with four weighted lines, whose rhythm struggles ostentatiously against the iambic tetrameter, as in "When the keen north-wind's freezing breath." Then, in the next four lines, as she moves to rhyming couplets, the rhythm becomes more regular, as if the tortured images of the first four lines were giving way to a more businesslike callousness about murder. Finally, in a dramatic slowing down of the poem's pace, Bannerman increases the meter first to a pentameter and then to an Alexandrine. The last line's three medial caesurae let the mermaid drag out the slow length of her vindictive triumph over her male victims.

In such poems, Bannerman demonstrated the different possibilities open to a writer assuming the role of female genius. In all cases, she suggested that she was beyond writing about the supposedly natural feminine desires for men, domesticity, and pious submission. Daring as her 1800 volume was, her 1802 *Tales of Superstition and Chivalry* pushed the role of the female genius in even more unconventional directions. Having established her promise with her *Poems*, Bannerman faced the challenge of outdoing her earlier self. I suspect that the *Tales* were intended to be her breakthrough since the volume's London publisher and four engravings marked it as an attempt to enter the company of major writers. She also published it anonymously, perhaps knowing how thoroughly her work was breaking the implicit rules that had been established for female poets.

Unfortunately, the *Tales'* 1802 appearance was poorly timed. In 1800, M. G. Lewis had edited a two-volume collection of Gothic ballads by him and others, including Walter Scott and John Leyden, called *Tales of Wonder*. Readers greeted the collection with derision because Lewis included well-known work by authors like Jonson and Dryden in a seemingly transparent attempt to pad the volumes; it was nicknamed "Tales of Plunder." The reception of this volume and the subsequent parodies of it demonstrated that by 1800, "the period of greatest fascination with the Gothic ballads had already passed."[71] Yet the chief obstacle to Bannerman's success, I suspect, was the strangeness of her tales themselves. Although reviewers had praised the sublime lyrics of her first volume, when she transferred that sublimity to narrative forms, she went beyond conventionally acceptable critical bounds. According to the volume's readers, "There [was] no Plot and Story made out at least no Denouement"; the tales were a "chaos of horrid images, without story, without connection, 'without form and void' "; the poet had "contrived to leap over, not the dull parts, but what would in ordinary hands have formed the main action."[72] No writer, not even a female genius, could be praised for transgressing narrative conventions so openly.[73]

In themselves, imitation Gothic ballads were not unusual. Since Bishop Percy's *Reliques* (1765), such imitations had played a large role in Romanticism because they countered the Augustan assumption that the classics provided the proper origins for English literature.[74] Anderson's inclusion of medieval authors in his anthology encouraged those in his circle, like Leyden, to explore imitation medievalism. While Anderson's commentary on medieval authors was not particularly enthusiastic, he nevertheless earned tributes for having in his anthology "mark'd the first beams of genius quiver bright / Through the mist of ages and of night!" (106), as Bannerman wrote.[75] She associated medievalism, rather than classical literature, with the origins of genius, and her ballads attempted to recapture the force of that original genius.

The Gothic ballad also offered special challenges to Bannerman as a specifically female genius. Although in recent years critics interested in gender and sexuality have studied Gothic novels almost exhaustively, Gothic ballads of the 1790s have received virtually no attention.[76] Eve Kosofsky Sedgwick's claim that "homophobia found in the paranoid Gothic a genre of its own" has proved an exceptionally helpful insight for linking the Gothic novel with emerging attitudes toward male homosexual roles.[77] Yet the Gothic novel, as a genre associated with the repetition of stock motifs and familiar "machinery," was too degraded a vehicle for would-be geniuses, although in some cases it provided a venue in which authors might criticize aspects of its cult, as in Mary Shelley's *Frankenstein*.

If, as critics have argued, Gothic novels permitted explorations of unorthodox sexual relationships, Gothic ballads were generally more conservative. While some ballads do not contain female characters ("The Erl-King," "The Wild Huntsman"), the narratives of the best known hinge on evil done by women. Human women, such as those in Bürger's "Leonore," Lewis's "Alonso the Brave and the Fair Imogene," and Scott's "The Eve of St. John," are punished for erotic misdeeds. Supernatural women, like those in Scott's "Glenfilas," Lewis's "The Earl-King's Daughter," and later Keats's "La Belle Dame Sans Merci," seduce or attempt to seduce men to their doom. In all cases, the perceived dangers of female sexuality dominate the Gothic ballad far more completely than they do the Gothic novel. This one-sidedness may arise, at least in part, because so few female authors wrote such ballads, and those who did, such as Joanna Baillie, did not depart from the conventions established by male authors.

Bannerman's friend Thomas Brown expressed concern at her turn to medievalism because during the age of chivalry, "In halls, and bowers, of stern delight, / Neglected female Genius lay."[78] If Bannerman had been alive in the Middle Ages, implied Brown, her voice would have been unheard. Her *Tales* imagine what the voice of female genius might have been if it had been able to speak during the age of chivalry. The resulting narratives radically alter the Gothic ballad's machinery, and, as in Bannerman's earlier work, this revision involves the unconventional representation of female desire. While the plots of previous ballads depended on punishing or demonizing female heterosexual desire, Bannerman instead creates female characters whose desires cannot be explained in heteronormative terms. Her tales demonstrate that conventional Gothic narratives become hieroglyphs once the women in them no longer conform to heterosexual expectations.

For students of British Romanticism, Bannerman's revision of the Gothic ballad has a special interest for the light that it casts on her better-known contemporaries. Early readers of Bannerman's poems explicitly compared her work to that of Wordsworth and Coleridge. The *Critical Review* described her tales as "imitations, chiefly from Mr. Scott's and Dr. Leyden's ballads, and the poems of Mr. Wordsworth."[79] In a cruel letter, Anna Seward wrote to Bannerman that she assumed the tales were burlesques "particularly aimed at Coleridge's *Ancient Mariner*, as the language, and phrase, and manner of writing, so often parody that composition."[80] Seward was right to note Coleridge's influence on Bannerman, which Bannerman herself foregrounded in her tale "The Dark Ladie." It continued a poem by Coleridge known today as "Love" but which first appeared as "Introduction to the Tale of the Dark Ladie" in the *Morning Post* in 1799. It was reprinted in the February 1800 issue of the *Edinburgh Magazine*, and the following March, Bannerman's "The Dark Ladie" appeared in the same periodical with a note referring the reader back to Coleridge's poem.[81] She later used a slightly longer version of her poem as the first of her *Tales* (139–48).[82]

Coleridge's "Introduction to the Tale of the Dark Ladie," like most imitation Gothic ballads, treated female heterosexual desire as a given. The poem contains two heterosexual love plots: the speaker wins his beloved Genevieve by telling her the story of the Ladie of the Land's devotion to a love-crazed Knight. Although the speaker ends by promising Genevieve "a sister tale / Of Man's perfidious Cruelty,"[83] Coleridge never wrote such a tale; Bannerman did, instead. Her poem describes how Sir Guyon, having returned from the Holy Land, invites his fellow knights to his castle. There, they are visited by the terrifying sight of a veiled lady:

> And to the alarmed guests she turn'd,
> No breath was heard, no voice, no sound,
> And in a tone, so deadly deep,
> She pledg'd them all around,
> That in their hearts, and thro' their limbs,
> No pulses could be found.
>
> (142)

After this, she disappears and the soldiers are haunted by the memory of her voice "that stopt / Thro' all their limbs the rushing blood" because "no human voice / Could ever reach that echo deep" (143). Unlike the feminine women in Coleridge's poem, who are dedicated to their men, the deep voice of Bannerman's Dark Lady confounds the knights so thoroughly that they take her to be inhuman.

In response, they hope to learn a narrative that would explain the lady's appearance. While they discover that she abandoned her husband and child for Sir Guyon, nothing they learn explains her weirdly deep voice. The poem ends confessing the Dark Lady's uninterpretability, since the knights never discover

> Whence those deep unearthly tones,
> That human bosom never own'd;
> Or why it cannot be removed,
> That folded veil that sweeps the ground?
>
> (148)

No story of sexual transgression and punishment explains the lady's unfeminine appearance. Instead, she remains permanently unreadable, an enigma that paralyzes male viewers. The lady with the deep voice appears as a Gothic version of the cross-gendered female genius who confounds her auditors by aspiring for masculine sublimity. While the two differ somewhat in that the Dark Lady's fate seems to have been thrust upon her and the genius chooses to present her work, both frustrate the expectations of their masculine audiences by not conforming to expected modes of feminine behavior.

The presence of non-heteronormative women in Bannerman's tales causes narrative disruptions in the form of odd gaps and explanations that do not explain. "The Prophetess of the Oracle of Seam" (188–201) describes a terrifying female figure who sacrifices men to a mysterious dark power, and the Queen of Beauty in "The Prophecy of Merlin" (202–12) suddenly metamorphoses into a male spirit to confirm to Arthur that he must die. Ellinor in "The Penitent's Confession" (158–65) dies to become a spectral "it" who reduces the male speaker's arm of "living flesh" to a "dry and wither'd bone" (164) with her touch. Bannerman's Gothic women possess the power to unman the men around them. Traditionally, male authors softened their representations of such unmanning women by suggesting that at least their sexual desires were heteroerotic, even if they devoured men like air. Yet Bannerman, in contrast, prefers to keep her female characters' sexuality far more elusive. She revises the "obscurity" associated with the Burkean sublime by suggesting that narrative logic breaks down as soon as the assumption of female heterosexuality vanishes.

Even in a tale like "The Perjured Nun," in which heterosexual love drives female characters, the end result is an encounter that suggests alternate paths for desire. Bannerman modeled "The Perjured Nun" on Lewis's "The Bleeding Nun" in the *Tales of Wonder*, which he based on a situation in his novel *The Monk*. In Lewis's ballad, Raymond plans to elope with Agnes by having Agnes disguise herself as the Bleeding Nun, only to learn that he has eloped with the Bleeding Nun herself.[84] Bannerman keeps the figure of the spectral nun, but revises the relations between the human man and woman. Lord Henrie, having caused a nun to forsake her vows, is doomed to be haunted by her ghost in his castle's eastern tower. He leaves his wife Geraldine so that he may watch the tower and warns her not to follow him. She disobeys him, goes to the tower, and, when she runs to meet him, encounters the nun instead:

> She burst thro' the door, to the eastern floor,
> To welcome her love again!
>
> But O! her shriek!—Like the dead from the grave
> Was the form she has clasp'd around!
> And the phantom turn'd, where the lamps had burn'd
> And stood on the marble ground.
>
> "You sought not me!" cries the hollow voice,
> "You came not to welcome me!
> Let your watching cease, and depart in peace,
> For him you shall never see.—"
>
> (176–77)

After the nun then explains that she was betrayed by Henrie, the poem ends without describing a reaction from Geraldine. This moment is striking in Bannerman's poetry because it is the only moment in which two female characters actually embrace. At the level of the plot, it is not a real embrace because, as the nun's response emphasizes, it is only Geraldine's mistake. Nevertheless, the scene tellingly reverses the conventional erotic situation in which a woman mediates relations between two men. Here, the man is conveniently eliminated and the two women are left alone in the castle.

The embrace conforms strikingly to Terry Castle's theory of the apparitional lesbian: "The kiss that doesn't happen, the kiss that *can't* happen, because one of the women involved has become a ghost . . . seems to me a crucial metaphor for the history of lesbian literary representation since the early eighteenth century."[85] Given the context that Castle traces, there may even be a nuance of erotic reproach in the nun's "You sought not me! . . . / You came not to welcome me." At the least, the nun partly occupies the place of a traditional male hero because she has dispatched a villain who threatened the heroine: "Let your soul be at peace, and your watching cease, / For his faithless heart is cold" (177). The moment is paradigmatic not just of the particular tale but of Bannerman's entire career. Without ever writing a love poem from one woman to another, she continually avoids heteronormativity.

Doing so, as I have argued, marks her implied superiority to other women writers as a female genius. Yet the rarity of the female genius also determined that Bannerman had to keep any character that might be read as a surrogate for her as a solitary. Only through such devices as a ghostly embrace, an impassioned address to an absent sister, or the spectral resurrection of a dead slave mother could Bannerman bring her voices of female genius into relations with other women. Castle's analysis suggests how the apparitional quality of lesbian representation in Bannerman's work was itself a condition of her authorial stance as a female genius.

In 1830, a year after Bannerman's death in obscurity, Walter Scott paid her tribute: "Miss Anne Bannerman likewise should not be forgotten, whose *Tales of Superstition and Chivalry* appeared about 1802. They were perhaps too mystical and too abrupt; yet if it be the purpose of this kind of ballad poetry powerfully to excite the imagination, without pretending to satisfy it, few persons have succeeded better than this gifted lady, whose volume is peculiarly fit to be read in a lonely house by a decaying lamp."[86] Since by 1830, poets such as Felicia Hemans and L.E.L. had perfected a mode of sentimental, feminine poetry, Scott's tribute is tinged with nostalgia not only for Bannerman but for a kind of woman's writing that had largely disappeared. As he notes, its salient characteristic was "to excite the imagination" without satisfying it. I have argued that what Bannerman uses for such excitement are representations of women who cannot be contained within heterosexual conventions.

Bannerman's strategy is interesting in its own right, but her career has larger significance for understanding women's writing during the Romantic period. Most recent criticism has focused on how gender conditioned women's writing. Anne Mellor has gone so far as to distinguish between masculine and feminine romanticisms for the period.[87] What Bannerman's work suggests is the difficulty of taking analytical categories like gender or sexuality for granted as origins for poetic representation. I have suggested instead that the literary system in which Bannerman tried and ultimately failed to have a career offered its own incentives for work that challenged contemporary heterosexual norms. Her unusual poems were less the mark of an alienated, marginalized writer than of one whose deviant representations were virtually mandated by her situation. Genius demanded that Bannerman push the limits of acceptable poetry in ways that most women writers never did.

CHAPTER SIX

Genius and the Blakean Ridiculous

The love affair between gay writers and William Blake has been long and happy. Allen Ginsberg, most famously, had Blakean visions in a Harlem basement and never let them go. For Robert Duncan, hearing the introduction to the *Songs of Experience* read in a "sublime and visionary manner" succeeded in "breaking the husk" of his "modernist pride and shame."[1] James Merrill and David Jackson used Merrill's copy of Blake's biography to hide the transcript of their first Ouija board sessions.[2] In discussing such poets, Maria Damon describes their love for the supernatural in ways that help explain their love for Blake. Noting that "angel" is gay slang for a young man, she argues that it "indicates an ethereal sense of belonging to multiple worlds, multiple planes of existence, of inhabiting space somewhere between the human and the divine."[3] Writing about angels gave gay poets a new vision of the double life. Instead of being a rigid split between gay ghetto and restrictive straight world, it became in their work a shimmering border between the real and the more than real. I would add to Damon's analysis that gay angels have a defensively campy edge. They belong to the most hallowed Christian traditions, and to steal them for gay writing rescues a set of images supposedly discarded by a secular society. While sane people are not supposed to take angels literally, they let a poet like James Merrill treat the doubleness of pre-Stonewall gay life as a blessing, not a curse.

For gay poets, Blake is on the side of the angels. Like them, he refuses the borders between the real and the extra-real. While nobody can quite take Blake or angels with an absolutely straight face (at least not all the time), they give their believers a chance for camp participation in myth that is more exalted than merely established belief. While many Blake readers first learn about him in school, to be a Blake fan transcends whatever is represented by the academy. All Blake's admirers presumably believe that they

have a special link to him, but love for such an odd writer may be especially valuable to gay readers alienated from traditional sites of adoration. Blake
is a ready-made patron saint for those wanting to elevate their marginality,
dissent, and queerness into strength. The relative futility of Blake's battle
during his lifetime makes him all the more attractive. In the intertextual
heritage of queer art, Blake has become an honorary icon.

In the finest traditions of camp, Blake's poetry demands to be taken seri-
ously and loses much of its power if so read. Yet few authors have spurred
academic criticism quite as poker-faced. Reading it, my mind wanders to
Blakean versions of questions usually associated with the Janeites: Who would
one cast in *Jerusalem: The Motion Picture*? What advice could Dr. Ruth give
Thel? How long would Urizen last as Chair of a Ways and Means Committee?
Such questions open up Blake's generous and ignored sense of the absurd.
Critics have agreed that Blake is a comic poet in a large sense.[4] He never
doubts that humanity can and will be redeemed through the oldest of comic
plots, the "torments of Love & Jealousy."[5] Yet the sheer gusto with which he
lets his mythic beings make fools of themselves is too often lost in commentary. A poet so conscious of imperfect strivings, mixed motives, and the bad
results of good intentions rarely lacks an ironic edge. I want to linger over the
almost conscious absurdity that laces Blake's most sublime moments, the
defensive fluidity that will not locate meaning in one place or time, and the
pathos of a system whose excesses guarantee that it will fail exactly when
Blake seems to need it most.

The Blakean ridiculous is not simply "in" Blake. Part of the fun of reading him is that his campiness shatters illusions about the reader's neutrali-
ty. Eve Kosofsky Sedgwick lists some questions upon which camp depends:
"What if the right audience for this were exactly *me*? What if, for instance,
the resistant, oblique tangential investments of attention and attraction
that I am able to bring to this spectacle are actually uncannily responsive to
the resistant, oblique, tangential investments of the person, or of some of
the people, who created it?"[6] For Sedgwick, camp needs a hidden, antiestablishment bond between the viewer and artwork. I would agree with a
slightly modified version of her definition that made more room for the
specificities of being gay. As she describes the experience, camp depends
only on individual fantasy. Yet the marginalized "me" may also wonder if
she / he shares the same tangential investments as other, similarly marginalized askers. Camp involves bonding not only with the work of art but also
with other gay viewers. The history of twentieth-century poetry reveals that
Blake has been peculiarly alive to the camp questions that gay readers have
brought.[7]

Blake's camp quotient skyrockets when he confronts sex / gender issues. For him, nothing is as serious and as silly as gender relations in a heterosexist, patriarchal culture. Gender relations for him are not simply one site of ridiculousness among many others. As Cate McClenahan has argued, gender is the source, not simply the model, for all bad power relations in Blake.[8] For him, injustices in the state, religion, economy, or education all spring from the sex / gender system. Most readers agree that Blakean revolution depends on breaking down the system, liberating desire, and finding a utopian space beyond genders. Yet since at least the late seventies, academic Blakeans have met such hopes with stern demystification. According to one, while "sexes vanish" in Blake's "culminating visions," his "most sympathetic female characters are victims, while his most monstrous ones represent a devouring and destructive 'Female Will' which as he grew older he represented as more and more frightening and abhorrent."[9] Blake's critics write as if an unwary reader might be deluded into thinking that Blake were more sexually liberating than he really is: "Despite critical claims that Blake anticipated the liberation of women from sexual repression and patriarchal tyranny, Blake shared his culture's denigration of the feminine gender."[10]

Taking this stance to its extreme, David Punter scorchingly describes the work of unrigorous Blakeans: "Blake becomes Protean.... In our admiration for and propagation of this Protean shape, we perform simultaneously a celebration of our own ability to survive, to adapt our threatened interpretative craft flexibly to changing circumstances, to institutional pressures." He wants critics to dismiss such appropriative nonsense and to attack the scandal of Blake's sexism. They must see that his works "are themselves politically subverted by the shapes imposed on and by sexuality." If they do not, they refuse "to recognise the exclusions which are nonetheless present"and thereby "settle for Blake's texts as applicable commodities rather than as themselves participants in the vicissitudes of history, politics, patriarchy."[11]

Punter writes as if putting Blake's texts in "history, politics, patriarchy" escaped treating them as "applicable commodities." My point is not that Blake criticism should ignore history but that Punter assumes that his historical Blake is somehow less Protean than any other. More problematically, he writes as if putting Blake in history necessarily transformed a visionary poet into a chauvinist creep. History makes obvious to him what is less obvious to me, that Blake's sex / gender system demands oppressive straightness.

I take as my test case Blake's epic *Milton*, which has been a magnet for critic gloom. The standard reading of gender in the poem stems from the influential work of Susan Fox. She splits the epic into masculine and feminine halves: "Book I is concerned with the 'masculine' assertiveness of the

poet, his responsibility to his vision and his compeers; Book II is concerned
with the 'feminine' portion which is his inspiration and support, the mercy
he learns to exercise in Book I."[12] For Fox, in Book I, Milton descends from
heaven to redeem his "sixfold female Emanation," his three wives and
daughters. In Book II, Ololon, identified as Milton's Emanation, descends
from heaven to redeem Milton. Such a scheme begs for a heterosexual cli-
max when Milton and Ololon at last unite. Critics who agree with this reading, at least in outline, have especially hated the way that Blake makes
Ololon submit to Milton. Instead of allowing her to have her own apocalyptic fulfillment, she seems to sacrifice herself for him. As Marc Kaplan
notes, "Blake wants to end the game of hunter and hunted by having the
prey willingly submit to the hunter." After having given a female character
center stage in Book II, Blake seems to undercut her. According to Margaret
Storch, "Ololon plays the role of compliant support of a male who has realized the full strength of his masculinity and has overcome the menace of
female power."[13] She is supposedly at her best only when at her weakest.

This reading depends on thinning *Milton* down to a peculiar courtship
plot: boy goes after girl; girl goes after boy; girl submits self to boy and
causes apocalypse. Ololon looks like a wife in a mythic but still recognizably patriarchal marriage, and *Milton* is made to seem an elaborately
obscure version of the same old heterosexist plot.[14] I only wish *Milton* were
so easy. But, whatever else it may be, the sheer, frustrating difficulty of its
narrative experiments prevents it from turning into such a tidy story. The
gap between the clarity of the standard critical narrative and the difficulty
of Blake's text is too large, and it has come about because certain much-
repeated assumptions have frozen into perceived fact.[15] In readings of *Milton*, the one that bothers me most is the identification of Ololon as Milton's
Emanation.[16] Emanations are the fallen, female portions of beings who, in
an unfallen state, supposedly have no sex, although Blake usually refers to
them as male even before they fall. If Ololon is Milton's Emanation, then
the whole poem looks like a natural progress toward heterosexual marriage.
Since she is part of Milton's unfallen self, it only makes heterosexist sense
that she should spend the poem searching for and at last uniting with him.

My difficulty with this reading is that Blake never actually identifies
Ololon as Milton's Emanation.[17] On the contrary, Ololon does not look
much like other female Emanations in his poetry. Unlike them, Ololon is
not a female but a "they" with both male and female members, both of
whom play roles in the poem. It is useful to return to some of the earliest,
nonacademic commentators on the poem, such as Algernon Swinburne,
Ellis and Yeats, and Pierre Berger, to see what the poem looked like to them.

None assumed that Ololon was Milton's Emanation. Yeats and Ellis, for example, noted that Ololon "appears at first as of both sexes, lamenting with its female tears that its male fires had driven Milton . . . into Ulro."[18] For them, Ololon was not Milton's female Emanation but an odd, omni-gendered character whose role in the poem was far less predictable.

Milton does not feel quite so oppressively heterosexist when Ololon looks less like an obedient wife and more like Sandy Stone's description of trans-sexual bodies, "a set of embodied texts whose potential for *productive* dis-ruption of structured sexualities and spectra of desire has yet to be explored."[19] Distinguishing Ololon from Milton's Emanation means getting rid of an assumption made in virtually all readings of the poem in the past fifty years. For me, what is most striking about Ololon is not *her* weakness but *their* unpredictability. Ololon lacks a stable gender identity, has no con-sistent motives for doing anything, and gives speeches that are weirdly inco-herent even for Blake. They guarantee that the poem does not work in straight terms.

In this chapter, I want to put Ololon in the wider context of Blakean camp, which, in *Milton*, has two forms. One parodies the conventional sex / gender system. In loving detail, Blake shows that following traditional roles reduces men to ineffective heaps of egomania. He punctures constricting gender roles with a sharp sense of how characters are never more absurd than when they keep up exhausted conventions. With Ololon, Blake moves to another mode, which revises the old assumption that any sexuality other than heterosexuality is inherently ridiculous. Many earlier comic works, such as Shakespeare's comedies, open up a brief space for sexual experi-ment, but eventually collapse it into happy marriages. With Ololon, Blake appropriates the comic space but rejects the final collapse. Ololon's gender-bending quest for Milton is apocalyptic, but not heavy-handed. The odd lightness of touch with which Blake characterizes it is one of *Milton*'s unex-pected pleasures, and one that deserves more recognition.

BLAKE AS GENIUS

Looking for Blake's queer appeal sounds like the kind of reading that David Punter dismisses as "*appropriative*" criticism, which means criticism that fits Blake into the trend of the month.[20] He prefers instead his own brand of historicism. Yet, given the understanding of genius developed in earlier chap-ters, a queer reading of Blake does not have to be ahistorical. Specifically, Blake's use of genius helps to locate *Milton* in eighteenth-century literary history as well as in postmodern queer space. From the beginning of his career, Blake believed in genius. In one of his first works, *All Religions are One*, he asserted "That the Poetic Genius is the true Man" (E 1). He lived the role of "Poetic Genius"so completely that he fit every cliché: radical originality, sublime goals, quasi-divine inspiration, and a life of poverty and neglect. Like William Beckford, he pushed genius to its limits in ways that invited critical condemnation. He might have taken for praise the words of one critic in 1806: "As an artist, he seems to be one of those who mistake extravagance for genius."[21] For Blake, such scorn proved that he indeed was better than his contemporaries: "My title as Genius thus is provd / Not Praisd by Hayley nor by Flaxman lovd" (E 505). With genius came the sex / gender experiments that, as I have argued, were de rigeur for many aspiring eighteenth-century geniuses. Iconoclastic sex / gender representations let Blake show that he, as a genius, put merely ordinary writers to shame. From early in his career, in works like *Visions of the Daughters of Albion*, he loudly opposed sexual respectability.

By the time he wrote *Milton*, his sexual radicalism faced its greatest challenge in the form of his employer, William Hayley, who was a paragon of patriarchal virtue. Hayley was a moderately popular poet and critic who dedicated his life to squelching whatever was daring in eighteenth-century theories of genius. He recognized Blake as a genius, but knew that Blake could never make a successful living as a visionary. Blake, in turn, could never forgive Hayley for pointing out the obvious. Although the exact date of *Milton* is uncertain, Blake seems to have written and revised it the height of his alienation from all that Hayley represented.[22]

Since Hayley had created his own version of Milton in his *Life of Milton* (1796), which Blake almost certainly knew, Blake's *Milton* responded not only to John Milton but also to Hayley's version of him. I think of Hayley's biography less as a source for Blake's epic than as a compendium of everything about genius and gender that Blake disliked. Next to Shakespeare, Milton was the exemplary British genius, and eighteenth-century theorists excerpted him often for examples of genius. By the beginning of the nineteenth century, it might have seemed as if Milton's genius needed no defense. Yet Hayley wrote his *Life of Milton* because he felt that Samuel Johnson's famous attack in his *Lives of the Poets* (1780) seriously threatened Milton's reputation.[23] In defending Milton, he recapitulated the gendered myths in which eighteenth-century writers described genius: heteroerotic (love for women inspired Milton); homosocial (male friends inspired Milton); and cross-gendered (Milton had in himself both the masculine and feminine qualities needed for great poetry). Although for other eighteenth-century writers, such myths were incompatible, Hayley's *Life* wove them into harmonious blandness. All three myths appear, but they never interfere with each other or threaten the overall impression of Milton's heterosexuality.

Given the background of Hayley's work, for Blake to write about Milton was inevitably to write about genius.[24] While Blake's *Milton* is not in dialogue only with Hayley, it from the start tears into Hayley's tepid generalizations. Blake's invocation begins with the last and most notorious myth about genius, its supposed combination of masculine and feminine traits. Hayley, who tried to soften Johnson's grimly masculine Milton, gave Milton neatly balanced gender qualities. In Milton's life and work, "the most engaging qualities are admirably united to the most awful—the graceful and the tender to the grand and the sublime." Admittedly, when he noted that Milton's nickname at Cambridge was "The Lady," he hastily added that Milton's "general appearance approached not in any degree to effeminacy." Nevertheless, his Milton is a model eighteenth-century gentleman uniting "real tenderness of heart to equal dignity of mind."[25]

Blake's invocation refuels the excitement of cross-gendered genius that Hayley had dampened. For him, inspiration demands exaggerating the conflict between genders that Hayley eliminated:

> Daughters of Beulah! Muses who inspire the Poets Song
> Record the journey of immortal Milton thro' your Realms
> Of terror & mild moony lustre, in soft sexual delusions
> Of varied beauty, to delight the wanderer and repose
> His burning thirst & freezing hunger! Come into my hand
> By your mild power; descending down the Nerves of my
>   right arm
> From out the Portals of my Brain, where by your ministry
> The Eternal Great Humanity Divine. planted his Paradise
>   (2:1–8, E 96)

For Hayley, Milton's cross-gendering was an image of dignified self-sufficiency. Blake celebrates his undignified muses because they throw gender out of kilter by combining masculine "terror" with feminine "delight." He exchanges Hayley's earnestness for the ridiculousness of muses who are almost more than he can handle. While the first two lines imitate a conventional epic voice, the Blakean ridiculous creeps in by line 3. The alliterations of "mild moony lustre" and "soft sexual delusions" introduce an affectionately mocking, almost teasing, quality in his relationship to them. He writes as if he knows every trick in their repertoire but nevertheless welcomes their "delusions" and "delight" as aids to his composition. From them he wants not just inspiration but full-fledged bodily invasion, as if previous poets had been too cerebral. Hayley's tidy gender relations give way to a poet who throws caution to the winds in embracing his muses' multifaceted "ministry."

In the Bard's Song that takes up the first half of Book I, Blake shows what happens when men are not open to such cross-gendering.[26] The result is the straight male mind, which for Blake is the mind that believes in its own self-sufficiency. Its dominant characteristics are the refusal to accept that it is part of anything else and a desire to see everything else as part of it. In rhetorical terms, it believes too little and too much in the possibilities of metonymy. As such, it uncovers the narcissism and egotism lurking behind the glorification of the eighteenth-century genius as all-encompassing male creativity. Through the figure of Satan, the genius is shown to be comically absurd, not sublimely noble.

Blake presents two stories to explain why he can parody the straight male genius so easily. The first blames the rise of pseudo-genius on the family, especially on father-son relations. According to Hayley, such relations were supposed to nourish genius. Milton's father, having been "driven from the pursuits of learning," decided "to exert uncommon liberality and ardour in the education of his son." Milton's friendships with elder poets like Manso, the "Nestor of Italy," had a great "tendency to preserve and strengthen the seeds of poetic enterprize in the mind of the young traveller."[27] Never once is Hayley's Milton bothered by the need to prove his genius against the blocking will of a father figure.

Blake has little patience with Hayley's idealizations. As represented by him, father-son relations are pitched battles. These Bloomian showdowns are ridiculous for Blake because they are based on a fundamentally impossible metonymic conflict: the structure of the family demands that the members see themselves as part of it, while the cult of genius demands that men believe themselves to be completely independent. In the Bard's Song, the conflict between family and genius arises in the fight between a father, Los, and his uncooperative son, Satan. Seeing that his brother Palamabron is "with labour wearied every evening," Satan asks Los if he can take his place. Los answers him sternly:

> If you account it Wisdom when you are angry to be
>   silent, and
> Not to shew it: I do not account that Wisdom but Folly.
> Every Mans Wisdom is peculiar to his own Individ[u]ality

> O Satan my youngest born, art thou not Prince of the
>   Starry Hosts
> And of the Wheels of Heaven, to turn the Mills day
>   & night?
> Art thou not Newtons Pantocrator weaving the Woof
>   of Locke
> To Mortals thy Mills seem every thing & the Harrow
>   of Shaddai
> A scheme of Human conduct invisible & incomprehensible
> Get to thy Labours at the Mills & leave me to my wrath.
>
> Satan was going to reply, but Los roll'd his loud thunders.
>
> Anger me not! thou canst not drive the Harrow in
>   pitys paths.
> Thy Work is Eternal Death, with Mills & Ovens &
>   Cauldrons.
> Trouble me no more. thou canst not have Eternal Life.
>
>   (4:6–18, E 98)

Los makes a thorough fool of himself because he believes in the fundamental tenet of the straight male genius, "Every Man's Wisdom is peculiar to his own Individuality." Such a belief precludes cooperation by glorifying the individual. While it might seem that Blake elsewhere supports Los's idea to justify romantic rebellions, in *Milton*, it makes Los into a petty tyrant, not the fire-breathing prophet that he should be. Trying to justify his behavior to Satan, he dwindles from an inspired creator to a harried father dealing with a problem child. He tells Satan that he can "not have Eternal Life" as if talking to a rebellious adolescent.

Satan knows that he can ignore Los's speech because Los praises individuality in theory while denying Satan's individuality in practice. Rather than letting Satan express his peculiar "Wisdom," Los wants to force him into a pre-assigned job, laboring "day & night" in the Mills of Eternity. Such "Labours" hardly deserve the name of wisdom since they are the least glamorous job in the Blakean universe. As Los himself admits, Satan's mills impress mortals only because they are too stupid to recognize truly important activities like those of the Harrow of Shaddai. Satan's response to his degradation is the bourgeois parent's worst nightmare. He becomes a comic parody of the eighteenth-century male genius, the all-encompassing, narcissistic creator: "I am God alone / There is no other! let all obey my principles of moral individuality / I have brought them from the uppermost innermost recesses / Of my Eternal Mind" (9:25–28, E 103). Blake's humor is particularly cutting with Satan's "uppermost innermost recesses," in which Satan's desire for transcendence appears only as inane repetition. Los had praised each man's individuality: Satan answers him by elevating his own individuality to a universal law. Blake rewrites the eighteenth-century cult of genius as naked egocentrism.

Having told one story about the birth of the Satanic ridiculous, Blake quickly tells another, thus guaranteeing that no one moment in his epic can ever be a metonymy for others. In his second story, pseudo-genius comes from heterosexual rather than from homosocial struggle. Milton had been a challenge for eighteenth-century authors who wanted to argue that heterosexuality inspired genius. Samuel Johnson's condemnation was notorious: "What we know of Milton's character in domestic relations is that he was severe and arbitrary. His family consisted of women; and there appears in his books something like a Turkish contempt of females, as subordinate and inferior beings."[28] Milton had such a bad time with his wives and daughters that he became an example for Isaac D'Israeli of the problems that domestic life created for male genius.[29]

Since Hayley wanted to represent Milton as a model heterosexual, he used all his rhetorical skill to argue that women really did inspire Milton's genius, but his evidence is less convincing than he wanted it to be. For example, to prove Milton's gallantry, Hayley instanced his behavior to his first wife. About to marry a second time, Milton suddenly experienced "an occurrence, which has the air of an incidence in romance." As he was talking with a relative, "the door of an adjoining apartment was suddenly opened: he beheld his repentant wife kneeling at his feet, and imploring his forgiveness." He forgave her, but only after "the natural struggles of honest pride and just resentment."[30] For Hayley, this scene showed that Milton was a good person because he was nice to women, especially to ones who conveniently prostrated themselves before him. Even better, he argued that Milton's first wife had inspired his genius because Milton used this biographical incident in *Paradise Lost* when he described Eve's repentance. Since Milton's failed marriages made it hard to maintain that good relations with women had inspired him, such a moment was the best Hayley could offer to link Milton's heterosexuality to his genius.

On the evidence of *Milton*, Blake found nothing more absurd than the idea that male creativity depended on female prostration. He undercuts the Hayleian presentation of genius and heterosexuality by introducing a character named Leutha, identified only as "a Daughter of Beulah" (11:28, E 105), who descends to announce that she has made Satan rebel against Los.

Leutha not only admits her guilt but also claims that she alone has caused the entire incident: "I am the Author of this Sin! by my suggestion / My Parent power Satan has committed this transgression" (11:35–36, E 105). It is as if Blake rewrites Hayley's scene so that Milton's first wife actually causes Milton's faults. He recognizes that the Hayleian desire to elevate women into the inspiration for genius only encourages a fruitless battle for power between the sexes. Men give women pseudo-power, and women compensate by grabbing any real power they can.

In the invocation, Blake invited his muses to invade him, thereby demonstrating his openness to outside influences, even dangerous ones. But in the darkly comic world of the Bard's Song, in which all characters believe in their absolute autonomy, Leutha's invasion of Satan is more threatening:

> entering the doors of Satans brain night after night
> Like sweet perfumes I stupified the masculine perceptions
> And kept only the feminine awake. hence rose his soft
> Delusory love to Palamabron: admiration join'd with envy
> Cupidity unconquerable! my fault . . .
>
> (12:4–8, E 105)

Her account jumbles the heterosexual model of genius with the cross-gendered one, since she is both inside and outside of Satan at once. Her "perfumes" are a little too external, too much like cheap stage props, to be taken seriously as agents in an internal, mental drama. Yet the confusion of internal and external is the essence of the Blakean ridiculous in the Bard's Song because it is the source of narcissistic pseudo-genius. Leutha wants to believe that she is responsible for everything that has happened to Satan, both internal and external. As a result, she ends up imitating Satan's egoism even as she blames herself for having caused it.

Leutha's feminization of Satan ultimately collapses. Just as Satan could not tolerate competition from Los, he also rejects her. He understands her feminine aspects in himself as unholy impurities: "In selfish holiness demanding purity / Being most impure, self-condemn'd to eternal tears, he drove / Me from his inmost Brain" (12:46–48, E 106). Like the closeted homophobe, Satan punishes in others what he cannot acknowledge in himself. In such a scene, Blake shows why the Hayleian treatment of heterosexuality and genius must always be a farce: a genius cannot admit the influence of anything outside himself. The straight male genius for Blake produces nothing but self-defeating assertions of individuality. Social relations that, according to Hayley, were supposed to inspire genius crumble before Satan's hunger for domination. By the end of the Bard's Song, Blake has so dismantled the aura of genius that, for creativity to continue, inspiration needs to be reimagined from its roots.

RIDICULOUS IMPASSES

Blake turns in the second half of Book I to a new kind of genius that might be able to break out of the restrictions imposed by a conventional sex / gender system. This new genius turns out to be an old one, John Milton, the very figure whom Hayley had so thoroughly tamed. Since Milton was the epitome of genius, letting him reform his own egoism allows Blake to criticize the Hayleian tradition from within. Milton learns from the Bard's Song that his egomania has been as bad as Satan's, and his separation from his Emanation proves it:

> What do I here before the Judgment? without my
>   Emanation?
> With the daughters of memory, & not with the daughters
>   of inspiration[?]
> I in my Selfhood am that Satan: I am that Evil One!
> He is my Spectre! in my obedience to loose him from
>   my Hells
> To claim the Hells, my Furnaces, I go to Eternal Death.
>
> (14:28–32, E 108)

With ringing rhetoric, Milton announces that he will leave behind the male selfhood that has kept him from his Emanation. Reuniting with her means giving up a self-glorifying straight male mind and going "to Eternal Death." Exactly what "Eternal Death" means in Blake is never quite clear, but Milton treats it as a mode of self-annihilation. If the Bard's Song has shown how thoroughly men can blunder, Milton's speech should point the way to male redemption.

Nevertheless, while Milton's grand speech contains none of the Bard's Song's black comedy, its high seriousness is itself suspicious. Given what happens to Milton in the rest of the poem, this moment retrospectively gains a trace of the absurd. If Satan represented the solipsistic straight mind, Milton demonstrates what happens when that mind tries to apologize.

Paradoxically, he is never more egocentric than when he says that he wants to eradicate his ego by going to "Eternal Death." He reproduces the male cult of genius even as he tries to repudiate it because he proclaims his sympathy for his victims without doing anything for them. As Stephen Vine notes, Milton's act "involves both a shedding of the self *and* a consummate act of apocalyptic will—as if it joined the height of willed power with the death of this power in self-sacrifice."[31] If problems of metonymy dominated the comedy of the Bard's Song, paradox turns Milton's sections of the poem into a comedy of the absurd. He is so enmeshed in the male will that abandoning it on his own is impossible. Where the Satanic ridiculous was parodic, the Miltonic ridiculous is self-canceling.

Blake represents this paradoxical comedy by summoning up a familiar comic image: the hermaphrodite. As I discuss in the chapter on Cowper, the hermaphrodite in the eighteenth century had a variety of meanings, including "sodomite." But for Blake, it stands not for sodomy but for a literal combination of genders: Milton "beheld his own Shadow; / A mournful form double; hermaphroditic: male & female / In one wonderful body. and he enterd into it" (14:36–38, E 108). This "Shadow" represents the impasses that ordinary gender creates. "Wonderful" though it is, it has none of the liberating power that twentieth-century critics like Judith Butler have associated with cross-dressing and that eighteenth-century critics associated with androgynous genius.[32] Instead, the hermaphrodite is a visual sign of Milton's self-canceling project.[33] Asserting his will at the same time he is denying it is like trying to be male and female at the same time, although assertion is not necessarily masculine and denial is not necessarily feminine. For Blake, since both genders are fundamentally wrong, combining them only compounds error.

Despite the paradoxes disabling his progress, Milton has moments of enlightenment. He recognizes that, without his Emanation, he cannot be fully human:

> Then Milton knew that the Three Heavens of Beulah
>   were beheld
> By him on earth in his bright pilgrimage of sixty years
> In those three females whom his Wives, & those three
>   whom his Daughters
> Had represented and containd . . .
>   . . . also Milton knew: they and
> Himself was Human
>
>   (15:51–17:2, 17:5–6, E 110)

This moment looks like Blake's wholesale endorsement of visionary heterosexuality because the highest state, that of being completely "human," occurs when Milton combines himself with his wives and daughters. But it is one thing to know that "they and / Himself was Human" and another thing to achieve it. Milton recognizes his goal but his self-assertive means of reaching it prevent him from getting there. Consequently, his Emanation remains alienated from him in the image of "those Female forms, which in blood & jealousy / Surrounded him, dividing & uniting without end or number" (17:7–8, E 110). Even to conceive of union as a joining of "they" and "Himself" makes Milton and his Emanation too much like the hermaphrodite because they retain the gendered roles that need to be transcended.

Some readers have argued that Blake turns to male homosexuality as a way out of the problems presented by heterosexuality. For them, he celebrates gay sex to avoid women entirely: "Blake uses homosexuality as trope in much the same manner as Byron, and to the same end: to assert his own masculine superiority."[34] The homophobic assumption behind such remarks is that gay sex is really about misogyny. It is seriously inadequate as a reading of Blake because it ignores his strenuous criticism of conventional male roles. Anyone wanting to explain Blake's queer allure by looking at relations between men in *Milton* will be disappointed. As the fight between Los and Satan demonstrates, two masculine wills are not better than one. Homosexuality for Blake is merely another version of the hermaphrodite, the doubling of a mistake.

The second half of Book I details the inadequacies of male-male unions. The first and most important occurs when Milton enters Blake's "left foot." Blake's illustration is quite graphic: it shows his figure bent backward in orgasmic bliss and, in some versions, with penis erect, while flames shoot from the star representing Milton.[35] The text, however, suggests that the sex is a grotesquely comic letdown: "And on my left foot falling on the tarsus, enterd there; / But from my left foot a black cloud redounding spread over Europe" (15:49–50, E 110). Penetrated by Milton, Blake produces not masculine superiority or even great poetry but a "black cloud." This cloud should give some pause to critics wanting to argue that Blake celebrates gay sex. As represented by Blake, union between men produces dark confusion, not enlightenment.

Blake repeats the letdown of the black cloud a few plates later when he admits that, although Milton's entry has produced new forms of vision for him and "all men on Earth, / And all in Heaven," they still see only "in the nether regions of the Imagination" (21:6, E 115). He revises God's description in Exodus 33:23 of his appearance to Moses: "I will take away mine hand, and thou shalt see my back parts; but my face shall not be seen." In Exodus, the moment describes the poignancy of an invisible God who cannot be seen face to face. Yet God's mention of his "back parts" is also faintly ridiculous, as if God were going to "moon" Moses. Since heterosexist codes demand that "back parts" be hidden, it seems perverse of God to expose areas that respectable behavior covers. He guarantees that viewing the divine form has the potential to be shadowed by the comedy of a gay innuendo. In Blake's revision, he links this innuendo to the outcome of the Blake-Milton union. The best that can come of a man's union with another man is to be stuck in the "nether regions." Even to conceive of the imagination as something tangible enough to have nether regions is to be trapped at its bottom rung.

Throughout Book I, Blake repeats the impasses of the Miltonic ridiculous, in which what look like triumphantly homoerotic encounters fizzle. When Milton meets Urizen, Urizen tries to halt him by taking "up water from the river Jordan: pouring on / To Miltons brain the icy fluid from his broad cold palm" (19:8–9, E 112). Milton responds with a humanizing gesture. Taking "the red clay of Succoth," he rebuilds Urizen, "Creating new flesh on the Demon cold, and building him, / As with new clay a Human form in the Valley of Beth Peor" (19:10, 13–14, E 112). Blake's illustration represents a nude, muscular Milton plunging between Urizen's outspread legs, as if to shatter Urizen's coldness with his sexual vitality (figure 3). Yet, as with Milton's enlightenment about his Emanation, even his best moments do not advance his quest. Try as he may, he remains blocked by Urizen because they are both trapped in the role of male genius: both want to create the other in his own image. Although Milton's intentions are more benevolent than Urizen's, he is enough like Urizen that he cannot get past him. Blake ends the episode by stating that "Urizen oppos'd" Milton's path in his journey to "the Universe of Los and Enitharmon" (19:26, 25, E 113), as if to freeze the two in permanent conflict. Morton Paley argues that the struggle is still going on by Plate 40 because of the "non-sequential, non-temporal nature of the events" in the poem.[36] Yet the poem as a whole, though nonsequential, is not unprogressive. For a fight to last as long as this one does, something is wrong. The two men cancel each other out because neither has found a way out of conventionally gendered creativity.

Likewise, in a fiercely homoerotic union, Los merges with Blake: "He kissed me and wishd me health. / And I became One Man with him arising in my strength: / Twas too late now to recede. Los had enterd into my soul" (22:11–13, E 117). Yet a few plates later, Blake shows this union to be as great

FIGURE 3.
William Blake, *Milton*, copy B, plate 15.
(Courtesy Huntington Library, San Marino, California)

a letdown as the others because Los / Blake as "One Man" prove as incapable of Milton of effective change. When they confront Los's sons, they are sadly unable to convince them of their good intentions: "Indignant. unconvinced by Los's arguments & thun[d]ers rolling / They saw that wrath now swayd and now pity absorbd him / As it was, so it remaind & no hope of an end" (24:45–47, E 120). To Los's sons, he and Blake appear as another version of the hermaphrodite, an emblem of two impulses, wrath and pity, working against one another. Los faces similar "lightnings of discontent" (25:63, E 122) when he tries to tell the laborers in Golgonooza that the apocalypse is at hand. Teaming up with Blake does not produce visionary power for Los but bungled attempts at persuasion.

Nothing that Milton does breaks the chain of the male selfhood that he shares with Satan. Eventually Blake abandons Milton at the end of Book I for an extended set piece, his description of the labor of Golgonooza. It contains some of his best poetry, but it also signals that, even though the poem is called *Milton*, Milton has not fulfilled his promise. What initially looked like a hopeful alternative to Satanic egotism remains unable to undo the privileges of male creativity.

ANNIHILATING GENDER

With Ololon, Blake turns to a more hopeful comedy that depends on the old tradition in which nothing is funnier than gender destabilization. Yet this tradition usually mandates that, in the end, gender roles sort themselves out to let heterosexuality win. In creating Ololon, Blake increases rather than eliminates this destabilization.[37] Ololon challenges what Judith Butler calls "a false stabilization of gender in the interests of the heterosexual construction and regulation of sexuality within the reproductive domain." The questions that Butler asks about Monique Wittig seem to be ones that Blake asks in creating Ololon: "What is left when the body rendered coherent through the category of sex is *dis*aggregated, rendered chaotic? . . . Are there possibilities of agency that do not require the coherent reassembling of this construct?"[38]

Blake and Butler reach different answers to these questions. For Butler, performativity is the new agency that comes from bodily disaggregation. She rejects gender as an expression of a preexistent reality for gender as "a *stylized repetition of acts.*" Effective politics, for her, aims "through a radical proliferation of gender, *to displace* the very gender norms that enable the repetition itself."[39] Yet she sternly limits the grounds on which such a "proliferation" might occur: "The account of agency conditioned by those very regimes of [regulatory] discourse / power cannot be conflated with voluntarism or individualism, much less with consumerism, and in no way presupposes a choosing subject." She writes as if believing in a "choosing subject" was an embarrassingly stupid position. Doing so evidently encourages one to believe that one might have "external opposition to power" instead of "a reiterative or rearticulatory practice, immanent to power."[40]

To an extent, Blake agrees. The Milton sections of the poem show the problems that result when Milton thinks he can simply abandon the gendered hierarchies that he himself has created. Even his assertion of his project proves that he is still enmeshed in his own hierarchies. At the same time, for Blake, a system of power so all-encompassing that one can never be outside it is not worth worrying about. The promise of Ololon is that, if one entirely reconceives character, motivation, and gender, one can change the dominant regimes of power. As Blake demonstrates, the results may look ridiculous, since sex / gender experimentation always does. Yet once *Milton* has shown the nonsense of ordinary gender roles, Ololon's ridiculousness makes good sense. Ololon is neither male nor female; their speeches are harder to follow than those of any other character in Blake; their motives for action are scarcely comprehensible; and, since Ololon appears only in *Milton*, Blake's other works cannot be used to gloss their behavior.

Postmodern as Ololon may sound, they can also be understood as Blake's revisionary return to eighteenth-century theories of genius. Blake uses Ololon, far more than Milton, to revise the watering down of genius in writers like Hayley. William Duff noted that, although "ordinary minds seldom rise above the dull uniform tenor of common sentiments, . . . the most lawless excursions of an original Genius . . . are towering, though devious; its path, as the course of a comet, is blazing, though irregular; and its errors and excellencies are equally inimitable".[41] In creating Ololon, Blake imagines a character who strives to live up to Duff's description, unlike the more conventional genius of Hayley's Milton. Blake's criticism of the cult of genius returns to the promise of genius betrayed by its circulation in eighteenth-century culture.

The critical difference between Ololon and the eighteenth-century genius is that Ololon does not try to reproduce themselves in art. Having shown in the first part of the poem how bound up such self-reproduction is with male egomania, Blake finds for Ololon other forms of productivity. Male creativity as represented by Los, Satan, and Milton depends on having a creative will and then asserting it through active labor and struggle. In all cases, this assertion occurs at the expense of other characters rather than with their cooperation, assistance, or guidance.[42] "Will" is an inappropriate term for a character as unstable as Ololon. Their speeches change directions so rapidly that it is impossible to imagine them as the translation of preverbal thought. Instead, Ololon produces their own improvisations, in which zigzags of thought forestall the narcissism of the other characters.

Blake sees the comedy in a character who goes on "lawless excursions" that are "towering, though devious." Getting rid of ordinary gender roles also rids Ololon of any established maps for behavior. Since, as Blake shows in the Milton sections of the poem, too much identity gets in the way, only a self as improvisatory as Ololon's can regenerate the universe. Where Butler's gender performers repeat culturally prescribed roles, Ololon admits no such prescriptions. Their performance demands daring lawlessness while rejecting the egomania of the poem's straight men. It also represents the poem's most benevolent version of the ridiculous, since from any conventional point of view, Ololon is an absurdly messy character. Ololon first appears in the appropriately fluid guise of a river:

> There is in Eden a sweet River, of mild & liquid pearl,
> Namd Ololon; on whose mild banks dwelt those who
> Milton drove
> Down into Ulro: and they wept in long resounding song
> For seven days of eternity
>
> (21:15–18, E 115)

The passage cleverly blurs Ololon's gender identity. The phrase "mild & liquid pearl" suggests both male semen and female milk. Unlike the hermaphrodite, the image of the river makes gender undecidable because both categories would be equally appropriate. Nevertheless, feminine traits dominate Ololon's first appearance because they engage in the traditional feminine activity of lamenting a fallen hero. With a gallant touch of excess, Blake even gives them good manners: "And when night came all was silent in Ololon: & all refusd to lament / In the still night fearing lest they should others molest" (21:26–27, E 116). The detail has a comic incongruity in this epic, as if Jane Austen's standards were allowed to intrude for a line and a half.

Yet Ololon's femininity is not all that it seems. Blake blows apart not just conventional characterization but conventional narrative patterns. The key to his experiment is the strange phrase, "those who Milton drove / Down into Ulro." Critics have argued that it refers to an earlier moment:

> But many of the Eternals rose up from eternal tables
> Drunk with the Spirit, burning round the Couch of death
>   they stood
> Looking down in to Beulah: wrathful, fill'd with rage!
> They rend the heavens round the Watchers in a fiery circle:
> And round the Shadowy Eighth: the Eight close up
>   the Couch
> Into a tabernacle, and flee with cries down to the Deeps:
> Where Los opens his three wide gates, surrounded by
>   raging fires!
> They soon find their own place & join the Watchers of
>   the Ulro.
>
> (20:43–50, E 114–15)

A group of "Eternals" gang up on Milton, rip up the "heavens" surrounding him, and toss him, Vulcan-like, into Ulro, the bottom of the Blakean universe. On first reading, this scene appears to be a standard moment of Blakean turmoil, in which the excessive literality—"Couch of death," "fiery circle," "raging fires"—takes the edge off the seriousness of the violence. Yet in retrospect, this moment is not just one more violent scene, but a critical turning point. The "Watchers" turn out to be Milton's guardian spirits, and "the Shadowy Eighth" is Milton himself. Critics explaining how Ololon drove Milton into Ulro identify the "Eternals" who "rend the heavens round the Watchers" with Ololon.[43] Later comments support them: Ololon "lamented that they had in wrath & fury & fire / Driven Milton into the Ulro" (21:31–32, E 116), and the singers of Beulah ask Ololon, "Are you the Fiery Circle that late drove in fury & fire / The Eight Immortal Starry-Ones down into Ulro dark" (34:3–4, E 133).

This identification makes sense of the plot, but it also makes Ololon incoherent. The ferocity of the Eternals who drive down Milton in no way resembles the sweetness of the lamenters at the river. Ololon is not a coherent whole but an identity suspended between two incompatible, Jekyll / Hyde appearances. If the Satanic ridiculous involves metonymy and the Miltonic ridiculous, paradox, the Ololonian ridiculous is about non sequiturs. One might invent a narrative to save the appearances: perhaps the Eternals, in reaction to their violence, coalesced to form Ololon and repent their deed. Doing so clarifies Blake at the cost of ignoring the Ololonian ridiculous, in which ordinary standards of coherence no longer apply. Unlike the hermaphrodite, whose genders contradicted each other, the relation between the two faces of Ololon is unclear, the gender identity asymmetrical, and the motivation nonexistent.

Unpromising as this description sounds, it prevents Ololon from succumbing to the traps that plague the other characters. A character whose
identity is so unstable can never succumb to egomania. Moreover, this scattered selfhood, far from crippling Ololon's potential for action, reinforces
it. After they hear from the "Family Divine" that "Milton goes to Eternal
Death!," they decide to follow him:

> Let us descend also, and let us give
> Ourselves to death in Ulro among the Transgressors.
> Is Virtue a Punisher? O no! how is this wondrous thing?
> This World beneath, unseen before: this refuge from
>   the wars
> Of Great Eternity! unnatural refuge! unknown by us
>   till now!
> Or are these the pangs of repentance? let us enter into them
>   (21:45–50, E 116)

As a coherent piece of rhetoric, this speech makes no sense. It moves from
thought to thought with no logical connections and with sharp qualifica-
tions or contradictions. But Blake's movement into the queer might be
encapsulated by Ololon's enthusiasm at entering an "unnatural refuge," by
which they mean the everyday world to which Milton has descended. Rather
than attacking the world for its unnaturalness, Ololon is naively excited
about the prospect of a visit. Looking forward to the most unnatural forms
of experience becomes an occasion for childlike enthusiasm ("let us enter
into them") rather than for prophetic gloom.

Although no moment in the poem can stand for all the others, if one is
looking for what in Blake has proved attractive to gay readers, Ololon's
enthusiasm is a more welcoming "in" to Blake than the overblown homoeroticism in the second half of Book I. Outside of Blake, an "unnatural
refuge" would almost always be stigmatized because the natural is supposedly better than the unnatural, and taking refuge is supposedly never as
good as confronting the enemy. Especially in a Protestant tradition, active
striving in the world should override the allure of monastic refuge. Gay
men have suffered from both associations. Because they do not conform to
compulsory heterosexuality, they are labeled unnatural. Because they supposedly prefer the adornments of gay sensibility to whatever the straight
world designates as manly, they are blamed for fleeing into a shadow world.
But in Ololon's brilliant reversal, active striving in the world is itself a
refuge, a turning "from the wars / Of Great Eternity." What we had thought
was the real world of struggle and pain suddenly turns out to be a vast hol-

iday. Nevertheless, refuge though it may be, Ololon has to steel their nerves to enter it because, as they know, the important work belongs there.

For his readers, Blake himself is such an unnatural refuge from whatever nature and the real world are presumed to be. Ololon's enthusiasm for a world hitherto unnoticed is the same excitement that Blake seems to demand: without it, his work degenerates into a heap of nonsense. Knowing that the refuge he offers is an unnatural one means that only those for whom nature offers few attractions will be at home in it. In real life, incoherence like Ololon's may be a fantasy or goal that can be achieved intermittently, at best. But in Blake, the burdens of the natural, the coherent, and the stigmatization of refuge are lightened. Ololon manifests an energy in the face of an unpromising situation that has been one of the hallmarks of camp idols, and it provides whatever coherence they have. Comprehensible motives are less valuable than the improvisatory zest with which Ololon, on the spur of the moment, decides to explore the unnatural. Whereas humans are usually thought of as rational next to the irrationality of nature, Blake reverses the assumption. For Ololon, nature and the wars of eternity mean regularity and repetition. Only in the unnatural refuges of a human world can their characteristic mode of improvisatory non sequitur flourish. Rather than performing conventional gender roles, Ololon improvises actions in ways that elevate them into the unnatural.

Having so little selfhood gives Ololon a wide range of sympathies. For example, on their journey, they recognize the tragic plight of subordinated women: "O dreadful Loom of Death! O piteous Female forms compelld / To weave the Woof of Death" (35:7–8, E 135). Through Ololon, Blake admits that the Female Will is not intrinsic to women, but is "compelld" behavior. Milton earlier noticed female suffering, but only because it belonged to his own Emanation. Ololon, less bound by self-consciousness, sees more clearly the failings of ordinary existence. Just in case such sympathy might make Ololon seem too stereotypically feminine, Blake notes that these observations come from "the Sons of Ololon" who have taken up "their abode / In Chasms of the Mundane Shell" (34:40–41, E 134).

The test of the Ololonian ridiculous comes in their final encounters with Milton. Ololon's justification for following Milton is the desire to apologize to him for an act that they may or may not have committed. Yet, as Ololon's speech earlier has made clear, the more powerful motive is the refuge of the unnatural world itself. Reconciling with Milton seems less like an end than the most exciting possibility opened up by this new refuge. Blake lets them reconcile twice. The first time is the less successful because both Ololon and Milton relapse into conventional roles. Ololon falls "prostrate before the

Starry Eight [Milton plus his seven guardian angels] asking with tears for-giveness / Confessing their crime with humiliation and sorrow" (35:32–33, E 135). Blake copies *Paradise Lost* and the Hayleian scene discussed earlier. Yet, in a comic twist, he complicates the reconciliation. The Starry Eight do not so much forgive Ololon as choose not to fight when they see that they are outflanked: "And all silent forbore to contend / With Ololon for they saw the Lord in the Clouds of Ololon" (35:40–41, E 136). In the abstract, this recogni-tion make conventional Christian sense: the Starry Eight see the divine voice in Ololon's repentance. Yet Blake's actual phrasing is less comforting because keeping silent is almost always a bad sign for him. "All silent forbore to con-tend" hints that the Starry Eight might have put up a fight if it were only up to them. Instead, seeing that Ololon has a major trump card up their sleeve in the form of "the Lord in the Clouds," the Starry Eight decide that discre-tion is the better part of valor. With a small comic nuance, Blake punctures the scene's seriousness by reminding us that this reconciliation is an offer that cannot be refused.

Having given us the serious reconciliation, Blake lowers the emotional temperature to a more earthly view, a smaller scale, and a lighter tone. Milton and Ololon meet again not in eternity but in Blake's own backyard. Ololon also loses their plural appearance because "Ololon and all its mighty Hosts" cannot appear in "Vegetable Worlds without becoming / The enemies of Humanity" (36:16, 14–15, E 136–37). They adopt the supposedly harmless guise of "a Virgin of twelve years" and seem to shed their dangerous fluidity (36:17, E 137). Although Ololon's disguise makes their encounter with Milton look like a simple man-woman discussion, the appearance is deceptive. In their first meeting, Ololon relapsed into a stereotypical feminine posture. In their second meeting in Blake's garden, Ololon looks like a conventional female, a twelve-year-old virgin, but retains their expanded, plural consciousness. Blake keeps the appearance of a heterosexual debate but not the expected behavior. Critics of the poem too often forget that Ololon's virginity is protective drag.

Blake signals a lighter tone by entering his poem to chat with Ololon. Addressing them "as a Daughter of Beulah," he asks them to pity another woman, his wife: "Pity thou my Shadow of Delight / Enter my Cottage, com-fort her, for she is sick with fatigue" (36:31–32, E 137). Ololon snaps back by calling Blake's bluff: "Knowest thou of Milton who descended / Driven from Eternity; him I seek! terrified at my Act / In Great Eternity which thou know-est! I come him to seek" (37:1–3, E 137). Since, according to Ololon, Blake knows about Milton and about their action in "Great Eternity," he knows that they are not a "Daughter of Beulah" and that they have more important goals than merely caring for another woman. At the same time, the comic gap between Blake's garden and "Great Eternity" has a touch of pathos. Blake, unlike Milton at the poem's start, is seriously worried about his wife, yet appears unable to help her. Catherine Blake's health is a slight reminder of the limits of vision. Ololon pities female forms compelled to weave the woof of death, but has no time for the sick Catherine Blake. Blake's visionary forms bring down the apocalypse, but do little for the wife in his cottage.

The poem soon moves past this pathos to the final encounter between Milton and Ololon. At its height, Milton demonstrates that he has learned virtually nothing. He repeats his usual message, which is that he annihilates himself to destroy the "Sexual Garments, the Abomination of Desolation / Hiding the Human Lineaments as with an Ark & Curtains / Which Jesus rent: & now shall wholly purge away with Fire" (41:25–27, E 142–43). The stereotypical maleness of his thundering rhetoric underscores that talking about shedding the sexual garment and doing so are not the same. As always, he is never more male than when talking about the need to give up his maleness. Yet he is lucky at last to have a discerning audience, Ololon, who can act on his message in a way that he cannot.

In response, Ololon, with a fine sense of melodrama, asks, "Is this our Femin[in]e Portion the Six-fold Miltonic Female? / Terribly this Portion trembles before thee O awful Man" (41:30–31, E 143). Critics have usually taken Ololon's first question as the moment in which they at last identify themselves as Milton's Emanation. But the speech does not quite do what critics want it to do. Ololon ventures a tentative question, not a firm identification, since, despite *Comus*, there is quite a difference between a twelve-year-old virgin and the "Six-fold Miltonic Female." They do not say, "Am I your Feminine Portion?" but "Is this our Feminine Portion?," as if to keep a narrator's distance on the action. It is as if Ololon has split themselves in two and comment on their disguised body while retaining their larger consciousness. In addition, while the feminine portion unsurprisingly trembles after Milton's long harangue, this trembling does not indicate that Blake endorses Milton's bullying speech. Ololon's comments are closer to criticizing the "awful Man" for having reduced the "Feminine Portion" to such a state than to praising him.

Rather than accepting Milton's analysis, Ololon offer a more perceptive reading of the problems that they and Milton have faced:

> Altho' our Human Power can sustain the severe contentions
> Of Friendship, our Sexual cannot: but flies into the Ulro.
> Hence arose all our terrors in Eternity! & now remembrance
> Returns upon us! are we Contraries O Milton, Thou & I
> O Immortal! how were we led to War the Wars of Death

In this the Void Outside of existence, which if enterd into
Becomes a Womb? & is this the Death Couch of Albion
Thou goest to Eternal Death & all must go with thee
(41:32–42:2, E 143)

Where Milton announced the need to get rid of the "sexual garments" as an abstract dogma, Ololon reaches a similar conclusion for a different reason. For them, "sexual" power undercuts the liberating power of the "severe contentions / Of Friendship" because it merely creates "terrors in Eternity" and forces the possessor to fly "into the Ulro." Blake does not define what the severe contentions of friendship are, but in the context of the epic as a whole, they seem to be moments like the one in which Ololon decides to descend and follow Milton. They are severe, among other reasons, because friendship demands abandoning the self-obsession characteristic of the male characters. Conventional gender roles preclude such openness by freezing selfhood into established, oppositional patterns.

Ololon acts vigorously on their realization. They end the wars of death by doing what Milton has only talked about, annihilating the sexual self:

So saying, the Virgin divided Six-fold & with a shriek
Dolorous that ran thro all Creation a Double Six-fold
    Wonder!
Away from Ololon she divided & fled into the depths
Of Miltons Shadow as a Dove upon the stormy Sea.

Then as a Moony Ark Ololon descended to Felphams Vale
In clouds of blood, in streams of gore, with dreadful
    thunderings
Into the Fires of Intellect that rejoic'd in Felphams Vale
Around the Starry Eight: with one accord the Starry
    Eight became
One Man Jesus the Saviour. wonderful! round his limbs
The Clouds of Ololon folded as a Garment dipped in blood
(42:3–12, E 143)

This scene has angered many critics because they have read it as Ololon's sex/death for the redemption of Milton. I see it rather as Blake's representation of a world in which gender roles have become irrelevant. The Virgin's sixfold division is a sexual image that ends conventional sexuality. Like the earlier reconciliation scene, this division works at two levels, both of which upset gender norms. At the spectral level of Milton's shadow, Blake upsets the hierarchies of *Paradise Lost*. According to Milton's invocation in *Paradise Lost*, God "dove-like" sat "brooding on the vast Abyss" and made it "pregnant."[44] In Blake's version, the male figure, Milton, becomes the vast abyss, while Ololon takes over the divine role of the "Dove." The image also recalls the dove that Noah sends from the ark to test for the presence of dry land. For Blake, keeping the Ololon-dove permanently skimming over the Milton-sea describes the fluidity and openness required by the severe contentions of friendship better than letting them reach dry land.

At a more exalted level, Milton becomes "One Man, Jesus." Ololon, having rid themselves of their disguise, becomes clouds worn by Jesus as a garment, "Written within & without in woven letters: & the Writing / Is the Divine Revelation in the Litteral expression" (42:13–14, E 143). As I noted earlier, part of Blake's revision of genius was not making Ololon a creative artist. Yet in their apotheosis, Ololon appears as writing. As such, they retain their characteristic fluidity, since the writing appears "within & without" so that meaning is never concentrated in one place. Milton, English literature's great poet-genius, gives way before the greater power of Ololon's literal expression of the "Divine Revelation."

In what looks like a repetition of the poem's earlier gay unions, Jesus then merges with Albion to bring about the apocalypse: "Jesus wept & walked forth / From Felphams Vale clothed in Clouds of blood, to enter into / Albions Bosom" (42:19–21, E 143). Blake has named Jesus as "One Man," and it seems that, after Ololon has put an end to sexuality, the redeemed order disappointingly succumbs to repetition by taking the male gender as its universal. Yet Blake immediately disrupts this impression by upsetting the conventional association between Christ and masculinity. On the poem's final plate, the line "To go forth to the Great Harvest & Vintage of the Nations" (43:1, E 144) appears above an image of a nude woman triumphantly bursting forth from the page while two plant people look on (figure 4). Although she is not identified, her image strongly suggests traditional Christian iconography. Her arms are spread above her in a version of the shape of Jesus's arms on the cross, and she has a wound on her right side, like the spear wound that traditionally appears in images of the Crucifixion. While the epic's first image is Milton, breaking his name to enter into the text, its last is this nameless woman, leading the poem into the apocalypse. The movement between them encapsulates the epic's progress from patriarchal associations of male genius and power to a world open to improvisation, in which the burdens of past gender mistakes have been wiped clean.[45]

FIGURE 4.
William Blake, *Milton*, copy B, plate 45.
(Courtesy Huntington Library, San Marino, California)

This female Jesus is Blake's final joke on epic seriousness. Jesus on the cross has always been the perfect closet image for gay culture. The frail, passive, penetrated, beautiful male body that can be held up for worship is an invaluable alternative to conventional images of warlike men.[46] In his art, Blake's Jesus is markedly androgynous: the *Antijacobin Review* complained of one of his images that "there is a prettiness about the face, which were it not for the beard would better consort with the graceful character of a young female, than with the majesty of" Christ.[47] At the end of *Milton*, Blake makes that androgyny even more combative by abandoning Jesus's masculinity altogether. The female Jesus shatters conventional gender hierarchies that elevate only a man to divinity.

She also appears as quite a surprise, since the image does not obviously correspond to any action in the text. Instead, it looks like a Blakean correlative to the improvisations of Ololon, an unexpected turn to "unnatural refuge" that is better than severe contentions ever could be. In the encounters between Milton and Ololon, the playful ridiculousness of earlier scenes fades before the intensity of the apocalyptic consequences. Yet Blake's lightness returns in this final image of a diva whose liberation is contemplated by the bizarre plant people who flank her. She is his answer to the most far-reaching potential in the eighteenth-century cult of genius, the possibility of recognizing that unnatural human endeavor is the only endeavor worth valuing. She stands not for the masculine, Blakean sublime, but the omnigendered Blakean ridiculous, the secret reward for readers retreading the Blakean labyrinth without customary, heterosexist guides.

CHAPTER SEVEN

"A Sight to Dream of, Not to Tell": Christabel, Pornography, and Genius

When *Christabel* appeared in 1816, it changed the history of lesbian representation. Previous works had treated sex between women as a matter for pornographic interest, satirical commentary, scandalous exploration, or titillating innuendo. *Christabel*, for the first time, made lesbianism sublime. What had been a mildly amusing or shocking topic became a matter of almost sacred mystery. In *Christabel*, sex between women loses the characteristic corporeality of eighteenth-century representation. Instead, a blank space in the text marks an event so burdened with sublime horror that it cannot even be spoken. Like a cultic rite that remains known only to initiates, lesbianism in *Christabel* points to mysteries forbidden to ordinary mortals.

But *Christabel*'s dramatic effect on the future of lesbian representation did not depend only on how it treated sex between women. It also revised where such representations could be found. Rather than appearing in political or religious satire, bawdy tales, or classical translations, *Christabel*'s lesbianism appeared in a poem that seemed "an end in itself and without ulterior purpose."[1] It was a highly elite work, appreciated mostly by other poets and roundly condemned by commonplace critics. Its elite status arose partly because it drew on representations that literal-minded, respectable readers might condemn as obscene. Suspicions of the poem's obscenity clustered around it from its first appearance. According to Alaric Watts, even William Wordsworth, who rejected the poem for the second edition of *Lyrical Ballads*, thought that it was "indelicate."[2] An anonymous author accused it of being "the most obscene poem in the English language."[3] William Hazlitt noted that "there is something disgusting at the bottom of his subject, which is but ill glossed over by a veil of Della Cruscan sentiment and fine writing."[4] Lesbianism in *Christabel* enabled more discriminating readers to demonstrate their finer aesthetic taste by recognizing Coleridge's alchemy of the obscene into the sublime. They could see what Wordsworth and Hazlitt could not: *Christabel*'s pioneering transformation of shocking or disreputable representations into high art.

COLERIDGE AS GENIUS

Christabel's uniqueness was no accident. Coleridge foregrounded it when he noted in his 1816 Preface that "if even the first and second part had been published in the year 1800, the impression of its originality would have been much greater" than it would be in 1816.[5] Although his explicit intention was to claim that the poem would have seemed more original sixteen years earlier, he actually suggested that it would be even more special when it appeared. By mentioning the gap between the poem's composition and appearance, he underscored that it was no ordinary piece of hackwork, ground out to make fast cash. Instead, it was a work so extraordinary that it needed to be kept from the public for sixteen years. The gap also emphasized that this poem relied on no local political references for its interest. Unlike Canto III of Byron's *Childe Harold's Pilgrimage*, also published in 1816, which is filled with discussions of contemporary politics, *Christabel* appears to be a more timeless poem that does not condescend to exploit merely local events. It was presumably so exceptional that it was worth publishing even though it was unfinished.

Although any claims by Coleridge about his originality should be treated with suspicion, he was right about *Christabel*. It would certainly have been a bolt from the blue in the 1790s, and even in the context of his own work during that decade, it seems sui generis. Most of Coleridge's poetry from the 1790s copies familiar literary trends, from Della Cruscan floweriness to the bombast of his political odes. To move from them to *Christabel* is to move to an entirely different aesthetic terrain. Even though the poem draws on motifs found elsewhere in his work, it functions as an odd parenthesis in his career, a perfect specimen of a mode of writing that seemed to come from nowhere and that he did not develop in his later work, although its effect on later writers was immense. The oddness of *Christabel* did not arise merely because it was a Gothic poem. No other Gothic poem from the 1790s remotely resembles it, and it owes less to Gothic novels than critics have sometimes claimed.[6] It reads as if Coleridge had taken an entirely different direction from anything he or his contemporaries had done.

The biographical background for *Christabel*'s novelty was a dramatic change in Coleridge's situation as a writer.[7] He wrote *Christabel* in circumstances that few other authors enjoyed. When patronage for literary activity was fast fading, he was lucky to find two generous men, Thomas and Josiah Wedgwood II, who were heirs to Josiah Wedgwood's vast porcelain fortune. Out of nowhere, Coleridge received a letter from them at the end of 1797 enclosing a check for £100. He was not sure if he could accept since he was also considering other ways to make money, such as becoming a Unitarian minister or tutoring Basil Montagu in topics like "the mathematical Branches, chemistry, Anatomy, the laws of Life, the laws of intellect."[8] With the possibility of such steady employment, he worried that he could not take the Wedgwoods' money in good faith.

Thomas Wedgwood quieted Coleridge's concerns by reassuring him that he knew about Coleridge's circumstances and still wanted him to have the money: "We have canvassed your past life, your present situation & prospect; your character & abilities. As far as certainty is compatible with the delicacy of the estimate, we have no hesitation in declaring that your claim upon the fund appears to come under more of the conditions we have prescribed to ourselves for it's [sic] disposal, & to be every way more unobjectionable than we could possibly have expected."[9] Rather than giving Coleridge a mere £100, the Wedgwoods even increased their gift to a £150 annuity. Coleridge could not refuse, even though, as he recognized, the annuity burdened him with expectations: "Disembarrassed from all pecuniary anxieties yet unshackled by any regular profession, with powerful motives & no less powerful propensities to honourable effort, it is my duty to indulge the hope that at some future period I shall have given a proof that as your intentions were eminently virtuous, so the action itself was not unbeneficent."[10] Coleridge knew that great things were expected of him.

Accepting the annuity put Coleridge in an odd relation to what, by the 1790s, had become the conventional image of the genius. He bought into the Wedgwoods' fantasy of him as a man with such outstanding abilities that he deserved to be freed from financial worries. As Thomas Wedgwood's biographer wrote, Wedgwood had "had the insight to discern, in the unknown young man of twenty-five . . . a rare and original genius" so that "when the opportunity came he did what he could to set that genius free for doing the highest service to the world."[11] Coleridge no longer had to employ himself as a political hack or as an occasional preacher, but could work as a full-time genius. Earlier in the 1790s, he had used "genius" to describe himself or his work only in jest. At Cambridge, for example, he wrote to his brother that his next ode would "aim at correctness & perspicu[ity], not *genius*" because his last one "was so *sublime* that nobody could understand it."[12] During Coleridge's Pantisocratic raptures, George

Caldwell told him that "he could not answer for his own Sanity sitting so near a madman of Genius!"[13] The tone of such comments resembles uses of "genius" by eighteenth-century authors who already had substantial claims to literary attention. If they linked themselves to genius, they did so in an amused, semiembarrassed way that acknowledged the claim's vanity, even as it let them take on a little of genius's aura. Their tone was as far as possible from the fierce assertions of a writer like Blake, who had nothing other than his rhetoric to back him up.

Yet Blake was a literary outsider, and Coleridge was not. His Cambridge education had given him the classical learning that still marked those who were and were not gentlemen. By the time he wrote *Christabel*, he had published many poems, run his own newspaper, given public lectures, and started his long association with Daniel Stuart's *Morning Post*. No marginal genius like Blake, he had earned a place in the literary circles of London and Bristol.[14]

Yet Coleridge's literary success had not brought him a steady income. He was as pressed for money as any stereotypical genius, and his letters show him counting every shilling: "After subtracting 40£ from C. Ll's [Charles Lloyd's] 80£ in return for the Review business, & then calculating the expence of a servant, a less severe mode of general Living, & Lloyd's own Board & Lodging, the remaining 40£. would make but a poor figure."[15] The Wedgwood annuity promised to free his imagination from such petty accounting. When he rejected the Wedgwoods' first offer of £100, he told them how frustrating it was to write for the newspapers: "If any idea of ludicrous personality, or apt antiministerial joke, crosses me, I feel a repugnance at rejecting it, because *something must be written*, and nothing else suitable occurs. The longer I continue a hired paragraph-scribbler, the more powerful these Temptations will become: and indeed nothing scarcely that has not a *tang* of personality or *vindictive* feeling, is pleasing or interesting, I apprehend, to my Employers."[16] With the Wedgwoods' money, he seemed at last free to avoid such temptations and to exercise his genius to the full.

What made Coleridge's position as genius peculiar was that the annuity complicated its traditional antiestablishment leanings. According to the cult of genius, geniuses existed on the margins of society and suffered from inadequate public recognition. Their status as geniuses was their only compensation for a life of neglect and incomprehension. Coleridge's annuity meant that he was supposed to produce the work of a genius without having to undergo the suffering and neglect that geniuses traditionally faced. On the contrary, his society actively supported his genius since no less than the Wedgwood brothers financed it. As a result, Coleridge confronted a greater burden of originality than that faced by more conventional geniuses. For all the novelty of writers like Bannerman and Blake, they did what geniuses were supposed to do by making grand, sublime gestures that advertised the stereotypical qualities of genius. Even a work as experimental as Blake's *Milton* took off from qualities that by the beginning of the nineteenth century had become clichés in the cult of genius.

Coleridge, in contrast, did not have to make such gestures. He already had recognition as a genius and did not need to perform for the same audience as Blake or Bannerman. Instead, he could confine himself to even more elite, select performances. Unlike the work of prior would-be geniuses, *Christabel* aims not at the grand gesture but at an eerily quiet, dreamlike atmosphere. Although it engages the sublime, it does so in a much quieter tone. Most shockingly, rather than tackling the grandiose topics traditionally associated with genius, it turns instead to obscene representation, the most culturally debased of forms, and uses it as a basis for poetic originality.

To underscore the novelty of Coleridge's self-fashioning as a genius, it is worth contrasting his efforts with those of William Wordsworth, with whom he was in close contact when he wrote *Christabel*.[17] Although Wordsworth ultimately crushed Coleridge's attempts at genius, for the brief space between Coleridge's receipt of the annuity in 1798 and Wordsworth's rejection of *Christabel* in 1800, it seemed that their partnership would foster Coleridge's poetry. The annuity allowed this partnership to take place because it gave Coleridge the financial wherewithal to live in the remote Lake District. As he wrote in his first extant letter to Wordsworth, dated January 23, 1798, the "unexpected event" of the annuity would allow him to "be able to trace the spring & early summer of Alfoxden."[18] The Wedgwoods had not been especially interested in Coleridge's poetry because what most impressed Thomas Wedgwood about Coleridge was his skill as a metaphysician.[19] Yet the Wedgwood annuity's greatest product would be poetry, not philosophy.

Wordsworth offered Coleridge one model of how to swim against the contemporary poetic tide. His poems for *Lyrical Ballads* have a complicated relation to the cult of genius as it had developed in the eighteenth century. Insofar as the cult had encouraged an interest in the primitive, the folkloric, and the anticlassical, Wordsworth's poems, as Marilyn Butler has argued, fit squarely in it.[20] Yet Wordsworth scrupulously avoided the wildness and stereotypical sublimity associated with genius. His description of his work in the preface to the 1800 edition proved that his poems were no mere effusions, despite his claims about the "spontaneous overflow of powerful feelings."[21] Wordsworth undercut the traditional cult of genius by insisting on the deliberate, purposive nature of his poetry and its role in a calculated strategy for healing damaged British sensibilities. Furthermore, for all his supposed denial of history, his *Lyrical Ballads* never presented themselves as self-sufficient works of art, as the works of genius supposedly did.[22] Even if the Preface had not made his social criticisms obvious, the poems alone would have been enough to convey a pointed message about rural life. When Wordsworth did not accept *Christabel* for the second edition of *Lyrical Ballads*, he substituted *Michael*, whose political implications were so strong that he sent the poem to Charles James Fox along with a letter about the plight of the rural poor. It would be impossible to imagine Coleridge sending *Christabel* to Fox with an accompanying letter about pressing social concerns.

Coleridge's anti-Wordsworthian achievement in *Christabel* was to create a poetry that did not subjectify politics. Instead, *Christabel* created its own distinctive world as a piece of art for art's sake. The key to the poem's distinctiveness was Coleridge's transformation of eighteenth-century obscene lesbian representation. Coleridge found in pornography a genre that was undergoing a critical transformation during his lifetime. As Lynn Hunt describes, consumption of obscene material had long been regulated "so as to exclude the lower classes and women," although these groups presumably had access to long-standing oral traditions of obscene songs, jests, stories, and riddles.[23] By the beginning of the nineteenth century, however, with the spread of literacy and increasing availability of obscene representations, pornography "as a regulatory category was invented in response to the perceived menace of the democratization of culture."[24]

Christabel provided a critical precedent for the migration of obscene materials from the miscellaneous forms of eighteenth-century bawdiness to high art. As I will argue, the key gesture in this migration was separating obscene representation from the layers of political, religious, and social meanings that it had acquired and treating it instead as pure enigma. This separation demanded removing lesbian representation from the traditional heterosexual contexts that had always defined it prior to *Christabel*.[25] The evidence for *Christabel*'s revisionary relation to such earlier contexts appears in Coleridge's letters. In his first extant letter to Wordsworth, he mentions two works often cited as inspirations for *Christabel*: M. G. Lewis's Gothic drama *The Castle Spectre*, and Bishop Percy's ballad of "Sir Cauline," in which the name "Christabelle" appears.[26] In Earl Leslie Griggs's standard edition of Coleridge's letters, both these works are footnoted, as if to draw the reader's attention to their importance for Coleridge. Yet Coleridge mentions another work that goes mysteriously unannotated. Writing about the weak humor in Lewis's play, Coleridge notes, "There is a book called the Frisky Songster, at the end of which are two chapters—the first containing *Frisky* Toasts & Sentiments—the second, *Moral* Toasts:—and from these chapters I suspect, that Mr Lewis has stolen all his sentimentality, moral & humorous."[27] Griggs's lack of annotation screens the possible significance of this work, and, despite the notorious energy of Coleridgean source studies, no critic of Coleridge has ever mentioned it.

The Frisky Songster, Being a Select Choice of Such Songs, as are Distinguished for their Jollity, High Taste and Humor, And above two hundred Toasts and Sentiments of the Most Delicious Order is one of many eighteenth-century collections of obscene songs, jests, and riddles that probably had their roots in men's urban drinking clubs. Unlike sophisticated French or French-inspired pornographic novels, it belongs to a coarser, less investigated English tradition of bawdry: "The bawdy songs and toasts of the drinking clubs were being published by the original 'men's magazines' of the 1780's and thereabouts, in volumes side-issued for the subscribers to these magazines in certain cases, under such titles as *The Buck's Delight* . . . , the *Covent Garden Repository* . . . , and, in particular, *The Frisky Songster*."[28] In *The Frisky Songster*, a typical song begins, "Now since you ask me for to sing, / It shall be a new and merry thing. / By me there lives a servant man, / That f—ks his fellow servant Nan, / And always does the best he can."[29]

Despite such crudeness and the poor quality of the volume's printing, some songs in *The Frisky Songster* indicate the elite audience for which it was intended. For example, it includes ribald, countercultural parodies of high art in such lyrics as "Eloisa to Abelard" and an opera libretto, *Cymon and Ephigene*, complete with airs and recitatives. Such works presumably only made sense to an audience with enough cultural knowledge to recognize the originals that were being parodied.

Two songs have particular relevance for *Christabel* because they represent women undressing in front of other women. In "The Dispute," four "lovely lasses" in a grove debate among themselves about who "was best supplied, / With that which pleases man." The male narrator, hidden in the bushes, watches while each disrobes for the others; for example,

> Eliza next disclos'd her parts,
>   And shew'd her circling hair;
> The vanquisher of mortal hearts,
>   Gods what a sign was there.
> The lucious, circling nut brown hair,
>   Which grew on belly high;
> Did like a sumptuous arch appear,
>   And reach'd from thigh to thigh.[30]

The hidden narrator decides in favor of the youngest, Kitty, but does nothing more than gaze at her body. At the end, he took his "fill of looking on, /And

slily sneak'd away" (60). The song presents a typical pattern of titillation without fulfillment. Although the women unclothe in a heterosexist context, since
they are looking for "that which pleases man," the all-female company hints
at lesbian undertones. The narrator's lustful gaze at Kitty counters these
undertones with more overtly heteroerotic possibilities, but no real sex
occurs. The hinted sexual potentials in the poem are presumably supposed to
be more suggestive than representations of actual physical contact could be.

In "The Crab-Tree," Sylvia similarly exposes herself to her sister Chloe:

> Come hither sister Chloe,
> I've learnt to stand upon my head,
>   Observe, my girl, I'll shew ye.
> She did what she design'd to do,
>   Her legs were wide extended,
> Her c—t expos'd to open view,
>   Since nothing could defend it.
>
> (45)

As in "The Dispute," a heterosexual frame quickly recuperates the lesbian
subtext lurking in this moment of female-female intimacy. It turns out that
Jack, who is "mounted" on a tree nearby, witnesses Sylvia's display. He
promptly "took the choicest fruit he could, / And fairly chuck'd it in."
Although he does not have sex with Sylvia, he figuratively penetrates her
and, in the poem's phantasmagoric vision, causes a tree to grow from her.
The tree sets up the song's feeble punch line: "For want of necessary care, /
Crabs were the only fruit on't" (46).

These obscene moments of women exposing themselves to women provide a hitherto unacknowledged background for Christabel's vision of the
disrobing Geraldine:

> Beneath the lamp the lady bowed,
> And slowly rolled her eyes around;
> Then drawing in her breath aloud,
> Like one that shuddered, she unbound
> The cincture from beneath her breast:
> Her silken robe and inner vest,
> Dropt to her feet, and full in view,
> Behold! her bosom and half her side—
> A sight to dream of, not to tell!
> And she is to sleep by Christabel.
>
> (*Christabel*, 245–54)

As in the obscene lyrics, the poem focuses on the exposure of one woman's body to another woman's gaze. In each, the poets linger on the unveiled female form as if it transfixed narrative attention. For the poets in *The Frisky Songster*, such exposure is the heart of their genre. In the two songs that I quoted, the fact that one woman gazes on another provides the excuse to heighten the sheer visibility of the naked female body, rather than its penetration. Lesbianism remains just beneath the surface of both poems in *The Frisky Songster*, but it is more suggestive because it is never treated graphically. Instead, the female-female situations encourage a fetishistic attention to the mere fact of the unclothed female body.

In *Christabel* as in *The Frisky Songster*, the unveiled female body acquires a special allure in an all-female context. Yet rather than describing Geraldine's body, the narrator breaks off at the climactic moment: "A sight to dream of, not to tell!" On the surface, Coleridge's narrative departs from *The Frisky Songster*'s precedent because it does not actually describe Geraldine's body. Yet the absence could be seen as providing a more powerful version of *The Frisky Songster*'s fetishism because it rivets attention even more compellingly on Geraldine's physicality. In most contexts, the line "A sight to dream of, not to tell!" if used to describe a female body, would describe one so beautiful that it defied language. In *Christabel* it describes the opposite, a sight so shocking that its horror demands silence. Yet Coleridge wisely cut a line specifying the ugliness of Geraldine's body and thereby ensured that, at least on first reading, the line would retain its ambiguity. Ugly or beautiful, Geraldine's unspeakable body usurps the imagination.

Of all the early responses to *Christabel*, the one most sensitive to its relation to eighteenth-century obscene representation was *Christabess*, an 1816 parody. *Christabess*, which was published by John Duncombe, takes *Christabel* back into traditional bawdry of the kind represented by *The Frisky Songster*. The title page announced its author as "S. T. Colebritche, Esq.," as if to play off the possible hearing of Coleridge's name as "cole-rich," and then debasing this "richness" by foregrounding Coleridge's "britches," which have turned suspiciously "coal" black. The title page also describes the work as "A Right Woeful Poem, Translated from the Doggerel, by Sir Vinegar Sponge." It is so nonsensical as to be "doggerel," and the fictitious Sir Sponge has presumably soaked up vinegary satiric spite that he is ready to squeeze onto the Coleridgean original through his translation.

In the work itself, Geraldine, renamed Adelaide, tells Christabess, "Oh! how we will hug tonight / With all the skill I have I'll try / To yield your little heart delight." Christabess then watches Adelaide disrobe:

> So up she sat upon her bum,
> And peep'd behind the curtain sly;
> And in the corner of the room,
> There she saw the maid untie
> A piece of hempen cord, that bound
> Her alabaster belly round!
> Down dropt her shift, and—O dear me!
> She's naked!—naked!!—naked!!!—see!—
> But, reader, turn away your view,
> She's not to sleep with me nor you.[31]

Christabess mocks the tradition of fetishistic female visibility by insisting on the banality of the exposed female: "She's naked!—naked!!—naked!!!—see!" The writer demystifies the sublime horror of Geraldine's body by reiterating the mere fact of nakedness. In his view, the female body does not deserve to be fetishized because it is only a body, and he has little patience for the claptrap of *Christabel*. Yet even as a parody, *Christabess* provides a contemporary interpretation of *Christabel* that links it back to the eighteenth-century tradition of obscene representation in a female homoerotic context. The presence of *Christabess* makes the link between *Christabel* and a work like *The Frisky Songster* even more compelling. *Christabel* arose in relation to such works, Coleridge's letters give evidence of it, and his contemporaries recognized it. Yet critics have never connected these texts, even though the letter in which Coleridge mentions *The Frisky Songster* has long been familiar.

On its own, *The Frisky Songster* would be nothing more than a titillating footnote if it did not help to locate *Christabel*'s lesbian representation in the context of Coleridge's career and his new role as acknowledged genius. I want to treat it less as a source than as a starting-point for Coleridge's revision of eighteenth-century obscenity into the materials for high art. The critical turn that Coleridge performed in *Christabel* on earlier obscene representation was to divorce it from what had become its traditional links to political, religious, or social satire. Obscene lesbian imagery had a place in the satiric tradition dating back to Juvenal. It was a standard item in anti-Catholic propaganda, as in Andrew Marvell's *Upon Appleton House* (1681), Laurence Sterne's *Tristram Shandy* (1759–1767), and Denis Diderot's *The Nun* (1798). In the chapter on Anne Damer, I have already discussed several examples of the political use of lesbian representation, in which writers attacked political parties by implying that women associated with it slept with other women. The general practice of using lesbianism as a political weapon continued into the 1790s, most obviously in such attacks on Marie Antoinette as the obscene *Memoirs of Antonina* (1790).[32]

Even a work as innocent of topical political concerns as *The Frisky Songster* could seem to authorities like a dangerously subversive text. In 1807, Edward Rich was indicted for publishing it because it "contained, amongst other things, divers wicked, false, feigned, lewd, impious, impure, gross, bawdy, and obscene manners." To the courts, *The Frisky Songster* looked politically dangerous because it had been published

> to the high displeasure of Almighty God, to the scandal and reproach of the Christian religion, in contempt of our said present sovereign the king, and his laws, and to the great offence of all civil governments, to the evil and pernicious example of all others, and against the peace of our said lord the king, his crown, and dignity.[33]

The Frisky Songster's obscenity threatened God, the church, and the state. With the possibility of such indictments from the courts, no one could pretend that obscenity was innocent or apolitical. As Iain McCalman has shown, during this period publishers of politically radical tracts and pamphlets also tended to publish pornography.[34] John Duncombe, *Christabess*'s publisher, was one of the most notorious of such radical pornographers. Since obscene and seditious works went hand in hand as proscribed forms of writing, *The Frisky Songster* was guilty by association.

What Katherine Binhammer has called the "sex panic" of the 1790s made obscene uses of the female body even more dangerous than they had been previously in the century. The revolutionary context called forth "pamphlets and tracts addressing such issues as the 'frightening' rise in divorces and cases involving criminal conversation . . . , fear over the basic degeneracy of the morals of the age, concern with the escalation of prostitutes invading the streets of London, anxiety over the impropriety of using male midwives and a heightened apprehension over the horrible dangers of seduction."[35] Coleridge's poetry of the 1790s responds vividly to this sex panic. For Coleridge as for many male writers of the 1790s, political corruption appears as female sexual corruption. He attacked Catherine the Great in *Religious Musings* as "that foul Woman of the North, / The lustful murderess of her wedded lord!" (171–72) and singled out for attention "the libidinous excesses of her private hours" (note to line 40) in "Ode to the Departing Year." In "France: An Ode," he treated France as a sexually loose woman who was "adulterous" (78) and was ruled by "the Sensual and the Dark" (85). In "Fears in Solitude," France appeared as an effeminate group of men "too sensual to be free" (143) against whom Britons must assert their masculinity ("Stand forth! be men!" [139]) and protect their "Mother Isle" (176).

Given the weight of tradition that had accrued to lesbian representation and to the representation of female sexual "perversity" more generally, nothing about *Christabel* is more striking than its success in leaving this tradition behind. Geraldine's actions with Christabel ought to be easily interpretable as a topical allegory. Like much else in *Christabel*, the image of her sleeping with Christabel seems to cry out for an analysis of what Keane has called "submerged politics."[36] What interests me about *Christabel* is that Coleridge makes such suggestions appear highly irrelevant. The poem is virtually immune to historical allegory of the kind that had traditionally been associated with lesbianism.[37] Even though it has at its center two women getting into bed together, it appeared to its admirers not as a threat to "the king, his crown, and dignity," like *The Frisky Songster*, but as high art. Even its detractors did not criticize it on political grounds, even though early nineteenth-century critics were adept in unearthing political aspects to poems that looked innocent. In the next section, I will discuss how Coleridge was able to transform the prior conventions of politicized lesbian representation so dramatically.

LESBIANISM AND THE PURIFICATION OF ART

Coleridge perceived as no one else had done that lesbianism could be a source of the sublime. This perception arose from the rhetorical challenge that lesbianism posed to eighteenth-century representation. As I argued in the chapter on Anne Damer, since writers assimilated virtually all sexual encounters to a heterosexual model of an active masculine partner and a passive feminine one, lesbianism was a potential enigma. Even though male homosexuality also supposedly could not be named, the law had precise terms (penetration and emission) for describing sodomy. Lesbianism was a different case because no such concrete language existed. Sometimes writers acknowledged its indescribability by gesturing to it vaguely, as when Queen Anne and Abigail Masham were accused of doing "some dark Deeds at Night."[38] Its unrepresentability could even be a source of comedy. For example, *An Authentic Narrative of the Celebrated Miss Fanny Davies, the Celebrated Modern Amazon* describes the escapades of Davies, who cross-dresses to further her schemes as a robber. In her disguise, she captivates "a lady of London" and arranges to meet her when her husband is not home. The author describes the ensuing scene as a titillating drama:

The room door is fastened.—A stately bed presents itself.—Courtship is unnecessary on the occasion.—The agreement is already made—The lady sits down on the couch—her brilliant eyes emit wild-fire.—All cupids play on her countenance.—Hah! A pistol!—Yes, madam, your money, or—mercy upon me, sir! is this the return for my unfeigned affection?—Hesitate not a moment, madam, I am *no man for you.*—Do you suppose that I would make your husband a monster?—I will not— *I cannot do it!*[39]

Readers who believed that Geraldine would eventually be unveiled as a man assimilated *Christabel* to such a plot. Without ever naming lesbianism, the narrator guarantees that its possibility remains present for the reader. Although in *An Authentic Narrative* the substitution of pistol for phallus switches the scene's manifest content from sex to money, lesbianism survives at the level of innuendo.

More frequently, bringing lesbianism into language demanded the rhetorical figure known as catachresis. Quintilian defines it as a "necessary misuse (*abusio*) of words" to describe what otherwise has no name.[40] To broaden Quintilian's definition with reference to lesbianism, heterosexuality was imported as a catachrestic means of describing sex between women. The absence of actual male and female figures meant that heterosexual imagery tended to dominate descriptions of lesbianism even more powerfully than it did descriptions of heterosexual sex. Eighteenth-century writers characteristically introduced a phallus substitute like a dildo, an enlarged clitoris, or some other phallic object, such as Fanny Davies' gun. If no such substitute was available, they at least made claims about the "masculinity" of one of the female partners. Lesbianism might also appear as an episode in a larger heterosexual context, as when Fanny Hill's first sexual experiences are with a woman to prepare her for the supposedly more substantial pleasures of heterosexual sex. Likewise, in the songs from *The Frisky Songster*, women undress for each other, but in so doing, they provide erotic pleasure chiefly to a hidden male viewer. In all cases, eighteenth-century lesbian representation was assimilated to the heterosexual imagination.

In *Christabel*, Coleridge goes against this tradition by dispensing with the traditional heterosexual context. When Geraldine gets into bed with Christabel, no pseudo-phallus appears to secure a heterosexual framework. No hidden man, as in *The Frisky Songster*, guarantees that erotic activities between two women would create male erotic pleasure. Whatever happens between Christabel and Geraldine, it has nothing to do with men, maleness, or heterosexuality in the way that traditional lesbian representation had.

I am not arguing that *Christabel* does not assume a male, heterosexual reader. Instead, I maintain that its lesbian representation does not pander to such a reader's expectations in the ways that previous writing had done. Much as later readers like Hazlitt wanted Geraldine to be a man, I agree with Karen Swann that "the *real* scandal of *Christabel*" is "that Geraldine is a woman."[41] As the anonymous author of *Christabess* tells the implicitly male reader in his parody, "But, reader, turn away your view, / She's not to sleep with me nor you." He registers how *Christabel* revises previous obscene representations, in which the exposed woman was depicted as an object for the male reader's fantasies. In *Christabel*, Geraldine is not available for such appropriation, and the poem forces the reader to "turn away" his view by keeping the contact between the women as a blank space. Coleridge's poem reveals the degree to which lesbian representation had always depended on a heterosexual catachresis by dispensing with it.

Since *Christabel* treats sex between two women as an activity that fits into no topical context and cannot be quickly assimilated to any tradition of representation, it became the perfect gesture with which Coleridge could demonstrate his originality as a would-be genius. Having been given an annuity that would supposedly free him from having to satisfy popular expectations, Coleridge created a poem showing that he had indeed been so freed. *Christabel*'s lesbianism guaranteed the poem's aesthetic autonomy because, without a heterosexual context, it seems to exist simply for itself. The poem's meanings came solely from the text and, implicitly, from its author, who appeared as its absolute originator. Without a heterosexual framework, lesbianism became original.

Part I of *Christabel* dramatizes the development that I have described in Coleridge's treatment of lesbianism. Initially, the female characters define themselves conventionally in relation to men. Christabel prays at midnight "for the weal of her lover that's far away" (30) and comforts Geraldine by promising that she will have "the service of Sir Leoline" (107). In almost her first words, Geraldine similarly announces that her "sire is of a noble line" (79) and that her distress has been caused by a gang rape of "five warriors" (81) who "choked" her cries "with force and fright" (83). Like Christabel, she defines herself in terms of paternity and erotic relations with men. Even their meeting-place, the "huge, broad-breasted, old oak tree" (42), establishes a looming phallic authority.

As Part I progresses, these signs of male, heterosexual authority slowly evaporate before a magical, otherworldly space dominated by women. Christabel prays not to Christ, her namesake, but to "the Virgin all divine" (139), although Geraldine cannot join the prayer. The "mastiff bitch" (149)

makes an "angry moan" (148) when Geraldine approaches, as if the subhuman female could detect the presence of the superhuman one without the
aid of male intermediaries. Christabel's bedroom, which one might expect
to be the most cozy space in the poem, instead possesses an eerie femininity. It is "carved so curiously, / Carved with figures strange and sweet"
(178–79). The conventionally feminine adjective "sweet" becomes disquiet-
ing through its alliteration with "strange." Although the room's carver presumably was male, his "strange and sweet" decorations denaturalize the
space and separate it from the solidity of Leoline's castle. Christabel intensifies the atmosphere of supernatural femininity by offering Geraldine magical wine made by her mother: "It is a wine of virtuous powers; / My mother made it of wild flowers" (192–93). The wine, in addition to its intoxicating
character, appears as link between dead and living women, since Christabel's mother has died in childbirth. Unable to provide her daughter with
mother's milk, Christabel's mother survives through the supernatural sus-
tenance of wine with "virtuous powers." Even the wine seems to be feminized by its ingredients, wild flowers, whose wildness has been harnessed
and made magical, but not eradicated, in the wine. Well before Geraldine
puts her spell on Christabel, the poem has surrounded Christabel's chamber and all in it with an aura of supernatural femininity. Geraldine only
intensifies this atmosphere by addressing Christabel's mother outright:
"Off, woman, off! this hour is mine— / Though thou her guardian spirit
be, / Off, woman off! 'tis given to me" (211–13). Her command makes clear
that her relation to Christabel is about relations between women, not
women and men.

As images of femininity come to dominate Part I, the possibility of reading *Christabel* as a topical allegory fades. The more the action concerns
itself exclusively with what goes on between women in a world whose
supernatural and subhuman characters are also female, the less it belongs
to the heterosexual context in which lesbian imagery had traditionally been
found. The heart of its autonomy is its silence at the moment at which the
two women touch. Geraldine announces that she is putting a spell on
Christabel, and the poem abruptly breaks off. The women's contact is a gap
on the page, an action that so challenges representation that even its absence
cannot be acknowledged. Sexual contact between women, which had been
supercharged with cultural meanings by its representational history, suddenly becomes unspeakable. When the poem resumes, the narrator broods
on the inexplicable gap between Christabel as she first appeared and as she
appears after the encounter with Geraldine: "O sorrow and shame! Can this
be she, / The lady, who knelt at the old oak tree?" (296–97). He cannot even

describe why Christabel now should be viewed with "sorrow and shame" except to speak accusingly to Geraldine, in language freighted with sexual overtones: "O Geraldine! one hour was thine— / Thou'st had thy will!" (305–306). No heterosexual context appears to make their union understandable in conventional terms.

After the scene between Geraldine and Christabel, Coleridge faced the challenge of sustaining his originality by not letting the relations between them lapse back into conventional modes of representation. In particular, since Geraldine magically possesses Christabel, it would have been easy to assimilate their relations to conventional heterosexual patterns of dominator and dominated. To do so would be to let his lesbian representation fall back into its traditional eighteenth-century mode as a warped version of heterosexuality. In particular, it would recall the commonplace of the seduction of a younger woman by an older one, as in Cleland's *Fanny Hill* or Diderot's *Nun*. In such works, the older woman becomes like the man; the younger woman, like the woman in a conventional, hierarchical relationship. Allowing *Christabel* to fall back into such a mode would have lessened the poem's claim to originality and Coleridge's claim to genius.

Yet Coleridge brilliantly avoids any such lapse. He does so by keeping the relations between Geraldine and Christabel ambiguous enough that they cannot fit easily into a pattern of dominator / dominated. Geraldine, for example, appears to be as much of a victim as an aggressor. In a late addition to the poem, Coleridge makes explicit that she acts partly against her will:

> Yet Geraldine nor speaks nor stirs;
> Ah! what a stricken look was hers!
> Deep from within she seems half-way
> To lift some weight with sick assay,
> And eyes the maid and seeks delay;
> Then suddenly, as one defied,
> Collects herself in scorn and pride,
> And lay down by the Maiden's side!—
>
> (255–62)

Geraldine's "stricken look" and her attempt to seek "delay" point to an internal struggle. Rather than appearing as a predatory, masculine lesbian, she involuntarily obeys forces beyond her control. Even in the first version of the poem, Geraldine's ambivalence is present, as when she tells Christabel, "Thou knowest to-night, and wilt know to-morrow, / This mark of my shame, this seal of my sorrow" (269–70). Her "shame" and "sorrow" disrupt Geraldine's heterosexualizing potential as an all-powerful being who dominates the helpless Christabel.[42] Lesbianism remains unassimilable to conventional patterns because Coleridge does not allow Geraldine to be seen as simply a masculinized aggressor.

Relations between women in *Christabel* are the terra incognita through which Coleridge's poem severs itself from eighteenth-century conventions of representation. Coleridge ends Part I by emphasizing that Christabel, in entering this all-female struggle, has become a complete enigma:

> And, if she move unquietly,
> Perchance, 'tis but the blood so free
> Comes back and tingles in her feet.
> No doubt, she hath a vision sweet.
> What if her guardian spirit 'twere,
> What if she knew her mother near?
>
> (324–28)

The narrator's faux-naif conjecture that Christabel moves unquietly because her feet have gone to sleep becomes eerie through his image of her "blood so free" and the peculiar tangibility of her feet. The freedom of Christabel's blood contrasts pointedly with the incarcerating image of Geraldine's arms as "the lovely lady's prison" (304). Geraldine's imprisoning of Christabel may have "freed" Christabel's blood in ways that heighten her erotic corporeality, which is made particularly vivid in the fetishistic detail of tingling feet. Yet, after having implicated Geraldine in Christabel's implied sexual awakening, the narrator imagines a different cause for Christabel's unquietness: her mother as her guardian spirit. It is unclear whether the narrator's conjecture is supposed to seem plausible or naively optimistic. Coleridge renders relations between women as a mystery that cannot be decrypted for the male reader's erotic pleasure.

In the poem's second part, written after Coleridge returned from Germany in 1799, he develops more explicitly the male viewer's relation to new possibilities of lesbian representation. Whereas the poem's first part was a nightpiece about women, the second is a day poem with three male characters: Sir Leoline, Bard Bracy, and Lord Roland, who never appears but whose memory shapes the action. If Coleridge had followed the conventional pattern of works like *The Frisky Songster*, the relations between Geraldine and Christabel would have been assimilated into a narrative that guaranteed male dominance and heterosexual pleasure. Yet it is typical of *Christabel*'s dramatic undermining of the male viewer's conventional relation to lesbianism that no such guarantee appears. On the contrary, the male world of Part II supports and even furthers the mysteriousness of Part I's lesbianism.

Geraldine turns the male world entirely to her advantage. The key to her success is homosocial desire. Merely with the mention of a name, Roland de Vaux of Tryermaine, Geraldine puts Sir Leoline under her spell:

> Sir Leoline, a moment's space,
> Stood gazing on the damsel's face:
> And the youthful Lord of Tryermaine
> Came back upon his heart again.
>
> (427–30)

The ensuing passage about Sir Leoline's affection for Lord Roland became the poem's most widely quoted and praised section. Walter Pater, for example, had little to say about the scenes between Geraldine and Christabel, but found in the passage about Sir Leoline and Lord Roland lines that "leave almost every reader with a quickened sense of the beauty and compass of human feeling."[43] Not coincidentally, it was the only passage that, when excerpted, seemed to have nothing to do with women. Excerpting the passage allowed readers to believe that *Christabel*, like traditional lesbian representation, was ultimately about men.

Yet in context, Sir Leoline's affection for Lord Roland is less independent of women than nineteenth-century readers wanted it to be. Initially, Geraldine's presence makes Sir Leoline's affection for Lord Roland look like another example of the triangulation of homosocial desire explored by Eve Kosofsky Sedgwick.[44] Yet the prior encounter between Geraldine and Christabel complicates the pattern. Erotic relations between daughters not only take narrative priority over the friendship between the fathers, they provide the context in which those relations can be perceived at all. Coleridge, having displaced the horror generically associated in the Gothic with male-male eroticism onto female-female eroticism, presents relations between men without much paranoia. The passage describing the ruined friendship between Sir Leoline and Lord Roland is as unabashed a declaration of the strength of male-male longing as can be found in any romantic narrative.

Instead of allowing male homosocial relations to banish lesbian ones, Coleridge presents them as unconsciously colluding with whatever forces compel Geraldine. The rhyming names of Geraldine and Leoline point to the magical link between them. The lovely Geraldine hides a "bosom old" and "bosom cold," and so does he, when, with only the faintest motivation, the loving father becomes the heartless domestic tyrant. His anger recalls the language describing Geraldine: "His heart was cleft with pain and rage, / His cheeks they quivered, his eyes were wild" (640–41). Geraldine is also cleft, breathes like one that shuddered, and has eyes that roll wildly. Also like Geraldine, Leoline fights off the claims of Christabel's mother, despite the narrator's pleas:

> O by the pangs of her dear mother
> Think thou no evil of thy child!
> For her, and thee, and for no other,
> She prayed the moment ere she died:
> Prayed that the babe for whom she died,
> Might prove her dear lord's joy and pride!
>
> (626–31)

Only the "gentle minstrel bard" Bracy (649), whose poetic powers feminize him by rendering him sensitive to music, dreams, and nature, knows that all is not well. Yet even he becomes the target of Leoline's anger as one more feminized being victimized by the homosocial desire between Leoline and Roland: " 'Why, Bracy! dost thou loiter here? / I bade thee hence!' The bard obeyed" (651–52). In driving away Bracy to seek Lord Roland, Leoline banishes the only character who attempted to make the link between Geraldine and Christabel comprehensible to men.

The forces driving Geraldine achieve total victory at the end of Part II: "The agéd knight, Sir Leoline, / Led forth the lady Geraldine!" (654–55). The poem ends with a union between a man and a woman, but heteroeroticism has failed to perform its traditional role of saving the day and banishing homosocial or homoerotic relationships. By leaving *Christabel* unfinished, Coleridge preserved its unconventional narrative pattern in which events involving men only accompany and enable the previously existing power struggle between Geraldine and Christabel. It may have been virtually impossible for Coleridge to complete *Christabel* without betraying its most original achievement, the unyoking of lesbian representation from its patriarchal contexts. Some male figure, perhaps Lord Roland or Christabel's lover, would have to be imported to create closure and to restore the poem to the expected male-dominated framework. By keeping the poem as a fragment, he preserved his claims to genius because he prevented his poem from lapsing into the clichés of convention.[45] Coleridge's transformation of the catachrestic aspects of lesbian representation allowed *Christabel* to make it a source of the sublime in a way that it had never been.

The result was that Coleridge fashioned himself as a new kind of genius. Rather than following clichéd paths to garner attention, as Blake did, he turned away entirely from contemporary expectations. *Christabel* removed itself at every level from contemporary contexts that might have overdetermined its meaning. So powerful was Coleridge's image of lesbianism as a source of the sublime that it became easy to forget that any other possibilities had ever existed. It succeeded so brilliantly in distinguishing itself from these contexts that scholars have only recently begun to recover the full range of meanings that lesbianism used to have.

RITUALIZING GENIUS

I have thus far emphasized how Coleridge's annuity allowed him to take genius in a different direction from that taken by artists like Blake or Bannerman, who did not have the prestige of an annuity to underwrite their efforts. Even an artist as independent as Blake was aware of the pressure to please his patrons and employers. Since Coleridge could afford far greater independence from public opinion, he had the privilege of not worrying about his audience. But *Christabel* does more than simply distinguish Coleridge from other writers of the 1790s. It also reflects critically on the cult of genius and the expectations that it created for writers. This cult had celebrated the liberatory powers of imaginative sympathy and the excitement of linguistic daring. *Christabel* responds by treating imaginative sympathy as a nightmarish prison, and by substituting trancelike repetition for the overheated diction that had become stereotypically associated with genius.

Associationists had praised geniuses for imagining objects so intensely that those who beheld their creations became possessed by them. Alexander Gerard, for example, wrote that passions and affections "can be expressed only by the person whose sensibility of heart enables him to conceive the passion with vivacity, to catch it as by infection, and whose imagination immediately receives an impulse from it." Such an artist could present a passion's "causes and objects in a way proper for infusing it into others."[46] Passion in Gerard works much like Geraldine's curse. It is an extra-human force that invades the artist's soul "as by infection" and then is passed on by "infusing" it into others. Mary Wollstonecraft echoed Gerard's associationist vocabulary when she described genius, but she intensified the viewer's unwilling complicity. She described geniuses as "glowing minds that concentrate pictures for their fellow-creatures; forcing them to view with interest the objects reflected from the impassioned imagination, which they passed over in nature."[47] For Wollstonecraft, the power of genius contained a hint of threat: its creations were so powerful that they compelled the viewer to look at them. What had been unremarkable when seen in nature became irresistibly attractive when reenvisioned by genius.

Geraldine herself can be seen as a demystifying allegory for the effects of genius. Like the genius, she has the power to compel her viewers and to force them to view what she wants them to view. In the poem's words, she demands "forced unconscious sympathy" (609). Yet this sympathy, far from being enriching or enlightening, is nightmarishly imprisoning. She transfuses her serpentine qualities into Christabel, who finds her own will annihilated by the power of Geraldine's spell. For a male genius to be able to enthrall his reader or even to project himself into his reader would be business as usual in eighteenth-century aesthetics. When such power was female, the results were far less reassuring, as the reactions of Coleridge's critics to *Christabel* showed.

At a formal level, the poem similarly draws back from the customary mannerisms of genius. It includes none of Bannerman's passionate, high-flown diction or Blake's visionary extravagance. It even avoids the tones of shock, scandal, or titillation in which sex between women was usually described in the eighteenth century. Instead, it presents the most appalling events with studied, deliberate inevitability, as if Geraldine's actions were a carefully planned ritual. This inevitability makes *Christabel* even more outrageous than the works of aspiring geniuses had usually been. Coleridge's poem explores the shock of not seeming to shock. It cultivates a lulling atmosphere of hypnotic repetition that bears little resemblance to the usual modes of genius.

The most important poetic device in creating this atmosphere is imposed repetition, by which I mean repetition that draws attention to its status as deliberate artifice. For example, the poem's first event, the cock's crowing, is immediately repeated: "And hark, again! the crowing cock, / How drowsily it crew" (4–5). Such drowsy repetitions appear throughout the early part of the poem, and they cumulatively slow down the narrative to a breathless crawl. Once Geraldine appears, they become especially sinister:

> So free from danger, free from fear,
> They crossed the court: right glad they were.
> And Christabel devoutly cried
> To the lady by her side,
> Praise we the Virgin all divine
> Who hath rescued thee from thy distress!
> Alas, alas! said Geraldine,
> I cannot speak for weariness.
> So free from danger, free from fear,
> They crossed the court: right glad they were.

(135–44)

The first two and last two lines are identical, but their meaning alters dramatically because of the events described between them. In the first two lines, Geraldine and Christabel are a simple unity, two women eagerly escaping from the midnight forest. Yet Geraldine's inability to pray shows that her connections with the supernatural are far more sinister than Christabel's. When the first two lines reappear, they have become ironic. Christabel still remains "right glad," but the words have a different sense for Geraldine, who is "right glad" because she has successfully penetrated Leoline's castle without giving herself away.

Such repetitions become the poem's master-trope for lesbianism. Lesbianism is supposedly unnatural because it involves repetition (a woman, and then another woman) where heterosexist expectations assume difference (a man, and then a woman). *Christabel* compounds this unnaturalness because Geraldine enforces exact repetition through her spell (one snake-woman, and then another snake-woman). In the second part of the poem, Coleridge uses linguistic repetition as a metaphor for the bodily repetitions of Geraldine's lesbianism. When Geraldine awakes, she rises up "fairer yet! and yet more fair!" (374), and when Christabel sees her embrace Sir Leoline: "Again she saw that bosom old, / Again she felt that bosom cold" (457–58). Such repetitions surround Geraldine's actions with a hypnotic, ritualistic character. When she appears as a snake to Christabel, Coleridge notes, "A snake's small eye blinks dull and shy; / And the lady's eyes they shrunk in her head, / Each shrunk up to a serpent's eye" (583–85). The repeated words slow down the temporal sequence to expand the moment in which the reader must take in the horror of Geraldine's transformation. In *Christabel*, the less overdetermined lesbian representation is by traditional historical associations, the more it acquires its own ineluctable, contagious magic.

Even at micro-levels of rhyme and meter, the poem, like Geraldine, avoids the sudden alterations and dramatic shifts of the rhetoric of genius and dramatizes instead repetition's hypnotic power. Coleridge's metrical experiment of letting the syllables in each line "vary from seven to twelve," although the accents are "only four," creates a far stronger metrical pulse than does regular iambic pentameter or tetrameter ("Preface"). The high point of Coleridge's metrical virtuosity comes with Geraldine's curse:

> And in her arms the maid she took,
>   Ah well-a-day!
> And with low voice and doleful look
> These words did say:
> 'In the touch of this bosom there worketh a spell,

> Which is lord of thy utterance, Christabel!
> Thou knowest to-night, and wilt know to-morrow,
> This mark of my shame, this seal of my sorrow.'
>
> (263–70)

As Geraldine begins to speak, Coleridge dramatically increases the number of syllables per line. Assuming that the timing of the beats in each line remains regular, fitting Geraldine's words into the space of four beats demands pronouncing them more quickly. Coleridge heightens the contrast between her lines and the narrator's by substituting two half lines in the quatrain before she begins to speak, so that her lines appear even longer than they would otherwise. Her curse becomes not a leisured piece of oratory but a rushed murmur, as if her "shame" and "sorrow" led her to thrust out her words as quickly as possible. Although her murmur grows even faster as the speech continues, the four-beat pulse prevents her speech from interrupting the poem's overall rhythmic monotony.

The point of these formal observations is that *Christabel* gave to lesbian representation not merely narrative conventions but a hypnotic mood and atmosphere quite unlike those in previous works belonging to the cult of genius. Coleridge replaces fiery rhetoric with ritualistic monotony, sudden changes of direction with enforced repetition, and male-dominated action with spectral relations between women. The poem earned its distance from topical associations partly through the virtuosity of its formal innovations. It created the precedent whereby the more obscene a work's content was, the more subtle and impressive its formal innovations could be. These innovations were not merely a way of making the outrageous content palatable. Instead, they suggested that appropriating obscenity demanded pushing the limits of conventional representation.

If Coleridge's artistic uses of obscenity were experimental, they were also rarefied. *Christabel* became an ideal cult item because of its combination of technical virtuosity and scandalous subject matter. Coleridge guaranteed *Christabel*'s quasi-mythic status by keeping it from publication for sixteen years, so that only those who had heard the poem read aloud from manuscript would know it. The storm of critical outrage that greeted the poem on its publication only increased its symbolic value as a work for the elite. As Paul Hamilton argues, it demanded special readers, the "membership of a learned class whose reflective habits and cultural priorities differentiate[d] them from the predominantly commercial interest of the rest of contemporary society."[48] Although some critics found it obscene, the most common charge was that it was incomprehensible: "balderdash," "profound nonsense," "wholly bottomless," and "a maze of impenetrable mystery."[49] Yet Lord Byron and Walter Scott had both admitted their admiration for and indebtedness to *Christabel*.[50] To approve of *Christabel* marked one as a reader who sided with artists rather than with mere critics. Percy Shelley's famous reaction to hearing *Christabel* read aloud proved how deeply the poem could affect the truly sensitive auditor, as opposed to dully unimaginative hacks.[51]

Later in the century, *Christabel* was especially popular among writers of the Aesthetic movement, who inherited and exploited the eighteenth-century link between genius and transgressive sexuality. For them, Coleridge had provided a model for the association between deviance and pure art central to late Victorian high culture. Tennyson alluded to *Christabel* prominently in his most homoerotic poem, *In Memoriam, A. H. H.*[52] Hall Caine and Dante Gabriel Rossetti discussed *Christabel* extensively, including the rumors that Geraldine was really a man, and even noted the existence of *Christabess*.[53] Swinburne praised *Christabel* as superior to "Kubla Khan" and the *Rime of the Ancient Mariner*: "The very terror and mystery of magical evil is imbued with this sweetness; the witch has no less of it than the maiden; their contact has in it nothing dissonant or disfiguring, nothing to jar or to deface the beauty and harmony of the whole imagination."[54] Swinburne foregrounded the beauty of the lesbianism that had so disturbed earlier readers, even as he de-eroticized it. Hall Caine similarly singled out "the marvellous passage in which Geraldine bewitches Christabel" not for its daring as a moment of sexual representation, but for its technical skill, or what he called its "dexterity of hand."[55] For these men, admiring *Christabel* cemented bonds between them as artists whose norms were not compromised by an allegiance to bourgeois codes of respectable sexual representation. I have argued that *Christabel* distinguished itself from earlier lesbian representation by not providing the expected heterosexual context. This absence paradoxically encouraged a different kind of masculine appropriation. Rather than providing erotic pleasure for the heterosexual male, it provided aesthetic pleasure for the members of an artistic, homosocial elite.

Lesbian writers eventually appropriated *Christabel* and its decadent tradition of lesbian representation. Renée Vivien's sonnet "Your Strange Hair . . . ," for example, addresses a woman whose appearance draws heavily on Geraldine's. Her "strange hair" has "pale glows," like Geraldine's hair, which "wildly glittered here and there" (64). Her "gown has the chill of the breeze and the woods," like Geraldine's, which "shadowy in the moonlight shone" (60). Most of all, she, like Geraldine, masks a terrible hideousness:

> The moon grazed you with a slanted glow . . .
> It was terrible, like prophetic lightning
> Revealing the hideous below your beauty.
>
> I saw—as one sees a flower fade—
> On your mouth, like summer auroras,
> The withered smile of an old whore.[56]

Vivien appropriates Geraldine's doubleness as a model for the deceptiveness of her beloved. The moon reveals not the withered serpentine bosom but the "smile of an old whore." The supernatural atmosphere of *Christabel* provides a vocabulary for describing the more mundane failures of a lesbian love affair.

By the early twentieth century, "Geraldine" had become a code among British modernists for older lesbians. In *Inclinations* (1916), for example, Ronald Firbank introduces "Geraldine O'Brookomore, the authoress of *Six Strange Sisters*." She invites the young Mabel (a diminished, domesticated, and secularized version of Christabel) to travel with her to Greece: " 'Was it solely Vampirism that made me ask her,' she queried, 'or is it that I'm simply bored?' "[57] Rosamond Lehmann's *Dusty Answer* (1927) presents a more serious character, Geraldine Manners, with whom the heroine Judith becomes obsessed when she meets her at Cambridge. Although Judith criticizes Geraldine's "broad heavy face and thick neck, those coarse and masculine features, that hothouse skin," she cannot deny her spell:

> In spite of all, she was beautiful: her person held an appalling fascination.
> She was beautiful, beautiful. You would never be able to forget her face,
> her form. You would see it and dream of it with painful desire: as if she
> could satisfy something, some hunger, if she would. But she was not for
> you. The secret of her magnetism, her rareness must be for ever beyond
> reach; but not beyond imagination.[58]

The magical power of Christabel's Geraldine becomes the frightening allure of an adult lesbian relationship for Lehmann's protagonist.

Aestheticism's influence on the academic canon also guaranteed *Christabel*'s inclusion in Romanticism anthologies and consequent availability to college-aged lesbian readers. Toni McNaron's memoir *I Dwell in Possibility* describes the poem's effect on her and her roommate: "In our romantic poetry course, we read Coleridge's 'Christabel' and decided we were very like the two women in that gothic tale of evil and forbidden fruits. Our nicknames became 'Chris' and 'Gere' . . . and we developed a private language around them and that poem."[59] For McNaron, this appropriation of homophobic representation was one step in her growing awareness of her own lesbianism. For her as for many readers, even a homophobic representation was better than complete silence.

In a way that few works have done, *Christabel* and its echoes have traced a distinct path through the canon of British literature as an iconic representation of transgressive desires. So powerful has been its hold on later imaginations that it has virtually erased earlier traditions of lesbian representation from critical memory. Even as contemporary writers break away from past homophobic traditions of representation and find new ways to represent lesbian experience, *Christabel* lingers as a haunting model for the lesbian sublime. It stands as the most influential example of the inexpressible possibilities that emerged when erotic relations between women were divorced from conventional heterosexual expectations.

Since this book's title mentions the prehistory of genius, it implies that, some time after the period covered by the book, a real history of homosexuality and genius begins. For the British tradition, I would locate the shift from prehistory to history in the life and work of George Gordon, Lord Byron. In making Byron's career a critical turning point, I do not mean to imply only that some readers perceived Byron as a man who had sex with other males and that many perceived him as a genius. Instead, as I have argued elsewhere, Byron's reception created, popularized, and disseminated an image of the "homosexualized" genius.[1] By this phrase, I mean an association between genius and mysteriously unfathomable depths of erotic transgression. In Byron's case, these depths were especially prominent because of his separation from his wife, which provided a rich source of gossip for most of literate England.

Byron's miserable, alienated heroes and early death clinched the connection between homosexualized genius and doom. His career forced his admirers and biographers to confront the supposed link between genius and sexual transgression more directly than that of any previous writer. Even though much nineteenth-century commentary on Byron had direct precedents in eighteenth-century works about genius, his life manifested eighteenth-century clichés so spectacularly that, after him, it could seem as if eighteenth-century writers had been describing him all along. His career scripted those of virtually all subsequent male artists aspiring to genius, especially those who ended in scandal, from Oscar Wilde to Kurt Cobain.

Since I have elsewhere treated Byron's influence on nineteenth-century writing, I want in this conclusion to look at three twentieth-century directions for the homosexualized genius. All three date from the 1920s: the genius as celebrity, as represented by Radclyffe Hall and *The Well of Loneliness* (1928); the genius as intellectual, as represented by Virginia Woolf and

A Room of One's Own (1929); and the genius as the gifted child, as described by Lewis Terman beginning in 1921. In terms of their larger effects on Anglo-American culture, all three models have had significant afterlives: Radclyffe Hall's continues to shape the aesthetics of fame; Woolf's, the path of queer theory; and Terman's, the goals of elementary education.

The connection between Radclyffe Hall and Virginia Woolf is familiar. In *A Room of One's Own*, Woolf refers explicitly to Sir Charles Biron, who prosecuted *The Well of Loneliness* for obscenity, when she begins her famous discussion of Chloe's liking for Olivia. Several critics have argued that Woolf's controversial treatment of androgyny in *A Room* and *Orlando* responds to Hall's treatment of lesbianism in *The Well*.[2] What has been less recognized is that Woolf's response to Hall is not only about lesbianism but also about the genius and sexuality. In looking at Hall's work and Woolf's response to it, critics sometimes forget that *The Well*'s heroine, Stephen Gordon, is a novelist and, according to some characters in the book, a genius.

Although as a young child, Stephen does not care about literature, as an adolescent, she found, "to her own deep amazement," that she "began to excel in composition" and wrote descriptions of her "queer hopes and queer longings, queer joys and even more curious frustrations."[3] Once Stephen becomes a writer, the vocabulary of genius runs throughout the novel, as when Stephen's teacher Puddle views Stephen as "true genius in bondage" (217) and when Pauline, Stephen's French servant, tells her, "Un grand génie doit nourrir le cerveau [A great genius must nurture her brain]" (370). Both of these characters are particularly fond of Stephen, so their views are not entirely trustworthy, but even the omniscient narrator claims that Stephen's work at moments "brushed the hem of greatness" (376).

Twice in the novel, Hall foregrounds the possible connection between Stephen's "inversion" and her genius. First, Puddle tells Stephen, "Why, just because you are what you are, you may actually find that you've got an advantage. You may write with a curious double insight—write both men and women from a personal knowledge" (208). She re-genders the eighteenth-century association between men of genius and androgyny to suggest that female inverts can write better than others because they will know both masculine and feminine characteristics from experience. For eighteenth-century writers, the male genius was androgynous because he transcended ordinary gender categories. For Hall, the invert had the potential for genius because she inhabits two gender categories and therefore has a wider range of insight.

Later in the novel, Hall allows a character to hope that inverts' outstanding abilities will lead the world to accept them: "For the sooner the world came to realize that fine brains very frequently went with inversion, the sooner it would have to withdraw its ban, and the sooner would cease this persecution" (413). Genius appears as the inverts' weapon with which to compel toleration. Stephen's duty is to use her genius to become such a representative "fine brain." As Adolphe Blanc, the "gentle and learned Jew" (394), tells her, "The doctors cannot make the ignorant think, cannot hope to bring home the sufferings of millions; only one of ourselves can some day do that. . . . It will need great courage but it will be done" (395). In encouraging Stephen, Blanc symbolically passes the torch of gay liberation from himself as a male homosexual to her as a lesbian. He represents gay male culture at its most intellectual, as signified, among other things, by his Jewishness, and at its most exhausted, as indicated by his name. "Blanc" points to his estrangement from the dominant white culture that stigmatizes Jews (he is white in name only) and indicates the evident "blankness" of the gay male voice, at least as a weapon for liberation. Recognizing his inadequacy, Blanc hopes to inspire Stephen, who, as an Englishwoman of impeccable breeding and a well-known writer, can take up liberation in a way that he cannot.

Yet, seriously as Hall treats Stephen's genius, she does not make it wholly positive. Like Anne Bannerman before her, Hall exacts a price for lesbian genius. In one of the most notorious turns of the novel's plot, Stephen martyrs herself by separating herself from the love of her life, Mary Llewellyn. Having decided that Paris's lesbian life is corrupting Mary, Stephen pretends to have an affair so that Mary will flee into the arms of a well-intentioned heterosexual man. Yet even before this dismal ending, the relationship between Mary and Stephen is not all it should be, and Stephen's genius is at fault. Convinced that she can protect Mary only if she becomes a famous novelist, Stephen buries herself in her work and lets their relationship stagnate. Although she writes "with the speed of true inspiration," she finds that "there were days when all that she did apart from her writing was done with an effort, with an obvious effort to be considerate" (346). Mary grows unhappy because she knows that she cannot compete with Stephen's artistic drive. Driven to Paris's underground lesbian bars, she begins the deterioration that Stephen determines to stop with her self-sacrifice.

As a result, the novel's gloom has two causes: Stephen's internalized homophobia and self-hatred, and the well-worn stereotype that the genius's solitude wrecks domestic happiness. Even when the genius is a female invert in an openly same-sex relationship, the egotism supposedly necessary for art corrodes romance. Following the logic of genius, Stephen recognizes her true artistic calling only once her personal life is wrecked. In the bizarre vision closing the novel, the Spirits of Inverts Past surround her and clamor "for their right to salvation" (446). They wish "to become articulate through her" (446), and she ends the book begging God to defend them. Having surrendered her personal relationship with Mary, Stephen rises to the more public voice in which her genius will find its true cause.

The grimness of *The Well* contrasts markedly with Hall's own life, her social success, and her long-term, happy, though not untroubled, partnership with Una Troubridge. Terry Castle's *Noël Coward and Radclyffe Hall* recreates the swirl of "literary gatherings, theatrical parties, and first nights" through which Radclyffe Hall in the 1920s became "the most easily-recognized artistic celebrity in London." Not coincidentally, she cultivated a "Byronese" appearance.[4] Like Byron and Wilde, her career as a celebrity had a scandalous public event as its defining moment: the trial of *The Well of Loneliness* for obscenity in 1928. The newspaper coverage of the trial spread the image of Hall as the mannish lesbian in much the same way the Wilde trial crystallized Wilde as the effeminate homosexual.[5]

Yet Hall was not merely a lesbian echo of Byron and Wilde. Unlike them, she survived her public ordeal. She never met the vehement condemnation that greeted Byron during the separation scandal and Wilde during his trial, although her novel certainly received scathing denunciations. The key difference was that they were men and were consequently more vulnerable. During their scandals, Byron and Wilde themselves were on trial, literally or figuratively, but Hall was not. The public scandal was about *The Well*, not about her. She was not even allowed to testify, although she made some widely publicized protestations in the courtroom. Although the English court condemned *The Well* for obscenity, the case against it was dismissed in New York, and the American press reviewed the novel enthusiastically. It continued to be widely available and sold thousands of copies.[6]

Hall proved that a lesbian writer could become an admired cultural icon, although she achieved her status partly at the cost of supporting homophobic myths about inverts. *The Well* gained sympathy for Stephen Gordon and her kind through a melodramatic plot, self-punishing representations, and a clunky essentialism that posed no serious threat to the sex/gender system. One of its most significant legacies may be the odd split in the way that celebrity itself has furthered the cause of gay rights. Celebrities who may or may not be gay and who may have perfectly happy personal lives can become icons for the gay movement if they portray unhappy gays and lesbians. Tom Hanks's Oscar-winning performance in the tear-jerker *Philadelphia* is one example. Another is the notorious coming-out episode of the television sitcom *Ellen*. Far as the light-hearted *Ellen* may seem from the gloom of *The Well*, this episode continued *The Well*'s long tradition by leaving its heroine without the woman of her dreams, although the actress playing Ellen was in a lesbian relationship that received widespread press coverage. Like *The Well*, the coming-out episode of *Ellen* assumed that a straight audience would have more sympathy with the fictional lonely lesbian than with the actual, partnered celebrity.

If the queer celebrity represents one development of the post-Byronic connection between genius and homosexuality, the queer intellectual is another. Although not usually recognized as such, Virginia Woolf's *A Room of One's Own* is a foundational text for queer as well as for feminist theory. The difference between Hall's text and Woolf's provides a provocative, early version of what has hardened into the clichéd split between essentialist "gay studies" and a more speculative and category-bending "queer theory." Woolf is no social constructionist, and in the context of her whole career, her positions about sexuality are far more complex than those in *A Room*. I concentrate on *A Room*, however, because of its huge influence in transmuting concepts of genius for the academy. It complicates any debate about homosexuality and art by positioning itself against representations like Hall's. In themselves, many of Woolf's aesthetic tenets are quite conservative and descend directly from Victorian aestheticism. What makes them interesting in the context of the 1920s is how they defined her against Hall's propaganda.

A Room of One's Own mulls over the status of the modern genius and broods on the artistic benefits that accrue to artists who, like Stephen Gordon, write not merely as a man or as a woman but as both. In chapter 5, Woolf fantasizes about the imaginary novelist Mary Carmichael, who, although she is "no 'genius,' " nevertheless deserves measured admiration because she writes "as a woman, but as a woman who had forgotten that she is a woman, so that her pages were full of that curious sexual quality which comes only when sex is unconscious of itself."[7] For Woolf, the female writer dare not descend to anything as blunt as polemical self-expression. The paradox she develops, which descends directly from eighteenth-century conceptions of genius, is that the author's personality shines through only when the author avoids direct self-expression.

In Carmichael, the proof of this "curious sexual quality" is that she dares to hint that "Chloe liked Olivia." Woolf finds this hint exciting because it admits the possibility of female intimacy, disrupts its almost complete absence from literature, and points to the desirability of lesbian fiction: "For if Chloe likes Olivia and Mary Carmichael knows how to express it she will light a torch in that vast chamber where nobody has yet been" (84).

Yet, to express such female-female liking, Carmichael need not descend to anything as blunt as lesbian polemics. Instead, her unconscious femininity will find its most vivid outlet in exploring little-known arenas of female experience.

Woolf expands upon the paradoxical need for Mary Carmichael to write as a woman and not as a woman in her final chapter, in which she describes her ideal of the androgynous artist:

> Coleridge certainly did not mean, when he said that a great mind is androgynous, that it is a mind that has any special sympathy with women; a mind that takes up their cause or devotes itself to their inter-pretation. Perhaps the androgynous mind is less apt to make these dis-tinctions than the single-sexed mind. He meant, perhaps, that the androgynous mind is resonant and porous; that it transmits emotion without impediment; that it is naturally creative, incandescent and undi-vided. In fact one goes back to Shakespeare's mind as the type of the androgynous, of the man-womanly mind. (98–99)

Like Hall in *The Well*, Woolf valorizes the mind that is not merely mascu-line or merely feminine. Yet the valorization differs in the two writers. For Hall, Stephen's inversion imposed on her the duty to polemicize. Because Stephen could see more than others, she was called to defend all inverts. Woolf's androgyny is more traditional and more purely aesthetic. For her, the androgynous mind resembles Schiller's naive poet who has not experi-enced the fall into self-consciousness. Her celebration of Shakespeare descends directly from the earlier monumentalization of him as the univer-sal genius who, in encompassing all experience, hid his own from view. The great, androgynous genius is precisely the one who rises above polemics to transmit a supposedly purer truth.

For Woolf, androgyny is a sign of freedom. In her view, too many women writers have been scarred by anger at oppression, which has led them to write self-consciously as women instead of freely as writers beyond sex. For Woolf, the true genius transcends specifically female or male experience. Hall had presented just the opposite case in *The Well*. Stephen realizes that her sexual frustration has begun to harm her art: "Why have I been afflict-ed with a body that must never be indulged, that must always be repressed. . . . What have I done to be so cursed? . . . I shall never be a great writer because of my maimed and insufferable body" (217). Whereas Woolf views the androgyny of genius as a paradise beyond gendered desire, Hall shows that the invert's genius requires sexual fulfillment for its flowering.

Woolf's influence on queer theory comes less from her particular positions about genius and androgyny, which rely on a high Victorian conception of pure art, than from her success in giving the academy a way to discuss lesbian aesthetics. Whereas Hall's book became the stuff of newspaper scandal, Woolf's debuted unspectacularly as an academic lecture at Newnham and Girton Colleges at Cambridge. As one auditor noted, "Her mellifluous cultivated voice *reading* from her manuscript added to the lullaby effect and I am deeply ashamed to confess that I slept right through it. If only I had known it was to become A Room of One's Own!"[8] The contrast between Woolf's lecture and the glare of the spotlight surrounding Hall could not have been more pronounced.

Whereas Hall's book became, for better or worse, the defining work of lesbian fiction for much of the century, *A Room of One's Own* waited until its academic, feminist recovery to have a substantial effect. Woolf explicitly distanced herself from the academic norms of the 1920s, but the academy had shifted enough by the 1980s that her book provided a model for how an academic inquiry into aesthetics and same-sex desire might avoid the supposed crudeness of outright advocacy. It may initially seem wrong to look at Woolf as a predecessor of queer theory since she seems so quick to transcend sex, while queer theory is so eager to talk about it. Yet *A Room* (though not necessarily Woolf's other work) shares with academic queer theory the preference for the speculative over the polemic, the complicated over the simple, and the ironic over the melodramatic.

Woolf's place in the movement to queer studies might be encapsulated by Ellen Bayuk Rosenman's essay "Sexual Identity and *A Room of One's Own*," published in *Signs* in 1989. In it, Rosenman positions herself against earlier gay studies, as represented specifically by Jane Marcus, in much the same way that Woolf positions herself against Hall:

> Jane Marcus has cogently analyzed Woolf's deliberate allusions to the Hall trial, which implicitly include Hall in *A Room of One's Own*'s female literary history. But this does not necessarily mean, as Marcus argues, that Woolf considered Hall "a martyr in [the] cause" of feminism. . . . With [*The Well*'s] realistic narrative conventions, its melodramatic plot, its explicit and heavy-handed moral stance, it hardly represented the ideal female sensibility defined by "suggestive power," "unconventionality," and "subtlety" postulated in *A Room of One's Own*.[9]

Whereas Marcus presented Woolf as a proto-feminist celebrating lesbian solidarity, Rosenman finds in Woolf a proto-queer sensibility that refuses to be pinned down to categories: "Woolf's notion of selfhood and relationships, nurtured in the freewheeling sexual permutations of Bloomsbury that she found so liberating, worked against the limited notions of the term 'lesbian.' "[10] For Rosenman, the fluidity of Woolf's emotional life provides a queer correction to Marcus/Hall's gayness. Rosenman finds in Woolf's life and work the complexity, depth, and ambiguity on which English studies thrives and which seem distressingly absent in Hall. Without quite having written queer theory, Woolf's turn away from Hall provided the model for an institutionally useful gesture of distinction. Woolf, like queer theory, fit the needs of disciplinarity in a way that Hall and essentialist gay politics did not.

No gay male writer from the 1920s wrote a novel that was outspokenly pro-gay as Hall, or developed a work of aesthetics as provocative as Woolf's for later scholars. It is difficult to explain why without making risky generalizations about lesbian versus gay male history. Yet, as Joseph Bristow has argued, the specter of the Wilde trials effectively forced much gay male writing underground.[11] Much, though not all, of the work of writers like E. M. Forster, Ronald Firbank, and Noël Coward remained coded. While this coding often encouraged witty and inventive literary experiments, it left the bigger risks to lesbian writers. They were the ones to take on the challenges of outing the homosexualized genius in a way that male writers did not.

Despite the immense influence of both Hall and Woolf, the figure who did even more than they to shape the twentieth-century homosexualized genius was not gay at all. Lewis Terman, the developer of the notorious Stanford-Binet IQ test, in 1922 "began the granddaddy of all longitudinal psychological studies, the first scientific study that attempted to divine the origin and outcome of genius."[12] He selected a large group of gifted children in California and collected data on them at regular intervals throughout their lives in order to track their progress. In so doing, he made a simple but critical intervention in the history of genius by developing a new category: giftedness. Whereas the genius was unpredictable, uncontrollable, potentially insane, and implicitly homosexual, the gifted person was the model of normality:

> Contrary to the theory of Lange-Eichbaum that great achievement is usually associated with emotional tensions which border on the abnormal, in our gifted group success is associated with stability rather than instability, with absence rather than presence of disturbing conflicts—in short, with well-balanced temperament and with freedom from excessive frustration.[13]

Giftedness sanitized genius of all its uncomfortable associations.

Terman's findings had obvious implications for the American educational system. Although tutoring genius looked like a bad investment because geniuses were unstable, disturbed, and implicitly homosexual, giftedness was a better bargain. Money for teaching gifted children would not be wasted because, far from becoming psychopathic weirdos, they would turn out to be model citizens. Terman's work catalyzed the American education system's numerous programs for gifted children. Against teachers who feared that outstandingly smart children would have unhappy lives and therefore should not have special treatment, he argued that giftedness should be measured, appreciated, and encouraged: "Gifted children who have been promoted more rapidly than is customary are as a group equal or superior to gifted nonaccelerates in health and general adjustment, do better schoolwork, continue their education further, marry a little earlier, and are more successful in their later careers" (377).

Nevertheless, despite Terman's efforts to eliminate the kinkiness of homosexualized genius, faint hints of the older association between genius and sex / gender deviance occasionally crop up in his detailed reports. For example, he created a list of play interests, hierarchized by gender. On the feminine end were such activities as playing school or cooking; on the masculine, garden work or marbles; and at the neutral middle, croquet and cards. Based on this scale, he decided that gifted boys were more masculine than a male control group, but that gifted girls "tended to be more masculine" (35). Even more interestingly, he noted that "one gifted boy received a masculinity rating lower than that of any girl in either [control or gifted] group" (36). Although the problematically masculine girl seemed to fade away with age, the questionably masculine boy haunted Terman's analysis.

In the volume devoted to the twenty-five-year follow-up of the children, the specter of the improperly masculine male genius appeared more tragically in a section describing suicides. Terman describes "M 913," whose paternal uncle "was described as 'decidedly queer' " (85). The subject himself

was rather undeveloped socially, and was in danger of becoming overly introverted. In high school he grew somewhat more sociable, but was shy with girls and disliked parties. . . . Worry over his responsibilities and the outlook for his future was accentuated by several weeks of illness from pneumonia. It was while convalescing from this illness that his depression led him to commit suicide. He was twenty-four years old at the time. (86)

Whether Terman suspected M 913 of being gay or not, the quiet, coded language of homosexuality ("introverted," "shy with girls," worry over "outlook for his future") lurks in this case study. Nothing about its chilly language is more revealing than its displacement of the motives for suicide
onto physical illness: depression arising from a bout of pneumonia. The
mere presence of M 913 shows that, much as Terman wanted to rescue
genius from perversion, his subjects did not escape at least momentary
lapses from his vision of normality.

Rather than simply denying the presence of homosexuality, Terman
included a section about it, but did so to emphasize how rare it was: "The
data we have show an incidence of about 1 percent for each sex" (120–21).
Given the difficulty of getting data on homosexuality in the 1940s, it is impressive that even eleven men in Terman's study admitted to having had sex with
other men. Their professions were largely in the arts: "Three are working in
the field of fine arts, 2 are musicians, 3 are writers, 1 is a scientist, 1 is a mechanic, and 1 has been employed chiefly in office work" (121). Terman also noted
that four had married "in a definite program to attain sexual normality" (121).
Nevertheless, his devotion to factual accuracy forced him to admit that "four
of the 11 men have been so outstanding in their achievement as to be rated
among the 150 most successful men of the gifted group" (121). He did not
include the potentially distressing corollary: in terms of percentages, gifted
male homosexuals were more likely to be outstandingly successful than gifted heterosexuals. To have admitted this conclusion would have threatened
the normality that mattered so much to him. Yet he did present the data, and
let readers interpret as they would.

The data on the six women who admitted that they had had sex with
another woman is less revealing. Terman, noting that five of the six had
married, concentrates almost entirely on the status of their marriages. For
example, he describes two who were married and divorced before they came
out. One was "a patient in a mental hospital for some years, and it was after
her hospitalization that her homosexual traits became most evident" (as if
staying in the mental hospital turned her into a lesbian) (122). For another,
"a brilliant and highly successful professional woman," her "homosexual
relationship" waited "until sometime after her divorce" (122). Whereas Terman admits that at least some of the homosexual men were exceptionally
successful, he is mostly concerned, when discussing lesbians, to find
whether or not they were married when they had sex with other women. As
Shurkin has noted, Terman's supposedly objective studies reveal their biases nowhere more clearly than in their treatment of women in general, and
these biases continue in his treatment of lesbians in particular. Shurkin

traces in moving detail the degree to which many of Terman's female subjects, lesbian and straight, did not lead perfectly well-adjusted lives, but
confronted the frustrations, disappointments, and bitterness that accompanied being a highly intelligent women in a society that still had no approved
outlets for them.[14]

Terman's efforts did not entirely kill off the older myth of the homosexualized genius, even in education. Instead, while "giftedness" became the label
for the smart but normal child, "creative" became the word for the smart but
queer one, especially in the arts. Herbert A. Carroll's *Genius in the Making*,
one of the prestigious McGraw-Hill Series in Education, drew heavily on
Terman's work and popularized it for a broader audience. For example, he
repeated Terman's findings about the masculine games of gifted boys in order
to counter the misguided "conviction that gifted boys are effeminate."[15] Yet
when he moved from raw intelligence to the "Special Gifts" chapter, which
dealt specifically with "genius in the arts," the older link between homosexuality and genius reappeared: "It is interesting to note that boys who are gifted
in art and music are much more likely to possess feminine traits than are
intellectually gifted boys or unselected boys. . . . It is possible, though not
likely, that an element of homosexuality profoundly influences all achievements in aesthetics" (193–94). He is more guarded about lesbianism, but does
note that "it may be that the ability to create is more closely linked with the
male sex hormones" (193). Paradoxically, while boys have to have "feminine"
traits to be creative, creativity also depends on male hormones. His implica-
tion is that female creativity is virtually impossible.

Carroll's book appeared in 1940, and we might hope that such stereotypes would have vanished from more recent work in educational research.
Yet, especially in investigations of creativity, they linger. In Robert S. Albert
and Mark A. Runco's article "The Achievement of Eminence" (1986), which
focuses on boys, the authors note that creative persons can "express both
masculine and feminine aspects to their personalities."[16] Although they
hastily add that this finding "does not mean that creative men or women
are more homosexual than less creative persons," they confirm that "creative persons as children often have a greater diversity of identification
models." As a result, they attain a "wider emotional and informational base"
as a resource for their creative endeavors.[17] Once intelligence is split off
from creativity, creativity can inherit all that once belonged to genius. However much critics may want to claim that postmodernism has debunked
every aspect of Enlightenment thought, the vocabulary and stereotypes of
eighteenth-century genius continue to shape elementary education at the
most basic level.[18]

Reading such works, it can seem that gay / lesbian children will almost inevitably find themselves doomed to the label "creative," regardless of whether they care about the arts or not. Like "genius," this label is not purely negative. Yet it automatically provides an institutional backing and legitimization to the social marginality that a gay / lesbian child is likely to encounter. Creativity politely dooms the gay child to perpetual difference. This doom is all the more frightening since such a child has no chance to protest an educational establishment eager to label anyone who challenges the tyranny of the normal.

The legacy of the link between homosexuality and genius must be a mixed one. The diminishment of genius into creativity can stand for the invitation that genius poses to a society eager to control, without quite denying, all forms of difference. For such a society, homosexualized geniuses are fun to have around because they create great art and because their sufferings are entertaining and instructive. Gay / lesbian / bisexual / transgender people may well feel that it is time to stop being the sacrificial clowns for a homophobic culture. If they want art, let them suffer for it. It might be pleasant for us to have some of the power, money, and control for a change.

Yet the prospect of shedding the mystique of genius entirely, of admitting that queers can be as dull as anyone else, does not inspire unmixed delight. It is still satisfying to know that in the theater, the art gallery, the bookstore, the ground will feel safe in a way it does not elsewhere. In response to the weak self-justification, "I can't help being what I am," genius offers the promise of self-determination, of at least being able to help what you create. The problem of genius as it was formulated in the eighteenth century and as it has descended to us is that it forces a choice: either you stand apart from the crowd or you do not. For the writers that I have discussed, the right choice was obvious. The gains and losses of post-Stonewall queer history might be encapsulated by observing that it no longer is.

NOTES

INTRODUCTION

1. "The Invisible Characteristics of Homosexuality and Genius—Detected at Birth!" (Internet). Online at: Http://www.usadvertiser.com/900/glo-ra.htm. Accessed September 11, 1997.

2. For information about the outstanding accomplishments of gays and lesbians, see Thomas Dale Cowan, *Gay Men and Women Who Enriched the World*, 2d ed. (Los Angeles: Alyson, 1996).

3. Sigmund Freud, *Leonardo da Vinci and a Memory of His Childhood* (1910), trans. Alan Tyson (New York: Norton, 1964), 30.

4. Edward Carpenter, *Intermediate Types Among Primitive Folk: A Study in Social Evolution* (1919) (New York: Arno, 1975), 62.

5. Prisoner quoted in George Chauncey, *Gay New York: Gender, Urban Culture, and the Making of the Gay Male World, 1890–1940* (New York: Basic Books, 1994), 285.

6. "Sexual Orientation" (Internet). Online at: Http://www.ice.net/public/acfhr/sexorien.htm. Accessed September 15, 1997.

7. I am grateful to John McAdam for making available to me a collection of Poffo's bouts on video.

8. Cesare Lombroso, *The Man of Genius* (New York: Scribner's, 1891), 316; William Hirsch, *Genius and Degeneration: A Psychological Study*, trans. anon. (New York: Appleton, 1896), 137.

9. Janine Chasseguet-Smirgel, *Creativity and Perversion* (New York: Norton, 1984), 90, 91.

10. Arnold M. Ludwig, *The Price of Greatness: Resolving the Creativity and Madness Controversy* (New York: Guilford, 1995), 73; Albert Rothenberg, *Creativity and Madness: New Findings and Old Stereotypes* (Baltimore: Johns Hopkins University Press, 1990), 110, 112.

11. Lori Reisenbichler, "Creative Tension: A Crucial Component of Creativity in the Workplace" (Internet). Online at: Http://www.workteams.unt.edu/reports/lreisenb.htm. Accessed September 15, 1997.

12. Ernst Kretschmer, *The Psychology of Men of Genius*, trans. R. B. Cattell (New York: Harcourt Brace, 1931), 14.

13. See Jeff Nunokawa, " 'All the Sad Young Men': AIDS and the Work of Mourning," in Diana Fuss, ed., *Inside / Out: Lesbian Theories, Gay Theories* (New York: Routledge, 1991), 311–23.

14. Christine Battersby, *Gender and Genius: Towards a Feminist Aesthetics* (Bloomington: Indiana University Press, 1989); Kretschmer, *The Psychology of Men of Genius*, 125–26.

15. For demystifications, see Michel Foucault, *"The Archaeology of Knowledge" and "The Discourse on Language,"* trans. A. M. Sheridan Smith (New York: Barnes and Noble, 1993), 21–30, and Pierre Bourdieu, *The Rules of Art: Genesis and Structure of the Literary Field*, trans. Susan Emanuel (Stanford, Calif.: Stanford University Press, 1996), 47–112.

16. *Webster's New World Dictionary of the American Language*, David B. Guralnik, ed., 2d College Edition (New York: William Collins and World Publishing, 1976), 582.

17. For recent work on the period, see the bibliography in Ian McCormick, ed., *Secret Sexualities: A Sourcebook of Seventeenth- and Eighteenth-Century Writing* (New York: Routledge, 1997), 249–54. See also Cameron McFarlane, *The Sodomite in Fiction and Satire, 1660–1750* (New York: Columbia University Press, 1997); Lisa L. Moore, *Dangerous Intimacies: Toward a Sapphic History of the British Novel* (Durham, N.C.: Duke University Press, 1997); Jon Thomas Rowland, *"Swords in Myrtle Dress'd": Toward a Rhetoric of Sodom* (Madison, N.J.: Fairleigh Dickinson University Press, 1998).

18. Wilde quoted in Richard Ellmann, *Oscar Wilde* (New York: Vintage, 1987), 160.

19. Michel Foucault, *The History of Sexuality*, vol. 1, *An Introduction*, trans. Robert Hurley (New York: Vintage, 1990), 68.

20. As such, the eighteenth century shares much with the system of gender described by Chauncey in *Gay New York*, 47–63.

21. "A Well-Wisher to Great-Britain," *The Ten Plagues of England, Of Worse Consequence Than Those of Egypt* (London: R. Withy, 1757), 10–14.

22. Susan C. Shapiro, " 'Yon Plumed Dandebrat': Male 'Effeminacy' in English Satire and Criticism," *Review of English Studies* 39 (1988): 400–12 (401).

23. Foucault, *History of Sexuality* 1:43.

24. For more information about the scenes that he describes, see Craig Patterson, "The Rage of Caliban: Eighteenth-Century Molly Houses and the Twentieth-Century Search for Sexual Identity," *Illicit Sex: Identity Politics in Early Modern Culture* (Athens: University of Georgia Press, 1997), 256–69.

25. Foucault, *History of Sexuality* 1:43.

26. See Randolph Trumbach, "The Birth of the Queen: Sodomy and the Emergence of Gender Equality in Modern Culture, 1660–1750," in Martin Duberman,

Martha Vicinus, and George Chauncey, Jr., eds., *Hidden from History: Reclaiming the Gay and Lesbian Past* (New York: New American Library, 1989), 129–40.

27. Randolph Trumbach, "London's Sapphists: From Three Sexes to Four Genders in the Making of Modern Culture," in Julia Epstein and Kristina Straub, eds., *Body Guards: The Cultural Politics of Gender Ambiguity* (New York: Routledge, 1991), 112–41.

28. Eve Kosofsky Sedgwick, *Epistemology of the Closet* (Berkeley: University of California Press, 1990), 44, 46, 47.

29. Patterson, "The Rage of Caliban," 257.

1. THE DANGER ZONE: EFFEMINATES, GENIUSES, AND HOMOSEXUALS

1. On developments in eighteenth-century masculinity, see Lawrence Stone, *The Family, Sex, and Marriage in England, 1500–1800*, abr. ed. (New York: Harper and Row, 1979), 217–99; John R. Gillis, "Bringing Up Father: British Paternal Identities, 1700 to the Present," *Masculinities* 3 (1995): 1–27; and Tim Hitchcock, "Redefining Sex in Eighteenth-Century England," *History Workshop Journal* 41 (1996): 73–90.

2. For a thorough discussion, see Christine Battersby, *Gender and Genius: Towards a Feminist Aesthetics* (Bloomington: Indiana University Press, 1989), 71–102.

3. The inspiration for separating the categories of sexuality and gender has come largely from Gayle S. Rubin's "Thinking Sex: Notes for a Radical Theory of the Politics of Sexuality," in Henry Abelove, Michèle Aina Barale, and David M. Halperin, eds., *The Lesbian and Gay Studies Reader* (New York: Routledge, 1993), 3–44. The best discussion of the impossibility of separating them when analyzing earlier historical periods appears in George Chauncey, *Gay New York: Gender, Urban Culture, and the Making of the Gay Male World, 1890–1940* (New York: Basic Books, 1994), 12–23.

4. Fielding, *Amelia* (1751), ed. Martin C. Battestin (Middletown, Conn.: Wesleyan University Press, 1983), 33; Fielding, "The Female Husband" (1746) in Lillian Faderman, ed., *Chloe Plus Olivia: An Anthology of Lesbian Literature from the Seventeenth Century to the Present* (New York: Viking, 1994), 143–57 (156).

5. For a useful attempt to chart these changes, see Michael McKeon, "Historicizing Patriarchy: The Emergence of Gender Difference in England, 1660–1760," *Eighteenth-Century Studies* 28 (1995): 295–322.

6. On the gender role of the rake, see Randolph Trumbach, "Sodomy Transformed: Aristocratic Libertinage, Public Reputation, and the Gender Revolution of the 18th Century," *Journal of Homosexuality* 19 (1990): 105–24.

7. See Emma Donoghue, *Passions Between Women: British Lesbian Culture, 1668–1801* (London: Scarlet Press, 1993), 202–206.

8. J. G. A. Pocock, *Virtue, Commerce, and History: Essays on Political Thought and History, Chiefly in the Eighteenth Century* (Cambridge: Cambridge University Press, 1985), 48; see also Catherine Gallagher, *Nobody's Story: The Vanishing Acts of*

Women Writers in the Marketplace, 1670–1820 (Berkeley: University of California Press, 1994), 107–10.

9. For an excellent discussion of the influence of this model on early eighteenth-century thought, see Carolyn D. Williams, *Pope, Homer, and Manliness: Some Aspects of Eighteenth-Century Classical Learning* (London: Routledge, 1993), 9–53.

10. Pope, "An Epistle from Mr. Pope, to Dr. Arbuthnot" (1735), ll. 400–401, *The Poems of Alexander Pope*, ed. John Butt (New Haven: Yale University Press, 1963), 611.

11. Pope, "Epistle to a Lady" (1735), l. 272 (*Poems*, 569).

12. Samuel Johnson, *Rambler* 191 (1752), *Selected Poetry and Prose*, ed. Frank Brady and W. K. Wimsatt (Berkeley: University of California Press, 1977), 222.

13. It is worth noting that the conservatism of writers like Johnson and Pope was never consistent or monolithic. In both cases, their lives offer interesting and telling contrasts with the heterocentrism of their most notorious works or comments.

14. Susan C. Shapiro, " 'Yon Plumed Dandebrat': Male 'Effeminacy' in English Satire and Criticism," *Review of English Studies* 39 (1988): 400–12 (400–401).

15. The best discussion of classical effeminacy is Michel Foucault, *The History of Sexuality*, vol. 2, *The Use of Pleasure*, trans. Robert Hurley (New York: Vintage, 1990), 78–93. I have also relied heavily on Williams, *Pope, Homer, and Manliness*, 111–15, and Linda Dowling, *Hellenism and Homosexuality in Victorian Oxford* (Ithaca, N.Y.: Cornell University Press, 1994), 1–31.

16. Thorold, "Agis" in *Plutarch's Lives Translated from the Greek by Several Hands*, 5 vols. (London: Jacob Tonson, 1685), 4:541.

17. Charles Wesley, *A Sermon Preached on Sunday, April 4, 1742*, 19th ed. (Wilmington, Del.: James Adams, 1770), 11.

18. Matthew Henry, *An Exposition of the Several Epistles Contained in the New Testament* (London: John Clarke, 1721), 94; E. Harwood, *A Liberal Translation of the New Testament*, 2 vols. (London: T. Becket, 1768), 2:53; John Guyse, *A Practical Exposition of the Acts of the Apostles, the Epistle to the Romans, and the First and Second Epistles to the Corinthians*, 2d ed. (London: Edward Dilly, 1761), 584.

19. Jonson, *Volpone* (1607), IV.i.48, in *Three Comedies*, ed. Michael Jamieson (Harmondsworth, Middlesex: Penguin, 1966), 127.

20. On this development, see Randolph Trumbach, "Gender and the Homosexual Role in Modern Western Culture: The 18th and 19th Centuries Compared," *Homosexuality, Which Homosexuality?* (London: GMP, 1989), 149–69.

21. Joseph Spence, *Observations, Anecdotes, and Characters*, ed. James Osborn, 2 vols. (Oxford: Clarendon Press, 1966), 1:80.

22. Cleland, *Fanny Hill, or Memoirs of a Woman of Pleasure* (1749), ed. Peter Wagner (Harmondsworth, Middlesex: Penguin, 1985), 196.

23. [Henry Carey], *Faustina; Or, the Roman Songstress, A Satyr on the Luxury and Effeminacy of the Age* (London: J. Roberts, 1726), 5; for discussion, see Cameron McFarlane, *The Sodomite in Fiction and Satire, 1660–1750* (New York: Columbia University Press, 1997), 31–33. See also Charles Churchill, "The Times" (1764) in *Poems*

of Charles Churchill, ed. James Laver (New York: Barnes and Noble, 1970), 404–27, and discussion in Jon Thomas Rowland, *"Swords in Myrtle Dress'd": Toward a Rhetoric of Sodom* (Madison, N.J.: Fairleigh Dickinson University Press, 1998), 183–95.

24. Alan Sinfield, *The Wilde Century: Effeminacy, Oscar Wilde, and the Queer Movement* (New York: Columbia University Press, 1994), 27.

25. Gallagher, *Nobody's Story*, 107.

26. See Pocock, *Virtue, Commerce, and History*, 114.

27. Gallagher, *Nobody's Story*, 108.

28. Ellen Messer-Davidow, " 'For Softness She': Gender Ideology and Aesthetics in Eighteenth-Century England," in Frederick M. Keener and Susan E. Lorsch, eds., *Eighteenth-Century Women and the Arts* (New York: Greenwood, 1988), 45–55 (45–46).

29. Addison, *Selections from "The Tatler" and "The Spectator" of Steele and Addison*, ed. Angus Ross (Harmondsworth: Penguin, 1982), 251.

30. On this aspect of the civil humanist model, see Linda Colley, *Britons: Forging the Nation, 1707–1837* (New Haven: Yale University Press, 1992), 273–81.

31. Lovibond, "On Men Being Deprived, From Custom and Delicacy, of Enjoying Social Friendship with the Fair-Sex," *The Works of the British Poets*, ed. Thomas Park, 42 vols. (London: J. Sharpe, 1808), 33:65–66.

32. For an excellent treatment of the relevance of this femininity to art history, see Chloe Chard, "Effeminacy, Pleasure, and the Classical Body," in Gill Perry and Michael Rossington, eds., *Femininity and Masculinity in Eighteenth-Century Art and Culture* (Manchester: Manchester University Press, 1994), 142–61.

33. The literature on the man of feeling is substantial. For one of the best treatments, see Patricia Meyer Spacks, *Desire and Truth: Functions of Plot in Eighteenth-Century English Novels* (Chicago: University of Chicago Press, 1990), 114–46; see also Janet Todd, *Sensibility: An Introduction* (London: Methuen, 1986); G. J. Barker-Benfield, *The Culture of Sensibility: Sex and Society in Eighteenth-Century Britain* (Chicago: University of Chicago Press, 1992); John Mullan, "Sentimental Novels," in John Richetti, ed., *The Cambridge Companion to the Eighteenth-Century Novel* (Cambridge: Cambridge University Press, 1996), 236–54; and Markman Ellis, *The Politics of Sensibility: Race, Gender, and Commerce in the Sentimental Novel* (Cambridge: Cambridge University Press, 1996).

34. Sterne, *A Sentimental Journey Through France and Italy* (1768), ed. Graham Petrie (Harmondsworth: Penguin, 1967), 45.

35. McKeon, "Historicizing Patriarchy," 314; Claudia L. Johnson, *Equivocal Beings: Politics, Gender, and Sentimentality in the 1790s* (Chicago: University of Chicago Press, 1995), 14.

36. *Hermsprong* (1792), quoted in Spacks, *Desire and Truth*, 184.

37. See Eve Kosofsky Sedgwick, *Between Men: English Literature and Male Homosocial Desire* (New York: Columbia University Press, 1985), 67–82.

38. George E. Haggerty, "*O lachrymarum fons*: Tears, Poetry, and Desire in Gray," *Eighteenth-Century Studies* 30 (1996): 81–95; 83.

39. On Juvenal in the eighteenth century, see Donoghue, *Passions Between Women*, 212–14, and Felicity Nussbaum, *The Brink of All We Hate: English Satires on Women, 1660–1750* (Lexington: University of Kentucky Press, 1984), 77–93.

40. For a discussion of this trend in lesbian history, see Judith C. Brown, "Lesbian Sexuality in Medieval and Early Modern Europe," in Martin Duberman, Martha Vicinus, and George Chauncey, Jr., eds., *Hidden from History: Reclaiming the Gay and Lesbian Past* (New York: New American Library, 1989), 67–75.

41. For Cleland and King, see Ian McCormick, ed., *Secret Sexualities: A Sourcebook of Seventeenth- and Eighteenth-Century Writing* (New York: Routledge, 1997), 223, 207–209.

42. James Fordyce, *Sermons to Young Women*, 2 vols., 7th ed. (London: Cadell and Dodsley, 1771), 1:104.

43. On this theatrical trend, see Kristina Straub, *Sexual Suspects: Eighteenth-Century Players and Sexual Ideology* (Princeton: Princeton University Press, 1992), 127–50.

44. William Blake, *The Marriage of Heaven and Hell* (1790) in *The Complete Poetry and Prose of William Blake*, ed. David V. Erdman, rev. ed. (Garden City, N.Y.: Anchor / Doubleday, 1982), 36.

45. See Donoghue, *Passions Between Women*, 25–58.

46. For the best account of conduct books and the eighteenth-century novel, see Nancy Armstrong, *Desire and Domestic Fiction: A Political History of the Novel* (Oxford: Oxford University Press, 1987), 59–95.

47. Spacks, *Desire and Truth*, 175–202; see also Jane Spencer, *The Rise of the Woman Novelist: From Aphra Behn to Jane Austen* (Oxford: Basil Blackwell, 1986), and Janet Todd, *The Sign of Angellica: Women, Writing, and Fiction, 1660–1800* (New York: Columbia University Press, 1989).

48. Radcliffe, *The Italian; Or, the Confessional of the Black Penitents* (1797), ed. Frederick Garber (Oxford: Oxford University Press, 1968), 91. Aikin is quoted in Lucy Aikin, *Memoir of John Aikin, M.D.* (Philadelphia: Abraham Small, 1824), 319.

49. See Claudia L. Johnson, *Equivocal Beings*.

50. See Polly Morris, "Sodomy and Male Honor: The Case of Somerset, 1740–1850," 383–406, and Randolph Trumbach, "Sodomitical Assaults, Gender Role, and Sexual Development in Eighteenth-Century London," 407–29, in Kent Gerard and Gert Hekma, eds., *The Pursuit of Sodomy: Male Homosexuality in Renaissance and Enlightenment Europe* (New York: Haworth, 1989).

51. Trumbach, "London's Sapphists: From Three Sexes to Four Genders in the Making of Modern Culture," in Julia Epstein and Kristina Straub, eds., *Body Guards: The Cultural Politics of Gender Ambiguity* (New York: Routledge, 1991), 112–41; Lisa L. Moore, *Dangerous Intimacies: Toward a Sapphic History of the British Novel* (Durham, N.C.: Duke University Press, 1997).

52. Coleridge quoted in H. J. Jackson, "Coleridge's Women, or Girls, Girls, Girls, Are Made to Love," *Studies in Romanticism* 32 (1993): 577–600 (594); see also Jean Watson, "Coleridge's Androgynous Ideal," *Prose Studies* 6 (1983): 36–56.

53. The literature on the history of genius is large. Some works that I have found useful include Battersby, *Gender and Genius*; Paul Kaufman, "Heralds of Original Genius," *Essays in Memory of Barrett Wendell* (Cambridge: Harvard University Press, 1926), 191–217; Herbert Dieckmann, "Diderot's Conception of Genius," *Journal of the History of Ideas* 2 (1941): 151–82; James Engell, *The Creative Imagination: Enlightenment to Romanticism* (Cambridge: Harvard University Press, 1981), 78–90; Ken Frieden, *Genius and Monologue* (Ithaca, N.Y.: Cornell University Press, 1985), 66–83; Jonathan Bate, "Shakespeare and Original Genius," 76–97, and Drummond Bone, "The Emptiness of Genius: Aspects of Romanticism," 113–27, in Penelope Murray, ed., *Genius: The History of an Idea* (Oxford: Basil Blackwell, 1989); David Bromwich, "Reflections on the Word *Genius*," *A Choice of Inheritance: Self and Community from Edmund Burke to Robert Frost* (Cambridge: Harvard University Press, 1989), 20–42.

54. Margaret Lee Wiley, "Genius: A Problem in Definition," *Studies in English* (Texas) 16 (1936): 77–83 (81).

55. [Anon.], "Character of Lord Bolingbroke," *Gentleman's Magazine* 23 (1753): 330–31 (331); Edward Young, "Conjectures on Original Composition" (1759), in Geoffrey Tillotson, Paul Fussell, Jr., and Marshall Waingrow, eds., *Eighteenth-Century English Literature* (New York: Harcourt Brace Jovanovich, 1969), 871–89 (876); William Duff, *An Essay on Original Genius* (1767) (New York: Garland, 1970), 85; Alexander Gerard, *An Essay on Genius* (1774) (New York: Garland, 1970), 17; William Jackson, "Whether Genius be born, or acquired," in *The Four Ages; Together with Essays on Various Subjects* (London: Cadell and Davies, 1798), 185–98 (196); William Wordsworth, "Essay, Supplementary to the Preface [of 1815]," in David Bromwich, ed., *Romantic Critical Essays* (Cambridge: Cambridge University Press, 1987), 29–51 (48).

56. Weinsheimer, "Conjectures on Unoriginal Composition," *The Eighteenth Century: Theory and Interpretation* 22 (1981): 58–73 (67).

57. Woodmansee, *The Author, Art, and the Market: Rereading the History of Aesthetics* (New York: Columbia University Press, 1994), 35–56; Gallagher, *Nobody's Story*, 145–202; Hiffernan, *Dramatic Genius* (London, 1770), 90.

58. [Anon.], *The Cabinet of Genius Containing Frontispieces and Characters Adapted to the Most Popular Poems &c. with the Poems &c. at Large* (London: C. Taylor, 1787); Tomkins, ed., *Rays of Genius Collected to Enlighten the Rising Generation*, 2 vols. (London: Longman, Hurst, Rees, and Orme, 1806), 1:10.

59. Cafarelli, *Prose in the Age of Poets: Romanticism and Biographical Narrative from Johnson to De Quincey* (Philadelphia: University of Pennsylvania Press, 1990), 58.

60. Jackson, *The Four Ages*, 216.

61. Hurd, *Letters on Chivalry and Romance* (1762) (New York: Garland, 1971), 4; Percy, *Reliques of Ancient English Poetry*, 3 vols. (London: Dodsley, 1765), 1:vii. On Percy's influence, see Kathryn Sutherland, "The Native Poet: The Influence of Percy's Minstrel from Beattie to Wordsworth," *Review of English Studies* 33 (1982): 414–33.

62. Duff, *Essay on Original Genius*, 186–87.

63. See Samuel Holt Monk, *The Sublime: A Study of Critical Theories in Eighteenth-Century England* (1935; rpt., Ann Arbor: University of Michigan Press, 1960), 101–33.

64. John Pinkerton, *Letters of Literature* (1785) (New York: Garland, 1970), 207–208.

65. Duff, *Essay on Original Genius*, 162.

66. Elizabeth Montague, *An Essay on the Writings and Genius of Shakespear* (1769) (New York: Augustus M. Kelley, 1970), 11.

67. For a sample, see Robert Lloyd, *The Triumph of Genius, A Dream: Sacred to the Memory of the Late Mr. Charles Churchill* (London: T. Jones, 1764); Courtney Melmoth (pseud. of Samuel Jackson Pratt), *The Tears of Genius, Occasioned by the Death of Dr. Goldsmith* (London: T. Becket, 1774); "Ode to Genius" in Francis Webb, *Poems* (Salisbury: E. Easton, 1790); George-Monck Berkeley, "Ode to Genius," *Gentleman's Magazine* 67 (1797): 405; Charles Symmons, "Genius: An Ode," *Gentleman's Magazine* 71 (1801): 644–45.

68. Combe, *The R[oya]l Register*, 9 vols. (London: J. Bew, 1784), 7:111; Burke, *A Philosophical Enquiry into the Origin of our Ideas of the Sublime and Beautiful* (2d ed., 1759), ed. James T. Boulton (Notre Dame: University of Notre Dame Press, 1958), 81.

69. For a paradigmatic analysis, see Anne K. Mellor, *Romanticism and Gender* (New York: Routledge, 1993), 85–87.

70. See Chard, "Effeminacy, Pleasure, and the Classical Body," 150.

71. Burke, *A Philosophical Enquiry*, 64, 69 (Burke's quotation from Lucretius is not exact), and 172.

72. Duff, *Essay on Original Genius*, 171.

73. Young, "Conjectures," 880; future page references to this work are cited in the text.

74. For a discussion of the androgyny of sublimity, see Warren Stevenson, *Romanticism and the Androgynous Sublime* (Madison, N.J.: Fairleigh Dickinson University Press, 1996).

75. D'Israeli, *An Essay on the Manners and Genius of the Literary Character* (1795) (New York: Garland, 1970), 106; Gerard, *Essay on Genius*, 356.

76. James Boswell, *Life of Johnson* (1791), ed. R. W. Chapman (Oxford: Oxford University Press, 1980), 1011.

77. For examples of genius as a female figure, see Courtney Melmoth, *The Tears of Genius*; Mary Julia Young, "Genius and Fancy; Or, Dramatic Sketches," in *Genius and Fancy* (London: H. D. Symonds, 1791); [Anon.], *What is Genius? A Poem* (London: Bowdery and Kerby, 1818).

78. Battersby, *Gender and Genius*, 72.

79. See Terry J. Castle, "Lab'ring Bards: Birth *Topoi* and English Poetics, 1660–1820," *Journal of English and Germanic Philology* 78 (1979): 193–208.

80. For other examples of this characterization, see [Anon.], "The Different Conduct of the Man of Genius, and the Man of Business accounted for," *Gentleman's Magazine* 12 (1742): 364–66; W. B. Sleath, "Letter to Mr. Urban," *Gentleman's Magazine* 77 (1807): 998.

81. D'Israeli, *Essay on the Manners and Genius of the Literary Character*, 52, 56, 57, 57–58.

82. Ibid., 127–28.

83. For more on this stereotype about genius, see "The Death of Genius: A Fable," *Gentleman's Magazine* 37 (1767): 271, and Everhard Ryan, *Reliques of Genius* (London: Edward and Charles Dilly, 1777), 6.

84. G. Gregory, *The Life of Thomas Chatterton, with Criticisms on his Genius and Writings* (London: G. Kearsley, 1789), 70.

85. Beattie, *The Minstrel; Or, the Progress of Genius. A Poem. The First Book*, 4th ed. (London: Edward and Charles Dilly, 1774), 27, 28.

86. For a good overview, see Roger Robinson, "The Progress of Genius?: James Beattie and *The Minstrel*," *Charles Lamb Bulletin* 86 (1994): 56–70.

87. Butler, "Satire and the Images of Self in the Romantic Period: The Long Tradition of Hazlitt's *Liber Amoris*," *Yearbook of English Studies* 14 (1984): 209–25 (213).

88. Wordsworth, *The Excursion* 1.57–58, 60–61 (*Poems*, 2 vols., ed. John O. Hayden [Harmondsworth: Penguin, 1977], 2.42). On Wordsworth and homoeroticism, see Wayne Koestenbaum, *Double Talk: The Erotics of Male Literary Collaboration* (New York: Routledge, 1989), 71–111; David Collings, *Wordsworthian Errancies: The Poetics of Cultural Dismemberment* (Baltimore: Johns Hopkins University Press, 1994); James Holt McGavran, "Defusing the Discharged Soldier: Wordsworth, Coleridge, and Homosexual Panic," *Papers on Language and Literature* 32 (1996): 147–65.

89. Colman, *The Genius* (pamphlet), June 11, 1761, 1, 2 (Bodleian fol. Θ 664 [14]); "A Genius" (James Bowell), *Observations Good or Bad, Stupid or Clever, Serious or Jocular, on Squire Foote's Dramatic Entertainment Intitled The Minor* (London: J. Wilke, 1761), 5–6.

90. Gilding, *The Breathings of Genius* (London: W. Faden, 1776), "Advertisement."

91. Colman, *The Genius*, 1.

92. Currie quoted in Nicholas Roe, "Authenticating Robert Burns," *Essays in Criticism* 46 (1996): 195–218 (203); see Roe throughout for the connection between Burns's sexuality and perceptions of his genius.

93. Gregory, *Life of Thomas Chatterton*, 1.

94. On the eighteenth-century interest in members of the working class as natural geniuses, see James M. Osborn, "Spence, Natural Genius, and Pope," *Philological Quarterly* 45 (1966): 123–44, and Annette Wheeler Cafarelli, "The Romantic 'Peasant' Poets and Their Patrons," *Wordsworth Circle* 26 (1995): 77–87.

95. Busby, *The Age of Genius!* (London: Harrison, 1786), 8, 41; for a similar satiric representation, see the letter from "No Genius" in the *Gentleman's Magazine* 69 (1799): 199–200.

96. See in particular two novels by Barbara Hofland, *The Son of a Genius* (London: J. Harris, 1812) and *The Daughter of a Genius* (London: J. Harris, 1823).

97. [Anon.], *On the Preference of Virtue to Genius* (London: Cadell, 1779), 9.

98. [Anon.], *A Few Well-Meant Observations Addressed to Young People of great genius in any art or science, (MUSICK in particular) who swallow praise too greadily: seeing that intoxication is not of drink alone* (London: E. Hodgson, 1790?).

99. Burney, *Camilla; Or, A Picture of Youth* (1796), ed. Edward A. Bloom and Lillian D. Bloom (London: Oxford University Press, 1972), 41; Edgeworth, *Belinda* (1801) (London: Pandora, 1986), 8; More, *Strictures on the Modern System of Female Education* (1799) in *The Complete Works of Hannah More*, 2 vols. (New York: Harper, 1841), 1:325 and note.

100. Downman, "On Genius" in *Infancy; Or, the Management of Children*, 6th ed. (Exeter: Trewman, 1803), 213–18.

101. Cawthorn, "The Birth and Education of Genius: A Tale," vol. 10 of *A Complete Edition of the Poets of Great Britain* (London: John and Arthur Arch; Edinburgh: Bell and Bradfute, and J. Mundell, 1794), 417; Purshouse, *An Essay on Genius* (London: Dodsley, 1782), 35.

102. Alan Richardson, *Literature, Education, and Romanticism: Reading as Social Practice, 1780–1832* (Cambridge: Cambridge University Press, 1994), 48.

103. Parsons, *Essays on Education* (London: Cadell, 1794), 218.

104. On Godwin's position, see James Malek, "Isaac D'Israeli, William Godwin, and the Eighteenth-Century Controversy Over Innate and Acquired Genius," *Rocky Mountain Review of Language and Literature* 34 (1980): 48–64.

105. For useful discussions of the literary marketplace at this date, see Brian Goldberg, "Romantic Professionalism in 1800: Robert Southey, Herbert Croft, and the Letters and Legacy of Thomas Chatterton," *ELH* 63 (1996): 681–706; Marilyn Butler, "Romanticism in England," in Roy Porter and Mikuláš Teich, eds., *Romanticism in National Context* (Cambridge: Cambridge University Press, 1988), 37–67; Cheryl Turner, *Living by the Pen: Women Writers in the Eighteenth Century* (London: Routledge, 1992).

2. WILLIAM BECKFORD AND THE GENIUS OF CONSUMPTION

1. [Anon.], *New Review* 9 (1786): 410–12 (410, 412).

2. [Anon.], *Augustan Review* 1 (1815): 843–48 (843); [Anon.], *Dublin Examiner* 1 (1816): 338–50 (350).

3. Reade quoted in Cyrus Redding, *Memoirs of William Beckford of Fonthill*, 2 vols. (London: Charles J. Skeet, 1859), 1:257.

4. Quotation from Robert Kiely, *The Romantic Novel in England* (Cambridge: Harvard University Press, 1972), 50.

5. "All the females in 'Vathek' were portraits of those in the domestic establishment of old Fonthill" (Beckford quoted by Cyrus Redding in "Recollections of the Author of 'Vathek,'" *New Monthly Magazine* 71 [1844]: 143–58 [150]).

6. See John W. Oliver, *The Life of William Beckford* (London: Oxford University Press, 1932), 277–78. For biographical information about Beckford throughout this chapter, I am primarily indebted to Oliver. I have also drawn on Guy Chapman,

Beckford (London: Jonathan Cape, 1937); Boyd Alexander, *England's Wealthiest Son: A Study of William Beckford* (London: Centaur Press, 1962); and Brian Fothergill, *Beckford of Fonthill* (London: Faber and Faber, 1979).

7. For paradigmatic biographical readings, see Fothergill, *Beckford of Fonthill,* 128–34, and Malcolm Jack, *William Beckford: An English Fidalgo* (New York: AMS, 1996), 19–21.

8. Haggerty, "Literature and Homosexuality in the Late Eighteenth Century: Walpole, Beckford, and Lewis," *Studies in the Novel* 18 (1986): 341–52 (348); Potkay, "Beckford's Heaven of Boys," *Raritan* 13 (1993): 73–86 (83); see also Rictor Norton, *Mother Clap's Molly House: The Gay Subculture in England, 1700–1830* (London: GMP, 1992), 222.

9. Weatherill, "The Meaning of Consumer Behaviour in Late Seventeenth- and Early Eighteenth-Century England," in John Brewer and Roy Porter, eds., *Consumption and the World of Goods* (London: Routledge, 1993), 206–27 (208).

10. Quoted in H. T. Dickinson, *Liberty and Property: Political Ideology in Eighteenth-Century Britain* (London: Wiedenfeld and Nicolson, 1977), 111. On civic humanism more generally, see J. G. A. Pocock, *Virtue, Commerce, and History: Essays on Political Thought and History, Chiefly in the Eighteenth Century* (Cambridge: Cambridge University Press, 1985).

11. Sheridan, *The Rivals* (1775), ed. Alan S. Downer (New York: Appleton-Century-Crofts, 1953), 3; Cowper, *The Task* (1785), in volume 2 of *The Poems of William Cowper,* ed. John D. Baird and Charles Ryskamp, 3 vols. (Oxford: Clarendon Press, 1980–1995), 4.534, 540, 545–46, 548–49; Johnson, *The Idler,* No. 40 (1759) in W. J. Bate, John M. Bullitt, L. F. Powell, eds., *The Idler and the Adventurer* (New Haven: Yale University Press, 1963), 126 (on advertising more generally, see Peter M. Briggs, " 'News from the Little World': A Critical Glance at Eighteenth-Century British Advertising," *Studies in Eighteenth-Century Culture* 23 [1994]: 29–45).

12. For a useful discussion, see Christopher J. Berry, *The Idea of Luxury: A Conceptual and Historical Investigation* (Cambridge: Cambridge University Press, 1994), esp. ch. 6.

13. Smith, *An Inquiry into the Nature and Causes of the Wealth of Nations* (1776) (New York: Knopf, 1991), 306; future references in the text are to this edition.

14. As James Raven has documented, Smith was not alone in trying to define what kinds of luxury were best for the nation. Numerous articles appeared in the London press from the 1750s to the 1780s that tried to distinguish "between innocent, beneficial luxury and a pernicious luxury of excess" (Raven, "Defending Conduct and Property: The London Press and the Luxury Debate," in John Brewer and Susan Staves, eds., *Early Modern Conceptions of Property* [London: Routledge, 1995], 301–19 [302]).

15. Zeynep Tenger and Paul Trolander, "Genius versus Capital: Eighteenth-Century Theories of Genius and Adam Smith's *Wealth of Nations,*" *Modern Language Quarterly* 55 (1994): 169–89 (171); I am indebted to this article throughout this paragraph.

16. Beckford, *Vathek* (1786), ed. Roger Lonsdale (Oxford: Oxford University Press, 1983), 25; future references in the text are to this edition.

17. Campbell, "Understanding Traditional and Modern Patterns of Consumption in Eighteenth-Century England: A Character-Action Approach," *Consumption and the World of Goods*, 40–57 (54).

18. Quotation from Pierre Bourdieu, *Distinction: A Social Critique of the Judgement of Taste*, ed. and trans. by Richard Nice (Cambridge: Harvard University Press, 1984), 414.

19. Albert Ten Eyck Gardner, "Beckford's Gothic Wests," *Metropolitan Museum of Art Bulletin* 13, no. 2 (October 1954): 41–49.

20. Oliver, *Life of William Beckford*, 3.

21. Combe, *The R[oya]l Register*, 9 vols. (London: J. Bew, 1784), 8:41.

22. Quotation from Boyd Alexander's typescript transcription of selections from Beckford's journal (Bod. MS. Eng. misc. d. 1289, p. 33).

23. Redding, "Recollections," 143.

24. Quotations from Lewis Melville (pseud. of Lewis Saul Benjamin), *The Life and Letters of William Beckford of Fonthill* (London: William Heinemann, 1910), 31–32.

25. Melville, *Life and Letters*, 96. On the man of feeling and childhood, see G. A. Starr, " 'Only a Boy': Notes on Sentimental Novels," *Genre* 10 (1977): 501–28; Potkay, "Beckford's Heaven of Boys."

26. Haggerty, "Beckford's Paederasty," in Thomas DiPiero and Pat Gill, eds., *Illicit Sex: Identity Politics in Early Modern Culture* (Athens: University of Georgia Press, 1997), 123–42.

27. Oliver, *Life of William Beckford*, 31–32; Melville, *Life and Letters*, 65–66.

28. Melville, *Life and Letters*, 48.

29. Ibid., 42.

30. See Brown, *Ends of Empire: Women and Ideology in Early Eighteenth-Century English Literature* (Ithaca, N.Y.: Cornell University Press, 1993); Kowaleski-Wallace, *Consuming Subjects: Women, Shopping, and Business in the Eighteenth Century* (New York: Columbia University Press, 1997).

31. Altman, *The Homosexualization of America, The Americanization of the Homosexual* (New York: St. Martin's, 1982), esp. ch. 3, "Sex and the Triumph of Consumer Capitalism."

32. Carter quoted in Alexander, *England's Wealthiest Son*, 110–11.

33. Oliver, *Life of William Beckford*, 54–55.

34. Melville, *Life and Letters*, 96.

35. For articles about aspects of Beckford's collections, see Francis J. B. Watson, "Beckford, Mme. de Pompadour, the Duc de Bouillon and the Taste for Japanese Lacquer in Eighteenth-Century France," *Gazette des Beaux-Arts* 6, no. 61 (1963): 101–27, and A. R. A. Hobson, "William Beckford's Binders," *Festschrift Ernst Kyriss* (Stuttgart: Max Hettler Verlag, 1961), 375–81.

36. From "Fonthill Foreshadowed," the name given by Boyd Alexander to his

typescript of Beckford's manuscripts, which he dates in the late 1770s (Bod. MS. Eng. misc. d. 1289, p. 112).

37. Stewart, *On Longing: Narratives of the Miniature, the Gigantic, the Souvenir, the Collection* (1984; rpt., Durham: Duke University Press, 1993), 151, 158; see also Bourdieu, *Distinction*, 281.

38. Quoted in Boyd Alexander, *Life at Fonthill, 1807–22, With Interludes in Paris and London* (London: R. Hart-Davis, 1957), 121.

39. Churchill, "The Times," *Poems of Charles Churchill*, ed. James Laver (New York: Barnes and Noble, 1970), 416.

40. Oliver, *Life of William Beckford*, 110, 111.

41. See Norton, *Mother Clap's Molly House*, 226–31.

42. Alexander, *England's Wealthiest Son*, 265; Chapman, *Beckford*, 83.

43. Alexander quoted from Bod. MS. Eng. misc. d. 1289, p. 84; this is a typescript of Beckford material that Alexander prepared for publication, although none of it was published.

44. William Duff, *An Essay on Original Genius* (1767) (New York: Garland, 1970), 162, 164, 168, 171.

45. Ibid., 162.

46. Redding, "Recollections," 152.

47. Cope, "Beckford and the Emerging Consciousness: Projective Collecting and the Aesthetic Dynamics of Acquisition," *Studies on Voltaire and the Eighteenth Century* 305 (1992): 1815–19 (1815).

48. Duff, *Essay on Original Genius*, 179, 187.

49. On the Eastern tale, see Martha Pike Conant, *The Oriental Tale in England in the Eighteenth Century* (1908; rpt., New York: Octagon, 1966); on its pornographic uses, see Peter Wagner, *Eros Revived: Erotica of the Enlightenment in England and America* (London: Secker and Warburg, 1988), 205–208.

50. Edward Young, "Conjectures on Original Composition" (1759), in Geoffrey Tillotson, Paul Fussell, Jr., and Marshall Waingrow, eds. *Eighteenth-Century English Literature* (New York: Harcourt Brace Jovanovich, 1969), 878–79.

51. George Eliot, *Daniel Deronda* (1876), ed. Barbara Hardy (Harmondsworth, Middlesex: Penguin, 1967), 646.

52. Oliver, *Life of William Beckford*, 129.

53. The definitive treatment of the circumstances surrounding the publication of *Vathek* appears in André Parreaux's *William Beckford: Auter de Vathek* (Paris: A. G. Nizet, 1960), 201–62; for a convenient summary, see Lonsdale's introduction to his edition of *Vathek*, xii–xviii.

54. Redding, "Recollections," 151. The *Episodes* were eventually translated and published in the early twentieth century (*The Episodes of "Vathek,"* trans. Frank T. Marzials [London: Stephen Swift, 1912]).

55. Liu, "Toward a Theory of Common Sense: Beckford's *Vathek* and Johnson's *Rasselas*," *Texas Studies in Literature and Language* 26 (1984): 183–217 (186).

56. For alternative views of the tale's female characters, see Colette Le Yaouanc,

"Le thème sexuel dans *Vathek*" in André Bordeaux, ed., *Linguistique, Civilisation, Littérature* (Paris: Didier, 1980), 257–64.

57. Liu, "Towards a Theory of Common Sense," 198.

58. Ibid., 187.

59. Irigaray, "When the Goods Get Together," trans. Claudia Reeder, in Elaine Marks and Isabelle de Courtivron, eds., *New French Feminisms: An Anthology* (Amherst: University of Massachusetts, 1980), 107–10 (107).

60. For another treatment of the relevance of Jamaica to *Vathek*, see P. H. Knox-Shaw, "The West Indian *Vathek*," *Essays in Criticism* 43 (1993): 284–307.

61. Borges, "About William Beckford's *Vathek*," *Other Inquisitions, 1937–1952*, trans. Ruth L. C. Simms (Austin: University of Texas Press, 1964), 137–40 (139).

62. Piozzi, *Thraliana: The Diary of Mrs. Hester Lynch Thrale*, ed. Katharine C. Balderston, 2 vols., 2d ed. (Oxford: Clarendon Press, 1951), 2:799.

63. Liu, "Towards a Theory of Common Sense," 196.

64. For critical discussion of the tone of Beckford's irony, see Frederick Garber, *Self, Text, and Romantic Irony: The Example of Byron* (Princeton: Princeton University Press, 1988), 70–79; Kenneth W. Graham, "Beckford's 'Vathek': A Study in Ironic Dissonance," *Criticism* 14 (1972): 243–52, and "Implications of the Grotesque: Beckford's *Vathek* and the Boundaries of Fictional Reality," *Tennessee Studies in Literature* 23 (1978): 61–74; Randall Craig, "*Vathek*: The Inversion of Romance," in Kenneth W. Graham, ed., *Vathek and the Escape from Time* (New York: AMS, 1990), 113–29.

65. [Anon.], Number 18 (Saturday, October 4, 1823) of *The Unique: A Series of Portraits of Eminent Persons* (London: George Smeeton; Limbird), 5.

66. "An Unpublished Episode of Vathek," *Weekly Entertainer; and West of England Miscellany* 9 (1824): 108–12 (112).

67. On the fate of aristocratic collections, see Linda Colley, *Britons: Forging the Nation, 1707–1837* (New Haven: Yale University Press, 1992), 174–77.

68. Redding, *Memoirs of William Beckford* 2:372.

69. Oliver, *Life of William Beckford*, 305.

70. Wilde, *The Picture of Dorian Gray* (1891), ed. Isobel Murray (Oxford: Oxford University Press, 1981), 120.

71. Ibid., 224.

3. THE DOMESTICATION OF GENIUS: COWPER AND THE RISE OF THE SUBURBAN MAN

1. On the rise of the suburbs, see Donald J. Olsen, *The Growth of Victorian London* (London: Batsford, 1976), 189–264; Walter L. Creese, "Imagination in the Suburb," in U. C. Knoepflmacher and G. B. Tennyson, eds., *Nature and the Victorian Imagination* (Berkeley: University of California Press, 1977), 49–67; Bruce Coleman, "The Idea of the Suburb: Suburbanization and Suburbanism in Victorian Britain," *London in Literature* (London: Roehampton Institute, 1979), 73–90; F. M. L. Thompson, ed., *The Rise of Suburbia* (Leicester: Leicester University Press, 1982),

1–26; Robert Fishman, *Bourgeois Utopias: The Rise and Fall of Suburbia* (New York: Basic Books, 1987), 39–72.

2.   Crompton, *Byron and Greek Love: Homophobia in Nineteenth-Century England* (Berkeley: University of California Press, 1985), 38.

3.   On the Labouchère amendment, see H. Montgomery Hyde, *The Love That Dared Not Speak Its Name: A Candid History of Homosexuality in Britain* (Boston: Little, Brown, 1970), 134–37; Ed Cohen, *Talk on the Wilde Side: Toward a Genealogy of a Discourse on Male Sexualities* (New York: Routledge, 1993), 491–93.

4.   Adam, "Structural Foundations of the Gay World," *Comparative Studies in Society and History* 27 (1985): 658–71 (663); Hocquenghem, *Homosexual Desire*, trans. Daniella Dangoor (1972; Durham, N.C.: Duke University Press, 1993), 93–112; Fernbach, "Toward a Marxist Theory of Gay Liberation," *Socialist Revolution* 6, no. 2 (1976): 29–41; D'Emilio, "Capitalism and Gay Identity" in *Making Trouble: Essays on Gay History, Politics, and the University* (New York: Routledge, 1992), 3–16.

5.   On masturbation, see Cohen, *Talk on the Wilde Side*, 35–68.

6.   *Times*, July 5, 1822, quoted in Crompton, *Byron and Greek Love*, 301.

7.   *Shelley's Prose*, ed. David Lee Clark (London: Fourth Estate, 1988), 222.

8.   *The Letters of Thomas Babington Macaulay*, ed. Thomas Pinney, 6 vols. (Cambridge: Cambridge University Press, 1974–81), 1:76; *The Diaries of William Charles Macready*, ed. William Toynbee, 2 vols. (London: Chapman and Hall, 1912), 1:243. On the rumors surrounding Byron's separation, see Crompton, *Byron and Greek Love*, 221–35, and Andrew Elfenbein, *Byron and the Victorians* (Cambridge: Cambridge University Press, 1995), 206–13.

9.   W. H. Thompson, *The Phaedrus of Plato* (1868; rpt., New York: Arno Press, 1973), 163*n*.

10.   Richardson, *Literary Leaves*, quoted in Peter Stallybrass, "Editing as Cultural Formation: The Sexing of Shakespeare's Sonnets," *MLQ* 54 (1993): 91–103 (101, 102); Henry Hallam, *Introduction to the Literature of Europe*, 3 vols. (1837–39; rpt., New York: Johnson, 1970), 2:504.

11.   Sedgwick, *Epistemology of the Closet* (Berkeley: University of California Press, 1990), 185, 186.

12.   The literature on nineteenth-century masculinity is substantial. Accounts that I have found particularly useful are David Newsome, *Godliness and Good Learning: Four Studies on a Victorian Ideal* (London: Cassell, 1961); Leonore Davidoff and Catherine Hall, *Family Fortunes: Men and Women of the English Middle Class, 1780–1850* (Chicago: University of Chicago Press, 1987), 229–71; Linda Colley, *Britons: Forging the Nation, 1707–1837* (New Haven: Yale University Press, 1992), 283–320; and James Eli Adams, *Dandies and Desert Saints: Styles of Victorian Manhood* (Ithaca, N.Y.: Cornell University Press, 1995), 1–20.

13.   For an appropriation of Bourdieu for the study of gender, see Toril Moi, "Appropriating Bourdieu: Feminist Theory and Pierre Bourdieu's Sociology of Culture," *New Literary History* 22 (1991): 1017–49; for Bourdieu and sexuality, see Elfenbein, *Byron and the Victorians*, 206–29.

14. Bourdieu, *Distinction: A Social Critique of the Judgement of Taste*, ed. and trans. by Richard Nice (Cambridge: Harvard University Press, 1984), 291, 414.

15. Hazlitt, *The Round Table* (1817) in *The Complete Works of William Hazlitt*, ed. P. P. Howe, 21 vols. (New York: AMS, 1967), 4:136; *Table Talk* (1822), 8:50.

16. Buzard, *The Beaten Track: European Tourism, Literature, and the Ways to "Culture,"* *1800–1918* (Oxford: Clarendon Press, 1993), 121–22; see more generally 80–154; Elfenbein, *Byron and the Victorians*, 58–74.

17. Bulwer, *England and the English* (1833), ed. Standish Meacham (Chicago: University of Chicago Press, 1970), 45; Smiles, from *Self-Help* (1859), quoted in *Culture and Society in Britain, 1850–1890*, ed. J. M. Golby (Oxford: Oxford University Press, 1986), 109; Mill, *On Liberty* (1859) (Indianapolis: Bobbs-Merrill, 1956), 76.

18. Bowdler, *Select Pieces in Verse and Prose*, 2 vols. (London: G. Davidson, 1816), 2:525.

19. Olsen, *Growth of Victorian London*, 221; Bulwer, *England and the English*, 23.

20. See H. J. Dyos, *Victorian Suburb: A Study of the Growth of Camberwell* (Leicester: Leicester University Press, 1961), 23.

21. John Archer, "Ideology and Aspiration: Individualism, the Middle Class, and the Genesis of the Anglo-American Suburb," *Journal of Urban History* 14 (1988): 214–53 (229).

22. Dickens, *Great Expectations* (1860–61), ed. Angus Calder (Harmondsworth, Middlesex: Penguin, 1965), 231.

23. Cohen, "The Double Lives of Man: Narration and Identification in Late Nineteenth-Century Representations of Ec-centric Masculinities," in Sally Ledger and Scott McCracken, eds., *Cultural Politics at the Fin de Siècle* (Cambridge: Cambridge University Press, 1995), 85–114.

24. *Don Leon* reprinted in Bernard Grebanier, *The Uninhibited Byron: An Account of His Sexual Confusion* (New York: Crown, 1970), 307–49 (308, 309).

25. Foucault, *The History of Sexuality*, vol. 1, *An Introduction*, trans. Robert Hurley (New York: Vintage, 1990), 43; Sedgwick, *Epistemology*, 44–48.

26. Cohen, *Talk on the Wilde Side*, 212.

27. Davidoff and Hall, *Family Fortunes*, 162–67.

28. For these terms, see Williams, *Marxism and Literature* (Oxford: Oxford University Press, 1977), 121–27.

29. For standard works on Cowper, see Patricia Meyer Spacks, *The Poetry of Vision: Five Eighteenth-Century Poets* (Cambridge: Harvard University Press, 1967), 178–94; Vincent Newey, *Cowper's Poetry: A Critical Study and Reassessment* (Totowa, N. J.: Barnes and Noble, 1982); Marvin Priestman, *Cowper's Task: Structure and Influence* (Cambridge: Cambridge University Press, 1983); Bill Hutchings, *The Poetry of William Cowper* (London: Croom Helm, 1983); Marshall Brown, *Preromanticism* (Stanford, Calif.: Stanford University Press, 1991), 58–81.

30. "Additional Particulars Relative to Mr. Cowper," *Monthly Magazine* 9 (1800): 498–500 (500); Jeffrey, "Hayley's *Life of Cowper*," *Edinburgh Review* 2 (1803): 64–86 (84).

31. "Cowper's Poems and Life," *Quarterly Review* 16 (1816): 117–29 (120); *Lives of Eminent and Illustrious Englishmen*, ed. George Godfrey Cunningham, 8 vols. (Glasgow: A. Fullarton, 1838), 6:327.

32. Fishman, *Bourgeois Utopias*, 51–62.

33. Melanie Louise Simo, *Loudon and the Landscape: From Country Seat to Metropolis, 1783–1843* (New Haven: Yale University Press, 1988), 41 (see also 28–29, 40, 197); Thomas B. Shaw, *A Complete Manual of English Literature*, ed. William Smith (New York: Sheldon, 1865), 359.

34. On bachelors as threats, see Sedgwick, *Epistemology*, 189–95.

35. On Cowper's use of this tradition, see Newey, *Cowper's Poetry*, 83–84; see also Dustin Griffin, "Redefining Georgic: Cowper's *Task*," *ELH* 57 (1990): 865–79.

36. Davidoff and Hall, *Family Fortunes*, 112.

37. All quotations from *The Task* are from volume 2 of *The Poems of William Cowper*, ed. John D. Baird and Charles Ryskamp, 3 vols. (Oxford: Clarendon Press, 1980–1995); refs. to book and line numbers.

38. On this tradition, see Linda H. Peterson, *Victorian Autobiography: The Tradition of Self-Interpretation* (New Haven: Yale University Press, 1986), 34–40.

39. For a discussion of secrecy in relation to Pater that has useful parallels with Cowper, see Adams, *Dandies and Desert Saints*, 194–205.

40. Foucault, *The Order of Things: An Archaeology of the Human Sciences* (New York: Random House, 1970), 251; Foucault, *The History of Sexuality* 1:59, 61.

41. Evidence of the popularity of Cowper's personality is abundant. In 1800 a Dr. Willowby published a sonnet to Cowper in which he noted, "At thy sad tale many a tear I've shed, / While down the vale I guide my pensive way" ("Sonnet to Mr. Cowper," *Gentleman's Magazine* 70 [1800]: 565). The Rev. Fellowes noted that *The Task* was so powerful a poem "as to overpower [him] with concern, and sympathy, and admiration" (quoted in *Letters of Anna Seward Written Between the Years 1784 and 1807*, 6 vols. [Edinburgh: A. Constable, 1811], 5:327). James Mackintosh "could not look at [Cowper's] writing without tears. So meek in his life!—so pure!—so tender!—so pious!—he surely never had his rival in virtue and misfortune" (Robert James Mackintosh, *Memoirs of the Life of the Right Honourable Sir James Mackintosh*, 2 vols., 2d ed. [London: Moxon, 1836], 1:148). Joseph Bringhurst was so concerned over reports of Cowper's illness that he wrote a letter to him explaining, "I admire thy poetical talents, but the efforts of thy mind in the cause of true virtue, have gained thee my love, and my veneration" (*Copy of a letter from a Young Man, A Quaker, in Pennsylvania, to the Late William Cowper, The Poet* [Chester: Brother and Son, 1800], 4–5). He added that in Philadelphia where he lived, there were "many amiable and some great minds, who love thee with true affection" (6).

42. For a complete discussion of this process, see my "Cowper's *Task* and the Anxieties of Femininity," *Eighteenth-Century Life* 13 (1989): 1–17.

43. Klancher, *The Making of English Reading Audiences, 1790–1832* (Madison: University of Wisconsin Press, 1987), 173.

44. On the importance of self-discipline to eighteenth-century understandings

of masculinity, see Carolyn D. Williams, *Pope, Homer, and Manliness: Some Aspects of Eighteenth-Century Classical Learning* (London: Routledge, 1993), 9–26.

45. Olsen, *Growth of Victorian London*, 214.

46. My understanding of the Evangelical movement and Cowper's relation to it is informed by Boyd Hilton, *The Age of Atonement: The Influence of Evangelicalism on Social and Economic Thought, 1795–1865* (Oxford: Clarendon Press, 1988), 3–35, and D. W. Bebbington, *Evangelicalism in Modern Britain: A History from the 1730s to the 1980s* (London: Unwin Hyman, 1989), 20–74.

47. Brydges, *The Autobiography, Times, Opinions, and Contemporaries of Sir Egerton Brydges, Bart.*, 2 vols. (London: Cochrane and M'Crane, 1834), 1:132.

48. Sedgwick, *Epistemology*, 3.

49. Patricia Meyer Spacks, *Desire and Truth: Functions of Plot in Eighteenth-Century English Novels* (Chicago: University of Chicago Press, 1990), 124.

50. See Claudia L. Johnson, *Equivocal Beings: Politics, Gender, and Sentimentality in the 1790s* (Chicago: University of Chicago Press, 1995), 1–22; Judith Frank, "'A Man Who Laughs is Never Dangerous': Character and Class in Sterne's *A Sentimental Journey*," *ELH* 56 (1989): 97–124.

51. "Review of Cowper's Poems," *Gentleman's Magazine* 55 (1785): 985–88 (987). By 1824, readers longed for a definitive source that would allow them to say, "Now, then, we shall probably be able to 'pluck out the heart of poor Cowper's mystery!'" ("Private Correspondence of Cowper," *New Monthly Magazine* 10 [1824]: 90–103 [92]). Readers were still wondering in 1854 when George Gilfillan asked, "Why did this man suffer thus? Why was he ever born to endure such wretchedness? What the *rationale* of his long martyrdom and darkness?" ("The Life of William Cowper" in *The Poetical Works of William Cowper* [Edinburgh: James Nichol, 1854], xxv). In 1874, M. Seeley likewise noted that "a mystery, a painful mystery, enveloped most part of poor Cowper's life and being" (*The Later Evangelical Fathers* [London: Seeley, Jackson, and Halliday, 1874], 82).

52. On the controversy, see Lodwick Hartley, "Cowper and the Evangelicals: Notes on Early Biographical Interpretations," *PMLA* 65 (1950): 719–31.

53. Linn, *The Powers of Genius, A Poem* (Philadelphia: Asbury Dickens, 1801), 36; William Hayley, *The Life and Posthumous Writings of William Cowper*, 3 vols. (London: John Johnson, 1803–1804), 1:206.

54. "Hayley's *Life and Posthumous Writings of William Cowper*, Vol. III," *Monthly Review* 44 (1804): 241–52 (241).

55. Hayley, *Life of Cowper* 2:222.

56. Bernard Barton, "Verses on Reading Hayley's Life of Cowper," *Metrical Effusions; Or, Verses on Various Occasions* (Woodbridge: S. Loder, 1812), 212–15 (214); R. R. Madden, *Infirmities of Genius Illustrated*, 2 vols. (London: Saunder and Otley, 1833), 2:1–104.

57. "Cowper's Poems and Life," *Quarterly Review*, 123; "The Rural Walks of Cowper," *Monthly Review* 100 (1823): 111–12 (111); Thomas Frognall Dibdin also noted that publishing the memoirs "could only lead to the debasement of that amiable creature, whom it was the bounden duty of the publisher to have kept ... free from all

NOTES TO PAGES 82–85

imputation" (*The Library Companion*, 2d ed. [London: Harding, Triphock, and Lepard, 1825], 547*n*).

58. Newey, *Cowper's Poetry*, 1–2.

59. For Blake and Cowper, see my "Cowper, Blake, and the Figure of the Invader," *The Friend* 1, no. 4 (1992): 10–19.

60. Hazlitt, *Lectures on the English Poets* (1818) in *Complete Works*, 5:91; Maurice, *The Friendship of Books and Other Lectures*, ed. Thomas Hughes, 2d ed. (London: Macmillan, 1874), 28.

61. Jeffrey, "Hayley's *Life of Cowper*," 80; Saintsbury, *Short History of English Literature* (New York: Macmillan, 1898), 590.

62. Madden, *Infirmities of Genius* 2:99; "Private Correspondence of William Cowper," *Somerset House Gazette* 1 (1824): 297–300 (298); "Cowper's Poems and Life," *Quarterly Review*, 120.

63. Samuel Holt Monk and Lawrence Lipking, in M. H. Abrams, ed., *The Norton Anthology of English Literature*, 6th ed., 2 vols. (New York: Norton, 1993), 1:2502.

64. "Private Correspondence of Cowper," *Quarterly Review* 30 (1823): 185–99 (185).

65. Dibdin, *The Library Companion*, 735*n*; John Wilson, "North's Specimens of the British Critics, No. VIII: Supplement to MacFlecnoe and the Dunciad," *Blackwood's* 58 (1845): 366–88 (388).

66. Maurice, *Friendship of Books*, 28.

67. *The Literary Remains of Henry Neele* (New York: Harper, 1829), 125; Thomas Babington Macaulay, *Critical and Historical Essays*, 2 vols. (London: Dent, 1967), 2:630; William Michael Rossetti, *Lives of Famous Poets* (London: E. Moxon, 1878), 186–87.

68. Thomas Campbell, *Specimens of British Poets*, 7 vols. (London: John Murray, 1819), 7:350; Macaulay, *Essays* 2:631.

69. *The Correspondence of Robert Southey with Caroline Bowles*, ed. Edward Dowden (London: Longmans, Green, 1881), 296.

70. *The Greville Memoirs, 1814–1860*, ed. Lytton Strachey and Roger Fulford, 8 vols. (London: Macmillan, 1938), 3:85.

71. Charles Ryskamp, *William Cowper of the Inner Temple, Esq.: A Study of His Life and Works to the Year 1768* (Cambridge: Cambridge University Press, 1959), 140.

72. Greville quoted in ibid., 139.

73. Dreger, "Doubtful Sex: The Fate of the Hermaphrodite in Victorian Medicine," *Victorian Studies* 38 (1995): 336–70.

74. *New Letters of Robert Southey*, ed. Kenneth Curry, 2 vols. (New York: Columbia University Press, 1965), 2:432.

75. Southey's letter printed in Ryskamp, *William Cowper*, 141; Southey, *Correspondence*, 300; see also Southey, *New Letters*, 433.

76. In Ben Jonson's *Volpone* (1607), when Lady Politic accuses her husband of consorting with "Your Sporus, your hermaphrodite" (IV.ii.48), the conjunction of the term with the name of a Roman catamite implies same-sex activity (*Three Comedies*, ed. Michael Jamieson [Harmondsworth, Middlesex: Penguin, 1966], 127). Yet in a pamphlet published in 1718, when Jonathan Wild asked if a group of "he-

whores" were "hermaphrodites," he was told, "No ye fool . . . they are sodomites"; the response implied that the two terms were not synonymous (*An Answer to a Late Insolent Libel*, quoted in Randolph Trumbach, "The Birth of the Queen: Sodomy and the Emergence of Gender Equality in Modern Culture, 1660–1750," in Martin Duberman, Martha Vicinus, and George Chauncey, Jr., eds., *Hidden from History: Reclaiming the Gay and Lesbian Past* [New York: New American Library, 1989], 129–40 [137]).

77. Crompton, *Byron and Greek Love*, 118–23, 196–235, 300–301.

78. On these cases, see Rictor Norton, *Mother Clap's Molly House: The Gay Subculture in England, 1700–1830* (London: GMP, 1992), 169–86, 226–31.

79. Southey, *Correspondence*, 346.

80. For the most complete account, see Ryskamp, *William Cowper*, 135–44; for a recent discussion of Cowper's possible homosexuality, see David Perkins, "Cowper's Hares," *Eighteenth-Century Life* 20 (1996): 57–69.

81. Sedgwick, *Epistemology*, 73.

82. On "character" in relation to nineteenth-century masculinity, see Stefan Collini, "The Idea of 'Character' in Victorian Political Thought," *Transactions of the Royal Historical Society* 35 (1985): 29–50, and J. W. Burrow, *Whigs and Liberals: Continuity and Change in English Political Thought* (Oxford: Clarendon Press, 1988), 77–100.

83. Carlyle, *Sartor Resartus* (1833–34), ed. Kerry McSweeney and Peter Sabor (Harmondsworth, Middlesex: Penguin, 1987), 115.

84. Hughes, *Tom Brown at Oxford* (1861) (New York: Macmillan, 1888), 543.

85. George Parker, *Views of Society and Manners in High and Low Life*, quoted in Norton, *Mother Clap's Molly House*, 185.

86. *The Yokel's Preceptor*, quoted in Hyde, *Love That Dared Not Speak Its Name*, 120.

87. *Punch*, quoted in Matthew Sturgis, *Passionate Attitudes: The English Decadence of the 1890s* (London: Macmillan, 1995), 226.

88. *Daily Telegraph*, April 6, 1895, quoted in Cohen, *Talk on the Wilde Side*, 172.

4. ANNE DAMER'S SAPPHIC POTENTIAL

1. Walpole quoted in Hugh Stokes, *The Devonshire House Circle* (London: H. Jenkins, 1917), 159; Walpole's manuscript notes to *A Description of the Villa of Horace Walpole* (Thomas Kirgate, 1774), at the Lewis-Walpole Library, Farmington, Connecticut.

2. Edward Jerningham, "The Shakespeare Gallery," in *Poems and Plays*, 4 vols., 9th ed. (London: Luke Hansard, 1806), 2:3–27 (2:23).

3. The best overall accounts of Damer's life, to which I am indebted here and in the following paragraphs, are Susan Benforado, "Anne Seymour Damer (1748–1828), Sculptor" (Ph.D. diss., University of New Mexico, 1986) and Percy Noble, *Anne Seymour Damer: A Woman of Art and Fashion, 1748–1828* (London: Kegan Paul, Trench, Trübner, 1908).

4. Randolph Trumbach, "London's Sapphists: From Three Sexes to Four

Genders in the Making of Modern Culture," in Julia Epstein and Kristina Straub, eds., *Body Guards: The Cultural Politics of Gender Ambiguity* (New York: Routledge, 1991), 112–41; revised version in Gilbert Herdt, ed., *Third Sex, Third Gender: Beyond Sexual Dimorphism in Culture and History* (New York: Zone, 1994), 111–36. For accounts of Damer stemming from Trumbach's work, see Rictor Norton, *Mother Clap's Molly House: The Gay Subculture in England, 1700–1830* (London: GMP, 1992), 234–35, and Emma Donoghue, *Passions Between Women: British Lesbian Culture, 1668–1801* (London: Scarlet Press, 1993), 145–48, 262–65.

5. Momigliano quoted by Carlo Ginzburg, "Checking the Evidence: The Judge and the Historian," in James Chandler, Arnold I. Davidson, and Harry Harootunian, eds., *Questions of Evidence: Proof, Practice, and Persuasion Across the Disciplines* (Chicago: University of Chicago Press, 1994), 290–303 (302).

6. For one of the best exchanges on this topic, see Lauren Berlant, "Evidences of Masturbation," and Eve Kosofsky Sedgwick, "Against Epistemology," in *Questions of Evidence*, 125–36.

7. Martha Vicinus, "Lesbian History: All Theory and No Facts or All Facts and No Theory?" *Radical History Review* 60 (1994): 57–75; 59, 58. For other discussions of lesbian historiography, see Sheila Jeffreys, "Does It Matter if They Did It?" in Lesbian History Group, ed., *Not a Passing Phase: Reclaiming Lesbians in History, 1840–1985* (New York: Women's Press, 1989), 19–28; Lisa Duggan, "The Discipline Problem: Queer Theory Meets Lesbian and Gay History," *GLQ* 2 (1995): 179–91; Donna Penn, "Queer: Theorizing Politics and History," *Radical History Review* 62 (1995): 24–42.

8. Vicinus, "Lesbian History," 58.

9. For more on eighteenth-century lesbians and lesbian representation in addition to Donoghue, Norton, and the Trumbach essay already cited, see Terry Castle, *The Apparitional Lesbian: Female Homosexuality and Modern Culture* (New York: Columbia University Press, 1993); Eve Kosofsky Sedgwick, "Privilege of Unknowing: Diderot's *The Nun*," *Tendencies* (Durham, N.C.: Duke University Press, 1993), 23–51; Martha Vicinus, " 'They Wonder to Which Sex I Belong': The Historical Roots of the Modern Lesbian Identity," in Henry Abelove, Michèle Aina Barale, and David M. Halperin, eds., *The Lesbian and Gay Studies Reader* (New York: Routledge, 1993), 432–52; Carolyn Woodward, " 'My Heart So Wrapt': Lesbian Disruptions in Eighteenth-Century Fiction," *Signs* 18 (1993): 838–65; Randolph Trumbach, "The Origin and Development of the Modern Lesbian Role in the Western Gender System: Northwestern Europe and the United States, 1750–1990," *Historical Reflexions / Réflections Historiques* 20 (1994): 287–320; A. D. Harvey, *Sex in Georgian England: Attitudes and Prejudices from the 1720s to the 1820s* (London: Duckworth, 1994); Claudia L. Johnson, *Equivocal Beings: Politics, Gender, and Sentimentality in the 1790s* (Chicago: University of Chicago Press, 1995); Lisa L. Moore, *Dangerous Intimacies: Toward a Sapphic History of the British Novel* (Durham, N.C.: Duke University Press, 1997).

10. Faderman, *Surpassing the Love of Men: Romantic Friendship and Love Between Women from the Renaissance to the Present* (New York: William Morrow, 1981).

11. Donoghue, *Passions Between Women*, 149–50.

12. Ibid., 11.

13. For material on Lister, see Castle, *Apparitional Lesbian*, 92–106; Anna Clark, "Anne Lister's Construction of Lesbian Identity," *Journal of the History of Sexuality* 7 (1996): 23–50.

14. On Conway, see Brian Fothergill, *The Strawberry Hill Set: Horace Walpole and His Circle* (London: Faber and Faber, 1983), 177–207.

15. On Damer in the 1770s, see Jonathan David Gross, *Byron's "Corbeau Blanc": The Life and Letters of Lady Melbourne* (Houston: Rice University Press, 1997), 20–22.

16. *The Letters and Journals of Lady Mary Coke*, 4 vols. (Bath: Kingsmead Reprints, 1970), 2:30, 4:128.

17. Quotation about plumes in Harlan W. Hamilton, *Doctor Syntax: A Silhouette of William Combe, Esq. (1742–1823)* (London: Chatto and Windus, 1969), 82.

18. Catherine Gallagher, *Nobody's Story: The Vanishing Acts of Women Writers in the Marketplace, 1670–1820* (Berkeley: University of California Press, 1994), 95.

19. "A New Ballad to the Tune of Fair Rosamund," quoted in ibid., 106–107.

20. Rachel Weil, "Sometimes a Scepter Is Only a Scepter: Pornography and Politics in Restoration England," in Lynn Hunt, ed., *The Invention of Pornography: Obscenity and the Origins of Modernity, 1500–1800* (New York: Zone, 1993), 125–53 (139).

21. William Combe, *The First of April; Or, The Triumphs of Folly* (London: J. Bew, 1777), 27–28.

22. For details, see Hamilton, *Doctor Syntax*, 60–64, 76–85, and Terry Castle, *Masquerade and Civilization: The Carnivalesque in Eighteenth-Century English Culture and Fiction* (Stanford, Calif.: Stanford University Press, 1986), 1–51.

23. Combe, *First of April*, 20.

24. Lady Harrington is identified in Hamilton; I thank Betty Rizzo for suggesting Sarah Horneck's identity. For details on Horneck's adultery, see *Trials for Adultery; Or, The History of Divorces*, 7 vols. (New York: Garland, 1985), 2:1–28; this facsimile reprint is the second case in this volume.

25. Ibid., 2:26–28.

26. James Perry, *Mimosa; Or, The Sensitive Plant, A Poem. Dedicated to Mr. Banks, and Addressed to Kitt Frederick, Dutchess of Queensberry, Elect* (London: W. Sandwich, 1779); subsequent page numbers are cited in the text.

27. For information on Damer and Du Barry, see *The Yale Edition of Horace Walpole's Correspondence*, ed. W. S. Lewis et al., 48 vols. (New Haven: Yale University Press, 1937–1983), 7:88, 184, 33:71.

28. [Anon.], *A Sapphick Epistle, from Jack Cavendish to the Honourable and Most Beautiful Mrs. D**** (London: M. Smith, 1778?).

29. On Cavendish, see the entry in the *Dictionary of National Biography*, ed. Leslie Stephen et al., 22 vols. (1885–1901; rpt., Oxford: Oxford University Press, 1921–22), 3:1262–64.

30. *Sapphick Epistle*, 5; subsequent page numbers are cited in the text.

31. "Review of *Sapphick Epistle*," *Monthly Review* 58 (March 1778): 235.

32. On the *Monthly Review*, see Frank Donoghue, *The Fame Machine: Book*

Reviewing and Eighteenth-Century Literary Careers (Stanford, Calif.: Stanford University Press, 1996), 16–55.

33. *The Life and Letters of Lady Sarah Lennox, 1745–1826*, ed. Countess of Ilchester and Lord Stavordale (London: John Murray, 1904), 286.

34. *Correspondence of Emily, Duchess of Leinster (1731–1814)*, ed. Brian Fitzgerald, 3 vols. (Dublin: Stationery Office, 1949–1957), 3:227; see also Gross, *Byron's "Corbeau Blanc,"* 71.

35. Howard, *Reading Gothic Fiction: A Bakhtinian Approach* (Oxford: Clarendon Press, 1994), 94–95.

36. See Stuart Curran, "Women Readers, Women Writers," in Curran, ed., *The Cambridge Companion to British Romanticism* (Cambridge: Cambridge University Press, 1993), 177–95; 184.

37. *The Berry Papers: Being the Correspondence Hitherto Unpublished of Mary and Agnes Berry (1763–1852)*, ed. Lewis Melville (pseud. of Lewis Saul Benjamin) (London: John Lane, 1914), 44–45.

38. Berry's letter quoted from extracts made by Anne Damer in four notebooks now in the Lewis-Walpole Library. The extracts are in chronological order in each notebook. This quotation appears on page 21 of the third one. Quotations from this material will be cited as *Damer Notebooks* with references to volume and page.

39. *Berry Papers*, 117.

40. Ibid., 59.

41. See Lewis Bettany, *Edward Jerningham and His Friends: A Series of Eighteenth-Century Letters* (London: Chatto and Windus, 1919), 185–86.

42. *Berry Papers*, 116.

43. *Damer Notebooks* 3:46–47.

44. Ibid., 3:82.

45. For more information about the Berry-Damer relationship, see *Extracts of the Journals and Correspondence of Miss Berry from the Year 1783 to 1852*, ed. Lady Theresa Lewis, 3 vols. (London: Longmans, Green, 1865); Noble, *Anne Seymour Damer*, 107–17; and volumes 11 and 12 of *The Yale Edition of Horace Walpole's Correspondence*.

46. *Berry Papers*, 113.

47. On Hosmer, see Dolly Sherwood, *Harriet Hosmer: American Sculptor, 1830–1908* (Columbia: University of Missouri Press, 1991).

48. *Berry Papers*, 40.

49. Ibid., 27.

50. For the information in this paragraph, I am indebted to the work of Benforado, "Anne Seymour Damer," which provides the most complete account available of Damer's work as an artist.

51. Noble, *Anne Seymour Damer*, 29–30.

52. See Suzanne Bloxam, *Walpole's Queen of Comedy: Elizabeth Farren, Countess of Derby* (Ashford, Kent: Suzanne Bloxam, 1988), 80–97.

53. For background on cross-dressing and eighteenth-century theater, see Kristina Straub, *Sexual Suspects: Eighteenth-Century Players and Sexual Ideology*

(Princeton: Princeton University Press, 1992), 127–50; Jill Campbell, *Natural Masques: Gender and Identity in Fielding's Play and Novels* (Stanford, Calif.: Stanford University Press, 1995), 19–60; Beth H. Friedman-Romell, "Breaking the Code: Toward a Reception Theory of Theatrical Cross-Dressing in Eighteenth-Century London," *Theatre Journal* 47 (1995): 459–79.

54. For a modern edition of Murphy, see *The Way to Keep Him and Five Other Plays*, ed. John Pike Emery (New York: New York University Press, 1956).

55. George Colman the Younger, *The Jealous Wife* (London: W. Lowndes, 1816), 77.

56. Mary Berry, *The Fashionable Friends*, 3d ed. (London: J. Ridgway, 1802), 82; subsequent page numbers are cited in the text.

57. Moore, *Dangerous Intimacies*, 8.

58. Other roles played by Damer included the Countess in her father's *False Appearances*, Donna Violante in Susanna Centlivre's *The Wonder*, and Lettice in Henry Fielding's *The Intriguing Chambermaid* (Noble, *Anne Seymour Damer*, 96–106, 166–73).

59. I have only seen the three-volume version of *Belmour*; my source for the existence of the two-volume version is Benforado, "Anne Seymour Damer," 302.

60. [Anon.], "Review of *Belmour*," *Monthly Review* ns, 38 (1802): 314.

61. Marilyn Butler, *Jane Austen and the War of Ideas* (Oxford: Clarendon Press, 1975); Gary Kelly, *The English Jacobin Novel, 1780–1805* (Oxford: Clarendon Press, 1976); Claudia L. Johnson, *Equivocal Beings*.

62. Quotation from "Della Crusca" (pseud. Robert Merry), *Diversity: A Poem* (London: J. Bell, 1788), 32; see also Erasmus Darwin, *The Botanic Garden: A Poem*, 2 vols., 4th ed. (London: J. Johnson, 1799), 1:81, and Edward Jerningham, "The Shakespeare Gallery," in *Poems and Plays*, 2:23–24.

63. "No. IX: The Honourable Anne Seymour Damer" in *The Annual Biography and Obituary* 13 (1829): 125–36; Samuel Mossman, *Gems of Womanhood; Or, Sketches of Distinguished Women in Various Ages and Nations* (Edinburgh: Gall, 1870), 123–34; Grace and Philip Wharton (pseud. A. T. and John Thomson), *Queens of Society* (New York: Harper, 1860), 383–401.

64. Allan Cunningham, *The Lives of the Most Eminent British Painters and Sculptors*, 5 vols. (New York: J. and J. Harper, 1831–1834), 3:214–36.

65. Ibid., 3:234.

66. Leslie Stephen, "Anne Seymour Damer," *Dictionary of National Biography*, 5:451.

67. Polwhele, *The Unsex'd Females* (London: Cadell and Davies, 1798), esp. 22–28.

68. *The Diary of Joseph Farington*, ed. Kenneth Garlick and Angus Macintyre, 16 vols. (New Haven: Yale University Press, 1978–1984), 3:1048.

69. [Anon.], "The Damerian Apollo" (London: William Holland, 1789).

70. For information on Holland and an image of his exhibition room, see Diana Donald, *The Age of Caricature: Satirical Prints in the Reign of George III* (New Haven: Yale University Press, 1996), 7–8.

71. Mary Robinson, *Modern Manners* (London: For the author, 1793), 18.

72. Cowley, *The Town Before You* (London: Longman, 1795), 17; subsequent page numbers are cited in the text. I am grateful to Margaret Doody for this reference.

73. *Memoir and Correspondence of Susan Ferrier, 1782–1854*, ed. John A. Doyle (London: John Murray, 1898), 103.

74. Susan Ferrier, *Marriage, A Novel* (1818), ed. Herbert Foltinek (London: Oxford University Press, 1971), 48; subsequent page numbers are cited in the text.

75. *Berry Papers*, 241.

76. *Damer Notebooks* 3:5, 15, 61.

77. Anne Seymour Damer, *Belmour, A Novel*, 3 vols. (London: J. Johnson, 1801), 2:279.

78. Ibid., 3:5.

79. For images of Damer's and Tresham's contributions, see Winifred H. Friedman, *Boydell's Shakespeare Gallery* (New York: Garland, 1976), plate 219 and plate 45; for discussion of Damer's contribution, see Benforado, "Anne Seymour Damer," 86–92.

80. For the tradition of lesbian censorship, see Castle, *Apparitional Lesbian*, 28–65.

81. *Berry Papers*, 93; subsequent page numbers are cited in the text.

82. [Charles Pigott], *The Whig Club; Or, A Sketch of the Manners of the Age* (London: For the author, 1794), 55; subsequent page numbers are cited in the text.

83. Identification of Sir William Mordaunt Milner from MS marginalia (hand unidentified) in Bodleian G. Pamph. 2676 (2).

84. Bloxam, *Walpole's Queen of Comedy*, 81.

85. On such rumors, see Emma Donoghue, *Passions Between Women*, 145–47.

86. Piozzi, *Thraliana: The Diary of Mrs. Hester Lynch Thrale*, ed. Katharine C. Balderston, 2 vols., 2d ed. (Oxford: Clarendon Press, 1951), 2:770.

87. Ibid., 2:949.

88. [Anon.], "Review of *Belmour*," 314.

89. Damer, *Belmour*, 1:152.

5. LESBIANISM AND ROMANTIC GENIUS: THE POETRY OF ANNE BANNERMAN

1. Christine Battersby, *Gender and Genius: Towards a Feminist Aesthetics* (Bloomington: Indiana University Press, 1989), 73.

2. Mary Robinson, "Ode to Genius," *The Poetical Works*, 3 vols. (1806; London: Routledge / Thoemmes, 1996), 1:91–96 (94).

3. Anna Seward, *The Poetical Works of Anna Seward*, ed. Walter Scott, 3 vols. (Edinburgh: John Ballantyne, 1810), 3:150.

4. John Milton, *Paradise Lost* (1674), 2.146–48, in *Complete Poems and Major Prose*, ed. Merritt Y. Hughes (Indianapolis: Bobbs-Merrill, 1957).

5. Ann Yearsley, "To Mr. ****, an unlettered Poet, on *Genius Unimproved*," *Poems on Various Subjects* (1787; Oxford: Woodstock, 1994), 77–82 (81).

6. Belsham, *Essays, Philosophical, Historical, and Literary* (1799), 2 vols. (New York: Garland, 1971), 2:459.

7. William Hayley, "Ode to the Countess de Genlis," *Poems and Plays*, 6 vols. (London: T. Cadell, 1788), 1:151–58 (157).

8. "Sappho and the Triumph of Female Genius" is Picture IV in Thomson's *Pictures of Poetry: Historical, Biographical, and Critical* (Edinburgh: Mundell; London: Longman and Rees, and J. Wright, 1799), 52–63 (63).

9. Piozzi, *Thraliana: The Diary of Mrs. Hester Lynch Thrale*, ed. Katharine C. Balderston, 2 vols., 2d ed. (Oxford: Clarendon Press, 1951), 2:730.

10. [Anon.], "Prologue" to Miss Cutherbertson's "Anna" (1793) (MS. Larpent Collection 969): on microprint card in Henry Willis Wells's edition of *Three Centuries of Drama* (New York: Readex Microprint, 1952–1954).

11. More, *Strictures on the Modern System of Female Education* (1799), in *The Complete Works of Hannah More*, 2 vols. (New York: Harper, 1841), 1:325 and note.

12. Polwhele, *The Unsex'd Females* (London: Cadell and Davis, 1798), 6.

13. Mary Poovey, *The Proper Lady and the Woman Writer: Ideology as Style in the Works of Mary Wollstonecraft, Mary Shelley, and Jane Austen* (Chicago: University of Chicago Press, 1984).

14. Mary Robinson, *Petrarch to Laura*, in *Poetical Works*, 1:5.

15. Wollstonecraft, *Mary: A Fiction*, in *"Mary" and "The Wrongs of Woman,"* ed. Gary Kelly (Oxford and New York: Oxford University Press, 1976), xxix.

16. Wollstonecraft, *Collected Letters of Mary Wollstonecraft*, ed. Ralph M. Wardle (Ithaca, N.Y.: Cornell University Press, 1979), 162.

17. Wollstonecraft, *Mary*, 26.

18. Claudia L. Johnson, *Equivocal Beings: Politics, Gender, and Sentimentality in the 1790s* (Chicago: University of Chicago Press, 1995), 57.

19. Godwin, *Memoirs of the Author of the "Rights of Woman,"* ed. Richard Holmes (Harmondsworth: Penguin, 1987), 210.

20. Bannerman, *Poems* (Edinburgh: Mundell, Doig, and Stevenson, 1807), 48; future references to page numbers in this edition will appear in the text.

21. Beattie, *Life and Letters of Thomas Campbell*, 3 vols. (London: Edward Moxon, 1849), 1:245.

22. The most detailed discussion of Anderson can be found in W. E. K. Anderson's "Introduction" to *The Correspondence of Thomas Percy and Robert Anderson*, ed. W. E. K. Anderson, vol. 9 of *The Percy Letters*, ed. David Nichol Smith, Cleanth Brooks, and A. F. Falconer, 9 vols. to present (New Haven: Yale University Press, 1944—), v–xvii.

23. See George Whalley's note on Anderson's edition in his edition of *Marginalia* (3 vols. to present), number 12 of *The Collected Works of Samuel Taylor Coleridge* (Princeton: Princeton University Press, 1980—), 1:37–38. Wordsworth later visited Anderson in Scotland; see *The Letters of William and Dorothy Wordsworth*, rev. ed., ed. Ernest de Selincourt, Chester L. Shaver, Mary Moorman, and Alan G. Hill, 8 vols. (Oxford: Clarendon Press, 1967–1993), 3:151–55, 193.

24. Although Johnson's *Lives of the Poets* was originally intended to cover authors from Chaucer to the eighteenth century, the booksellers decided on a starting date of 1660 when they realized the magnitude of such an undertaking (see Alvin Kernan, *Samuel Johnson and the Impact of Print* [Princeton: Princeton University Press, 1987], 264–82).

25. For information on Campbell and others in the Anderson circle, see Beattie, *Life and Letters* 1:234–69.

26. For the Rousseau translation, see *Edinburgh Magazine* 11 (1798): 63–64; for the sonnets, see *Edinburgh Magazine* 11 (1798): 141–42; these poems appear in the 1807 volume as "To the Nightingale" (28–31); "To the Owl" (98); and an untitled sonnet (101).

27. She had William Erskine write to Cadell and Davies to ask if they would consider her volume (Erskine to Cadell and Davies, June 25, 1799, National Library of Scotland [NLS] MS. 3112, ff. 204–205).

28. For reviews, see *British Critic* 16 (1800): 139–41; *Critical Review*, 2d ser., 31 (1801): 435–38; *Monthly Magazine* Suppl. 10 (1801): 610; *New Annual Register* 21 (1800): 327; *New London Review* 3 (1800): 407–10. For positive reviews from Anderson's friends, see the letter of Thomas Park to Anderson, March 20, 1800, ADV. MS. 22.3.11, f. 47; in Joseph Cooper Walker's letter to Anderson of September 1800, he notes that all his friends have admired the volume (ADV. MS. 22.4.15, f. 19). Joseph Martin's letter to Anderson, September 27, 1800 (ADV. MS. 22.4.12, f. 79) notes the appearance of extracts from Bannerman's "Verses on an Illumination for a Naval Victory" in the *Morning Chronicle*; "ADV. MS." refers to MS. in NLS.

29. Reprinted poems in the *Edinburgh Magazine* include "Verses on an Illumination for a Naval Victory," 15 (1800): 301–302; "Ode: The Spirit of the Air," 15 (1800): 378–79; "Sonnet: The Soldier," 15 (1800): 379; "Sonnet: To the Cypress," 15 (1800): 379–80; "Sonnet: From Ossian," 15 (1800): 381; all appear in the 1807 volume.

30. For Bannerman's contributions to the *Poetical Register*, see "Exile," 1 (1801): 12–13; "Sonnet: At the Sepulchre of Petrarch," 1 (1801): 142; "The Fall of Switzerland," 2 (1802): 56–57; "The Nereid," 2 (1802): 64–65; "Sonnet: Good Friday," 3 (1803): 166; "Sonnet: Easter," 3 (1803): 167; all are reprinted in the 1807 volume. For correspondence related to this publication, see Richard Davenport to Anderson (February 11, 1802, ADV. MS. 22.4.12, f. 32). Bannerman's translations of the "Chorus of Dryads" in Politiano's *Orfeo* and "The Car of Death" by Antonio Allamanni both appear in Joseph Cooper Walker's *An Historical and Critical Essay on the Revival of the Drama in Italy* (Edinburgh: Mundell; London: Longman, Hurst, Rees, and Orme, 1805), appendix, 26–28 and 30–31; Walker mentions her on ix and xvii. Both translations appear in the 1807 volume. Walker mentions Bannerman frequently in his correspondence with Anderson; in his posthumous *Memoirs of Alessandro Tassoni*, edited by his brother Samuel Walker (London: Longman, Hurst, Rees, Orme, and Brown, 1815), her presentation copies to him are noted (lxxiv).

31. On Bloomfield, see Annette Wheeler Cafarelli, "The Romantic 'Peasant' Poets and Their Patrons," *Wordsworth Circle* 26 (1995): 77–87.

32. For reviews, see *Annual Review* 1 (1802): 720–21; *British Critic* 21 (1803): 78–79; *Critical Review*, 2d ser., 38 (1803): 110–13; *Monthly Mirror* 15 (1803): 102–103; *New Annual Register* 23 (1802): 318; *Poetical Register* 2 (1802): 431–32.

33. See Anderson's letters to Percy in W. E. K. Anderson, ed., *Correspondence*, 140, 162–63.

34. For their efforts, see Thomas Park to Anderson, May 23, 1803 (ADV. MS. 22.4.10, f. 242); Joseph Cooper Walker to Anderson, December 24, 1803 (ADV. MS. 22.4.15, f. 73); William Preston to Anderson, July 4, 1804 (ADV. MS. 22.3.11, f. 68); Walker to Anderson, July 5, 1804 (ADV. MS. 22.4.15, f. 84); William Richardson to Anderson, September 12, 1804 (ADV. MS. 22.4.13, f. 256).

35. See Walker's letter to Anderson, December 2, 1804 (ADV. MS. 22.4.15, f. 96). Lady Charlotte Rawdon (1769–1834) was a patron of the arts and supported Thomas Moore's early career; he wrote a poem to her. She is also mentioned in the letters of Walter Scott (*The Letters of Sir Walter Scott*, ed. H. J. C. Grierson, 12 vols. [London: Constable, 1932–1937], 1:235*n*, 2:221 and note, 242, 323).

36. For the political background of the period, see Michael Fry's *Patronage and Principle: A Political History of Modern Scotland* (Aberdeen: Aberdeen University Press, 1987), 6–29, and David Masson, *Edinburgh Sketches and Memories* (London and Edinburgh: Adam and Charles Black, 1892), 141–203. Anderson and his circle were the Whig predecessors to the younger Whigs who would become famous through the *Edinburgh Review*.

37. See W. E. K. Anderson, ed., *Correspondence*, 237–38. When Bannerman published "The Dark Ladie" in the *Edinburgh Magazine*, it appeared with the initial "B." The following poems appeared in the *Edinburgh Magazine* above the same initial, but not in any of Bannerman's actual volumes; they may possibly be hers: "The Father's Farewell to his Son," 17 (1801): 50–51; "On a young Lady, who died in her eighteenth year, after a lingering illness," 17 (1801): 145; "Verses: On four young Ladies planting a tree to Friendship," 17 (1801): 386; "Verses on the Earl of Buchan's Birth-Day," 17 (1801): 466–67; "On a Visit to Roslin," 18 (1801): 221; "To the Genius of Britain," 22 (1803): 55; and "To the Memory of James Beattie, L.L.D., Author of 'The Minstrel,'" 22 (1803): 377–78; the two latter are signed "A.B." I am baffled by the *Epistle from the Marquis de Lafayette, to General Washington* (Edinburgh: Mundell; London: Longman and Rees, and J. Wright, 1800), which is attributed in some catalogues to Bannerman and in others to George Hamilton. I have found no references confirming her authorship in any published or unpublished sources.

38. W. E. K. Anderson, ed., *Correspondence*, 256–57; see also Walker's letter to Anderson, April 13, 1807 (ADV. MS. 22.4.15, f. 132).

39. For her possible return to Edinburgh, see Robert Forrester to Anderson, September 28, 1810 (ADV. MS. 22.4.11, f. 233); for her residence with Mr. Hope (possibly a relative of the Beresford family), see Thomas Park to Anderson, January 24, 1811 (ADV. MS. 22.4.10, f. 257).

40. Richard Davenport in his letter to Anderson, February 14, 1815 (ADV. MS. 22.4.12, f. 55).

41. For this incident, see Robert Anderson to James Morton, February 22, 1816 (NLS MS. 3381, ff. 56–57); Morton to Anderson, August 14, 1816 (ADV. MS. 22.4.13, f. 267); Robert Leyden to Anne Bannerman, March 7, 1818 (NLS MS. 3381, f. 114). Bannerman is not thanked in James Morton's memoir of Leyden prefixed to *The Poetical Remains of the Late Dr. John Leyden* (London: Longman, Hurst, Rees, Orme, and Brown; Edinburgh: Constable, 1819).

42. Grant, *Memoir and Correspondence of Mrs. Grant of Laggan*, ed. J. P. Grant, 3 vols. (London: Longman, Brown, Green, and Longmans, 1844), 3:67; see also 3:162.

43. "They Only May Be Said to Possess a Child For Ever Who Have Lost One in Infancy" appears attributed to Bannerman in *The Casket: A Miscellany, Consisting of Unpublished Poems* (London: John Murray, 1829), 349–50. "The Exile" appeared in *The Laurel: Fugitive Poetry of the XIXth Century* (London: John Sharpe, 1830), 290–91; it appears in the 1807 volume.

44. I thank Hamish Whyte, Senior Librarian of the Arts Department of Glasgow's Mitchell Library, for information on Irving's correspondence, which makes clear that he knew Bannerman well.

45. Smith, *The Letters of Sydney Smith*, ed. Nowell C. Smith, 2 vols. (Oxford: Clarendon Press, 1953), 1:105.

46. Walker to Anderson, May 15, 1800 (ADV. MS. 22.4.15, f. 15).

47. *Critical Review*, 2d ser., 31 (1801): 435.

48. Preston, "An Epistle to Robert Anderson, M. D. On Receiving from Him a Present of various Poetical Works," *Poetical Register* 5 (1805): 166–70 (168).

49. *British Critic* 16 (1800): 139; *Monthly Magazine* Suppl. 10 (1801): 610; *New London Review* 3 (1800): 408; *New Annual Register* 21 (1800): 327.

50. "Lines Occasioned by the Perusal of *Tales of Superstition and Chivalry* by Miss Bannerman," included in Preston to Anderson, April 9, 1803 (ADV. MS. 22.4.14, f. 82).

51. Brown, "On an Elegant Production of a Female Friend," *Poems*, 2 vols. (Edinburgh: Mundell; London: Longman and Rees, 1804), 1:108–11 (111).

52. Park to Anderson, February 15, 1806 (ADV. MS. 22.4.10, f. 243).

53. W. E. K. Anderson, ed., *Correspondence*, 170.

54. Park to Anderson, November 29, 1802 (ADV. MS. 22.4.10, ff. 232–33); the engraving is still extant in some copies of the *Tales* and appears opposite the beginning of "The Prophecy of Merlin."

55. Walker to Anderson, December 24, 1803 (ADV. MS. 22.4.15, f. 73).

56. W. E. K. Anderson, ed., *Correspondence*, 256.

57. For information on Stewart, see W. E. K. Anderson, ed., *Correspondence*, 106.

58. Bannerman cited her borrowing from Smith in her translation from Rousseau (*Poems* [1807], 216).

59. For an examination of sonnets during the period, see Stuart Curran, *Poetic Form and British Romanticism* (New York and Oxford: Oxford University Press, 1986), 29–55.

60. *The Poems of Charlotte Smith*, ed. Stuart Curran (New York and Oxford: Oxford University Press, 1993), 21.

61. Bannerman, *Poems* (Edinburgh: Mundell, 1800), 94; this sonnet, a translation of "Sento l'aura mia antica, é i dolci colli," does not appear in the 1807 volume.

62. For "sickly delicacy," see Wollstonecraft, *Vindication of the Rights of Woman*, ed. Miriam Brody (Harmondsworth: Penguin, 1986), 112, 220.

63. *New London Review* 3 (1800): 407, 410.

64. For reference, see *Critical Review*, 2d ser., 31 (1800): 438.

65. Bannerman interestingly never tried the drama, although she addressed one of her poems to the most famous female dramatist of her day, Joanna Baillie ("To Miss Baillie, on the Publication of Her First Volume of Plays on the Passions," 108–10). Bannerman describes Baillie as an inheritor of "Genius, bursting from the depth of night" (108).

66. The passage about the sisters was cut from the 1807 version; it appears in the 1800 volume, 49.

67. Bannerman, *Poems* (1800), 42.

68. De Genlis, "Cécile; Ou, Le Sacrifice de l'Amitié," *Théatre à l'Usage des Jeunes Personnes*, 4 vols. (Paris: M. Lambert and F. J. Baudouin, 1780), 2:78, 89.

69. Homans, *Women Writers and Poetic Identity: Dorothy Wordsworth, Emily Brontë, and Emily Dickinson* (Princeton: Princeton University Press, 1980), 12–40.

70. For Burke's discussion, see *A Philosophical Enquiry into the Origins of our Ideas of the Sublime and Beautiful* (2d ed., 1759), ed. James T. Boulton (Notre Dame: University of Notre Dame Press, 1958), 144–45; for the figure of the African mother in abolitionist poetry, see Moira Ferguson, *Subject to Others: British Women Writers and Colonial Slavery, 1670–1834* (New York: Routledge, 1992).

71. Robert H. O'Connor, "Matthew Gregory Lewis and the Gothic Ballad," *Lamar Journal of the Humanities* 18 (1992): 5–26 (12).

72. Preston to Anderson, April 9, 1803 (ADV. MS. 22.4.14, f. 82); Anna Seward to Bannerman, July 22, 1803 (ADV. MS. 22.4.10, f. 236); *Critical Review*, 2d ser, 38 (1803), 110–11. Bannerman never received Seward's letter because Thomas Park never delivered it. He copied it for Anderson at Anderson's request on the condition that the copy would then be destroyed. For Seward's other scathing comments on Bannerman, see *Letters of Anna Seward*, 6 vols. (Edinburgh: Constable, 1811), 5:323–26, 335–42.

73. Thomas Park guessed at other problems: the volume was anonymous and therefore could not capitalize on the success of the 1800 volume, and the publisher, encouraged by the success of Bloomfield's *The Farmer's Boy*, had made too many copies (Park to Anderson, May 23, 1803, ADV. MS. 22.4.10, f. 242).

74. For the standard account, see Albert B. Friedman, *The Ballad Revival: Studies in the Influence of Popular on Sophisticated Poetry* (Chicago: University of Chicago Press, 1961).

75. Jessie Stewart similarly praised Anderson because for him "Thro' the drear regions of monastic night, / Where SUPERSTITION form'd her potent spell, / Wild FANCY pauses in her dubious flight / And wakes the music of her votive shell" ("To

Robert Anderson" prefixed to her *Ode to Dr. Thomas Percy* [Edinburgh: Mundell; London: Longman and Rees, 1804]).

76. Virtually the only detailed discussions of the Gothic ballad are O'Connor, "Lewis and the Gothic Ballad," and John William Ruff, "A Study of Walter Scott's *Apology for Tales of Terror*," Ph.D. diss., Yale University, 1930, 1–66.

77. Sedgwick, *Epistemology of the Closet* (Berkeley: University of California Press, 1990), 186.

78. Brown, "To a Defender of the Age of Chivalry," in *Poems* 1:140–42 (141).

79. *Critical Review*, 2d ser., 38 (1803), 110.

80. Seward to Bannerman, July 22, 1803 (ADV. MS. 22.4.10, f. 236).

81. Coleridge's poem appears in the *Edinburgh Magazine* 15 (1800): 141–42; Bannerman's, 15 (1800): 218–20.

82. The National Library of Scotland contains a copy of the *Edinburgh Magazine* version of "The Dark Ladie" with the added verses in a manuscript hand, possibly Bannerman's, on the back (NLS MS. 1001, f. 63).

83. Coleridge, "Love," *Poetical Works*, ed. Ernest Hartley Coleridge (Oxford: Oxford University Press, 1969), 335.

84. O'Connor, "Lewis and the Gothic Ballad," 19–20.

85. Castle, *The Apparitional Lesbian: Female Homosexuality and Modern Culture* (New York: Columbia University Press, 1993), 30.

86. Scott, "Essay on Imitations of the Ancient Ballad," in *Minstrelsy of the Scottish Border*, 4 vols. (London: Adam and Charles Black, 1880), 4:25–26.

87. Mellor, *Romanticism and Gender* (New York: Routledge, 1993), 1–12.

6. GENIUS AND THE BLAKEAN RIDICULOUS

1. For Ginsberg's relation to Blake, see his *Your Reason & Blake's System* (Madras: Hanuman Books, 1988); Robert Duncan, *Fictive Certainties* (New York: New Directions, 1985), 30.

2. Stephen Yenser, *The Consuming Myth: The Work of James Merrill* (Cambridge: Harvard University Press, 1987), 253.

3. Damon, *The Dark End of the Street: Margins in American Vanguard Poetry* (Minneapolis: University of Minnesota Press, 1993), 169.

4. See, for example, W. J. T. Mitchell, "Blake's Radical Comedy: Dramatic Structure as Meaning in *Milton*," in Stuart Curran and Joseph Anthony Wittreich, Jr., eds., *Blake's Sublime Allegory: Essays on "The Four Zoas," "Milton," "Jerusalem"* (Madison: University of Wisconsin Press, 1973), 281–309.

5. William Blake, *The Complete Poetry and Prose of William Blake*, ed. David V. Erdman, rev. ed. (Garden City, N.Y.: Anchor / Doubleday, 1982), 300. Future references to this edition will be in the text. I will follow standard practice of giving plate and line numbers, followed by the page number in the Erdman edition.

6. Sedgwick, *Epistemology of the Closet* (Berkeley: University of California Press, 1990), 156.

7. On camp generally, see the essays in David Bergman, ed., *Camp Grounds* (Amherst: University of Massachusetts Press, 1993).

8. McClenahan, "Made in the 'Sexual Machine': Blake, Gender, and the Politics of Empire," in Jackie DiSalvo, Christopher Hobson, and G. Anthony Rosso, eds., *Blake, Politics, and History*, forthcoming.

9. Alicia Ostriker, "The Road of Excess: My William Blake," in Gene W. Ruoff, ed., *The Romantics and Us: Essays on Literature and Culture* (New Brunswick, N.J.: Rutgers University Press, 1990), 67–90 (75). For variations on this view, see Brian Wilkie, "Epic Irony in *Milton*," in David V. Erdman and John E. Grant, eds., *Blake's Visionary Forms Dramatic* (Princeton: Princeton University Press, 1970), 359–72; Brenda S. Webster, *Blake's Prophetic Psychology* (Athens: University of Georgia Press, 1983), 250–71; Alan Richardson, "Romanticism and the Colonization of the Feminine," in Anne K. Mellor, ed., *Romanticism and Feminism* (Bloomington: Indiana University Press, 1988), 13–25; Margaret Storch, *Sons and Adversaries: Women in William Blake and D. H. Lawrence* (Knoxville: University of Tennessee Press, 1990), 131–46; Robert N. Essick, "William Blake's 'Female Will' and its Biographical Context," *Studies in English Literature, 1500–1900* 31 (1991): 615–30; Marc Kaplan, "Blake's *Milton*: The Metaphysics of Gender," *Nineteenth-Century Contexts* 19 (1995): 151–78; Betsy Bolton, " 'A Garment dipped in blood': Ololon and the Problems of Gender in Blake's *Milton*," *Studies in Romanticism* 36 (1997): 61–101.

10. Anne K. Mellor, *Romanticism and Gender* (New York: Routledge, 1993), 22.

11. David Punter, *The Romantic Unconscious: A Study in Narcissism and Patriarchy* (New York: New York University Press, 1989), 85, 101.

12. Susan Fox, *Poetic Form in Blake's "Milton"* (Princeton: Princeton University Press, 1976), 127; see also Fox's "The Female as Metaphor in William Blake's Poetry," *Critical Inquiry* 3 (1977): 507–19.

13. Kaplan, "Blake's *Milton*," 174; Storch, *Sons and Adversaries*, 140.

14. For a larger perspective on narrative and heterosexism, see Judith Roof, *Come As You Are: Sexuality and Narrative* (New York: Columbia University Press, 1996).

15. For some of the many useful arguments about the general difficulties of reading Blake, see Jerome J. McGann, "The Aim of Blake's Prophecies and the Uses of Blake Criticism," in Curran and Wittreich, eds., *Blake's Sublime Allegory*, 3–21, and *Towards a Literature of Knowledge* (Chicago: University of Chicago Press, 1988), 17–37; and Stephen D. Cox, "Methods and Limitations," in Dan Miller, Mark Bracher, and Donald Ault, eds., *Critical Paths: Blake and the Argument of Method* (Durham, N.C.: Duke University Press, 1987), 19–40.

16. This assumption has proved especially durable because it appears in the poem's best editions. Harold Bloom calls Ololon "the aggregate of Milton's sixfold emanation" in his notes to the poem (Erdman, ed., *Complete Poetry and Prose*, 918), and the editors of the William Blake Trust edition claim that "Milton's 'Emanation'

is Ololon" (*Milton: A Poem*, ed. Robert N. Essick and Joseph Viscomi [Princeton: Princeton University Press, 1993], 139).

17. For one of the few discussions of Ololon that complicates her supposed identity as Milton's Emanation, see Nelson Hilton, *Literal Imagination: Blake's Vision of Words* (Berkeley: University of California Press, 1983), 39–44.

18. John Ellis and William Butler Yeats, *The Works of William Blake, Poetic, Symbolic, and Critical*, 3 vols. (London: Bernard Quadritch, 1893), 2:285; see also Algernon Charles Swinburne, *William Blake: A Critical Essay* (London: William Heinemann, 1868), 261–76; Pierre Berger, *William Blake: Poet and Mystic*, trans. Daniel H. Conner (1914; rpt., New York: Haskell House, 1968), 361–68.

19. Sandy Stone, "The *Empire* Strikes Back: A Posttranssexual Manifesto," in Julia Epstein and Kristina Straub, eds., *Body Guards: The Cultural Politics of Gender Ambiguity* (New York: Routledge, 1991), 280–304 (296).

20. Punter, *Romantic Unconscious*, 101.

21. Anonymous critic, quoted in G. E. Bentley, Jr., *Blake Records* (Oxford: Clarendon Press, 1969), 181.

22. The story of the Blake-Hayley quarrel has been discussed often; for a recent account, see Peter Ackroyd, *Blake* (New York: Knopf, 1996). For a discussion of the poem's dates, see Essick and Viscomi's introduction to their edition, 35–41.

23. For Hayley's biography, see Joseph Anthony Wittreich, Jr.'s "Introduction" to his edition of *The Life of Milton* (1796) (Gainesville, Florida: Scholars' Facsimiles, 1970), v–xiv, and his *Angel of Apocalypse: Blake's Idea of Milton* (Madison: University of Wisconsin Press, 1975), 229–36. I disagree strongly, however, with his claim that Hayley's biography "forges an attitude toward the poet [Milton] compatible with Blake's own" (231).

24. For other works on *Milton* that concentrate on the Blake-Milton relationship, see in addition to Wittreich, Leslie Brisman, *Milton's Poetry of Choice and Its Romantic Heirs* (Ithaca, N.Y.: Cornell University Press, 1973), 192–212; David E. James, *Written Within and Without: A Study of Blake's "Milton"* (Frankfurt: Peter Lang, 1977), 55–103; David Riede, "Blake's *Milton*: On Membership in the Church Paul," in Mary Nyquist and Margaret W. Ferguson, eds., *Re-membering Milton: Essays on the Texts and Traditions* (New York: Methuen, 1987), 257–77.

25. Hayley, *Life of Milton*, 229, 196, 92.

26. For a useful discussion of the Bard's Song, see James Rieger, " 'The Hem of Their Garments': The Bard's Song in *Milton*," in Curran and Wittreich, eds., *Blake's Sublime Allegory*, 259–80.

27. Hayley, *Life of Milton*, 5, 46, 49.

28. Samuel Johnson, "John Milton" (1783), in *Selected Poetry and Prose*, ed. Frank Brady and W. K. Wimsatt (Berkeley: University of California Press, 1977), 424.

29. See D'Israeli, *An Essay on the Manners and Genius of the Literary Character* (1795) (New York: Garland, 1970), 58.

30. Hayley, *Life of Milton*, 91.

31. Vine, *Blake's Poetry: Spectral Visions* (Basingstoke: Macmillan, 1993), 142.

32. See Judith Butler, *Gender Trouble: Feminism and the Subversion of Identity* (New York: Routledge, 1990), 128–41.

33. For an illuminating discussion of the hermaphrodite and of gender-crossing in *Milton*, see Bolton, " 'A Garment dipped in blood,' " 71–78.

34. Kaplan, "Blake's *Milton*," 168; for a similar reading, see Storch, *Sons and Adversaries*.

35. On sexuality and the illustrations for *Milton*, see W. J. T. Mitchell, "Style and Iconography in the Illustrations of Blake's *Milton*," *Blake Studies* 6 (1973): 47–71, and Stephen C. Behrendt, *Reading William Blake* (New York: St. Martin's, 1992), 161–65.

36. Morton D. Paley, *Energy and the Imagination: A Study of the Development of Blake's Thought* (Oxford: Clarendon Press, 1970), 243.

37. On Ololon and destabilization, see Thomas A. Vogler, "Re:Naming *MIL/TON*," in Nelson Hilton and Thomas A. Vogler, eds., *Unnam'd Forms: Blake and Textuality* (Berkeley: University of California Press, 1986), 141–76, esp. 161–66.

38. Butler, *Gender Trouble*, 135, 127.

39. Ibid., 140, 148.

40. Butler, *Bodies That Matter: On the Discursive Limits of "Sex"* (New York: Routledge, 1993), 15.

41. William Duff, *An Essay on Original Genius* (1767) (New York: Garland, 1970), 167–68.

42. For discussion of the relevance of such assertions to romanticism generally, see Marlon B. Ross, *The Contours of Masculine Desire: Romanticism and the Rise of Women's Poetry* (New York: Oxford University Press, 1989), 15–55.

43. See notes of Essick and Viscomi in their edition of *Milton*, 191.

44. John Milton, *Paradise Lost* (1674), 1:21–22, in *Complete Poems and Major Prose*, ed. Merritt Y. Hughes (Indianapolis: Bobbs-Merrill, 1957), 212.

45. See John Grant, "The Female Awakening at the End of Blake's *Milton*: A Picture Story, with Questions," in John Karl Franson, ed., *Milton Reconsidered: Essays in Honor of Arthur E. Baker* (Salzburg: University of Salzburg, 1976), 78–102, and Eugenie R. Freed, *"A Portion of His Life": William Blake's Miltonic Vision of Woman* (Lewisburg, Pa.: Bucknell University Press, 1994), 104–06.

46. On the potential homoeroticism of Christ, see Sedgwick, *Epistemology of the Closet*, 140.

47. *Antijacobin Review* quoted in Bentley, *Blake Records*, 203.

7. "A SIGHT TO DREAM OF, NOT TO TELL": *CHRISTABEL*, PORNOGRAPHY, AND GENIUS

1. Karl Kroeber, *Romantic Narrative Art* (Madison: University of Wisconsin Press, 1966), 64.

2. Alaric Alfred Watts, *Alaric Watts: A Narrative of His Life*, 2 vols. (London: Richard Bentley, 1884), 1:239.

NOTES TO PAGES 177–182

3. Quoted in A. H. Nethercot, *The Road to Tryermaine* (Chicago: University of Chicago Press, 1939), 28.

4. Hazlitt, *Coleridge: The Critical Heritage*, ed. J. R. de J. Jackson, 2 vols. (London: Routledge, 1970–1991), 1:207.

5. Coleridge, "Preface" to *Christabel* in *Poetical Works*, ed. Ernest Hartley Coleridge (Oxford: Oxford University Press, 1969), 214. Future references to this poem and others by Coleridge will be by line number in this edition.

6. For critics who consider *Christabel*'s relation to the Gothic more thoroughly than I do, see Edward Dramin, " 'Amid the Jagged Shadows': *Christabel* and the Gothic Tradition," *Wordsworth Circle* 13 (1982): 221–28, and Andrew M. Cooper, *Doubt and Identity in Romantic Poetry* (New Haven: Yale University Press, 1988), 107–29.

7. For a biographical account, I rely on Richard Holmes, *Coleridge: Early Visions* (New York: Viking, 1989), 174–82.

8. Coleridge, *Collected Letters of Samuel Taylor Coleridge*, ed. Earl Leslie Griggs, 6 vols. (Oxford: Clarendon Press, 1956–1971), 1:361.

9. Coleridge, *Collected Letters* 1:373.

10. Ibid., 374.

11. R. B. Litchfield, *Tom Wedgwood, the First Photographer* (London: Duckworth, 1903), 63

12. Coleridge, *Collected Letters* 1:80.

13. Ibid., 1:103.

14. For a full account of Coleridge's literary activities in the late 1790s and early 1800s, see David V. Erdman's introduction to Coleridge's *Essays on His Times*, 3 vols. (Princeton: Princeton University Press, 1978), 1:lix–cxxi.

15. Coleridge, *Collected Letters* 1:273.

16. Ibid, 1:365.

17. For discussions of *Christabel* in the context of Wordsworth-Coleridge relations, see Paul Magnuson, *Coleridge and Wordsworth: A Lyrical Dialogue* (Princeton: Princeton University Press, 1988), 120–38, and Susan Eilenberg, *Strange Power of Speech: Wordsworth, Coleridge, and Literary Possession* (New York: Oxford University Press, 1992), 97–107.

18. Coleridge, *Collected Letters* 1:377–78.

19. For more on Thomas Wedgwood's relation to Coleridge, see Francis Doherty, "Tom Wedgwood, Coleridge, and 'Metaphysics,' " *Neophilologus* 71 (1987): 305–15.

20. Marilyn Butler, *Romantics, Rebels, and Reactionaries: English Literature and its Background, 1760–1830* (Oxford: Oxford University Press, 1981), 57–68.

21. Wordsworth, "Preface to the Second Edition of *Lyrical Ballads*" (1800, 1802), *Selected Poems and Prefaces*, ed. Jack Stillinger (Boston: Houghton Mifflin, 1965), 460.

22. For the most complete presentation of Wordsworth's poetry as a denial of history, see Alan Liu, *Wordsworth: The Sense of History* (Stanford, Calif.: Stanford University Press, 1989).

23. Hunt, "Introduction: Obscenity and the Origins of Modernity, 1500–1800" in Lynn Hunt, ed., *The Invention of Pornography* (New York: Zone, 1993), 12.

24. Hunt, ibid., 12–13; her formulation is indebted to Walter Kendrick, *The Secret Museum: Pornography in Modern Culture* (New York: Viking, 1987).

25. For the best discussion of eighteenth-century obscene representation in general, see Peter Wagner, *Eros Revived: Erotica of the Enlightenment in England and America* (London: Secker and Warburg, 1988).

26. For discussions of *Christabel* and its sources, see D. R. Tuttle, "*Christabel*: Sources in Percy's *Reliques* and the Gothic Romance," *PMLA* 53 (1938): 445–74; Nethercot, *Road to Tryermaine*; Michael D. Patrick, *Christabel: A Brief Critical History and Reconsideration* (Salzburg: University of Salzburg, 1973); Lore Metzger, "Modifications of Genre: A Feminist Critique of 'Christabel' and 'Die Braut von Korinth,'" *Studies in Eighteenth-Century Culture* 22 (1992): 3–19.

27. Coleridge, *Collected Letters* 1:378–79.

28. G. Legman, *The Horn Book: Studies in Erotic Folklore and Bibliography* (New Hyde Park: University Books, 1964), 375.

29. [Anon.], *The Frisky Songster, Being a Select Choice of Such Songs, as are Distinguished for their Jollity, High Taste and Humor, And above two hundred Toasts and Sentiments of the Most Delicious Order*, 9th ed. (London, 1802), 35.

30. *The Frisky Songster*, 58; subsequent page numbers are cited in the text.

31. [Anon.], *Christabess* (London: J. Duncombe, 1816), 21–22.

32. See Wagner, *Eros Revived*, 99–100.

33. Quoted in Joseph Chitty, *A Practical Treatise on the Criminal Law*, 5th American ed., 3 vols. (New York: Banks, Gould, 1847), 2:42; for the identification of Rich, see Donald Thomas, *A Long Time Burning: The History of Literary Censorship in England* (London: Routledge, 1969), 194.

34. McCalman, *Radical Underworld: Prophets, Revolutionaries, and Pornographers in London, 1795–1840* (Cambridge: Cambridge University Press, 1988), 204–31.

35. Binhammer, "The Sex Panic of the 1790s," *Journal of the History of Sexuality* 6 (1996): 409–34 (414–15).

36. See Patrick J. Keane, *Coleridge's Submerged Politics: The Ancient Mariner and Robinson Crusoe* (Columbia: University of Missouri Press, 1994), 167–353.

37. For examples, see Andrea Henderson, "Revolution, Response, and 'Christabel,'" *ELH* 57 (1990): 881–900, and Daniel P. Watkins, *Sexual Power in British Romantic Poetry* (Gainesville: University of Florida Press, 1996), 62–87.

38. "A New Ballad to the Tune of Fair Rosamund," quoted in Catherine Gallagher, *Nobody's Story: The Vanishing Acts of Women Writers in the Marketplace, 1670–1820* (Berkeley: University of California Press, 1994), 107.

39. [Anon.], *An Authentic Narrative of the Most Remarkable Adventures . . . of Miss Fanny Davies, the Celebrated Modern Amazon*, 2d ed. (London, n.d.), 34.

40. Quintilian quoted in T. V. F. Brogan, ed., *The New Princeton Handbook of Poetic Terms* (Princeton: Princeton University Press, 1994), 34.

41. Karen Swann, "Literary Gentleman and Lovely Ladies: The Debate on the Character of *Christabel*," in Karl Kroeber and Gene W. Ruoff, eds., *Romantic Poetry: Recent Revisionary Criticism* (New Brunswick, N.J.: Rutgers University Press, 1993), 204–220 (211).

42. For a discussion of Geraldine's ambiguity, see Michael E. Holstein, "Coleridge's *Christabel* as Psychodrama: Five Perspectives on the Intruder," *Wordsworth Circle* 7 (1976): 119–28.

43. Walter Pater, *Three Major Texts: "The Renaissance," "Appreciations," and "Imaginary Portraits,"* ed. William E. Buckler (New York: New York University Press, 1986), 454.

44. Eve Kosofksy Sedgwick, *Between Men: English Literature and Male Homosocial Desire* (New York: Columbia University Press, 1985), 21–27.

45. See William Galperin, "Coleridge and Critical Intervention," *Wordsworth Circle* 22 (1991): 58–64.

46. Alexander Gerard, *An Essay on Genius* (1774) (New York: Garland, 1970), 357.

47. Mary Wollstonecraft, *Vindication of the Rights of Woman* (1792), ed. Miriam Brody (Harmondsworth: Penguin, 1986), 220.

48. Paul Hamilton, "Coleridge," in David B. Pirie, ed., *The Penguin History of Literature: The Romantic Period* (Harmondsworth: Penguin, 1994), 185–220 (210).

49. [Various critics, as follows], *Coleridge: The Critical Heritage*, 1:220 (anonymous review in *The Anti-Jacobin*); 1:224, 225 (William Roberts in *The British Review*); 2:251 (anonymous review in *The Champion*).

50. For Byron, see his note to *The Siege of Corinth* in *Selected Poems*, ed. Susan J. Wolfson and Peter J. Manning (Harmondsworth: Penguin, 1996), 375; for Scott, see his 1830 introduction to *The Lay of the Last Minstrel* in *The Poetical Works of Sir Walter Scott* (London: Frederick Warne, n.d.), 5.

51. For this story, see *His Very Self and Voice: Collected Conversations of Lord Byron*, ed. Ernest J. Lovell, Jr. (New York: Macmillan, 1954), 186.

52. Tennyson, *In Memoriam, A. H. H.* (1850), 15:3, in *Tennyson's Poetry*, ed. Robert W. Hill, Jr. (New York: Norton, 1971), 128.

53. T. Hall Caine, *Recollections of Dante Gabriel Rossetti* (London: Eliot Stock, 1882), 151–62.

54. A. C. Swinburne, "Coleridge," *The Complete Works of Algernon Charles Swinburne*, ed. Edmund Gosse and Thomas James Wise, 20 vols. (London: W. Heinemann, 1925–1927), 15:146.

55. Caine, *Recollections*, 153.

56. Renée Vivien, *The Muse of the Violets*, trans. Margaret Porter and Catharine Kroger ([Bates City, Mo.]: Naiad Press, 1977), 53.

57. Ronald Firbank, *3 More Novels* (New York: New Directions, 1986), 205, 211.

58. Rosamond Lehmann, *Dusty Answer* (New York: Henry Holt, 1927), 193.

59. Toni McNaron, *I Dwell in Possibility* (New York: Feminist Press, 1992), 102.

CONCLUSION

1. See my *Byron and the Victorians* (Cambridge: Cambridge University Press, 1995), esp. ch. 1, "Byron and the Secret Self," 13–46.

2. See Ellen Bayuk Rosenman, "Sexual Identity and *A Room of One's Own*: 'Secret Economies' in Virginia Woolf's Feminist Discourse," *Signs* 14 (1989): 634–50; Jane Marcus, "Sapphistory: The Woolf and the Well," in Karla Jay, Joanne Glasgow, and Catharine R. Stimpson, eds., *Lesbian Texts and Contexts: Radical Revisions* (New York: New York University Press, 1990), 164–79; Adam Parkes, "Lesbianism, History, and Censorship: *The Well of Loneliness* and the Suppressed Randiness of Virginia Woolf's *Orlando*," *Twentieth-Century Literature* 40 (1994): 434–60.

3. Hall, *The Well of Loneliness* (1928) (London: Hammond, 1956), 67; future references are cited in the text.

4. Terry Castle, *Noël Coward and Radclyffe Hall: Kindred Spirits* (New York: Columbia University Press, 1996), 19, 33.

5. See Esther Newton, "The Mythic Mannish Lesbian: Radclyffe Hall and the New Woman," in Martin Duberman, Martha Vicinus, and George Chauncey, Jr., eds., *Hidden from History: Reclaiming the Gay and Lesbian Past* (New York: New American Library, 1989), 281–93; Ed Cohen, *Talk on the Wilde Side: Toward a Genealogy of a Discourse on Male Sexualities* (New York: Routledge, 1993).

6. For discussion of the trial, see Vera Brittain, *Radclyffe Hall: A Case of Obscenity?* (London: Femina, 1968), and Leigh Gilmore, "Obscenity, Modernity, Identity: Legalizing *The Well of Loneliness* and *Nightwood*," *Journal of the History of Sexuality* 4 (1994): 603–24.

7. Woolf, *A Room of One's Own* (1929) (New York: Harcourt Brace, 1989), 93; future references are cited in the text.

8. Marna Sedgwick, quoted in Hermione Lee, *Virginia Woolf* (London: Chatto and Windus, 1996), 565.

9. Rosenman, "Sexual Identity and *A Room of One's Own*," 641–42.

10. Ibid., 643.

11. Joseph Bristow, *Effeminate England: Homoerotic Writing After 1885* (New York: Columbia University Press, 1995).

12. Joel N. Shurkin, *Terman's Kids: The Groundbreaking Study of How the Gifted Grow Up* (Boston: Little, Brown, 1992), 3.

13. Lewis M. Terman and Melita H. Oden, *The Gifted Child Grows Up: Twenty-Five Years' Follow-Up of a Superior Group* (Stanford, Calif.: Stanford University Press, 1959), 352; future references are cited in the text.

14. Shurkin, *Terman's Kids*, 227–44.

15. Herbert A. Carroll, *Genius in the Making* (New York: McGraw-Hill, 1940), 101; subsequent pages are cited in the text.

16. Robert S. Albert and Mark A. Runco, "The Achievement of Eminence: A Model Based on a Longitudinal Study of Exceptionally Gifted Boys and Their Families," in Robert J. Sternberg and Janet E. Davidson, eds., *Conceptions of Giftedness* (Cambridge: Cambridge University Press, 1986), 332–57 (342).

17. Ibid., 343.

18. For other recent work on giftedness, see Frances Degen Horowitz and Marion O'Brien, eds., *The Gifted and Talented: Developmental Perspectives* (American Psychological Association, 1985); Rena F. Subotnik and Karen D. Arnold, eds., *Beyond Terman: Contemporary Longitudinal Studies of Giftedness and Talent* (Norwood, N.J.: Ablex, 1994).

INDEX

Cavendish, John, 100
Cawthorn, James, 37
Ceracchi, Giuseppe, 96, 106
Chasseguet-Smirgel, Janine, 3
Chatterton, Thomas, 33, 34, 36, 133
Chauncey, George, 215*n*5, 216*n*20, 217*n*3
Christabess, 185–86, 190
Churchill, Charles, 46
civic humanism, 19–21, 22–23
civil humanism, 22–23, 26
Cleland, John, 19 , 21, 25, 97, 192
Cohen, Ed, 70, 71, 229*nn*3&5
Coleridge, Samuel Taylor, 14 and 15
    (mentioned); and Anne Banner-
    man, 143; and annuity, 179–82; and
    associationists, 196; and genius, 16,
    27, 179–82, 196–99, 208; and lesbian-
    ism, 188–202; and obscenity, 177–78,
    182–88; and reception, 199–202; and
    repetition, 197–99; and Robert
    Anderson, 130; and sources, 182–88;
    and William Wordsworth, 177, 178,
    181–82
——, *Works: Christabel*, 16, 177–202;
    "Fears in Solitude," 187–88; "France:
    An Ode," 187; "Introduction to the
    Tale of the Dark Ladie" ("Love"),
    143–44; "Kubla Khan," 200; "Ode to
    the Departing Year," 187; *Religious
    Musings*, 187; *Rime of the Ancient
    Mariner*, 143, 200
Colley, Linda, 219*n*30, 228*n*67, 229*n*12
Collings, David, 223*n*88
Colman, George (the Younger),
    35, 36, 107
Combe, William, 30, 43–44, 98–99,
    103–105
Conolly, Lady Louisa, 102
Conway, Henry Seymour, 96, 106
Cope, Kevin L., 48
Courtenay, William, 40, 43, 47, 93
Coward, Noël, 210
Cowley, Hannah, 113, 134
Cowper, William: and genius, 14–15, 16,

63–64, 77–80, 91; and model subur-
    ban man, 72–74, 87–89; and secrecy,
    75–77; and Evangelicals, 79, 81, 83;
    and deviance, 79–80; and reception,
    81–89, 114; and insanity, 81–83; and
    femininity, 83–85; and hermaphro-
    ditism, 84–87
——, *Works: Memoirs*, 82; *The Task*,
    14, 41, 71–82
Crompton, Louis, 64, 229*n*8
Cunningham, Allan, 110
Currie, James, 36
Cuthbertson, Miss, 127

Damer, Anne, 186 and 188 (mentioned);
    and acting, 106–108, 120–21; and
    attacks on, 98–102, 111–15, 120–22;
    and genius, 15, 91–92, 96, 109–10,
    115–18, 125; and marriage, 96, 118–19;
    and money, 118–20, 122–24, 133, 134;
    and response to "abuse," 103–109;
    and sapphism, 14, 26, 92–93, 97–103,
    115–24; and sculpture, 96–97,
    105–106, 116
——, *Works: Belmour*, 14, 92, 97,
    108–109, 116, 122
Damer, John, 96, 98–99, 102–103
"Damerian Apollo, The," 111
Damon, Maria, 149
Darwin, Erasmus, 109
Davenport, Richard, 131, 132,
    241*nn*30&40
Davidoff, Leonore, 72, 73, 74,
    229*n*12
Davy, Sir Humphry, 106
Della Cruscans, 177, 178
d'Emilio, John, 64
Derby, Edward, 12th Earl of, 120–22
de Staël, Germaine, 129
Devonshire, Georgiana, Duchess of,
    96, 97, 100
Dickens, Charles, 69–70
Diderot, Denis, 186, 192
Disraeli, Benjamin, 59

D'Israeli, Isaac, 31, 32–33, 34, 38, 63, 135, 158
Don Leon, 70
Donoghue, Emma, 92, 94–95, 217*n*7, 220*nn*39&45, 235*n*4, 239*n*85
Downman, Hugh, 37
Dreger, Alice Domerat, 85
Dryden, John, 27, 141
Du Barry, Viscountess, 99–100
Duff, William, 28, 29, 30, 31, 48, 49, 166
Duncan, Robert, 149
Duncombe, John, 185, 187
Dyos, Harold James, 230*n*20

Edgeworth, Maria, 36
Edinburgh Magazine, 130–31, 143
effeminacy, 8, 10–12, 20–22. *See also* Beckford, William
Eliot, George, 49
Ellis, John, 152–53
Evangelicalism, 72, 79, 81

Faderman, Lillian, 94
Farington, Joseph, 111
Farren, Elizabeth, 120–22
Fawkener, William, 118–19
Fernbach, David, 64
Ferrier, Susan, 114
Fielding, Henry, 19, 55, 97, 102
Firbank, Ronald, 201, 210
Fishman, Robert, 73, 229*n*1
Foote, Samuel, 35
Fordyce, James, 25
Forster, E. M., 210
Foucault, Michel, 6–7, 11, 12, 71, 76, 93, 216*n*15, 218*n*15
Fox, Charles James, 96, 97, 106, 109, 182
Fox, Susan, 151–52
Freud, Sigmund, 1–2, 47, 54, 76
Frisky Songster, The, 182–88, 189, 193

Gallagher, Catherine, 19–20, 22, 23, 28, 97–98, 217*n*8

genius: and academy, 207–10; and antidomesticity, 32–34; and bourgeois aesthetics, 5–6; and capitalism, 4–6; and celebrity, 203–207; and definition, 5, 27; and femininity, 30–31, 34; and homosexuality, 1–6, 34–35; and literary outsiders, 13–16, 18–19; and madness, 2–3; and originality, 28–29; and politics, 36–38; and popular culture, 1–3; and psychology, 1–5; and resemblance to sodomite, 17–19; and schools, 210–14; and sublimity, 29–31; and women, 5, 31–32, 35–36. *See also individual authors*
Genlis, Stephanie Felicité, Comtesse de, 137–39
George III, King, 106
Gerard, Alexander, 28, 31, 196
Gilding, Elizabeth, 35, 125
Ginsberg, Allen, 149
Godwin, William, 37, 129
Goethe, Johann Wolfgang von, 128, 129, 130, 136
Gore, Catherine, 59
Grahame, James, 130
Grant, Anne, 132, 133
Gray, Thomas, 37, 77, 80
Gregory, George, 36
Greville, Charles, 85–86, 87
Griggs, Earl Leslie, 182–83
Grimshawe, Thomas Shuttleworth, 83
Guyse, John, 21

Haggerty, George, 25, 40, 44
Hall, Catherine, 72, 73, 74, 229*n*12
Hall, Radclyffe, 203, 204, 206
———, *Works: The Well of Loneliness*, 111, 203, 204–206, 207, 208, 209, 210
Hallam, Henry, 66
Hamilton, Mary, 123
Hamilton, Paul, 199
Harrington, Caroline, Lady, 98–99
Harwood, E., 21

BETWEEN MEN ~ BETWEEN WOMEN

Lesbian and Gay Studies   *Lillian Faderman and Larry Gross, Editors*

Richard D. Mohr, *Gays/Justice: A Study of Ethics, Society, and Law*

Gary David Comstock, *Violence Against Lesbians and Gay Men*

Kath Weston, *Families We Choose: Lesbians, Gays, Kinship*

Lillian Faderman, *Odd Girls and Twilight Lovers: A History of Lesbian Life in Twentieth-Century America*

Judith Roof, *A Lure of Knowledge: Lesbian Sexuality and Theory*

John Clum, *Acting Gay: Male Homosexuality in Modern Drama*

Allen Ellenzweig, *The Homoerotic Photograph: Male Images from Durieu/ Delacroix to Mapplethorpe*

Sally Munt, editor, *New Lesbian Criticism: Literary and Cultural Readings*

Timothy F. Murphy and Suzanne Poirier, editors, *Writing AIDS: Gay Literature, Language, and Analysis*

Linda D. Garnets and Douglas C. Kimmel, editors, *Psychological Perspectives on Lesbian and Gay Male Experiences*

Laura Doan, editor, *The Lesbian Postmodern*

Noreen O'Connor and Joanna Ryan, *Wild Desires and Mistaken Identities: Lesbianism and Psychoanalysis*

Alan Sinfield, *The Wilde Century: Effeminacy, Oscar Wilde, and the Queer Moment*

Claudia Card, *Lesbian Choices*

Carter Wilson, *Hidden in the Blood: A Personal Investigation of AIDS in the Yucatán*

Alan Bray, *Homosexuality in Renaissance England*

Joseph Carrier, *De Los Otros: Intimacy and Homosexuality Among Mexican Men*

Joseph Bristow, *Effeminate England: Homoerotic Writing After 1885*

Corinne E. Blackmer and Patricia Juliana Smith, editors, *En Travesti: Women, Gender Subversion, Opera*

Don Paulson with Roger Simpson, *An Evening at The Garden of Allah: A Gay Cabaret in Seattle*

Claudia Schoppmann, *Days of Masquerade: Life Stories of Lesbians During the Third Reich*

Chris Straayer, *Deviant Eyes, Deviant Bodies: Sexual Re-Orientation in Film and Video*

Edward Alwood, *Straight News: Gays, Lesbians, and the News Media*

Thomas Waugh, *Hard to Imagine: Gay Male Eroticism in Photography and Film from Their Beginnings to Stonewall*

Judith Roof, *Come As You Are: Sexuality and Narrative*

Terry Castle, *Noel Coward and Radclyffe Hall: Kindred Spirits*

Kath Weston, *Render Me, Gender Me: Lesbians Talk Sex, Class, Color, Nation, Studmuffins . . .*

Ruth Vanita, *Sappho and the Virgin Mary: Same-Sex Love and the English Literary Imagination*

renée c. hoogland, *Lesbian Configurations*

Beverly Burch, *Other Women: Lesbian Experience and Psychoanalytic Theory of Women*

Jane McIntosh Snyder, *Lesbian Desire in the Lyrics of Sappho*

Rebecca Alpert, *Like Bread on the Seder Plate: Jewish Lesbians and the Transformation of Tradition*

Emma Donoghue, editor, *Poems Between Women: Four Centuries of Love, Romantic Friendship, and Desire*

James T. Sears and Walter L. Williams, editors, *Overcoming Heterosexism and Homophobia: Strategies That Work*

Patricia Juliana Smith, *Lesbian Panic: Homoeroticism in Modern British Women's Fiction*

Dwayne C. Turner, *Risky Sex: Gay Men and HIV Prevention*

Timothy F. Murphy, *Gay Science: The Ethics of Sexual Orientation Research*

Cameron McFarlane, *The Sodomite in Fiction and Satire, 1660–1750*

Lynda Hart, *Between the Body and the Flesh: Performing Sadomasochism*

Byrne R. S. Fone, editor, *The Columbia Anthology of Gay Literature: Readings from Western Antiquity to the Present Day*

Ellen Lewin, *Recognizing Ourselves: Ceremonies of Lesbian and Gay Commitment*

Ruthann Robson, *Sappho Goes to Law School: Fragments in Lesbian Legal Theory*

Jacquelyn Zita, *Body Talk: Philosophical Reflections on Sex and Gender*

Marilee Lindemann, *Willa Cather: Queering America*

George E. Haggerty, *Men in Love: Masculinity and Sexuality in the Eighteenth Century*